AN INTRODUCTION TO

BUDDHISM

Teachings, history and practices

This book provides a comprehensive introduction to the Buddhist tradition as it has developed in three major cultural areas in Asia, and to Buddhism as it is now developing in the West. It is intended to be a textbook for students of Religious or Asian Studies, but will also be of interest to those who want a general survey of Buddhism and its beliefs.

Unlike many other general books about Buddhism, it not only explores the world-views of the religion but also seeks to show how Buddhism functions as a set of *practices*. It thus includes chapters on devotion, ethics, monastic practice (of nuns as well as monks) and meditation, and relates each of these to Buddhist teachings and historical developments. While describing thought and practice, the book sets out at the same time to convey something of the emotional tone or 'flavour' of Buddhism; and emphasising as it does the diversity found within different Buddhist traditions, it aims throughout to highlight the common threads of belief, practice and historical continuities which unify the Buddhist world.

Dr Harvey has sought to answer questions that are often asked by people on first meeting the tradition, and has tried, where appropriate, to relate Buddhism to modern ways of thinking, while taking account of the most recent scholarship in the field. In his section on *Nirvāṇa* the author offers a novel interpretation of this ultimate, transcendent mystery.

The 'Peace Pagoda' in Battersea Park, London.

AN INTRODUCTION TO BUDDHISM

Teachings, history and practices

PETER HARVEY

CAMBRIDGE
UNIVERSITY PRESS

PUBLISHED BY THE PRESS SYNDICATE OF THE UNIVERSITY OF CAMBRIDGE
The Pitt Building, Trumpington Street, Cambridge, United Kingdom

CAMBRIDGE UNIVERSITY PRESS
The Edinburgh Building, Cambridge CB2 2RU, UK
40 West 20th Street, New York, NY 10011–4211, USA
10 Stamford Road, Oakleigh, VIC 3166, Australia
Ruiz de Alarcón 13, 28014 Madrid, Spain
Dock House, The Waterfront, Cape Town 8001, South Africa

http://www.cambridge.org

First published 1990
Reprinted 1991, 1992, 1993 (twice), 1994, 1995, 1996, 1997, 1998, 2000

Printed in the United Kingdom at the University Press, Cambridge

British Library Cataloguing in Publication data
Harvey, Peter (Brian Peter), 1951–
An introduction to Buddhism: teachings,
history and practices.
1. Buddhism
1. Title
294.3

Library of Congress Cataloguing in Publication data
Harvey, Peter
An introduction to Buddhism: teachings, history and practices/
B. Peter Harvey.
p. cm.
Bibliography.
includes index.
ISBN 0 521 30815 1 (hardback) ISBN 0 521 31333 3 (paperback)
1. Buddhism. 1. Title.
PQ4022.H37 1990
294.3–dc20 89-7317 CIP

ISBN 0 521 30815 1 hardback
ISBN 0 521 31333 3 paperback

UP

May any auspicious purifying power (*puñña*) generated by writing this work be for the benefit of my parents, wife and daughter, all who read this book, and indeed all beings.

Namo tassa Bhagavato Arahato Sammā-sambuddhassa

Honour to the Lord, *Arahat*,
perfectly and completely Enlightened One!

CONTENTS

List of illustrations — *page* xi
Acknowledgements — xiii
List of abbreviations — xiv
A note on language and pronunciation — xx
Introduction — 1

1 THE BUDDHA AND HIS INDIAN CONTEXT — 9
Background to the life of the Buddha — 9
The life of the Buddha — 14
The nature and role of the Buddha — 28
The nature and style of the Buddha's teaching — 29

2 EARLY BUDDHIST TEACHINGS: REBIRTH AND KARMA — 32
Rebirth and cosmology — 32
Karma — 39
Belief in rebirth and karma — 44

3 EARLY BUDDHIST TEACHINGS: THE FOUR HOLY TRUTHS — 47
The First Holy Truth: suffering — 47
The Second Holy Truth: the origin of suffering — 53
The Third Holy Truth: *Nibbāna* — 60
The Fourth Holy Truth: the Path — 68

4 EARLY DEVELOPMENTS IN BUDDHISM — 73
The early *Sangha* — 73
Emperor Asoka and Buddhism — 75
Devotion and symbolism in early Buddhism — 77
The *Abhidhamma* — 83
The early schools and their doctrines — 85
The rise of the Mahāyāna — 89

5 MAHĀYĀNA PHILOSOPHY 95
The Perfection of Wisdom literature and the Madhyamaka school 95
The Yogācāra school 104
Tathāgata-garbha thought 113
The *Avataṃsaka Sūtra* and the Hua-yen School 118

6 MAHĀYĀNA HOLY BEINGS 121
The path of the *Bodhisattva* 121
The Mahāyāna Buddhology 125
The Mahāyāna pantheon 129
The Tantric perspective 133

7 THE LATER HISTORY AND SPREAD OF BUDDHISM 139
Buddhism in India and Central Asia 139
Sri Lanka 141
South-east Asia excluding Vietnam 143
The lands of Northern Buddhism 144
China 148
Vietnam and Korea 159
Japan 161

8 BUDDHIST PRACTICE: DEVOTION 170
Focuses and locations of devotional acts 170
Bowing, offerings and chanting 172
The refuges 176
Attitudes to images 179
Protective chanting 180
Devotion to Avalokiteśvara 182
Devotion to Amitābha 187
Devotion to Bhaiṣajya-guru 189
Devotion to the Lotus *Sūtra* 190
Pilgrimage 190
Festivals 191

9 BUDDHIST PRACTICE: ETHICS 196
The role and basis of ethics in Buddhism 196
Giving 198
Keeping the precepts 199
Lovingkindness and compassion 209
Care for the dying and the dead 211
The ethics of social relationships 213

10 BUDDHIST PRACTICE: THE *SANGHA* 217
The role of monasticism 217
Patterns of ordination 220
Nuns 221
The monastic code of discipline 224
The economic base of the monastic life 229
Study and meditation 231
Communal life 236
Relations with the laity 240

11 BUDDHIST PRACTICE: MEDITATION AND THE DEVELOPMENT OF WISDOM 244
The approach to meditation 244
The practice of Calm meditation in Southern Buddhism 246
The practice of Insight meditation in Southern Buddhism 253
The classical path of Calm and Insight in Northern and Eastern Buddhism 257
Pure Land visualizations 258
Tantric visualizations 260
Tantric techniques of spontaneity 268
Zen meditation 270

12 THE MODERN HISTORY OF BUDDHISM IN ASIA 280
Communist Asia: Buddhism under a cloud 280
The continuing tradition and its modern varieties 283
Recovering old ground 296

13 BUDDHISM BEYOND ASIA 300
Scholarship 300
The influence of Buddhism through literature and philosophy 302
The Theosophical Society: a bridge between East and West 303
Immigration, foreign wars and travel 304
Buddhist missions and organizations 307

Appendix on Canons of Scriptures 322
Notes 325
Bibliography 326
Indices 344

ILLUSTRATIONS

The 'Peace Pagoda' in Battersea Park, London. *Frontispiece*

MAPS

1 Current location of Buddhism in Asia. *page* 6
2 The region where the Buddha lived and taught. 12

FIGURES

1 Sāñcī Stūpa. (Adapted from A. Volwahsen, *Living Architecture – India*, Macdonald, 1969, p. 91.) 79
2 Gotama's former wife presenting his son to him, from a second century AD carved relief. 80
3 Chart showing the presence, dominance and residual survival of Buddhism in different lands. 169

PLATES

1 A nineteenth-century Burmese image, showing Gotama at his 'conquest of Māra', just prior to his enlightenment. (Reproduced by kind permission of Durham University Oriental Museum.) 20
2 An image from Sārnāth, showing the Buddha making the gesture of 'Setting in motion the *Dhamma*-wheel', symbolizing his first sermon (fifth or sixth century AD). (Reproduced by kind permission of Ann and Bury Peerless Slide Resources and Picture Library.) 82
3 A *thang-ka*, or hanging scroll, depicting the *Bodhisattva* Mañjuśrī, at the Manjushri Institute, a Tibetan Buddhist College in the Lake District, England. (Reproduced by kind permission of Andy Weber.) 132

4 A *Vajra*-sceptre and *Vajra*-bell. (Reproduced by kind permission of Durham University Oriental Museum.) 136

5 An image of Tārā in the courtyard of a temple in Kathmandu, Nepal. 137

6 The Shwe-dāgon *Stūpa*, Rangoon, Burma, complete with scaffolding for re-gilding. (Reproduced by kind permission of Ann and Bury Peerless Slide Resources and Picture Library.) 171

7 A Thai Buddha-image and offerings, in the shrine-room of a meditation centre in Manchester, England. 174

8 A modern porcelain figure of Kuan-yin. 184

9 A *thang-ka* depicting Avalokiteśvara, with offering bowls in front of it. (Reproduced by kind permission of Andy Weber, on behalf of Peter Iseli.) 185

10 A small Japanese shrine depicting Amitābha and his two *Bodhisattva* helpers. Lacquered wood, with sandalwood figures. (Reproduced by kind permission of the Trustees of the British Museum.) 188

11 A Tibetan image of the *Heruka* Yamāntaka and his female consort. (Reproduced by kind permission of the Ashmolean Museum, Oxford.) 263

12 A *thang-ka* showing a *maṇḍala* surrounded by a number of Vajrayāna deities and spiritually realized beings. (Reproduced by kind permission of Durham University Oriental Museum.) 265

13 *Landscape with Pine Trees and Hut*, by Bunsei, fifteenth-century Japan. (Reproduced by kind permission of Special Chinese and Japanese Fund, Museum of Fine Arts, Boston.) 278

TABLES

1 States developed on the basis of Calm meditation. 251

2 Largest Buddhist groups in the USA (excluding the Buddhist Churches in America). 309

3 Largest Buddhist groups in Great Britain 312

ACKNOWLEDGEMENTS

I would like to express my gratitude to Lance S. Cousins, of Manchester University, for his very valuable comments on a draft of this work. I would also like to thank Ajahn Tiradhammo for his comments on the chapter on the *Sangha*, and Stewart McFarlaine, of Lancaster University, for his help with one or two points on Eastern Buddhism.

ABBREVIATIONS

Note that below:
Th. = a text of Pali Canon or later Theravādin literature
My. = a Mahāyāna text in Sanskrit, Chinese or Tibetan

A.	*Aṅguttara Nikāya* (Th.); (tr. F. L. Woodward and E. M. Hare), *The Book of Gradual Sayings*, 5 vols., London, PTS, 1932–6.
Asl.	*Aṭṭhasālinī* [Buddhaghosa's commentary on the *Dhamma-saṅgaṇī*] (Th.); (tr. Pe Maung Tin), *The Expositor*, 2 vols, London, PTS, 1920 and 1921.
Asta.	*Aṣṭasāhasrikā Prajñā-pāramitā Sūtra* (My.); (tr. E. Conze), *The Perfection of Wisdom in Eight Thousand Lines, and its Verse Summary*, Bolinas, Four Seasons Foundation, 1973.
BPS	Buddhist Publication Society.
Bvms.	*Buddhavaṃsa* (Th.); (tr. I. B. Horner) in *Minor Anthologies*, vol. III, London, PTS, 1975. Also includes translation of *Cariyā-piṭaka*.
c.	*circa.*
Ch.	Chinese.
D.	*Dīgha Nikāya* (Th.); (tr. by T. W. and C. A. F. Rhys Davids), *Dialogues of the Buddha*, 3 vols., London, PTS, 1899–1921.
Dhp.	*Dhammapada* (Th.); (tr. Nārada Thera), *The Dhammapada*, London, John Murray, 1954 (the same translation, accompanied by the Pali text, is also published by the Buddhist Missionary Society, Kuala Lumpur, 1978 – available from Wisdom Publications); (tr. Acharya Buddharakkhita), *The Dhammapada: The Buddha's Path of Wisdom*, Kandy, Sri Lanka, BPS, 1985.

Dhp. A. *Dhammapada Commentary* (Th.); (tr. E. W. Burlingame), *Buddhist Legends*, 3 vols., Harvard Oriental Series, Harvard University Press, 1921; repr. London, PTS, 1979.

Dhs. *Dhamma-saṅgaṇi* (Th.); (tr. C. A. F. Rhys Davids), *Buddhist Psychological Ethics*, London, PTS, 1900, 3rd edn 1974.

Dial. Ling, T., *The Buddha's Philosophy of Man: Early Indian Buddhist Dialogues* [selected from *D.*, using the Rhys Davids's translations, with revisions], London, Dent, 1981.

Essays Suzuki, D. T., *Essays in Zen Buddhism*, First, Second and Third Series, London, Luzac & Co., 1927, 1933 and 1934; Rider, 1949, 2nd edn 1970.

FWBO Friends of the Western Buddhist Order.

It. *Itivuttaka* (Th.); (tr. F. L. Woodward), in *Minor Anthologies*, vol. II, London, PTS, 1935.

Jap. Japanese.

Jat. *Jātaka with Commentary* (Th.); (tr. by various hands under E. B. Cowell), *The Jātaka or Stories of the Buddha's Former Births*, 6 vols., London, PTS, 1895–1907.

JIABS *Journal of the International Association of Buddhist Studies.*

JPTS *Journal of the Pāli Text Society.*

Khp. *Khuddaka-pāṭha* (Th.); (tr. with its commentary, Bhikkhu Ñāṇamoli), *Minor Readings and Illustrator*, London, PTS, 1960.

Khp. A. Commentary on *Khp.*: see last item for translation.

Kor. Korean.

Kvu. *Kathāvatthu* (Th.); (tr. S. Z. Aung and C. A. F. Rhys Davids), *Points of Controversy*, London, PTS, 1915.

Lanka. *Lankāvatāra Sūtra* (My.); (tr. D. T. Suzuki), *The Lankavatara Sutra*, London, Routledge & Kegan Paul, 1932.

Lotus *Sūtra* *Saddharma-puṇḍarīka Sūtra* (My.); (tr. H. Kern, from Sanskrit), *The Saddharma-puṇḍarīka* or *The Lotus of the True Law*, Sacred Books of the East, vol. XXI, Oxford, Clarendon Press, 1884; repr. Delhi, MB, 1968; (tr. B. Kato *et al.*, from Chinese), *The Threefold Lotus Sūtra*, New York and Tokyo, Weatherhill/Kosei, 1975.

M. *Majjhima Nikāya* (Th.); (tr. by I. B. Horner), *Middle Length Sayings*, 3 vols., London, PTS, 1954–9.

MB Motilal Banarsidass (publisher).

MBS Mahā Bodhi Society.

Medit. Conze, E., *Buddhist Meditation* [anthology], New York, Harper Torchbooks, 1969, and London, Allen & Unwin, 1972.

Mk. *Mūla-madhyamaka-kārikā* [of Nāgārjuna] (My.); translation included in F. J. Streng, *Emptiness: A Study in Religious Meaning*, Nashville, Tenn., Abingdon Press, 1967; (tr. K. K. Inada), *Nāgārjuna: A Translation of his Mūlamadhyamaka-kārikā, with an Introductory Essay* [and Sanskrit text], Tokyo, Hokuseido Press, 1970.

Miln. *Milindapañha* (Th.); (tr. I. B. Horner), *Milinda's Questions*, 2 vols., London, PTS, 1963 and 1964.

Ms. *Mahāyāna-saṃgraha* [of Asaṅga] (My.); (tr. E. Lamotte), *La Somme du Grande Véhicule d'Asanga*, 2 vols., Louvain, Bureaux du Muséon, 1938–9.

Mv. *Madhyānta-vibhāga* [of Asaṅga/Maitreya] (My.); (tr. T. Stcherbatsky), *Madhyānta-vibhāga, Discourse on Discrimination Between Middle and Extremes*, Bibliotheca Buddhica, 30, 1936; repr. Delhi, MB, no date.

Mvkb. *Madhyānta-vibhāga-kārikā-bhāṣya* [of Vasubandhu] (My.); ch. 1 translated in T. A. Kochumuttom, *A Buddhist Doctrine of Experience: A New Translation and Interpretation of the Works of Vasubandhu the Yogācārin*, Delhi, MB, 1982. All translated in S. Anacker, *Seven Works of Vasubandhu*, Delhi, MB, 1984.

Mvs. *Mahāvastu* [of the Lokottaravāda school]; (tr. J. J. Jones), *The Mahāvastu, Translated from the Buddhist Sanskrit*, 3 vols, London, PTS, 1949–56.

Panca. *Pañcaviṃśati-sāhasrikā Prajñā-pāramitā Sūtra* (My.); (tr. E. Conze), *The Large Sutra on Perfect Wisdom*, London, Luzac & Co., 1961–4; repr. Delhi, MB, 1979, and Berkeley, Calif., Center for South and Southeastern Asia Studies, University of California, 1985.

Pati. *Paṭisambhidā-magga* (Th.); (tr. Bhikkhu Ñāṇamoli), *The Path of Discrimination*, London, PTS, 1982.

Plat. *The Platform Sutra of the Sixth Patriarch*, (tr. from Chinese by P. B. Yampolsky), New York, Columbia University Press, 1967.

pron. pronounced.

PTS Pāli Text Society.

Rv. *Ratnagotra-vibhāga* [of Asaṅga/Maitreya, or Sthiramati/Saramati] (My.); (tr. from Tibetan by K. H. and K. Holmes), *The Changeless Continuity: Mahayana Uttara Tantra Sastra*, 2nd edn, Eskdalemuir, Dumfriesshire, Scotland, Karma Drubgyud Darjay Ling, 1985; (tr. from Sanskrit by J. Takasaki), *A Study of the Ratnagotravibhāga (Uttaratantra): Being a Treatise on the Tathāgatagarbha Theory of Mahāyāna Buddhism*, Rome, Series Orientales Rome XXIII, 1966.

S. *Saṃyutta Nikāya* (Th.); (tr. by C. A. F. Rhys Davids and F. L. Woodward), *The Book of Kindred Sayings*, 5 vols., London, PTS, 1917–30.

Script. Conze, E., *Buddhist Scriptures*, [anthology], Harmondsworth, Penguin, 1959.

Skt Sanskrit.

Sn. *Sutta-nipāta* (Th.); (tr. K. R. Norman), *The Group of Discourses*, in paperback *The Rhinoceros Horn and Other Early Buddhist Poems*, London, PTS, 1984; (tr. H. Saddhatissa), *The Sutta-Nipāta*, London, Curzon Press, 1985.

Sources Beyer, S. V. *The Buddhist Experience: Sources and Interpretations* [anthology], Encino, Calif., Dickenson, 1974.

Srim. *Śrīmālā-devī Siṃhanāda Sūtra* (My.); (tr. D. M. Paul), *The Buddhist Feminine Ideal: Queen Śrīmālā and the Tathāgatagarbha*, American Academy of Religion Dissertation Series, no. 30, Missoula, Mont., Scholar's Press, 1980; (tr. A. & H. Wayman), *The Lion's Roar of Queen Śrīmālā*, New York and London, Columbia University Press, 1974; repr. Buddhist Traditions Series, vol. 4, Delhi, MB, 1989.

Texts Conze, E., Horner, I. B., Snellgrove, D., and Waley, A. (eds.) *Buddhist Texts Through the Ages* [anthology, references are to the number of the text], Cassirer, Oxford, 1954; London, Luzac & Co., and New York, Harper Torchbooks, 1964.

Thag. *Thera-gāthā* (Th.); (tr. K. R. Norman), *Elders' Verses*, vol. I, London, PTS, 1969.

Thig. *Therī-gāthā* (Th.); (tr. K. R. Norman), *Elders' Verses*, vol. II, London, PTS, 1971.

Tib. Tibetan.

Trad. De Bary, W. T. (ed.) *The Buddhist Tradition in India, China and Japan* [anthology with introductory essays], New York, The Modern Library, 1969, Vintage, 1972.

Trims. *Triṃśatikā-kārikā* [of Vasubandhu] (My.); see under *Mvkb.* for translations.

Tsn. *Trisvabhāva-nirdeśa* [of Vasubandhu] (My.); see under *Mvkb.* for translations.

Ud. *Udāna* (Th.); (tr. F. L. Woodward), in *Minor Anthologies*, vol. II, London, PTS, 1935.

Vc. *Vajracchedikā Prajñā-pāramitā Sūtra* (My.); (tr. and explained by E. Conze), in *Buddhist Wisdom Books: The Diamond Sutra and the Heart Sutra*, London, George Allen & Unwin, 1958.

Vibh. *Vibhaṅga* (Th.); (tr. U. Thittila), *The Book of Analysis*, London, PTS, 1969.

Vibh. A. Commentary on *Vibh.* (Th.); (tr. Ñāṇamoli), *Dispeller of Delusion*, 2 vols., London, PTS, 1988 and 1989.

Vims. *Viṃśatikā-kārikā* [of Vasubandhu] (My.); see under *Mvkb.* for translations.

Vin. *Vinaya Piṭaka* (Th.); (tr. I. B. Horner), *The Book of the Discipline*, 6 vols., London, PTS, 1938–66.

Vism. *Visuddhimagga* [of Buddhaghosa] (Th.); (tr. Bhikkhu Ñāṇamoli), *The Path of Purification*, 3rd edn, Kandy, Sri Lanka, BPS, 1975, and, 2 vols., Berkeley, Calif., Shambhala, 1976.

Vrtti. *Viṃśatikā-vṛtti* [of Vasubandhu] (My.); see under *Mvkb.* for translations.

Vv. *Vigraha-vyāvartanī* [of Nāgārjuna] (My.); translation included in F. J. Streng, *Emptiness: A Study in Religious Meaning*, Nashville, Tenn., Abington Press, 1967.

Wheel *The Wheel*: a series of booklets produced by the BPS.

Most of these works are still in print; reprints have only been mentioned where the publisher differs from the original one. Translations published by the PTS are from the editions of the text published by them. Other translations are from various editions. Translations given in this book are not necessarily the same as those in the cited translations, particularly in the case of translations from Pali.

Reference is generally to volume and page number in original text; but for *Dhp.*, *Sn.*, *Thag.*, and *Thig.*, it is to verse number, and Mahāyāna works other than *Sūtras* are referred to by chapter (ch.) and verse number. For *Kvu.*, reference is either to the page number or the number of the 'book' and the discussion point within it. *Dhs.*, *Plat.* and *Vc.* are referred to by section (sec.) number in text.

The page numbers of the relevant edition of an original text are generally given in brackets in its translation, or at the top of the page. In translations of the Pali Canon, the volume number of the translation generally corresponds to the volume of the PTS edition of the texts, except that *Vin.* III, IV, and V are translated as *Book of the Discipline*, vols. I, II and III, and *Vin.* I and II are translated as *Book of the Discipline*, vols. IV and V.

A NOTE ON LANGUAGE AND PRONUNCIATION

Most of the foreign words in this work are from Pali and Sanskrit, which are closely related languages of ancient India. Pali is the scriptural, liturgical and scholarly language of Southern Buddhism, one of the three main cultural traditions of Buddhism. Sanskrit, or rather 'Buddhist Hybrid Sanskrit', is the language in which many of the scriptures and scholarly treatises of Mahāyāna Buddhism came to be written in India. Northern and Eastern Buddhism, where the Mahāyāna form of Buddhism predominates, generally use the Tibetan or Chinese translations of these texts. Many works on Buddhism give only Sanskrit versions of words, but this is artificial as Sanskrit is no longer used by Buddhists (except in Nepal), but Pali is still much in use. This work therefore uses the Pali version of terms for most of early Buddhism, for Southern/Theravāda Buddhism, and when discussing Buddhism in general. Sanskrit versions are used when particularly discussing Mahāyāna forms of Buddhism, for some early schools which also came to use Sanskrit, and when discussing Hinduism. The Sanskrit term '*Stūpa*', referring to a relic mound, is also used in preference to the less well-known Pali term '*Thūpa*'. Sanskrit '*karma*' is also used instead of Pali '*kamma*', as it is now also an English word. In many cases, Pali and Sanskrit terms are spelt the same. Where the spellings are different, the Pali spelling is the simpler one.

Both Pali and Sanskrit have more than twenty-six letters, so to write them in the roman alphabet means that this needs to be expanded by the use of diacritical marks. Once the specific sounds of the letters are known, Pali and Sanskrit words are then pronounced as they are written, unlike English ones. It is therefore worth taking account of the diacritical marks, as they give a clear guide to pronunciation. The letters are pronounced as follows:

(i) ***a*** is short and flat, like the *u* in 'hut' or 'utter'
i is short, like *i* in 'bit'
u is like *u* in 'put', or *oo* in 'foot'
e is like *e* in 'bed', only pronounced long
o is long, like *o* in 'note' (or, before more than one consonant, more like *o* in 'not' or 'odd').

(ii) A bar over a vowel makes it long:
ā is like *a* in 'barn'
ī is like *ee* in 'beet'
ū is like *u* in 'brute'.

(iii) When there is a dot under a letter (***ṭ, ḍ, ṇ, ṣ, ṛ, ḷ***), this means that it is a 'cerebral' letter. Imagine a dot on the roof of one's mouth that one must touch with one's tongue when saying these letters. This produces a characteristically 'Indian' sound. It also makes ***ṣ*** into a *sh* sound, and ***ṛ*** into *ri*.

(iv) ***ś*** is like a normal *sh* sound.

(v) Aspirated consonants (***kh, gh, ch, jh, ṭh, ḍh, th, dh, ph, bh***) are accompanied by a strong breath-pulse from the chest, as when uttering English consonants very emphatically. For example:
ch is like *ch-h* in 'church-hall'
th is like *t-h* in 'hot-house'
ph is like *p-h* in 'cup-handle'
When aspirated consonants occur as part of a consonant cluster, the aspiration comes at the end of the cluster.

(vi) ***c*** is like *ch* in 'choose'.

(vii) ***ñ*** is like *ny* in 'canyon', ***ññ*** is like *nnyy*.

(viii) ***ṃ*** is a pure nasal sound, made when the mouth is closed but air escapes through the nose, with the vocal chords vibrating; it approximates to *ng*.

(ix) ***ṅ*** is an *ng*, nasal sound said from the mouth, rather than the nose. It is omitted here, though (except in the Appendix, Abbreviations and Bibliography), as an *n* before a *g*, *gh*, *k* or *kh* (gutterals, as is *ṅ*) is always in this form, as, for example in *Sangha*.

(x) ***v*** may be somewhat similar to English *v* when at the start of a word, or between vowels, but like *w* when combined with another consonant.

(xi) Double consonants are always pronounced long, for example *nn* is as in 'unnecessary'.

All other letters are pronounced as in English.

ō is used to denote a long *o* in Japanese (as in 'note', rather than 'not').

For Tibetan words, the direct transcription is given followed (on first use, and in the index) by the pronunciation in brackets (as in G. Tucci's *The Religions of Tibet*), for pronunciations are often hard to deduce.

For foreign words in any language, when their first occurrence is in the plural, this will be indicated by an ending ....'s, for example *peta*'s, to indicate that the English plural ending is not part of the original word. Plurals of foreign words will also appear in the Indices in this form, in their main entry.

INTRODUCTION

The history of Buddhism spans almost 2,500 years from its origin in India with Siddhattha Gotama (Pali; Siddhartha Gautama in Sanskrit), through its spread to most parts of Asia and, in the twentieth century, to the West. While its fortunes have waxed and waned over the ages, over half of the present world population live in areas where Buddhism is, or has been, a dominant cultural force.

The English term 'Buddhism' correctly indicates that the religion is characterized by a devotion to 'the Buddha', 'Buddhas' or 'buddhahood'. 'Buddha' is not, in fact, a proper name, but a descriptive title meaning 'Awakened One' or 'Enlightened One'. This implies that most people are seen, in a spiritual sense, as being asleep – unaware of how things really are. As 'Buddha' is a title, it should not be used as a name, as in, for example, 'Buddha taught that...'. In many contexts, 'the Buddha' is specific enough, meaning the Buddha known to history, Gotama. From its earliest times, though, the Buddhist tradition has postulated other Buddhas who have lived on earth in distant past ages, or who will do so in the future. The later tradition also postulated the existence of many Buddhas currently existing in other parts of the universe. All such Buddhas, known as *sammā-sambuddha*'s, or 'perfect fully Awakened Ones', are nevertheless seen as occurring only rarely within the vast and ancient cosmos. More common are those who are 'buddhas' in a lesser sense, who have awakened to the truth by practising in accordance with the guidance of a perfect Buddha such as Gotama.

As 'Buddha' does not refer to a unique individual, Buddhism is less focussed on the person of its founder than is, for example, Christianity. The emphasis in Buddhism is on the *teachings* of the Buddha(s), and the 'awakening' of human personality that these are seen to lead to.

Nevertheless, Buddhists do show great reverence to Gotama as a supreme teacher and an exemplar of the ultimate goal that all strive for, so that probably more images of him exist than of any other historical figure.

In its long history, Buddhism has used a variety of teachings and means to help people first develop a calmer, more integrated and compassionate personality, and then 'wake up' from restricting delusions: delusions which cause attachment and thus suffering for an individual and those he interacts with. The guide for this process of transformation has been the '*Dhamma*' (Skt *Dharma*): meaning the eternal truths and cosmic law-orderliness discovered by the Buddha(s), Buddhist teachings, the Buddhist path of practice, and the goal of Buddhism, the timeless *Nibbāna* (Skt *Nirvāṇa*). Buddhism thus essentially consists of understanding, practising and realizing *Dhamma*.

The most important bearers of the Buddhist tradition have been the monks and nuns who make up the Buddhist *Sangha* or 'Community'. From approximately a hundred years after the death of Gotama, certain differences arose in the *Sangha*, which gradually led to the development of a number of monastic fraternities (*nikāya*'s), each following a slightly different monastic code, and to different schools of thought (*vāda*'s). All branches of the *Sangha* trace their ordination-line back to one or other of the early fraternities; but of the early schools of thought, only that which became known as the Theravāda has continued to this day. Its name indicates that it purports to follow the 'teaching' which is 'ancient' or 'primordial' (*thera*): that is, the Buddha's teaching. While it has not remained static, it has kept close to what we know of the early teachings of Buddhism, and preserved their emphasis on attaining liberation by one's own efforts, using the *Dhamma* as guide. Around the beginning of the Christian era, a movement began which led to a new style of Buddhism known as the Mahāyāna, or 'Great Vehicle'. This has been more overtly innovative, so that for many centuries, Indian Mahāyānists continued to compose new scriptures. The Mahāyāna is characterized, on the one hand, by devotion to a number of holy saviour beings, and on the other by several sophisticated philosophies, developed by extending the implications of the earlier teachings. In the course of time, in India and beyond, the Mahāyāna produced many schools of its own, such as Zen. One group of these which developed by the sixth century in India, and is sometimes seen as separate from the Mahāyāna, is known as the Mantrayāna, or the '*Mantra* Vehicle'. It is mostly the same as the Mahāyāna in its doctrines, but developed a range of powerful new *practices* to attain the goals of the Mahāyāna, such as the meditative repetitions of sacred words of power (*mantra*'s) and complex visualization practices.

Our knowledge of the teachings of the Buddha is based on several canons of scripture, which derive from the early *Sangha's* oral transmission of bodies of teachings agreed on at several councils. The Theravādin 'Pali Canon' is preserved in the Pali language, which is based upon a dialect close to that spoken by the Buddha, Old Māgadhī. It is the most complete extant early canon, and contains some of the earliest material. Most of its teachings are in fact the common property of all Buddhist schools, being simply the teachings which the Theravādins preserved from the early common stock. While parts of the Pali Canon clearly originated after the time of the Buddha, much must derive from his teachings. There is an overall harmony to the Canon, suggesting 'authorship' of its system of thought by one mind. As the Buddha taught for forty-five years, some signs of development in teachings may only reflect changes during this period. The most promising attempts at relative dating rely on criteria of style; comparisons of different canons are also useful. These canons gradually diverged as different floating oral traditions were drawn on, and systematizing texts peculiar to each school were added. Many of the minor differences within and between canons, however, can be seen to be due to the way in which oral traditions always produce several different permutations of essentially the same story or teachings.

The early canons contain a section on *Vinaya*, or monastic discipline, one on *Sutta*'s, or 'discourses' of the Buddha, and some contain one on *Abhidhamma*, or 'further teachings', which systematizes the *Sutta*-teachings in the form of detailed analyses of human experience. The main teachings of Buddhism are contained in the *Suttas*, which in the Pali Canon are divided into five *Nikāya*'s or 'Collections', the first four (sixteen volumes) generally being the older. The Pali Canon was one of the earliest to be written down, this being in Sri Lanka in around 80 BC, after which little, if any, new material was added to it. There are also sections of six non-Theravādin early canons preserved in Chinese and Tibetan translations, fragments of a Sanskrit Canon still existing in Nepal, and odd texts in various languages of India and Central Asia found in Tibet, Central Asia, and Japan.

The extensive non-canonical Pali literature includes additional

Abhidhamma works, historical chronicles, and many volumes of commentaries. An extremely clear introduction to many points of Buddhist doctrine is the *Milindapañha*, which purports to record conversations between a Buddhist monk and Milinda (Menander; *c.* 155–130 BC), a king of Greek ancestry. Another is the *Visuddhimagga*, a very influential Theravāda compendium of meditation practices and doctrine, written by Buddhaghosa (fifth century AD).

Mahāyāna texts were composed from around the first century BC, originating as written, not oral, works. In time, they were recorded in a form of the Indian prestige language, Sanskrit. While many are attributed to the Buddha, their form and content clearly show that they were later re-statements and extensions of the Buddha's message. The main sources for our understanding of Mahāyāna teachings are the very extensive Chinese and Tibetan Buddhist Canons. While most of the Pali Canon has been translated into English, only selected texts from these have been translated into Western languages, though much progress is being made. For some details on the three main extant Canons, see Appendix.

While Buddhism is now only a minority religion within the borders of modern India, its spread beyond India means that it is currently found in three main cultural areas. These are those of: 'Southern Buddhism', where the Theravāda school is found, along with some elements incorporated from the Mahāyāna; 'Eastern Buddhism', where the Chinese transmission of Mahāyāna Buddhism is found; and the area of Tibetan culture, 'Northern Buddhism', which is the heir of late Indian Buddhism, where the Mantrayāna version of the Mahāyāna is the dominant form.

Buddhism's concentration on the essentials of spiritual development has meant that it has been able to co-exist with both other major religions and popular folk traditions which catered for people's desire for a variety of rituals. There has hardly ever been a 'wholly' Buddhist society, if this means a kind of religious one-party state. Buddhism has been very good at adapting to different cultures while guarding its own somewhat fluid borders by a critical tolerance of other traditions. Its style has been to offer invitations to several levels of spiritual practice for those who have been ready to commit themselves. In Southern Buddhist lands, worship of pre-Buddhist nature gods has continued in South-east Asia, while, in Sri Lanka, Buddhists often worship gods whose cults are indigenous or Indian in origin. Most Buddhists would not see this as a betrayal of Buddhism, but just an attempt to interact with minor powers of the cosmos for some worldly advantage: like a person asking a member of parliament to try and help him. In Northern Buddhism, a similar relationship exists with the indigenous Bon religion of Tibet. In China, Taiwan, Korea and Vietnam, Buddhism has co-existed with Confucianism – more a system of social philosophy than a religion – the Taoist religion, and much folk religion. People would often partake of elements of all these traditions. In Japan, Buddhism has existed alongside the indigenous nature-orientated religion of Shintō, and the Confucianism that it brought with it from China. Traditionally, people would be married by Shintō rites and buried with Buddhist ones. In China (which now includes Tibet), Mongolia, regions of the Soviet Union, North Korea, Vietnam, Cambodia, and Laos, Buddhism now exists under Communist governments which do not favour religion. Chinese Communists persecuted Buddhism and vandalized its temples during the Cultural Revolution, but the government now seems to be easing up on it, so as to allow a gentle resurgence in China proper, and a continuation of the very strong Buddhist culture of Tibet.

The Buddhist population of Asia (excluding Western and Asian Buddhists in the West) is as follows. There are approximately 105 million Buddhists of the Southern tradition (figures in brackets are 1985 total populations of each country): Sri Lanka, 11m. (16m.); Burma, 30m. (37m.); Thailand, 47m. (51m.); Cambodia, 6m. (7m.) and Laos, 3·5m. (4m.). Minority populations also exist in: southern Vietnam bordering Cambodia, 0·7m; south-west China (Yunnan) bordering Laos and Burma, 0·85m.; regions bordering Burma in Chittagong, Bangladesh, 0·4m., and India, 0·25m.?; northern Malaysia, 0·5m.?, and recent converts in India, 4·5m., Indonesia, 1m.?, and Nepal, 0·2m.?.

Northern Buddhism has approximately 25 million followers: Tibet, 1·6m. (2m.); Tibetan and Mongol people in (the rest of) north-west China, 14m.?? (62m.?); Mongolia, 1·2m. (1·9m.); Bhutan, 1·4m. (1·4m.); Nepal, 6m. (17m.), and the Buryat, Tuva, and Kalmyk Republics of the Soviet Union, 0·3m. (1·3m.). Minority populations also exist in north and north-east India, 0·35m., and Bali, Indonesia 0·5m.?, and 0·08m. Tibetan exiles live in India and Nepal.

It is difficult to give a figure for the number of 'Buddhists' of the Eastern tradition, particularly China, due to traditional multi-religion

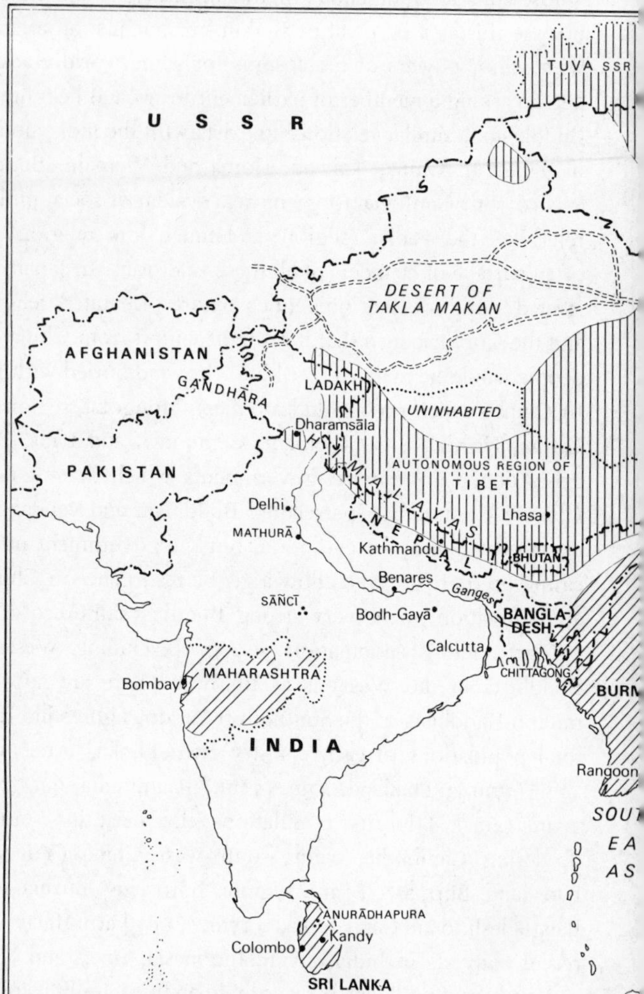

Map 1 Current location of Buddhism in Asia.

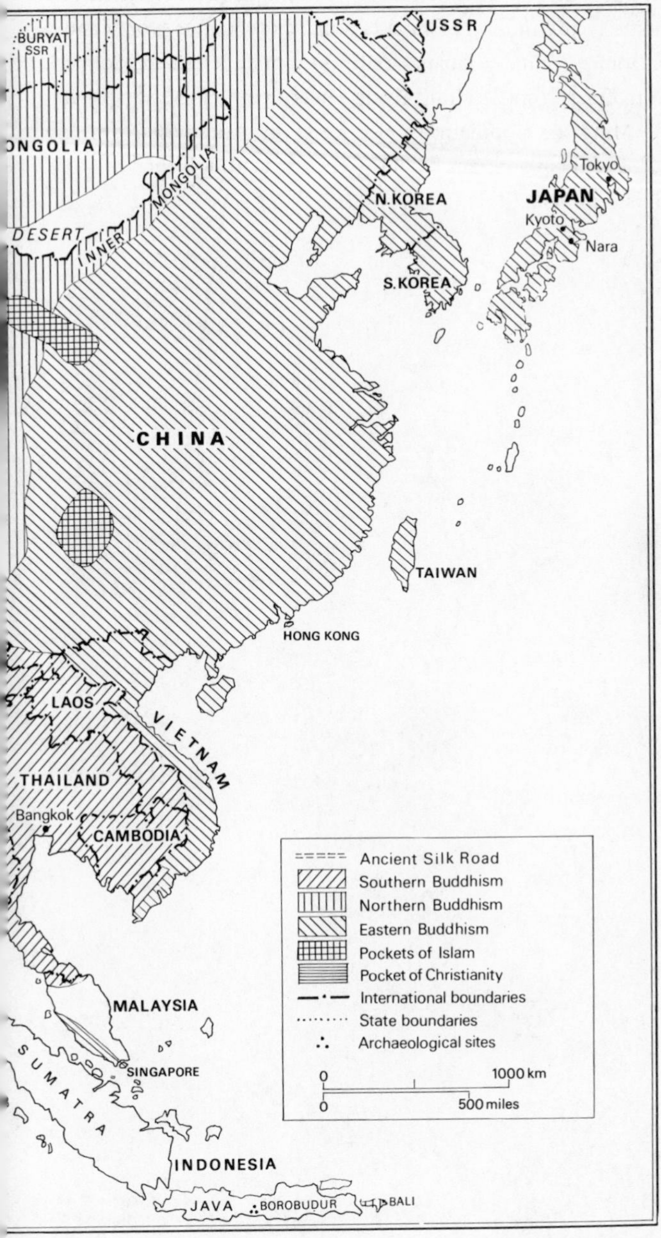
BURYAT SSR
USSR
MONGOLIA
INNER MONGOLIA
DESERT
N.KOREA
S.KOREA
JAPAN
Tokyo
Kyoto
Nara
CHINA
TAIWAN
HONG KONG
LAOS
VIETNAM
THAILAND
Bangkok
CAMBODIA
MALAYSIA
SINGAPORE
SUMATRA
INDONESIA
JAVA
BOROBUDUR
BALI
Ancient Silk Road
Southern Buddhism
Northern Buddhism
Eastern Buddhism
Pockets of Islam
Pocket of Christianity
International boundaries
State boundaries
Archaeological sites
0 1000 km
0 500 miles

allegiance and the current dominance of Communism. A somewhat arbitrary estimate is 365 million: China, 250m.?? (1060m.); North and South Korea, 20m.? (62m.); Japan, 40m.? (121m.); Vietnam, 40m.? (60m.); Taiwan, 6m.? (19m.); Hong Kong, 2m.? (5m.), and Singapore, 1m.? (2·5m.). Minority populations also exist in: Indonesia, 1m.?; Malaysia, 3m.?, and Thailand, 2m.? This gives a very rough total of 495 million Buddhists in Asia.

I

THE BUDDHA AND HIS INDIAN CONTEXT

Indian culture has not been as concerned with recording precise dates as have Chinese or Graeco-Roman culture, so datings can not always be arrived at with accuracy. The Buddhist sources say that Gotama died either 218 or 100 years before the consecration of emperor Asoka. From references in Asokan edicts to certain Greek kings, this can be dated at *c.* 268 BC. As all sources agree that Gotama was eighty when he died, his dates would be either *c.* 566–486 BC or 448–368 BC. In the past, modern scholars have generally accepted the earlier dates, but the consensus is now that they rest on evidence which is too flimsy. Something approaching the later dates is seen as more likely, perhaps *c.* 480–400 BC.

BACKGROUND TO THE LIFE OF THE BUDDHA

Brahmanism

The Buddha taught in the region of the Ganges basin in north-east India, where the dominant religion was Brahmanism, administered by priests known as Brahmins (Skt *Brāhmaṇa*'s). Later, around 200 BC, this tradition began to develop into the religion now known as Hinduism. Brahmanism had entered the north-west of the Indian sub-continent by around 1500 BC, brought by a nomadic people who seem to have come from an area now in eastern Turkey, southern Russia and northern Iran. In this area, people spoke a postulated Aryan (Skt *Ārya*) language, the basis of a number of 'Indo-European' languages spread by migration from there to India, Iran, Greece, Italy and other parts of Western Europe. The form of the language spoken in India was Sanskrit (from which Pali is derived), which is thus linked, through Greek and Latin, to modern European languages such as English. The influx of the

Aryans brought to an end the declining Indus Valley Civilization, a sophisticated city-based culture which had existed in the region of Pakistan since around 2500 BC. The religion of the Aryans was based on the *Veda*, a body of 'revealed' oral teachings and hymns: the *Ṛg Veda Saṃhitā* (*c.* 1500–1200 BC), three other *Veda Saṃhitā*'s, and later compositions known as *Brāhmaṇa*'s and *Upaniṣad*'s. The Aryans worshipped thirty-three gods known as *deva*'s, anthropomorphized principles seen as active in nature, the cosmos, and human life. The central rite of the religion was one in which the priests sang the praises of a particular *deva* and offered him sacrifices by placing them in a sacrificial fire. In return, they hoped for such boons as health, increase in cattle, and immortality in the afterlife with the *devas*. In the *Brāhmaṇas* (*c.* 1000–800 BC), animal sacrifices came to be added to the earlier offerings, such as grain and milk. The enunciation of the sacred sacrificial verses, known as *mantra*'s, was also seen as manipulating a sacred power called *Brahman*, so that the ritual was regarded as actually coercing the *devas* into sustaining the order of the cosmos and giving what was wanted. The great responsibility of the priests in this regard was reflected in them placing themselves at the head of what was regarded as a divinely-ordained hierarchy of four social classes, the others being those of the *Kṣatriya*'s or warrior-leaders of society in peace or war, the *Vaiśya*'s, or cattle-rearers and cultivators, and the *Śūdra*'s, or servants. A person's membership of one of these four *varṇa*'s, or 'complexions' of humanity, was seen as determined by birth; in later Hinduism the system incorporated thousands of lesser social groupings and became known as the caste, or *jāti*, system.

Brahmins learnt of yogic techniques of meditation, physical isolation, fasting, celibacy and asceticism from ascetics whose traditions may have gone back to the Indus Valley Civilization. Such techniques were found to be useful as spiritual preparations for performing the sacrifice. Some Brahmins then retired to the forest and used them as a way of actually carrying out the sacrifice in an internalized, visualized form. Out of the teachings of the more orthodox of these forest dwellers were composed the *Upaniṣads*, only two of which are certainly pre-Buddhist. In these, *Brahman* is seen as the substance underlying the whole cosmos, and as identical with the *ātman*, the universal self which the yogic element of the Indian tradition had sought deep within the mind. By true knowledge of this identity, it was held that a person could attain liberation from reincarnation after death, and merge back into *Brahman*. The idea of reincarnation seems to have developed as an extension of the idea, found in the *Brāhmaṇas*, that the power of a person's sacrificial action might be insufficient to lead to an afterlife that did not end in another death. The *Upaniṣads*, perhaps due to some non-Aryan influence, saw such a death as being followed by reincarnation as a human or animal. Non-Aryan influence was probably more certain in developing the idea that it was the quality of a person's *karma*, or 'action', that determines the nature of their reincarnation in an insecure earthly form; previously, '*karma*' had only referred to sacrificial action. Nevertheless, Brahmanism continued to see karma in largely ritual terms, and actions were judged relative to a person's *varṇa*, their station in society.

At the time of the Buddha, most Brahmins aimed at attaining the heaven of the creator god Brahmā by means of truthfulness, study of the Vedic teachings, and either sacrifice or austerities. Some were saintly, but others seem to have been haughty and wealthy, supporting themselves by putting on large, expensive and bloody sacrifices, often paid for by kings. At its popular level, Brahmanism incorporated practices based on protective magic spells, and pre-Brahmanical spirit-worship no doubt continued.

The *Samaṇas*

The time of the Buddha was one of changing social conditions, where the traditions of small kin-based communities were being undermined as these were swallowed up by expanding kingdoms, such as those of Magadha and Kosala. A number of cities had developed which were the centres of administration and of developing organized trade, based on a money economy. The ideas expressed in the *Upaniṣads* were starting to filter out into the wider intellectual community and were being hotly debated, both by Brahmins and wandering philosophers known as *Samaṇa*'s, who were somewhat akin to the early Greek philosophers and mystics. The *Samaṇas* rejected the Vedic tradition and wandered free of family ties, living by alms, in order to think, debate and investigate. Many came from the new urban centres, where old certainties were being questioned, and increasing disease from population-concentration may have posed the universal problem of

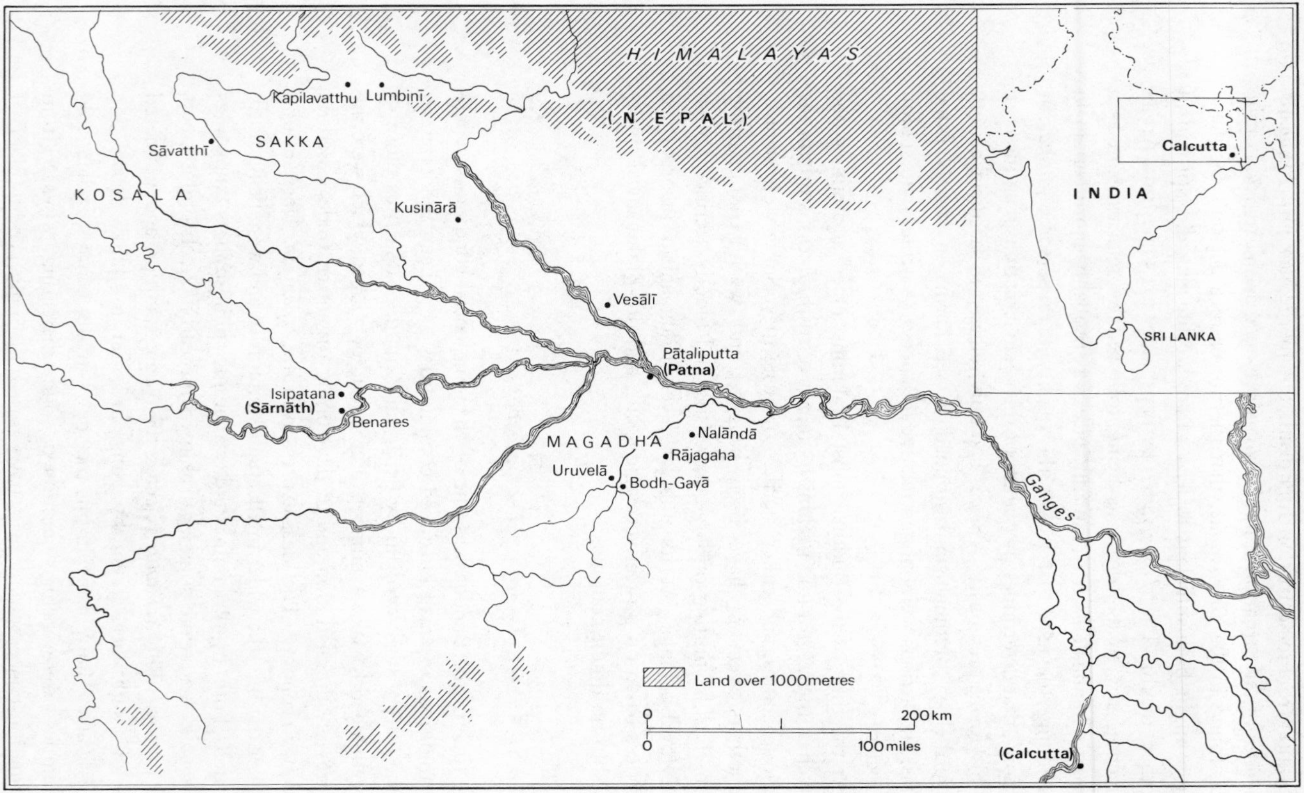

Map 2 The region where the Buddha lived and taught.

human suffering in a relatively stark form. They therefore sought to find a basis of true and lasting happiness in a changing and insecure world.

In its origin, Buddhism was a *Samaṇa*-movement. Its description and assessment of the other *Samaṇa* groups is contained in the *Sāmañña-phala Sutta* (*D*.I.47–86). One of the major *Samaṇa* groups was that of the Jains (referred to in the Buddhist *Suttas* as Nigaṇṭha's). Jainism was founded, or at least led in the Buddha's day, by Vardhamāna the Mahāvīra, or 'Great Hero'. It teaches that all things, even stones, are alive, each containing a *jīva*, or 'life-principle'. These are seen as individually distinct, unlike the universal *ātman* of the *Upaniṣads*, and to be naturally bright, omniscient and blissful. The aim of Jainism is to liberate the *jīva* from the round of rebirths by freeing it from its encrustation of karma, seen as a kind of subtle matter. The methods of doing so are primarily wearing out the results of previous karma by austerities such as fasting, going unwashed, and pulling out the hair, and also, to avoid the generation of new karma, self-restraint, total non-violence (Skt *ahiṃsā*) to any form of life, and vegetarianism. The free-will of the *jīva* is emphasized, though even actions such as unintentionally killing an insect are held to generate karma. While the Buddha agreed with the Jains on such matters as rebirth and non-violence, he saw their theory of karma as somewhat mechanical and inflexible, and opposed their asceticism as too extreme.

A group of *Samaṇas* that rivalled the Buddhists and Jains in their early centuries was that of the Ājīvaka's. Their founder was Makkhali Gosāla, but they also drew on ideas from Pūraṇa Kassapa and Pakudha Kaccāyana (according to the Pali tradition). Gosāla's key doctrine was that *niyati*, or impersonal 'destiny', governed all, such that humans had no ability to affect their future lives by their karma: actions were not freely done, but themselves determined by *niyati*. Gosāla thus believed in rebirth, but not in the principle of karma as that which regulates the level of a person's rebirth. The souls of living beings are driven by *niyati* alone through a fixed progression of types of rebirths, from a low form of animal to an advanced human who becomes an Ājīvaka ascetic. The Ājīvakas practised rigorous asceticism such as fasting, nakedness, and perhaps disfiguring initiations, and aimed to die by self-starvation (as Vardhamāna in fact did), as a fitting way to end their last rebirth. Both Vardhamāna, who had originally been on good terms with Gosāla, and the Buddha criticized Ājīvaka fatalism as a pernicious denial of human potential and responsibility.

Two other small groups of *Samaṇas* were the Materialists and the Skeptics. According to the Pali tradition, in the Buddha's day their main spokesmen were, respectively, Ajita Kesa-Kambala and Sañjaya Belaṭṭhaputta. The Materialists denied any kind of self other than one which could be directly perceived, and held that this was annihilated at death. They therefore denied the idea of rebirth, and also those of karma and *niyati*. Each act was seen as a spontaneous event without karmic effects, and spiritual progression was not seen as possible. The Buddha characterized the Materialists' theory as the extreme view of 'annihilationism', and saw most other views of the day as some form of the opposite extreme, 'eternalism', which says that what survives death is some eternal self, soul or life-principle. The Materialists' aim was to lead an abstemious, balanced life which enjoyed simple pleasures and the satisfaction of human relationships. The Skeptics responded to the welter of conflicting theories on religious and philosophical issues, and the consequent arguments, by avoiding commitment to *any* point of view, so as to preserve peace of mind. They held that knowledge was impossible, and would not even commit themselves to saying that other people's views were wrong. The Buddha saw this evasive stance as 'eel-wriggling', though he shared the wish to step aside from the 'jungle' of conflicting views, and avoid dogmatic assertions built in flimsy grounds. This common emphasis is perhaps reflected in the fact that the Buddha's two chief disciples, Sāriputta and Moggallāna, were originally Skeptics. The Buddha also shared the Materialists' emphasis on experience as the source of knowledge, and thus shared a critical evaluation of current beliefs on rebirth, karma and self. He saw the Materialists and Skeptics as going too far, however, in denying or doubting the principles of karma and rebirth, which he held were shown to be true by (meditative) experience (*M*.I.402). Buddhism, then, did not uncritically absorb belief in karma and rebirth from existing Indian culture, as is sometimes held. These ideas were very much up for debate at the time.

THE LIFE OF THE BUDDHA

We know that Gotama was born in the small republic of the Sakka (Skt Śākya) people, which straddles the present border with Nepal and had Kapilavatthu as its capital. From his birth among these people, Gotama is known in Mahāyāna tradition as Śākya-muni, 'the Śākyan sage'. The republic was not Brahmanized, and rule was by a council of household-heads, perhaps qualified by age or social standing. Gotama was born to one of these rulers, so that he described himself as a *Kṣatriya* when talking to Brahmins, and later tradition saw him as the son of a king.

In the early Buddhist texts, there is no *continuous* life of the Buddha, as these concentrated on his teachings. Only later, between 200 BC and 200 AD, did a growing interest in the Buddha's person lead to various schools producing continuous 'biographies', which drew on scattered accounts in the existing *Sutta* and *Vinaya* collections, and floating oral traditions. These 'biographies' include the Sarvāstivādins' *Lalitavistara*, the Theravādins' *Nidānakathā*, and Aśvaghoṣa's poem, the *Buddha-carita*. The details of these are in general agreement, but while they must clearly be based around historical facts, they also contain legendary and mythological embellishments, and it is often not possible to sort out one from the other. While the bare historical basis of the traditional biography will never be known, as it stands it gives a great insight into Buddhism by enabling us to see what the *meaning* of the Buddha's life is to Buddhists: what lessons it is held to contain.

The traditional biography does not begin with Gotama's birth, but with what went before it. It is held that a 'hundred thousand eons ago', in one of his past lives, Gotama was an ascetic named Sumedha who met and was inspired by a previous Buddha, Dīpankara. He therefore resolved to strive for Buddhahood, by becoming a *Bodhisatta*, a being (Pali *satta*) who is dedicated to attaining perfect enlightenment (*bodhi*) (*Bvms.* ch. 2). He knew that, while he could become an enlightened disciple of Dīpankara, the path he had chosen instead would take many lives to complete. It would, however, culminate in his becoming a perfect Buddha, one who would bring benefit to countless beings by rediscovering and teaching the timeless truths of *Dhamma* in a period when they had been forgotten by the human race. He then spent many lives, as a human, animal and god, building up the moral and spiritual perfections necessary for Buddhahood. These lives are described in what are known as *Jātaka* stories. Over the ages, he also met other past Buddhas, six of whom are named in the *Dīgha Nikāya* (*D.*II.2–9), and twenty-three in the *Buddhavaṃsa*. In his penultimate life he was born in the Tusita heaven, the realm of the 'delighted' gods. This is said to be the realm where the *Bodhisatta* Metteyya (Skt Maitreya) now lives, ready for a future period in human history when Buddhism will have become extinct, and he can become the next Buddha (*D*.II.76). The *Lalitavistara* tells that Gotama chose the time in human history in which to be reborn for the last time, while the *Suttas* say that he was 'mindful and fully aware' when he passed away from the Tusita heaven and was conceived in his mother's womb (*M*.III.119).

The early texts clearly see the conception and the other key events of Gotama's life, such as his birth, enlightenment, first sermon, and death, as events of cosmic importance; for at all of them they say that light spread throughout the world and the earth shook. The *Nidānakathā* relates that at the time of the conception, Mahāmāyā, his mother, dreamt that she was transported to the Himālayas where a being in the form of an auspicious white elephant entered her right side. On recounting this dream to her husband, Suddhodana, he had it interpreted by sixty-four Brahmins. They explained that it indicated that his wife had conceived a son with a great destiny ahead of him. Either he would stay at home with his father and go on to become a *Cakkavatti*, a universal emperor – which the *Suttas* say that he had been six times in previous lives – or he would become a wandering ascetic and become a great religious teacher, a Buddha.

This paralleling of a *Cakkavatti* and a Buddha is also made in relation to other events of Gotama's life, and indicates the idea of a Buddha having universal spiritual 'sovereignty' – i.e. influence – over humans and gods. It also indicates that Gotama renounced the option of political power in becoming a Buddha. He certainly had no political pretensions, as Muhammad had, and was not seen as a political threat by the rulers of his day, as was Jesus. He did, however, teach kings and give teachings on how best to govern a realm.

The *Nidānakathā* account relates that, near the end of her pregnancy, Mahāmāyā journeyed from Kapilavatthu to the home of her relatives to give birth, as was the custom. On the way, she and her party passed the pleasant Lumbinī grove, where she stopped to enjoy the flowers and birdsong. Here she went into labour and, holding onto a Sāl tree, gave birth standing up. The birth of Gotama under a tree fits the pattern of the other key events in his life: attaining enlightenment under another tree, giving his first sermon in an animal park, and dying between two trees. This suggests his liking for simple natural environments where he could be in harmony with all forms of life. The *Sutta* accounts say that the baby was set down on the ground by four *devas*, and that a warm and cool stream of water appeared from the sky as a water-libation for mother and child. He immediately stood, walked seven paces, scanned in all directions, and said in a noble voice that he was the foremost being in the world, and that this would be his last rebirth (*M.*III.123).

As his mother had died a week after giving birth (*M.*III.122), Gotama was brought up by his father's second wife, his mother's sister. The early texts say little on his early life, except that it was one of lily pools, fine clothes and fragrances, with female musicians as attendants in his three palaces (*A.*I.145). The later biographies portray him as having been an eager, intelligent, and compassionate youth. They relate that his father was keen that he should stay at home to become a great king, and so surrounded him with luxuries to ensure that he remained attached to the wordly life. At sixteen, he was married to Yasodharā, and at twenty-nine they had a son named Rāhula.

The renunciation and quest for enlightenment

It was from a pleasant and wealthy background, then, that Gotama renounced the worldly life of pleasure and set out on his religious quest. The lead-up to this crucial transition is described in different ways in the early and later texts. The *Suttas* portray it as the result of a long consideration. Even from his sheltered existence, he became aware of the facts of ageing, sickness and death. Realizing that even he was not immune from these, the 'vanities' of youth, health, and life left him (*A.*I.145–6). He therefore set out to find the 'unborn, unageing, undecaying, deathless, sorrowless, undefiled, uttermost security from bondage – *Nibbāna*' (*M.*I.163). He realized, though, that: 'House life is crowded and dusty; going forth [into the life of a wandering *Samaṇa*] is wide open. It is not easy, living life in a household, to lead a holy-life as utterly perfect as a polished shell. Suppose I were to shave off my hair and beard, put on saffron garments, and go forth from home into homelessness?' (*M.*I.240).

The later texts say that the transition occurred at the age of twenty-nine, just after the birth of his son, portraying it as arising from a sudden realization rather than from a gradual reflection. In this, they follow the model of a *Sutta* story of a previous Buddha (*D.*II.22–9), which sees the lives of all Buddhas as following a recurring pattern. The *Nidānakathā* relates that, on three consecutive days, Gotama visited one of his parks in his chariot. His father had the streets cleared of unpleasant sights, but the gods ensured that he saw a worn-out, grey-haired old man, a sick man and a corpse. Amazed at these new sights, his charioteer explained to him that ageing, sickness and death came to all people, thus putting him in a state of agitation at the nature of life. In this way, the texts portray an example of the human confrontation with frailty and mortality, for while these facts are 'known' to us all, a clear realization and acceptance of them often does come as a novel and disturbing insight. On a fourth trip to his park, Gotama saw a saffron-robed *Samaṇa* with a shaven head and a calm demeanour, the sight of whom inspired him to adopt such a life-style. That night, he left his palace, taking a long last look at his son, who lay in his sleeping wife's arms, knowing it would be difficult for him to leave if she awoke. The Buddhist tradition sees his leaving of his family as done for the benefit of all beings; moreover, after he became a Buddha, he is said to have returned to his home town and taught his family, with his son ordaining under him as a monk. His renunciation of family life stands as a symbolic precedent for the monastic life of Buddhist monks and nuns.

The *Suttas* say that Gotama sought out teachers from whom he could learn spiritual techniques, going first to Āḷāra the Kālāma (*M*.I.163 ff.). He soon mastered his teachings and then enquired after the meditational state on which they were based. This was the 'sphere of nothingness', a mystical trance attained by yogic concentration, in which the mind goes beyond any apparent object and dwells on the thought of nothingness. After Gotama quickly learned to enter this state, Āḷāra offered him joint leadership of his group of disciples, but he turned down the offer as he felt that, while he had attained a refined inner calmness, he had not yet attained enlightenment and the end of suffering. He then went to another yoga teacher, Uddaka the son of Rāma, and again quickly grasped his doctrine and entered the meditational state on which it was based, the 'sphere of neither-cognition-nor-non-cognition'. This went beyond the previous state to a level of mental stilling where consciousness is so attenuated as to hardly exist. In response, Uddaka acknowledged him as even his own teacher, for only his dead father had previously attained this state. Again Gotama passed up a chance of leadership and influence on the grounds that he had not yet reached his goal. Nevertheless, he later incorporated both the mystical states that he had attained into his own meditational system, as possible ways to calm and purify the mind in preparation for developing liberating insight. He in fact taught a great variety of meditational methods, adapting some from the existing yogic tradition, and can be seen as having been one of India's greatest practitioners of meditation.

After having experimented with one of the methods of religious practice current in his day, Gotama went on to try ascetic self-mortification as a possible route to his goal. The *Suttas* tell that he settled in a woodland grove at Uruvelā and resolved to strive earnestly to overcome attachment to sensual pleasures by intense effort, trying to dominate such tendencies by force of will (*M*.I.240 ff.). He practised non-breathing meditations, though they produced fierce headaches, stomach pains, and burning heat all over his body. He reduced his food intake to a few drops of bean soup a day, till he became so emaciated that he could hardly stand and his body hair fell out. At this point, he felt that it was not possible for anyone to go further on the path of asceticism and still live. Nevertheless, though he had developed clarity of mind and energy, his body and mind were pained and untranquil, so that he could not carry on with his quest. He therefore abandoned his practice of harsh asceticism, which the later texts say lasted for six years.

At this point, he might have abandoned his quest as hopeless, but he thought 'might there be another path to awakening?' (*M*.I.246). He then remembered a meditative state that he had once spontaneously entered while concentrating on the earth being cut by a plough. He recollected that this state, technically known as the 'first *jhāna*', was beyond involvement in sense-pleasures, which he had been attempting to conquer by painful asceticism, but was accompanied by deep calm, blissful joy, and tranquil happiness. He remembered having wondered whether it was a path to awakening, and as he now saw that it was, he resolved to use it. On his taking sustaining food to prepare himself for this meditation, his five companions in asceticism shunned him in disgust, seeing him as having abandoned their shared quest and taken to luxurious living.

One *Sutta* (Sn. 425–49) outlines a temptation sequence which the later texts put at this juncture. It refers to a Satan-like figure known as Māra, a deity who has won his place by previous good works, but who uses his power to entrap people in sensual desire and attachment, so as to stay within his realm of influence. This is the round of rebirth and repeated death, so that Māra is seen as the embodiment of both desire

Plate 1 A nineteenth-century Burmese image, showing Gotama at his 'conquest of Māra', just prior to his enlightenment.

and death. Māra came to the emaciated ascetic with honeyed words. He urged him to abandon his quest and take up a more conventional religious life of sacrifice and good works, so as to generate good karma, or 'merit'. In response, Gotama replied that he had no need of more 'merit', and scorned the 'squadrons' of Māra: sense-desire, jealousy, hunger and thirst, craving, sloth and torpor, cowardice, fear of commitment, belittling others, obstinate insensitivity, and self-praise. Māra then retreated in defeat.

This account, clearly portraying the final inner struggle of Gotama, gains dramatic colour in the later texts, where Māra's 'army' of spiritual faults bore witness to the fact that he had done many charitable acts in previous lives. Taunting Gotama that he had no-one to bear witness to *his* good deeds, Māra tried to use the power of his own 'merit' to throw Gotama off the spot where he was sitting. Gotama did not move, however, but meditated on the spiritual perfections that he had developed over many previous lives, knowing that he had a right to the spot where he sat. He then touched the earth for it to bear witness to his 'merit'. The earth quaked, and the earth goddess appeared, wringing from her hair a flood of water, accumulated in the past when Gotama had formalized good deeds by a simple ritual of water-pouring. At the quaking and flood, Māra and his army fled. This 'conquest of Māra' is commemorated as a victory over evil by countless images and paintings. These show Gotama, as in Plate 1, seated cross-legged in meditation with his right hand touching the earth: the 'earth-witness' gesture.

The enlightenment and after

Free of spiritual hindrances, Gotama then developed deep meditations as a prelude to enlightenment, seated under a species of tree (the *Assattha* or *Pipala*) which later became known as the *Bodhi*, or 'Enlightenment' tree. The *Sutta* account (*M*.I.247–9) describes how he entered the first *jhāna*, and then gradually deepened his state of concentrated calm till he reached the fourth *jhāna*, a state of great equanimity, mental brightness and purity. Based on this state, he went on to develop, in the course of the three watches of the moon-lit night, the 'threefold knowledge': memory of previous lives, seeing the rebirth of others according to their karma, and the destruction of spiritual faults which fester in the mind and keep it unenlightened. The third knowledge, completed at dawn, brought the perfect enlightenment he had been seeking, so that he was now, at the age of thirty-five, a Buddha. The *Dhammapada* verses 153–4 are said to record his words of joyful exultation at this achievement of the end of craving and spiritual ignorance, and attaining the unconditioned *Nibbāna*, beyond ageing, sickness and death.

The Canonical account (*Vin*.I.1 ff., *M*.I.167 ff.) then says that the new Buddha stayed under or near the *Bodhi* tree for four or more weeks, at the place now called Bodh-Gayā. After meditatively reflecting on his enlightenment, he pondered the possibility of teaching others, but thought that the *Dhamma* he had experienced was so profound, subtle, and 'beyond the sphere of reason', that others would be too subject to attachment to be able to understand it. At this, the compassionate god Brahmā Sahampati became alarmed at the thought that a fully awakened person had arisen in the world, but that he might not share his rare and precious wisdom with others. He therefore appeared before the Buddha and respectfully asked him to teach, for 'there are beings with little dust in their eyes who, not hearing the *Dhamma*, are decaying...'. The Buddha then used his mind-reading powers to survey the world and determine that some people were spiritually mature enough to understand his message. On deciding to teach, he declared, 'Opened for those who wish to hear are the doors of the Deathless'. The entreaty of the compassionate Brahmā is seen by Buddhists as the stimulus for the unfolding of the Buddha's compassion, the necessary complement to his enlightened wisdom for his role as a perfect Buddha, a 'teacher of gods and humans'.

Gotama wished to teach his two yoga teachers first of all, but gods informed him that they were now dead, a fact which he then confirmed by his meditative knowledge. He therefore decided to teach his former companions in asceticism. Intuiting that they were currently in the animal park at Isipatana (now called Sārnāth) near Benares, he set out to walk there, a journey of about one hundred miles.

The first sermon and the spread of the teachings

The Canonical account (*Vin*.I.8 ff.) relates that, on arriving at the animal park, his five former companions saw him in the distance, and resolved to snub him as a spiritual failure. As he approached, however, they saw that a great change had come over him and, in spite of themselves, respectfully greeted him and washed his feet. At first they addressed him as an equal, but the Buddha insisted that he was a *Tathāgata*, a 'Thus-gone' or 'Truth-attained One', who had found the Deathless and could therefore be their teacher. After he twice repeated his affirmation, to overcome their hesitation, the ascetics acknowledged that he had a new-found assurance and were willing to be taught by him.

Gotama, usually referred to as the 'Lord' or 'Blessed One' (*Bhagavat*) in the Pali Canon, then gave his first sermon. This commences with the idea that there is a 'Middle Way' for those who have gone forth from the home life, a way which avoids both the extremes of devotion to mere sense-pleasures and devotion to ascetic self-torment. Gotama had himself previously experienced both of these spiritual dead-ends. The Middle Way which he had found to lead to enlightenment was the *Ariya*, or Holy, Eightfold Path (*Magga*). He then continued with the kernel of his message, the Four Holy Truths. In brief, these are that suffering is inherent in life, that suffering and repeated lives are caused by craving, that craving and thus suffering can be destroyed, and that the Holy Eightfold Path is the course leading to this. He then emphasized the liberating effect on him of his full insight into these truths, such that he was now a Buddha.

As a result of this instruction, one member of Gotama's audience, Koṇḍañña, gained experiential insight into the truths taught, so that Gotama joyfully affirmed his understanding. This insight is described as the gaining of the stainless '*Dhamma*-eye', by which Koṇḍañña 'sees', 'attains' and 'plunges into' the *Dhamma*, free from all doubt in the Buddha's teachings. This experience is technically known as 'stream-entry', a crucial spiritual transition brought about by the first glimpse of *Nibbāna*. Koṇḍañña's gaining of the *Dhamma*-eye is clearly seen as the climax of the first sermon, for as soon as it occurs, the exultant message is rapidly transmitted up through various levels of gods that 'the supreme *Dhamma*-wheel' had been set in motion by the 'Lord', and could not be stopped by any power. The 'Setting in motion of the *Dhamma*-wheel' (*Dhamma-cakka-pavattana*) thus became the title of the *Sutta* of the first sermon (*S*.v.420–4). The image of setting a wheel in motion is intended to symbolize the inauguration of an era of the spiritual influence of the *Dhamma*.

After Koṇḍañña was ordained, thus becoming the first member of the *Sangha*, the Buddha gave more extensive explanations of his teachings to the other four ascetics, so that, one by one, they attained the *Dhamma*-eye and were then ordained. Later the Buddha gave his 'second' sermon (see p. 51), at which his disciples all attained the full experience of *Nibbāna* – as he himself had done at his enlightenment – so as to become *Arahat*'s, the highest grade of Buddhist saints.

Other disciples, monastic and lay, followed, so that soon there were sixty-one *Arahats*, including the Buddha. Having such a body of enlightened monk-disciples, the Buddha sent them out on a mission to spread the *Dhamma*: 'Walk, monks, on tour for the blessing of the manyfolk, for the happiness of the manyfolk, out of compassion for the world, for the welfare, the blessing, the happiness of gods and humans' (*Vin*.I.21). As the teaching spread, Gotama in time gained his two chief disciples, Sāriputta, famed for his wisdom and ability to teach, and Moggallāna, famed for his psychic powers developed by meditation. Five years after first ordaining monks, Gotama initiated an order of nuns, in response to the repeated requests of his foster-mother Mahāpajāpati, and the suggestion of his faithful attendant monk Ānanda.

The Canon gives only incidental reference to events between the sending out of the sixty *Arahats* and the last year of the Buddha's life. The general picture conveyed is that he spent his long teaching career wandering on foot, with few possessions, around the Ganges basin region. Though he was of a contemplative nature, loving the solitude of natural surroundings, he was generally accompanied by many disciples and spent much of his time in or near the new towns and cities, especially Sāvatthī, Rājagaha and Vesālī. Here, there were many people of a questioning nature looking for a new spiritual outlook. The commentary to the *Thera-gāthā* and *Therī-gāthā* describes the background of 328 monks and nuns and indicates that over two-thirds came from urban areas. It also indicates that, as to their social backgrounds, 41 per cent were Brahmin, 23 per cent *Kṣatriya*, 30 per cent *Vaiśya*, 3 per cent *Śūdra*, and 3 per cent 'outcaste' (below the *Śūdras* in the Brahmanical hierarchy). Of these, the Brahmins do not generally appear to have been traditional village priests, but urban dwellers perhaps employed as state officials. State officials and merchants were the dominant groups in urban society, but neither had an established niche in the *varṇa* system (though merchants later came to be seen as *Vaiśyas*). These groups seem to have been particularly attracted to the

Buddha's message, which addressed people as individuals in charge of their own moral and spiritual destiny, rather than as members of the *varṇa* system. Respect should be based on moral and spiritual worth, not birth: it had to be earned (*Sn*.136). Indeed, in urban society, people's worldly attainments increasingly depended on personal effort, rather than on traditionally ascribed social position. The Buddhist emphasis on karmic results as depending on adhering to universal, rather than *varṇa*-bound, moral norms was thus congenial. The Buddha taught all who came to him without distinction: men, women, rich merchants, servants, Brahmins, craftsmen, ascetics, kings and courtesans, and made a point of insisting that social background was irrelevant to the position of individuals within the *Sangha* (*A*.IV.202). He also urged his disciples to teach in the local languages or dialects of their hearers (*Vin*.II.139). In contrast, the Brahmins taught in Sanskrit, which had by now become unintelligible to those who had not studied it, and only made the Vedic teachings available to males of the top three *varṇas*.

The Buddha's charisma and powers

The early texts portray the Buddha as a charismatic, humanitarian teacher who inspired many people. He even elicited a response from animals; for it is said that an elephant once looked after him by bringing him water when he was spending a period alone in the forest (*Vin*.I.352). A person who bore enmity towards him, however, was his cousin Devadatta, one of his monks. Jealous of his influence, Devadatta once suggested that the ageing Buddha should let him lead the *Sangha*, and then plotted to kill him when the request was turned down (*Vin*.II.191–5). In one attempt on his life, Devadatta asked his friend, prince Ajātasattu, to send soldiers to waylay and assassinate the Buddha. Sixteen soldiers in turn went to do this, but all were too afraid to do so, and became the Buddha's disciples instead. In another attempt, the fierce man-killing elephant Nālāgiri was let loose on the road on which the Buddha was travelling. As the elephant charged, the Buddha calmly stood his ground and suffused the elephant with the power of his lovingkindness, so that it stopped and bowed its head, letting the Buddha stroke and tame it.

In gaining hearers for his message, the Buddha did not always rely on his charisma, reputation and powers of persuasion. Occasionally he had recourse to his psychic powers, though he forbade the mere display of these by his disciples (*Vin*.II.112). The results of such powers are not seen as supernatural miracles, but as the supernormal products of the great inner power of certain meditations. A late Canonical passage (*Pati*.I.125) describes his 'marvel of the pairs', which later legendary material ascribes to the Buddha while staying at Sāvatthī (*Dhp.A*.III.204–16). This describes a public challenge in which the Buddha was asked to display his psychic powers in the hope that he would abstain and thus appear to lack such abilities. The Buddha therefore agreed to meet the challenge at a later date, when he rose into the air and produced both fire and water from different parts of his body. Occasionally, he used his powers for physically healing one of his devout supporters, such as bringing a long and very painful childbirth to an end (*Ud*.15–16), or curing a wound without leaving even a scar (*Vin*.I.216–18). The Buddha generally regarded psychic powers as dangerous, however, as they could encourage attachment and self-glorification. In a strange parallel to the temptation of Jesus in the desert, it is said that he rebuffed Māra's temptation to turn the Himālayas into gold (*S*.I.116). Another time, on meeting an ascetic who had been meditating for years so as to be able to cross a river by walking on water (a power attributed to the Buddha), he said that for a few pennies, he could cross the river by the ferry!

The passing away of the Buddha

The *Mahā-parinibbāna Sutta* (*D*.II.72–167) deals with the last year of the Buddha's life. During this period, he suffered an illness, and Ānanda asked about the fate of the *Sangha* after his death, clearly wondering who would lead it. In reply, the Buddha said that he had taught the *Dhamma* without holding anything back, and that the *Sangha* depended on the *Dhamma*, not on any leader, even himself. Members of the *Sangha* should look to their own self-reliant practice, with the clearly taught *Dhamma* as guide: with themselves and the *Dhamma* as 'island' and 'refuge' (*D*.II.100). Later the Buddha specified that, after his death, the *Sangha* should take both the *Dhamma* and monastic discipline (*Vinaya*) as their 'teacher' (*D*.II.154).

Though unwell for the last three months of his life, the Buddha continued to wander on foot. Finally, he could only continue by overcoming his pain through the power of meditation. His journey ended at the small village of Kusinārā, where he lay down on a couch between two trees, in bloom out of season. The text says that gods from ten regions of the universe assembled to witness the great event of a Buddha's final passing into *Nibbāna* at death (*parinibbāna*) (*D*.II.138–9).

When asked what should be done with his remains after his death, the Buddha remarked that this was the concern of the laity, not the *Sangha*, but that his body should be treated like that of a *Cakkavatti* emperor. It should be wrapped in cloth, placed in a coffin and cremated. The relics remaining should then be placed in a *Stūpa* (Pali *Thūpa*), or burial mound, at a place where four roads meet. He then said, 'And whoever shall put flowers or scents on it, or whitewash, or shall express devotion or feel confidence in his heart there, that will be long for his welfare and happiness' (*D*.II.142). After his cremation, the Buddha's relics were placed in eight *Stūpas*, with the bowl used to collect the relics and the ashes of the funeral fire in two more. Such *Stūpas*, which could alternatively contain relics of *Arahats*, later became the focus of much devotion.

Even on his death-bed, the Buddha continued to teach. A wanderer asked whether other *Samaṇa* leaders had attained true knowledge. Rather than say that their religious systems were wrong and his right, the Buddha simply indicated that the crucial ingredient of any such system was the Holy Eightfold Path: only then could it lead to full Arahatship. He saw such a Path as absent from other teachings that he knew of.

Not long after this, the Buddha asked his monks if any had final questions that they wanted answering before he died. When they were silent, he sensitively said that, if they were silent simply out of reverence for him, they should have a friend ask their question. They remained silent. Seeing that they all had a good understanding of his teachings, he therefore gave his final words: 'All conditioned things are subject to decay. Attain perfection through diligence!' (*D*.II.156). He then made his exit from the world, in the fearless, calm and self-controlled state of meditation. He passed into the first *jhāna*, and then by degrees through the three other *jhānas*, four 'formless' mystical states, and then the 'cessation of cognition and feeling' (see p. 250 ff.). He then gradually descended back to the first *jhāna*, moved back up to the fourth *jhāna*, and attained *parinibbāna* from here (*D*.II.156). Buddhists see this event not so much as a 'death' as a passing into the Deathless *Nibbāna*.

THE NATURE AND ROLE OF THE BUDDHA

While modern Theravādins sometimes say that the Buddha was 'just a human', such remarks have to be taken in context. They are usually intended to contrast the Buddha with Jesus, seen as the 'Son of God', and to counter the Mahāyāna view of the Buddha's nature, which sees it as far above the human. These remarks may also be due to a somewhat demythologized view of the Buddha. In the Pali Canon, Gotama was seen as *born* a human, though one with extraordinary abilities due to the perfections built up in his long *Bodhisatta* career. Once he had attained enlightenment, though, he could no longer be called a 'human', as he had perfected and transcended his humanness. This idea is reflected in a *Sutta* passage where the Buddha was asked whether he was a god (*deva*) or a human (*A*.II.37–9). In reply, he said that he had gone beyond the deep-rooted unconscious traits that would make him a god or human, and was therefore to be seen as a *Buddha*, one who had grown up in the world but who had now gone beyond it, as a lotus grows from the water but blossoms above it unsoiled.

The mysterious nature of a Buddha is indicated by the Buddha's chiding of a monk who had too much uncritical faith in him, so as to be always following him round: 'Hush, Vakkali! What is there for you in seeking this vile visible body? Vakkali, whoever sees *Dhamma*, sees me; whoever sees me, sees *Dhamma*' (*S*.III.120). This close link between the Buddha and *Dhamma* is reinforced by another *Sutta* passage, which says that a *Tathāgata* can be designated as one who 'has *Dhamma* as body' (*Dhamma-kāya*) and who is '*Dhamma*-become' (*Dhamma-bhūta*) (*D*.III.84). These terms indicate that a Buddha has fully exemplified the *Dhamma*, in the sense of the Path, in his personality or 'body'. Moreover, he has fully realized *Dhamma* in the supreme sense by his experience of *Nibbāna*, the equivalent of the supreme *Dhamma* (*A*.I.156 and 158). The *Arahat* is no different in these respects, for he is described as 'become the supreme' (*brahma-bhūta*) (*S*.III.83), a term which is used as an equivalent to '*Dhamma*-become' in the above passage. Any enlightened person is one who is 'deep, immeasurable, hard-to-fathom as is the great ocean' (*M*.I.487). Having 'become *Dhamma*', their enlightened nature can only really be fathomed by one who has 'seen' *Dhamma* with the '*Dhamma*-eye' of stream-entry. While Christians see Jesus as God-become-man, then, Buddhists see the Buddha (and *Arahats*) as man-become-*Dhamma*.

In the early Buddhist texts, the Buddha is himself said to be an *Arahat*, and to be in most respects like other *Arahats*. Any *Arahat's* experience of *Nibbāna* is the same; however, a perfect Buddha is seen as having more extensive knowledge than other *Arahats*. For example, he can remember as far back into previous lives as he wants, while other *Arahats* have limitations on such a power, or may not even have developed it. A perfect Buddha is seen as one who can come to know anything he pleases about the past and present, and can make many valid predictions about the future, such as how a person will be reborn if they have acted in a certain way. What he teaches is just a small portion of his huge knowledge (*S*.v.438), for he only teaches what is both true and spiritually useful (*M*.I.395).

A second key difference between a Buddha and an *Arahat* is that a Buddha is someone who, by his own efforts, rediscovers the Path after it has been lost to human society. Having discovered it for himself, he skilfully makes it known to others so that they can fully practise it for themselves and so become *Arahats* (*M*.III.8). He is a rediscoverer and teacher of timeless truths (*A*.I.286–7). As founder of a monastic *Sangha*, and propounder of the rules of conduct binding on its members, a Buddha also fulfils a role akin to that of 'law-giver'.

THE NATURE AND STYLE OF THE BUDDHA'S TEACHING

The Buddha's style of teaching was generally one of skilful adaptation to the mood and concerns of his hearers, responding to the questions and even the non-verbalized thoughts of his audience and taking cues from events. By means of a dialogue with his questioners, he gradually moved them towards sharing his own vision of truth. When Brahmins asked him about how to attain union with the god Brahmā after death, he did not say that this was impossible, but that it could be attained by meditative development of deep lovingkindness and compassion, rather than by bloody Vedic sacrifices. He often gave old terms new meanings, for example calling the *Arahat* the 'true Brahmin', and using the term *ariya*, equivalent to the Sanskrit term for the 'noble' Aryan people, in the sense of spiritually noble, or holy.

The Buddha treated questions in a careful, analytic way. Some he answered directly, others he answered after first analysing them so as to clarify the nature of the question. Some he answered with a counter-question, to reveal concealed motives and presuppositions; others again he 'set aside' as question-begging and fraught with misconceptions (*A*.II.46). He did not mind if others disagreed with him, but censured misinterpretations of what he taught. He showed even-mindedness when gaining disciples. A general Sīha, who was a great supporter of Jain monks, once decided to become a lay disciple, but the Buddha advised him that such a prominent person as himself should carefully consider before changing his religious allegiances (*Vin*.I.236). Already impressed by the Buddha's teaching, Sīha was even more impressed by the fact that he did not jump at the chance of gaining an influential disciple. On affirming that he still wished to be a disciple, the Buddha advised him that he should not deprive Jain monks by withdrawing his generous support, but continue this while also supporting Buddhist monks, as he now wished to do.

The Buddha emphasized self-reliance and the experiential testing-out of all teachings, including his own. He was well aware of the many conflicting doctrines of his day, a time of intellectual ferment. Rejecting teachings based on authoritative tradition, or mere rational speculation, he emphasized the examination and analysis of actual experience. This is seen in a famous *Sutta* passage where he spoke to the Kālāma people, who had had a string of teachers visiting them, speaking in praise of their own teachings and disparaging those of others (*A*.I.189). In response to their perplexity over what is true or false, the Buddha said that they were right to feel uncertain. They should not accept anything:

> on the grounds of revelation, tradition or report, or because it is a product of mere reasoning, or because it is true from a standpoint, or because of a superficial assessment of the facts, or because it conforms with one's preconceived notions, or because it is authoritative, or because of the prestige of your teacher.

They should assess teachings for themselves by reference to their own experience, also taking note of the opinion of wise people, rejecting unskilful teachings whose practice conduced to harm and suffering, and accepting those that conduced to true benefit and happiness. Only occasionally, for example before his first sermon, did the Buddha use his authority, but this was not to force people to agree with him, but to get them to listen so that they could then gain understanding. He also advised his disciples not to react emotionally when they heard people speaking in blame or praise of him, but to assess calmly the degree to which what was said was true or false (*D*.I.3).

The Buddha emphasized that his teachings had a practical purpose, and should not be blindly clung to. He likened the *Dhamma* to a raft made by a man seeking to cross from the dangerous hither shore of a river, representing the conditioned world, to the peaceful further shore, representing *Nibbāna* (*M*.1.134–5). He then rhetorically asked whether such a man, on reaching the other shore, should lift up the raft and carry it around with him there. He therefore said, '*Dhamma* is for crossing over, not for retaining'. That is, a follower should not grasp at Buddhist ideas and practices, but *use* them for their intended purpose, and then let go of them when they had fully accomplished their goal. Many ordinary Buddhists, though, do have a strong attachment to Buddhism.

While the Buddha was critical of blind fath, he did not deny a role for soundly based faith or 'trustful confidence' (*saddhā*); for to test out his teachings, a person had to have at least some initial trust in them. The early texts envisage a process of listening, which arouses *saddhā*, leading to practice, and thus to partial confirmation of the teachings, and thus to deeper *saddhā* and deeper practice until the heart of the teachings is directly experienced. A person then becomes an *Arahat*, one who has replaced faith with knowledge. Even in Theravāda Buddhism, which often has a rather rational, unemotional image, a very deep faith in the Buddha, *Dhamma* and *Sangha* is common. Ideally, this is based on the fact that some part of the Buddha's path has been found to be uplifting, thus inspiring confidence in the rest. Many people, though, simply have a calm and joyful faith (*pasāda*) inspired by the example of those who are well established on the path.

2

EARLY BUDDHIST TEACHINGS: REBIRTH AND KARMA

In this and the following chapter, the central doctrines of early Buddhism, as presented primarily in the Pali Canon, will be outlined. While the Mahāyāna developed a new orientation towards some of these early teachings, and new doctrines of its own, such developments can only be understood against the background of these teachings. In the Theravāda, they remained the guiding framework for all new developments.

In a sense, Buddhism begins and ends with the Buddha's enlightenment experience, for this is the ultimate source of Buddhist teachings, and these are a means towards moral and spiritual development culminating in an experience of a like nature. At his enlightenment, the Buddha gained direct knowledge of rebirth, karma and the Four Holy Truths. All of the central teachings of early Buddhism can be arranged under one or other of these three heads.

REBIRTH AND COSMOLOGY

One word used to refer to the cycle of rebirths is *saṃsāra*, 'wandering on', which indicates that the process is seen as a long and often aimless process. It is not just said that we have had 'many' past lives, but that we have had *innumerable* ones. On the night of his enlightenment, the Buddha is said to have remembered more than a hundred thousand (*M*.I.22). The Buddhist view, in fact, is that there is no known beginning to the cycle of rebirths and the world: 'Inconceivable is any beginning of this *saṃsāra*; an earliest point is not discerned of beings who, obstructed by spiritual ignorance and fettered by craving, run and wander on' (*S*.II.178). However far back in time one goes, there must have been a prior cause for whatever beings existed at that time.

The earliest the Buddha is specifically said to have remembered is ninety-one 'eons' (*kappa*'s) ago (*M*.I.483). An 'eon' is a vast unit of time used for measuring the coming and going of world-systems. The physical universe is said to consist of countless world-systems spread out through space. Each is roughly equivalent to a planet, but they also exist in thousand-fold clusters, galactic groupings of these clusters, and super-galactic groupings of these galaxies (*A*.I.227). Within this vast universe, with no known limit, are other inhabited worlds where beings also go through the cycle of rebirths. Just as beings go through a series of lives, so do world-systems: they evolve, remain for a period, come to an end, and are then quiescent before re-evolving. Each phase takes an 'incalculable' eon, and the whole cycle takes a 'great' eon. The huge magnitude of this period is indicated by various suggestive images. For example, if there were a seven-mile high mountain of solid granite, and once a century it was stroked with a piece of fine cloth, it would be worn away before a great eon would pass (*S*.II.181–2). Nevertheless, more eons have passed than there are grains of sand on the banks of the river Ganges (*S*.II.183–4)!

The cycle of rebirths is thus seen as involving innumerable lives over vast stretches of time. If the cycle only involved human rebirths, it would be hard for a Buddhist to explain the human population explosion. As it is, however, the cycle is seen to involve many other forms of life, such as animals, so that re-adjustment between populations is quite feasible. This then introduces the idea of different realms of rebirth.

The first two of these realms are those of humans and the animal kingdom. The latter includes sentient creatures as simple as insects. Plants are not included, though they are seen as having a very rudimentary consciousness, in the form of sensitivity to touch (*Vin*.I.155–6). There are also realms of beings who are not (normally) visible. One of these is the realm of *peta*'s, the 'departed'. As these are seen as having bodies made of 'subtle' matter, such a rebirth does not involve 're-incarnation', that is, getting a gross physical body again. *Petas* are seen as frustrated ghostly beings who frequent the human world due to their strong earthly attachments, not unlike the ghosts of Western literature. One type of *peta*, generally known as a 'hungry ghost', is portrayed as having a huge stomach, racked by hunger, and a tiny neck that allows little sustenance to pass.

The worst realm is the hell-realm (*niraya*), comprising a number of hellish rebirths. These are described as involving experiences of being burnt up, cut up, frozen, or eaten alive, yet being revived to re-experience these (e.g. *M*.III.183). They are, then, realms in which a tortured consciousness experiences abominable nightmares, where every object of the senses appears repulsive and ugly (*S*.IV.126). Some hells are worse than others, but all are seen as appropriate to the evil deeds which led to them. While life in the hells is measured in millions of years, no rebirth is eternal, so a being from hell will in time reach the human level again.

The animal, *peta* and hell realms are the lower rebirths, where beings suffer more than human beings. The higher, more fortunate realms of rebirth are those of humans and *devas*, 'illustrious ones' or gods. Together these comprise the five realms. The realm of gods is sometimes divided into two, to make six realms, the two divisions being those of the gods proper and the *asura*'s, or 'titans', seen as proud, fierce, power-hungry divine beings (counted among the lower rebirths). Gods proper are said to live in twenty-six heavens, which are grouped according to a three-fold classification of rebirths. The lowest of these is the 'realm of sense-desire' (*kāma-avacara*), which includes all the rebirths mentioned so far and the six lowest heavens. In all of these realms, beings perceive sensory objects in such a way as to particularly notice their qualities of desirability or undesirability. More subtle than and 'above' the realm of sense-desire is the 'realm of (pure) form' (*rūpa-avacara*). Here dwell more refined gods, who are known in general as *brahmā*'s, in contrast to the *devas* proper of the six lower heavens. In the realm of pure form there are said to be sixteen heavens of a progressively more refined and calm nature. Beings at this level of existence are aware of objects in a pure way devoid of sensuous desire, and are without the senses of touch, taste and smell. They suffer from other attachments and limitations, however. More refined than the realm of pure form is the 'formless realm' (*arūpa-avacara*), which is comprised of the four most refined forms of rebirth. They are purely mental 'spheres' (*āyatana*'s) devoid of all hints of anything visible or physical, beyond all shape or form. They are named after the characteristic states of consciousness of the *brahmās* reborn 'there'. In the first, they have the experience of 'infinite space'; in the second they dwell on the 'infinite consciousness' which can contemplate infinite space; in the third, they experience the apparent 'nothingness' of their level of existence; in the last, their resting state of consciousness is so subtle that their sphere is that of 'neither-cognition-nor-non-cognition'. This last rebirth, the 'summit of existence', comprises the highest and most subtle form of life in the cosmos, with a huge life-span of 84,000 eons, and yet even this eventually ends in death. Under his yoga teacher Uddaka, Gotama is said to have attained a meditation which would have led to rebirth in this realm, but rejected it as falling short of his goal (see p. 18).

Descending from the highest to the lowest heavens, the life-span gradually decreases. In the 'lowest' formless heaven, it is 20,000 eons; in the realm of pure form, it varies from 16,000 down to one-third eons; in the realm of sense-desire, it varies from 9,216 million years down to 9 million years (*Vibh*.422–7). Nevertheless, it is emphasized that the experience of time is relative, so that even such large periods are felt to pass quite quickly. For example in the lowest heaven, fifty human years pass in one divine 'day', so that 9 million human years pass in 500 divine 'years'.

Among the sense-desire heavens are several significant ones. On the fringes of the sixth and highest one dwells the tempter Māra. The structure of things is such that there will nearly always be a Māra, but the particular incumbents of this cosmic position are born and die, as in the case of all other gods. They can perhaps be likened to particular people who hold an office such as that of mayor. The fourth heaven is that of the Tusita gods, being the realm in which *Bodhisattas* spend their penultimate life, and in which Metteyya now dwells. The second heaven is that of the Tāvatiṃsa gods, the 'thirty-three' gods of the pre-Buddhist Vedic pantheon. The chief Vedic god Indra, often known as Sakka in Buddhist texts, is said to have become a 'Stream-enterer' and thus a protector of Buddhism (*D*.II.288).

The top five pure form heavens are known as the 'pure abodes' (*suddhāvāsa*'s), and are only attainable by persons, known as Non-returners, who are almost *Arahats*. The remaining eleven pure form heavens parallel the four deep meditational states known as *jhāna*'s, and are reached by people mastering such a state during life, which 'tunes' their minds into a certain level of existence. Of the beings of these heavens, perhaps the most significant is Great Brahmā, who dwells in the upper heaven of the first *jhāna*, whose sphere of influence takes in one thousand 'world-systems', and whose life-span is one great eon. In the bottom two pure form heavens dwell the ministers and retinue of Great Brahmā.

The essential details of the levels of rebirth are thus:

Formless realm: four types of purely mental rebirths.

Pure form realm: the five pure abodes, below which are eleven other heavens parallelling the *jhānas*, with Great Brahmā, his ministers, and retinue in the bottom three.

Sense-desire realm: six heavens in which dwell the *devas*, below which dwell humans, *asuras*, animals, *petas* and hell-beings.

The questions of a creator God and the origins of human life

Buddhism sees no need for a creator of the world, as it postulates no ultimate beginning to the world, and regards it as sustained by natural laws. Moreover, if there were a creator of the world, he would be regarded as responsible for the suffering which is found throughout it (*Jat*.v.238). The nearest thing to God in the early texts is the Great Brahmā of our world-system, who was seen by some Brahmins as having created the world. While the Buddha regarded him as a long-lived glorious being, he still saw him as mistaken in his belief that he was an all-powerful creator. A *Sutta* passage in fact tells an ironic story of why he believed he was (*D*.I.18). Periodically, a physical world-system and the lower heavens associated with it come to an end. At this time, beings from these lower levels are generally reborn as 'Radiant' (*Ābhassara*) gods, in a second *jhāna* heaven. After a long period, the three lowest pure form heavens appear, and a Radiant god dies and is reborn here as a Great Brahmā. After some time, he becomes lonely and longs for the presence of others. Soon his wish is fulfilled, simply because other Radiant gods die and happen to be reborn, due to their karma, as his ministers and retinue. Not remembering his previous life, Great Brahmā therefore thinks, 'I am Brahmā, Great Brahmā... the All-seeing, the Controller, the Lord, the Maker, the Creator... these other beings are my creation'. His ministers and retinue agree with this erroneous conclusion, and when some of them eventually die and are reborn as humans, they develop the power to remember their previous life, and consequently teach that Great Brahmā is the eternal creator of all beings. Another ironic story illustrates Great Brahmā's limitations. A monk with a philosophical question about the transcending of all worlds meditates so as to be able to contact gods and ask them his question. None of the gods from the lowest heaven, or any up to that of the retinue of Brahmā, are able to help him, but he is assured that Great Brahmā will be able to. After a while, Great Brahmā makes himself visible and the monk asks his question. All he gets in reply, however, is Brahmā's proud assertion of his creatorship. After responding three times in this way, Brahmā takes the monk on one side and says that he could not disillusion his retinue by publicly admitting that he did not know the answer; the monk had best go to the Buddha, who would surely know the answer (*D.*I.215–23).

Brahmā is thus seen as inferior to the Buddha in wisdom. While being somewhat proud, however, he is seen as a kind and compassionate being. He is, then, a god of love who thinks he created the world but who in fact did not. There is thus no theological problem of evil in Buddhism, namely the problem of how an all-powerful, all-knowing, all-loving God could create a world in which evil and suffering exists.

The nearest thing to a creation story in Buddhism is its account of how beings come to populate a world-system as it starts up in a new cycle of existence. The *Aggañña Sutta* (*D.*III.80–98) says that, at this time, Radiant gods die and are reborn hovering over the re-evolving physical world, then an expanse of water in complete darkness. The reborn beings are seen as sexless, self-luminous and still semi-divine. After a long time, a crust of 'savoury earth' spreads out on the waters, and a greedy being tastes it and craves for it. This primaeval act of desire is imitated by others, till the beings lose their self-luminosity, become more solid and proud of their appearance, and so eventually develop into two sexes. Their environment is rich in food, but the more they greedily gather in its bounty, the less it gives. Eventually the idea of private property develops, and theft, lying and violence come in its train. By now recognizably human, the people then form a social contract to choose a king who will rule over them and punish wrong-doers. Thus goes the Buddhist account of a 'fall', due to greed and pride, and of the development of sexuality, human beings and society.

The implications of the rebirth perspective

The Buddhist perspective on rebirth is that it is not a pleasant affair, but that all unenlightened people are reborn whether they like it or not, and whether they believe in rebirth or not. The process of life and rebirth has no inherent purpose; for it was not designed and created by anyone. Thus the only sensible aim, for one who understands it to some extent, is to strive, firstly, to avoid its more unpleasant realms, and ultimately to transcend it altogether, and to help others to do so. Most Buddhists therefore aim for attaining a heavenly or a human rebirth, with the *Arahat's* liberating experience of *Nibbāna* as the long-term goal; the goal of full Buddhahood is an even higher goal, which is emphasized in Mahāyāna Buddhism. Buddhist heavens, then, are *this* side of salvation; for *Nibbāna* is beyond the limitations of both earthly and heavenly existence.

Within the round of rebirths, all beings are part of the same cycle of lives. Each human being has been an animal, ghost, hell-being and god in the past, and is likely to be so again at some time in the future. Any form of suffering one witnesses in another human or other being has been undergone by oneself at some time (*S*.II.186): thus one should not cling to rebirths and should have compassion for other sentient beings. In one's innumerable past lives, the law of averages dictates that most beings one comes across, however one may dislike them now, have at some time been a close relative or friend (*S*.II.189–90), so that lovingkindness towards them is appropriate.

Such teachings, of course, urge a kindness and non-violence towards all forms of life. Humans are part of the same cycle of lives as other beings, and are not separated from them by a huge gulf. Nevertheless, the more complex and developed a being is, the worse it is to harm or kill it; so it is worse to kill a human than an animal. It is, in fact, seen as particularly fortunate to be born as a human being. In the lower realms, there is much suffering and little freedom of action. In the heavenly realms, life is blissful in comparison with human life, but this tends to make the gods complacent, and they may also think they are eternal, without need of liberation. The human realm is a middle realm, in which there is enough suffering to motivate humans to seek to transcend it by spiritual development, and enough freedom to be able to act on this aspiration. It is thus the most favourable realm for spiritual development.

A human rebirth is relatively rare, however (*A*.I.35). While the human population has been increasing, there are still many more animals, birds, fishes and insects, for example. The Tibetan Buddhists talk of having attained a 'precious human rebirth': a marvellous opportunity for spiritual growth that should be used wisely and respected in others. As it may be cut short at any time by death, it should not be frittered away.

KARMA

The movement of beings between rebirths is not a haphazard process but is ordered and governed by the law of karma, the principle that beings are reborn according to the nature and quality of their past actions; they are 'heir' to their actions (*M*.III.203). It is said that acts of hatred and violence tend to lead to rebirth in a hell, acts bound up with delusion and confusion tend to lead to rebirth as an animal, and acts of greed tend to lead to rebirth as a ghost. A person's actions mould their consciousness, making them into a certain kind of person, so that when they die their outer form tends to correspond to the type of nature that has been developed. If bad actions are not serious enough to lead to a lower rebirth, they affect the nature of a human rebirth: stinginess leads to being poor, injuring beings leads to frequent illnesses, and anger leads to being ugly – an extension of the process whereby an angry person gradually develops ugly features during their present life (*M*.III.203–6). Poor, ill or ugly people are not to be presently blamed for their condition, however, for the actions of a past life are behind them, and the important thing is how they act and others treat them now. Acts of moral restraint, kindness and generosity are seen as tending to rebirth as a human or sense-desire realm god, while the attainment of the meditative calm of *jhāna* tends to rebirth in a corresponding heaven. In order to attain *Nibbāna*, a person must be able to perform a transcendental action, namely the attainment of deep insight into reality. All intentional actions, good or bad, *matter*; for they leave a trace on the psyche which will lead to future results.

The law of karma is seen as a natural law inherent in the nature of things, like a law of physics. It is not operated by a God, and indeed the gods are themselves under its sway. Good and bad rebirths are not, therefore, seen as 'rewards' and 'punishments', but as simply the natural results of certain kinds of action. Karma is often likened to a seed, and the two words for a karmic result, *vipāka* and *phala*, respectively mean 'ripening' and 'fruit'. An action is thus like a seed which will sooner or later, as part of a natural maturation process, result in certain fruits accruing to the doer of the action.

What determines the nature of a karmic 'seed' is the will or intention behind an act: 'It is will (*cetanā*), O monks, that I call karma; having willed, one acts through body, speech or mind' (*A*.III.415). It is the psychological impulse behind an action that is 'karma', that which sets going a chain of causes culminating in a karmic fruit. Actions, then, must be intentional if they are to generate karmic fruits: accidentally treading on an insect does not have such an effect, as the Jains believe. Thinking of doing some bad action is a bad (mental) karma, however, especially when one gives energy to such a thought, rather than just letting it pass. Deliberately putting such a thought down is a good mental karma. Regretting a past bad (or good) action, and resolving not to do it again lessens its karmic result as it reduces the psychological impetus behind the act. However, while painful feelings at the thought of a past act may be part of its karmic result, an active feeling of guilt is seen as associated with (self-)hatred, and as being an anguished state which is not conducive to calm, clarity, and thus spiritual improvement.

While belief in the law of karma can sometimes degenerate into a form of fatalism, the Buddha emphasized that deterministic fate (*niyati*) and karma are very different concepts; for the idea of karma emphasizes the importance of human action and its effects: people make their own 'destiny' by their actions. The aspects of life which are seen as the result of past karma include one's form of rebirth, social class at birth, general character, crucial good and bad things which happen to one, and even the way one experiences the world. Out of the mass of sense-data, one only ever gets 'edited highlights' of what lies around one. Some people tend to notice pleasant things, while others tend to notice unpleasant things; these differences are said to be due to karma. Results of past actions do not include *present* intentional actions, however, though karmic results may influence the type of action that a person tends to think of doing.

As a person never knows what aspect of any situation may have been determined by karma, difficult situations are not to be passively accepted, but a person should do his best to improve them; only when things happen in spite of efforts to avert them might they be put down to past karma. If the situation can be averted or changed, fine, but then any anxiety or suffering it led to may be still seen as due to past karma.

As an aid to planning courses of action in a karma-influenced world, many Buddhists use divination methods such as astrology at certain points in their lives, so as to try to gauge what their karma has in store for them. The idea of the influence of karma, while not fatalistic, does encourage a person to live patiently with a situation. Rather than making new bad karma by getting angry with society, family, or other people, blaming them for his lot, this can be viewed as the result of his own actions of the past. This attitude arises from a person taking responsibility for the shape of his life. Like people of other religions, however, Buddhists sometimes have an idea of fate, in parallel with their idea of karma, or they may even use past karma as an excuse for continuing with present bad karma.

It is mostly at the human level that good and bad actions are performed. The gods generally have little scope for doing either good or evil, and most simply enjoy the results of the previous good actions which led to their existence. Animals, ghosts and hell-beings have little freedom for intentional good or bad actions, though the higher animals can sometimes act virtuously, if not in a self-consciously moral way. Beings in the lower rebirths generally just reap the results of previous bad actions. When these results come to an end, the results of some previous good actions will come to fruition and buoy up the being to some better form of life, sooner or later reaching the human level again. This illustrates that karma does not just bring results in the next life: an action is said to have effects later in the present life, the next life, and also in some subsequent ones.

The law of karma is not regarded as rigid and mechanical, but as the flexible, fluid and dynamic outworking of the fruits of actions. The full details of its working out, in specific instances, are said to be 'unthinkable' (*acinteyya*) to all but a Buddha (*A*.IV.77). A moral life is not necessarily immediately followed by a good rebirth, if a strong evil action of a past life has not yet brought its results, or a dying person regrets having done good. Similarly, an immoral life is not necessarily immediately followed by a bad rebirth (*M*.III.209–15). The appropriate results will come in time, however (*Dhp*.71).

In Buddhism, a 'good' action is generally referred to as *kusala*: 'skilful' in producing an uplifting mental state in the doer, or 'wholesome', in that it involves a healthy state of mind. A 'bad' action is *akusala*: 'unskilful' or 'unwholesome'. The main criterion in deciding whether an action is 'unskilful' is to see whether it conduces to the harm of oneself, of others, or of both (*M*.I.415–16), and whether it is 'destructive of intuitive wisdom, associated with distress, not conducive to *Nibbāna*' (*M*.I.115). Correspondingly, a 'skilful' action does not conduce to any such harm, but does conduce to the growth of wholesome states of mind (*M*.II.114). The 'harm' to oneself which is relevant here is spiritual harm, or material harm if this arises from self-hatred. An act which benefits others at the expense of material harm to oneself is certainly not unskilful.

As well as this result-orientated criterion for the skilfulness of an action, there is also one which is based on motive. The three possible motivating 'roots' of 'unskilful' action are: (i) greed, which covers a range of states from mild longing up to full-blown lust, avarice, fame-seeking and dogmatic clinging to ideas; (ii) hatred, which covers mild irritation through to burning resentment and wrath, and (iii) delusion, the veiling of truth from oneself, as in dull, foggy states of mind through to specious doubt on moral and spiritual matters, distorting the truth, and turning away from it. The opposites of these are the three 'roots' of skilful action: (i) non-greed, covering states from small generous impulses through to a strong urge for renunciation of worldly pleasures; (ii) non-hatred, covering friendliness through to forbearance in the face of great provocation, and deep lovingkindness for all beings, and (iii) non-delusion, covering clarity of mind through to the deepest insight into reality. While phrased negatively, these three are nevertheless seen as positive states.

Auspicious actions and 'merit'

A 'skilful' action is also described as *puñña*: that which is 'auspicious' or 'fortunate', as it purifies the mind and thus leads to future good fortune. *Puñña* is generally translated as 'merit', but this imports an idea of 'deserving' into Buddhism, when what is alluded to is the natural effect of certain actions. An 'unskilful' action is described as *apuñña*, 'inauspicious', or as *pāpa*: 'bringing ill fortune', 'infertile' – an act from which beneficial results do not grow. Buddhists are keen to perform auspicious actions, such as supporting Buddhist monks by donating alms, or listening to sermons; for *puñña* is an unlosable 'treasure' (*Khp*.7). Any act of giving is seen as auspicious, even giving in the hope of some return, or giving purely to get the karmic result of giving. A purer motive, however, is seen as leading to a better karmic result. Thus it is particularly good to give from motives such as the appreciation of a gift as helping to support a holy way of life, or of the calm and joy that giving naturally brings (*A*.VI.60–3). While a large gift is generally seen as more auspicious than a small one, purity of mind can also make up for the smallness of a gift, for 'where there is a joyful heart, no gift is small' (*Jat*.II.85). Indeed, a person with nothing to give can act auspiciously by simply rejoicing at another person's giving. In Theravāda lands, this is expressed by uttering of the ritualized expression *sādhu*, meaning 'it is good!', when others give.

In Theravāda tradition, an auspicious act may not only be performed by empathizing (*anumodanā*) with someone else's auspicious deed, but also by the transference to or sharing of the auspicious quality of an act (*patti* – what has been gained) with another being. This practice may have originated as a Buddhist adaptation of the Brahmanical *śrāddha* ceremony, in which gifts were seen as transferred to deceased relatives by giving them to Brahmins at memorial rites at various intervals after a death in the family. In an early text, a Brahmin asks the Buddha if *śrāddha* rites bring benefit to the dead, and the Buddha replies that the dead will benefit only if reborn as *petas*, for these ghostly beings live either on the putrid food of their realm or on what is provided by gifts from relatives and friends (*A*.V.269–72). The *Petavatthu*, a late Canonical text, accordingly describes a number of instances where a gift is given in the name of a suffering *peta*, so that they attain rebirth as a god due to the auspicious quality of the giving. Theravāda rites for the dead therefore include the feeding of monks and the transference of the auspicious quality of the deed ('merit') to the deceased, or whatever other ancestors may be *petas*, in the hope that this will ease their lot as *petas* or help them to a better rebirth. This is done especially seven days after a death, but also in yearly memorial services. Another early text has the Buddha say that it is wise to support monks and to dedicate the gift to the local gods, so that they will look with favour on the donor (*D*.II.88). Accordingly, Theravādin donations to monks often conclude with a verse transferring the auspicious quality of the gift to gods. These are seen as having less opportunity to do auspicious deeds themselves, but can benefit from transferred 'merit', which helps maintain them in their divine rebirth; in return, it is hoped that they will use whatever powers they have to aid and protect Buddhism and the person making the donation. A boy ordaining as a novice or full monk will also share the 'merit' of this act with his mother. Here, her 'merit' will come from both the act of 'giving up' her son to the monkhood, and her rejoicing at his auspicious act.

Given the Buddhist stress on the idea that a person can only generate 'merit' by their own deeds, the idea of 'transferring' it is potentially anomalous. To avoid such an anomaly, the Theravādin commentaries, dating from the fifth century AD or earlier, developed an orthodox interpretation. This was that no 'merit' was actually transferred, but that the food, etc. donated to monks was dedicated, by the performer of the auspicious donation, to an ancestor or god, so that the donation was done on their behalf, with their property. Provided that they assented to this donation by rejoicing at it, they would themselves make 'merit', both from the donation-by-proxy and the mental act of rejoicing. In sharing 'merit', a person does not lose any himself, for his sharing is itself auspicious. 'Merit' sharing is simply a way of spreading the karmic benefits of good deeds to others, as a gesture of goodwill. This is expressed in the traditional simile to explain such sharing: lighting many lamps from one. In Mahāyāna tradition, 'merit' is often transferred to 'all sentient beings'; such an aspiration is found not only in Northern and Eastern, but also in Southern Buddhism.

BELIEF IN REBIRTH AND KARMA

While Buddhism holds that the existence of rebirth and the efficacy of karma can be confirmed by experiences in deep meditation, most Buddhists have not attained these. They therefore only have *belief* in these principles, not direct knowledge of their reality, and use these beliefs to provide a perspective on life and action in it. The reasonableness of the beliefs is nevertheless argued for in the Buddhist tradition. In one early text (*M*.I.403), the Buddha says that to believe in these principles, and so live a moral life, will lead to a good rebirth *if* rebirths exist. If rebirths do not exist, nothing will have been lost, and the person will in any case have been praised by wise people. The 'best bet' is thus to believe in and act on these principles. Past karma also offers perhaps the only religiously satisfactory explanation of the suffering of people who have done nothing to deserve it in this life.

Nevertheless, part of the working out of karma is said to come in this life, and people can observe that the results of good and bad actions very often catch up with a person even during one life. In a similar way, an aspect of the rebirth doctrine relates to what can be observed in one life. Probably from the time of earliest Buddhism, rebirth was seen both as a process which takes place after death, and also as a process taking place during life. That is, we are constantly changing during life, 'reborn' as a 'different' person according to our mood, the task we are involved in, or the people we are relating to. Depending on how we act, we may experience 'heavenly' or 'hellish' states of mind. The Buddhist would say that it is reasonable to suppose that this process of change, determined by the nature of our actions, does not abruptly stop at death, but carries on.

Modern Buddhists also point to certain data which apparently supports the theory of rebirth. Much of this has been researched by Professor Ian Stevenson, an American psychiatrist who has published the results of his investigations in such works as *20 Cases Suggestive of Reincarnation*. These detail studies of young children, from places such as India, Sri Lanka, the Lebanon, Brazil and Alaska, who apparently have spontaneous recall of past human lives. In the typical case, the child starts referring, not long after he can talk, to events, relations and possessions that he had when he was 'big'. These 'memories' generally fade as the child grows up. The previously personality is often locatable as having lived some way away, unknown to the child's family, and to have died not long before the child was conceived. The child often knows intimate details of the person's life, has similar character traits, and can even recognize past 'relatives' in a crowd, correctly name them, and react to them with strong and appropriate emotion. Sometimes, birthmarks correspond in location and even appearance to wounds or surgical incisions associated with the previous personality's death. Stevenson holds, after much probing analysis, that explanations such as fraud, wish-fulfilling fantasy, overhearing information about a dead person, or telepathy, are inadequate. He therefore regards rebirth as probably the best hypothesis to explain such phenomena, though possession would also explain some cases. It is unlikely that such cases are a purely modern phenomenon, and it seems reasonable to suppose that their occurrence in the past has helped sustain belief in rebirth in Buddhist cultures.

While teachings on karma and rebirth are an important part of Buddhist belief, they are not the *most* crucial, nor the most specifically Buddhist. They act, though, as the lead-up to, and motivator for the most important teachings, those on the Four Holy Truths. When teaching lay persons, the Buddha frequently began with a 'step-by-step discourse': (i) on giving and moral observance as leading to a heavenly rebirth, and then, (ii) on the advantages of renouncing sense-pleasures (by meditative calming of the mind). Such teachings were used to inspire his hearers and help them gain a state of mind which was calm, joyful and open. In this state of readiness, they would then be taught the Four Holy Truths relating to suffering (e.g. *Vin*.I.15–16). The teachings of the 'step-by-step discourse' and the Four Holy Truths correspond, respectively, to two levels of 'right view', or 'right understanding' of reality (*M*.III.72). The second type is wisdom and insight which directly perceives the Holy Truths. As it leads beyond suffering and rebirth in any world, it is seen as transcendent (*lokuttara*) and truly Holy (*ariya*). The first type is seen as ordinary (*lokiya*), as it supports actions leading to good rebirths. It is described as belief in the efficacy of karma, in the reality of rebirth, in the benefit of helping one's parents, in the existence of levels of rebirth invisible to normal vision, and in the existence of virtuous religious practitioners who have direct knowledge of other worlds. Practice based on such beliefs is seen as creating a good basis for the additional development of wisdom. Thus the overall path of Buddhism is seen as a training which gradually moves towards the profounder teachings, just as the ocean bottom shelves down gradually from the shore into the depths (*Vin*.II.238). Many Buddhists may not get beyond the shallows, but the invitation and opportunity to go deeper are always there.

3

EARLY BUDDHIST TEACHINGS: THE FOUR HOLY TRUTHS

The Four Holy Truths comprise the more advanced teachings of the Buddha, intended for those who have prepared themselves by previous moral and spiritual development. Stated briefly in the Buddha's first sermon, they form the structural framework for all higher teachings. The fourfold structure parallels the practice of doctors of the Buddha's day: (i) diagnose a disease, (ii) identify its cause, (iii) determine whether it is curable, and (iv) outline a course of treatment to cure it. The first Truth concerns the 'illness' of *dukkha*, the 'suffering' that we are all subject to. The second concerns the cause of this 'illness': craving. The third affirms that by removing the cause of the 'illness', a cure is possible: from the cessation of craving, in the experience of *Nibbāna*, suffering ceases. The fourth outlines the way to full health: the Holy Eightfold Path, or Middle Way. The Buddha, then, is seen as fulfilling the role of a spiritual physician. Having 'cured' himself of *dukkha*, he worked to help others to do likewise. The problem of suffering had prompted his own quest for enlightenment, and its solution naturally became the focus of his teachings. He sometimes summarized these by saying simply, 'Both in the past and now, I set forth just this: *dukkha* and the cessation of *dukkha*' (e.g. *M*.I.140). The appropriate response to the Four Holy Truths is to understand phenomena as *dukkha*, abandon the cause of *dukkha*, and experience the cessation of *dukkha*, by developing the Path to this.

THE FIRST HOLY TRUTH: SUFFERING

In his first sermon, the Buddha formulated the first Truth as follows:

(i) Birth is *dukkha*, ageing is *dukkha*, sickness is *dukkha*, death is *dukkha*; (ii) sorrow, lamentation, pain, grief and despair are *dukkha*; (iii) association with what one dislikes is *dukkha*, separation from what one likes is *dukkha*, not to get what one wants is *dukkha*; (iv) in short, the five groups of grasping (which make up a person) are *dukkha* [numbers added].

Here the word *dukkha* refers to all those things which are unpleasant, imperfect, and which we would like to be otherwise. It is both 'suffering' and the general 'unsatisfactoriness' of life. The first Truth essentially points out that suffering is inherent in the very fabric of life.

The first features described as *dukkha* are basic biological aspects of being alive, each of which can be painful and traumatic. The *dukkha* of these is compounded by the rebirth perspective of Buddhism, for this involves repeated re-birth, re-ageing, re-sickness and re-death. The second set of features refer to physical or mental pain that arises from the vicissitudes of life. The third set of features described as *dukkha* point to the fact that we can never wholly succeed in keeping away things, people and situations that we dislike, in holding on to those we do like, and in getting what we want. The changing, unstable nature of life is such that we are led to experience dissatisfaction, loss, and disappointment: in a word, frustration.

Is Buddhism 'pessimistic' in emphasizing the unpleasant aspects of life? Buddhism's reply is that the transcending of suffering requires a fully realistic assessment of its pervasive presence in life. One must accept one is 'ill' if a cure is to be possible: ignoring the problem only makes it worse. The path to the end of suffering, moreover, is one in which the deep calm and joy of devotion and meditation play an important part. Buddhism, then, does not deny the existence of happiness in the world – it provides ways of increasing it – but it does emphasize that all forms of happiness (bar that of *Nibbāna*) do not last. Sooner or later, they slip through one's fingers and leave an aftertaste of loss and longing. In this way, even happiness is to be seen as *dukkha*. This can be more clearly seen when one considers another classification of forms of *dukkha*: *dukkha* as physical pain, *dukkha* due to change, and the *dukkha* of conditioned phenomena (*S*.IV.259). When a happy feeling passes, it often leads to *dukkha* due to change, and even while it is occurring, it is *dukkha* in the sense of being a limited, conditioned, imperfect state, one which is not truly satisfactory. This most subtle sense of *dukkha* is sometimes experienced in feelings of a vague unease at the fragility and transitoriness of life.

The five factors of personality

When the first sermon summarizes its outline of *dukkha* by saying 'in short, the five groups of grasping are *dukkha*', it is referring to *dukkha* in the subtlest sense. The five 'groups of grasping' (*upādāna-khandha*'s) are the five factors which go to make up a 'person'. Buddhism holds, then, that none of the phenomena which comprise personality is free from unsatisfactoriness. Each factor is a 'group' or 'aggregate' (*khandha*) of related states, and each is an object of 'grasping' (*upādāna*) so as to be identified as 'me', 'I', 'myself'.

To aid understanding of *dukkha*, Buddhism gives details of each of the five factors that it analyses personality into. The first is *rūpa*, 'material shape' or 'form'. This refers to the material aspect of existence, whether in the outer world or in the body of a living being. It is said to be comprised of four basic elements or forces, and forms of subtle, sensitive matter derived from these. The four basics are solidity (literally 'earth'), cohesion ('water'), energy ('fire') and motion ('wind'). From the interaction of these, the body of flesh, blood, bones, etc. is composed.

The remaining four personality factors are all mental in nature; for they lack any physical 'form'. The second factor is *vedanā*, or 'feeling'. This is the hedonic tone or 'taste' of any experience: pleasant, unpleasant, or neutral. It includes both sensations arising from the body and mental feelings of happiness, unhappiness or indifference. The third factor is *saññā*, which processes sensory and mental objects, so as to classify and label them, for example as 'yellow', 'a man', or 'fear'. It is 'cognition', recognition and interpretation – including misinterpretation – of objects. Without it, a person might be conscious but would be unable to know *what* he was conscious of. The fourth personality factor is the *sankhāra*'s, or 'constructing activities'. These comprise a number of states which initiate action or direct, mould and give shape to character. They include very active states such as determination, joy and hatred, and also more passive states such as attention and sensory stimulation. While some are ethically neutral, many are ethically 'skilful' or 'unskilful'. The most characteristic 'constructing activity' is *cetanā*, 'will' or 'volition', which is identified with karma (see p. 40).

The fifth and final factor of personality is *viññāṇa*, '(discriminative) consciousness'. This includes both the basic awareness of a sensory or mental object, and the discrimination of its basic aspects or parts, which are actually recognized by *saññā*. It is of six types according to whether it is conditioned by eye, ear, nose, tongue, body or mind-organ. It is also known as *citta*, the central focus of personality which can be seen as 'mind', 'heart' or 'thought'. This is essentially a 'mind set' or 'mentality'; some aspects of which alter from moment to moment, but others recur and are equivalent to a person's character. Its form at any moment is set up by the other mental *khandhas*, but in turn it goes on to determine their pattern of arising, in a process of constant interaction.

Much Buddhist practice is concerned with the purification, development and harmonious integration of the factors of personality, through the cultivation of virtue and meditation. In time, however, the five-fold analysis is used to enable a meditator to gradually transcend the naive perception – with respect to 'himself' or 'another' – of a unitary 'person' or 'self'. In place of this, there is set up the contemplation of a person as a cluster of changing physical and mental processes, or *dhamma*'s, thus undermining grasping and attachment, which are key causes of suffering.

Phenomena as impermanent and not-self

Though the first sermon emphasizes *dukkha*, this is in fact only one of three related characteristics or 'marks' of the five *khandhas*. These fundamental 'three marks' of all conditioned phenomena are that they are impermanent (*anicca*), *dukkha*, and not-self (*anatta*). Buddhism emphasizes that change and impermanence are fundamental features of *everything*, bar *Nibbāna*. Mountains wear down, material goods wear out, and all beings, even gods, die. The gross form of the body changes relatively slowly, but the matter which composes it is replaced as one eats, excretes, and sheds skin cells. As regards the mind, character patterns may be relatively persistent, but feelings, moods, ideas, etc. can be observed to constantly change.

It is because of the fact that things are impermanent that they are also *dukkha*: potentially painful and frustrating. Because they are impermanent and unsatisfactory, moreover, they are to be seen as not-self: not a permanent, self-secure, happy, independent self or I. They are 'empty' (*suñña*) of such a self, or anything pertaining to such a self.

This important teaching was introduced by the Buddha in his second sermon, the *Anattā-lakkhaṇa Sutta* (*Vin*.I.13–14, *S*.II.66–8). Here he explained, with respect to each of the five *khandhas*, that if it were truly self, it would not 'tend to sickness', and it would be totally controllable at will, which it is not. Moreover, as each *khandha* is impermanent, *dukkha*, and of a nature to change, it is inappropriate to consider it as 'This is mine, this am I, this is my self'.

In the Buddha's day, the spiritual quest was largely seen as the search for identifying and liberating a person's true self (Skt *ātman*, Pali *atta*). Such an entity was postulated as a person's permanent inner nature, the source of true happiness and the autonomous 'inner controller' of action. In Brahmanism, this *ātman* was seen as a universal Self identical with Brahman, while in Jainism, for example, it was seen as the individual 'life principle' (*jīva*). The Buddha argued that anything subject to change, anything not autonomous and totally controllable by its own wishes, anything subject to the disharmony of suffering, could not be such a perfect true self. Moreover, to take anything which was not such a self as if it were one, is to lay the basis for much suffering. This arises when what one fondly takes as one's permanent, essential self changes in undesired ways.

The teaching on phenomena as not-self is not only intended to undermine the Brahmanical or Jain concepts of self, but also much more commonly held conceptions and deep-rooted feelings of I-ness. To feel that, however much one changes in life from childhood onwards, some part remains unchanged as the 'real me', is to have a belief in a permanent self. To act as if only *other* people die, and to ignore the inevitability of one's own death, is to act as if one had a permanent self. To relate changing mental phenomena to a substantial self which 'owns' them: '*I* am worried... happy... angry', is to have such a self-concept. To identify with one's body, ideas, or actions, etc. is to take them as part of an 'I'.

The not-self teaching can easily be misunderstood and misdescribed; so it is important to see what it is saying. The Buddha accepted many conventional usages of the word 'self' (also '*atta*'), as in 'yourself' and 'myself'. These he saw as simply a convenient way of referring to a particular collection of mental and physical states. But within such a conventional, empirical self, he taught that no permanent, substantial, independent, metaphysical self could be found. This is well explained by an early nun, Vajirā. Just as the word 'chariot' is used to denote a collection of items in functional relationship, but not a special part of a chariot, so the conventional term 'a being', is properly used to refer to the five *khandhas* relating together (*S.*I.135, cf, *Miln.*25–8). None of the *khandhas* is a 'being' or 'self', but these are simply conventional terms used to denote the collection of functioning *khandhas*.

The not-self teaching does not deny that there is continuity of character in life, and to some extent from life to life. But persistent character-traits are merely due to the repeated occurrence of certain *cittas*, or 'mind-sets'. The *citta* as a whole is sometimes talked of as an (empirical) 'self' (e.g. *Dhp.*160 with 35), but while such character traits may be long-lasting, they can and do change, and are thus impermanent, and so 'not-self', insubstantial. A 'person' is a collection of rapidly changing and interacting mental and physical processes, with character-patterns re-occurring over some time. Only partial control can be exercised over these processes; so they often change in undesired ways, leading to suffering. Impermanent, they cannot be a permanent self. Suffering, they cannot be an autonomous true 'I', which would contain nothing that was out of harmony with itself.

While *Nibbāna* is beyond impermanence and *dukkha*, it is still not-self. This is made clear in a recurring passage (e.g. at *A.*I.286–7), which says that all *sankhāra*'s, or conditioned phenomena, are impermanent and *dukkha*, but that 'all *dhammas*' are not-self. '*Dhamma*' is a word with many meanings in Buddhism, but here it refers to any basic component of reality. Most are conditioned, but *Nibbāna* is the unconditioned *dhamma*; both conditioned and unconditioned *dhammas* are not-self. While *Nibbāna* is beyond change and suffering, it has nothing in it which could support the feeling of I-ness; for this can only arise with respect to the *khandhas*, and it is not even a truly valid feeling here (*D.*II.66–8).

The not-self teaching is not in *itself* a denial of the existence of a permanent self; it is primarily a practical teaching aimed at the overcoming of attachment. It urges that all phenomena that we *do* identify with as 'self', should be carefully observed and examined to see that they cannot be taken as such. In doing this, a person finally comes to see *everything*, all *dhammas*, as not-self, thereby destroying all attachment and attaining *Nibbāna*. In this process, it is not necessary to give any philosophical 'denial' of self; the idea simply withers away, as it is seen that no actual instance of such a thing can be found anywhere. Buddhism sees no need to postulate a permanent self, and accounts for the functioning of personality, in life and from life to life, in terms of a stream of changing, conditioned processes. As seen below, rebirth does not require a permanent self or substantial 'I', but *belief* in such a thing is one of the things that causes rebirth.

THE SECOND HOLY TRUTH: THE ORIGIN OF SUFFERING

In the first sermon, the Buddha identifies the 'origin' (*samudaya*), or cause, of *dukkha* as follows: 'It is this craving (*taṇhā*), giving rise to rebirth, accompanied by delight and attachment, finding delight now here, now there...'. '*Taṇhā*' literally means 'thirst', and clearly refers to demanding desires or drives which are ever on the lookout for gratification. These lead to suffering in a number of ways. Firstly, they lead to the suffering of frustration, as their demands for lasting and wholly satisfying fulfilment are perpetually disappointed by a changing and unsatisfactory world. Secondly, they motivate people to perform various actions, whose karmic results lead on to further rebirths, with their attendant *dukkha*. Thirdly, they lead to quarrels, strife and conflict between individuals and groups.

The first sermon identifies three types of craving: craving for sensual pleasures, craving for existence, and craving for non-existence. The second type refers to the drive for self-protection, for ego-enhancement, and for eternal life after death as *me*. The third is the drive to get rid of unpleasant situations, things and people. In a strong form, it may lead to the impulse for suicide, the rejection of one's whole present life situation. Such a craving, ironically, helps cause a further rebirth, whose problems will be as bad as, or worse than, the present ones. In order to overcome *dukkha*, the Buddhist path aims not only to limit the expression of craving, but ultimately to use calm and wisdom to completely uproot it from the psyche.

Besides craving, two other important causes of *dukkha* are 'views' (*diṭṭhi*) and 'conceit' (*māna*). The first refers to speculative view-points, theories or opinions, especially when they become dogmatic, narrowing a person's whole outlook on life. Such views are seen as hidden forms of self-assertion, which lead to conflict with those of other opinions, be this in the form of verbal wrangling or ideological wars and bloody revolutions. In this context, it is worth noting that the atrocities carried out by Hitler, Stalin and the Khmer Rouge were initiated by people who were convinced of a theory which demanded and 'justified' their actions. The Buddha focussed much critical attention on views concerning 'self', which he saw as leading to attachment and thus suffering. Such views can take many forms, but the Buddha felt that all of them locate a substantial self somewhere in the five *khandhas*, so that each is known as a 'view on the existing group' (*sakkāya-diṭṭhi*). Even when such specific views have been transcended, 'conceit' still remains as a vague and non-specific feeling of I-ness with respect to the *khandhas* (*S*.III.127–32). This is the basic attitude of 'I am': deep-rooted self-assertion or egoism, which is concerned about how 'I' measure up to 'others'.

Conditioned Arising

A doctrine strongly related to the Four Holy Truths, particularly the second, is that of 'Conditioned Arising' (*paṭicca-samuppāda*; also translated as 'Dependent Origination'). The key sources for this doctrine are the *Nidāna Saṃyutta* (*S*.II.1–133) and the *Mahā-nidāna Sutta* (*D*.II.55–71). The understanding of Conditioned Arising is so central to Buddhist practice and development that the Buddha's chief disciple, Sāriputta, said, 'Whoever sees Conditioned Arising sees *Dhamma*, whoever sees *Dhamma* sees Conditioned Arising' (*M*.I.191). Moreover, the Buddha referred to it and *Nibbāna* as the 'profound, difficult to see' *Dhamma* understood by him at his enlightenment (*M*.I.167), and taught that rebirth continues until such understanding is attained (*D*.II.55).

In its abstract form, the doctrine states: 'That being, this comes to be; from the arising of that, this arises; that being absent, this is not; from the cessation of that, this ceases' (*S*.II.28). This states the principle of conditionality, that all things, mental and physical, arise and exist due to the presence of certain conditions, and cease once their conditions are removed: nothing (except *Nibbāna*) is independent. The doctrine thus complements the teaching that no permanent, independent self can be found. The main concrete application of the abstract principle is in the form of a series of conditioned and conditioning links (*nidāna*'s), culminating in the arising of *dukkha*. A standard formula of twelve *nidānas* is most common, but there are also variations on this, which emphasize the contribution of other conditions. These variations show that the 'that' of the abstract formula is not a single determining cause, but a major condition, one of several. Each is a necessary condition for the arising of 'this', but none is alone sufficient for this to happen. The standard formula begins 'Conditioned by spiritual ignorance are the constructing activities; conditioned by the constructing activities is consciousness', and then continues through a series of other conditions. The series thus runs: (1) spiritual ignorance→ (2) constructing activities→ (3) (discriminative) consciousness→ (4) mind-and-body→ (5) the six sense-bases→ (6) sensory stimulation→ (7) feeling→ (8) craving→ (9) grasping→ (10) existence→ (11) birth→ (12) ageing, death, sorrow, lamentation, pain, grief and despair, 'Thus is the origin of this whole mass of *dukkha*'. After the formula is given in forward order, it follows in 'reverse' order. In this form, it describes how the cessation of *dukkha* comes about due to the complete cessation of spiritual ignorance and the consequent cessation of each following *nidāna* (e.g. *Vin.*I.1).

Before looking at details of this formula, some general remarks are in order. It explains how *dukkha*, the subject of the first Holy Truth, comes about, this origination being the subject of the second Truth. The formula in reverse order describes the cessation of *dukkha*, namely *Nibbāna*, the subject of the third Truth (*A.*I.177). It is also said that the Holy Eightfold Path, the subject of the fourth Truth, is the way going to the cessation of each of the twelve links, and thus of *dukkha* (*S.*II.43). There is even a version of Conditioned Arising which continues beyond link twelve to say that, based on *dukkha*, faith arises (*S.*II.30). That is, faith in the Buddha's teaching arises from the experience and understanding of *dukkha*. From faith, other states successively arise which are part of the path to the end of *dukkha*: gladness, joy, serenity, happiness, meditative concentration, and deepening states of insight and detachment. The doctrine thus unites the four Truths, and makes possible a methodological science of moral and spiritual life. By becoming aware of how one is conditioned, one can come to alter the flow of conditions by governing, suspending or intensifying them so as to reduce *dukkha*, and ultimately stop it entirely by transcending the conditions.

Besides explaining the origin of *dukkha*, the formula also explains karma, rebirth and the functioning of personality, all without the need to invoke a permanent self. No substantial self can be found which underlies the *nidānas*, owning and operating them: they simply occur according to conditions. Thus it is inappropriate to ask, for example, 'who craves?', but appropriate to ask what craving is conditioned by, the answer being 'feeling' (*S*.II.14). While the five *khandha* doctrine is an analysis of the components of personality in static form, the twelve *nidāna* formula is a synthesis, which shows how such components dynamically interact to form the living process of personality, in one life and from life to life. Each of the five *khandhas* also occurs in the *nidāna* formula. (Discriminative) consciousness, constructing activities and feeling occur in both lists. Material shape is the same as the 'body' (part of link 4), and cognition is part of 'mind'; in the form of misinterpretation, it is also tantamount to spiritual ignorance.

The *nidāna* of spiritual ignorance (*avijjā*) is defined as unknowing with regard to the Four Holy Truths (*S*.II.4). As the principle of Conditioned Arising underlies these Truths, the first link can be seen, ironically, to be ignorance of this very principle. Conditioned Arising, then, is a process which can only operate in ignorance of itself. Once a person fully understands it, it can be stopped. The 'ignorance' referred to is not lack of information, but a more deep-seated misperception of reality, which can only be destroyed by direct meditative insight. It is given as the first link due to its fundamental influence on the process of life, but is itself conditioned by sensual desire, ill-will, laziness, agitation and fear of commitment: five hindrances which are in turn conditioned by unskilful conduct (*A*.V.113).

Buddhism, then, sees the basic root of suffering as spiritual ignorance, rather than sin, which is a wilful turning away from a creator God. Indeed, it can be regarded as having a doctrine of something like 'original sinlessness'. While the mind is seen as containing many unskilful tendencies with deep roots, 'below' these roots it is pure: 'Monks, this mind (*citta*) is brightly shining (*pabhassara*), but it is defiled by defilements which arrive' (*A*.I.10). That is, the deepest layer of the mind is bright and pure – representing, in effect, the potentiality for attaining *Nibbāna* – but defilements arise through interaction of the mind with the world. Even a newborn child is not seen as having a wholly pure mind, however, for it is said to have unskilful latent tendencies which are carried over from a previous life (*M*.I.433). In the calm of deep meditation, the depth-purity of mind is experienced at a conscious level, as the process of meditation suspends the defiling five hindrances, just as a smelter purifies gold-ore so as to attain pure gold (*S*.v.92). More than a temporary undefiled state of mind is necessary for enlightenment, however. For this, there must be destruction of the four 'cankers' (*āsava*'s): the most deeply-rooted spiritual faults, which are likened to festering sores, leeching off energy from the mind, or intoxicating influxes on the mind. These are the cankers of sense-desire, (desire for) existence, views, and spiritual ignorance, which are seen as conditioning, and being conditioned by, spiritual ignorance (*M*.I.54–5).

The second *nidāna*, 'constructing activities', is that which is expressed in both 'inauspicious' and 'auspicious' actions of body, speech and mind. In a person who has destroyed spiritual ignorance, actions no longer have the power to 'construct' any karmic results. Prior to that, actions can be auspicious if they are based on *some* degree of insight into reality, such as the principles of karma or impermanence. The main 'constructing activity' is will, that which initiates actions. As it is conditioned, but not rigidly determined by past events, it has a relative freedom. For example, the arising of anger need not lead on to angry behaviour, if a person becomes watchfully aware of it, so as to lessen its power. This is because the act of mindfulness brings about a change in the current conditions operating in the mind.

Constructing activities condition '(discriminative) consciousness'; for actions generate tendencies whose momentum tends to make a person become aware of, or think of certain objects. For example, if one has decided (a mental action) to look for a certain article to buy, such as a house, one's mind will automatically notice related things, such as advertisements and 'for sale' notices, that were previously not even registered. 'That which we will, and that which we intend to do, and that for which we have a latent tendency, this is an object for the persistence of consciousness. If there is an object, there is a support for consciousness…' (*S*.II.65). What one is conscious of, and thus the form of one's consciousness, depends on one's volitions and tendencies. As consciousness is also conditioned by its objects (and the sense-organs), the version of Conditioned Arising at *D*.II.63 gives mind-and-body, i.e. mental and physical phenomena as objects, as the first link in the chain, followed by consciousness and on through the remaining links as in the standard version.

The most important context in which constructing activities

condition consciousness is in the generation of consciousness in a future life; for it is said that the 'evolving' or 'conducive' (*saṃvattanika*) consciousness is the crucial link between rebirths (*M.*II.262). At death, the momentum set up by constructing activities (and craving) is not cut off, but impels the evolving flux of consciousness to spill over beyond one life and help spark off another. Conditioned Arising is here a 'Middle Way' which avoids the extremes of 'eternalism' and 'annihilationism': the survival of an eternal self, or the total annihilation of a person at death. Of a person in two consecutive rebirths, it is said, 'He is not the same and he is not different' (*Miln.*40): 'he' neither retains any unchanging essence, nor is wholly different. No unchanging 'being' passes over from one life to another, but the death of a being leads to the continuation of the life process in another context, like the lighting of one lamp from another (*Miln.*71). The 'later' person is a continuation, or evolute of the 'earlier' one on which he is dependent. They are linked by the flux of consciousness and the accompanying seeds of karmic results, so that the character of one is a development of the character of the 'other'.

The fourth *nidāna* is 'mind-and-body', literally 'name-and-form' (*nāma-rūpa*), consisting of feeling, cognition, will, stimulation, and attention ('mind'), and the physical elements ('body') (*S.*II.3). As such, it can be seen as the sentient organism. This develops once the flux of consciousness 'descends' into the womb (*D.*II.62–3), which is when there has been intercourse at the right time of the month (*M.*I.265–6). Outside the womb, mind-and-body continues unless consciousness is cut off (*D.*II.63): for consciousness, vitality (*āyu*) and heat make a body alive and sensitive (*M.*I.295–6). Together, consciousness and mind-and-body encompass all five *khandhas* of personality, and the interaction between them is seen to be the crux of the process of life and suffering:

> Indeed, consciousness turns back round onto mind-and-body, it does not go beyond. Only in this way can one be born, or grow old, or die, or fall away from one's past existence, or be reborn: that is to say, insofar as consciousness is conditioned by mind-and-body, mind-and-body is conditioned by consciousness, the six sense-bases are conditioned by mind-and-body...' (*D.*II.32).

The six sense-bases (*āyatana*'s) are the five physical sense organs and the mind-organ (*mano*), the latter being seen as that which is sensitive to mental objects, i.e. objects of memory, thought, imagination, and the input of the senses. They are conditioned by mind-and-body as they can only exist in a living sentient organism. Buddhism emphasizes that, whatever the external physical world is like, the 'world' of our actual lived experience is one built up from the input of the five senses, interpreted by the mind-organ (*S*.IV.95). As this interpretation is, for most people, influenced by spiritual ignorance, our 'lived world' is skewed and not in harmony with reality. Such a world is fraught with unsatisfactoriness, but it is conditioned and can be transcended: 'I declare that this fathom-long carcase, which is cognitive and endowed with mind-organ, contains the world, and the origin of the world, and the cessation of the world [*Nibbāna*], and the way leading to the cessation of the world' (*S*.I.62). This can be seen as a formulation of the Four Holy Truths, with 'the world' replacing '*dukkha*'.

The following *nidānas* show how the world of suffering is built up. Only if there are sense-bases can there be 'stimulation' (*phassa*) of these: the coming together of a sense-base, its object, and the appropriate kind of consciousness. When there is stimulation, feeling arises. Depending on what feelings arise, there is craving to enjoy, prolong, or get rid of them. While one cannot help what feelings arise, the extent of craving in response to them is modifiable. Craving is thus one of the two weak points in the twelvefold chain, the other being spiritual ignorance. The Buddhist path aims to undermine craving by moral discipline and meditative calming, and then destroy craving and ignorance by the development of wisdom.

From a 'thirst' for something arises 'grasping' (*upādāna*) at it, a more active involvement with and clinging to the object of craving. Grasping then leads on to 'existence' (*bhava*), that is, to the continuation of the whole changing process of life. The Theravādin *Abhidhamma* explains this as having two aspects: 'karma-existence', i.e. auspicious and inauspicious volitions, and 'resultant-existence', existence in some world as a result of grasping and karma (*Vibh*.137). Such a world is primarily meant as a new rebirth but, arguably, it can also be seen as applying to a 'world' in this life, i.e. a situation one finds oneself in as a result of one's grasping and actions. 'Existence' may also have been intended to refer to an 'intermediary existence' (*antarā-bhava*), a period of transition between rebirths. About half the pre-Mahāyāna schools, including the Theravādins, held that the moment of death was immediately followed by the moment of conception, with no intervening period. The other schools, and later the Mahāyāna, believed in such an existence. Some *Sutta* passages seem to indicate that the earliest Buddhists believed in it. One refers to a time when a being has laid aside one body and has not yet arisen in another (*S.*IV.399–400). Another refers to a subtle-bodied *gandhabba*, or spirit-being, as needing to be present if sexual intercourse is to lead to conception (*M.*I.265–6).

From 'existence' comes 'birth' (*jāti*), in the sense of the very start of a rebirth, conception. It might additionally be interpreted as referring to the constant re-arising, during life, of the processes comprising the five *khandhas*. Once birth has arisen, 'ageing and death', and various other forms of suffering naturally follow, for suffering is inherent in life, as explained in the First Holy Truth. While saying that birth is the cause of death may sound rather simplistic, in Buddhism it is a very significant statement; for there is an alternative to being born. This is to attain *Nibbāna*, so bringing an end to the process of rebirth and redeath. *Nibbāna* is not subject to time and change, and so is known as the 'unborn'; as it is not born it cannot die, and so it is also known as the 'deathless'. To attain this state, all phenomena subject to birth – the *khandhas* and *nidānas* – must be transcended.

The Theravādin tradition emphasizes the twelvefold-chain as an explanation of the working of personality over any three lives: past, present and future (*Pati.*I.52, *Vism.*578–81). Spiritual ignorance and constructing activities are karmically active states from one's past life, which lead to the arising of karmically passive states in this life: consciousness, mind-and-body, the sense-bases, stimulation, and feeling. In response to feeling, the karmically active states of craving, grasping and (karma-)existence arise, which then determine the karmically passive states of one's future life, namely birth, and ageing and death. Of course, spiritual ignorance and constructing activities are present in this life as well as in one's last life, working in union with the other karmically active states; and consciousness, etc. arise in one's next life as well as in this.

THE THIRD HOLY TRUTH: NIBBĀNA

The third Truth is expressed in the first sermon as follows: 'This, monks, is the Holy Truth of the cessation (*nirodha*) of *dukkha*: the utter cessation, without attachment, of that very craving, its renunciation, surrender, release, lack of pleasure in it'. That is, when craving, and other related causes come to an end, *dukkha* ceases. This is equivalent to *Nibbāna* (Skt *Nirvāṇa*), also known as the 'unconditioned' or 'unconstructed' (*asankhata*), the ultimate goal of Buddhism. To strive for this, admittedly a subtle craving for it is needed, which helps in the overcoming of other cravings. On the brink of *Nibbāna*, however, even this craving must be transcended: *Nibbāna* is only attained when there is total non-attachment and letting go.

Nibbāna literally means 'extinction' or 'quenching', being the word used for the 'extinction' of a fire. The 'fires' of which *Nibbāna* is the extinction are described in the 'fire sermon' (*Vin.* I.34–5). This teaches that everything internal and external to a person is 'burning' with the 'fires' of attachment, hatred, and delusion, and of birth, ageing and death. Here the 'fires' refer both to the causes of *dukkha* and to *dukkha* itself. Attachment and hatred are closely related to craving for things and craving to be rid of things, and delusion is synonymous with spiritual ignorance. *Nibbāna* during life is frequently defined as the destruction of these three 'fires' or defilements (e.g. *S.*IV.251). When one who has destroyed these dies, he cannot be reborn and so is totally beyond the remaining 'fires' of birth, ageing and death, having attained final *Nibbāna*.

Both during life and beyond death, *Nibbāna* pertains to the *Arahat*, one who has direct knowledge that he or she has destroyed the four 'cankers' (see p.57). The first aspect of *Nibbāna* is described as 'with remainder of what is grasped at' (*sa-upādi-sesa*), meaning that the *khandhas*, the result of past grasping, still remain for him; the second is described as 'without remainder of what is grasped at' (*an-upādi-sesa*) (*It.*38–9).

Nibbāna during life

It is often thought that *Nibbāna* during life is an ever-present state of the *Arahat*, but it would seem that this cannot be so. As *Nibbāna* is synonymous with the cessation of all *dukkha*, and *Nibbāna* during life is not seen as inferior to *Nibbāna* beyond death in any respect (*Sn.*876–7), it cannot be ever-present; for the *Arahat* will at some time experience physical pain. Moreover, simply to walk down the road is to have such states as feeling and consciousness occurring. As the cessation of *dukkha* involves the stopping of each of the *nidānas* and *khandhas*, *Nibbāna* lies beyond the occurrence of such states. One must therefore see *Nibbāna* during life as a specific experience, in which the defilements are destroyed forever, and in which there is a temporary stopping of all conditioned states (*Sn*.732–9). Such a destruction-of-defilements is clearly a transcendent, timeless experience, for it is said to be 'deathless' (*S*.v.8) and 'unconditioned' (*S*.IV.362). During life or beyond death, *Nibbāna* is the unconditioned cessation of all unsatisfactory, conditioned phenomena. During life, it is where these phenomena stop, followed by their recurrence in the arising of normal experiences of the world; once attained, this stopping can be returned to. Beyond death, it is where they stop for good.

Descriptions of the Nibbanic experience stress its 'otherness', placing it beyond all limited concepts and ordinary categories of thought. This is clearly shown in a description in the *Udāna* (p.80). This begins by firmly asserting the existence of that which lies beyond all *dukkha*. It then says that this is a sphere where there are neither the four physical elements (see p.49), nor the four formless mystical states, and corresponding heavenly levels of rebirth where only mental phenomena exist (see pp.34ff.). This indicates that it is beyond mind-and-body (*nāma-rūpa*). Further, it is said to be beyond this world or any other world of rebirth, and beyond the arising and ceasing of phenomena in the process of life and rebirth. It is without any 'support' (*patiṭṭhā*) on which it depends, and is without any mental 'object' (*ārammaṇa*). In the face of *Nibbāna*, words falter, for language is a product of human needs in this world, and has few resources with which to deal with that which transcends all worlds. *Nibbāna*, it is said, is an aspect of the *Dhamma* which is 'difficult to understand ... beyond abstract reasoning, subtle ...' (*Vin*.I.4). The most accurate and least misleading descriptions are negative, saying what it is *not*. Thus, above, there is an affirmation of existence followed by a string of negations. Most synonyms of *Nibbāna* are also negative: the stopping of *dukkha*, the unborn, the unbecome, the unmade, the unconditioned, the deathless, stopping (*nirodha*), detachment (*virāga*), the unelaborated (*nippapañca*). *Nibbāna* is also seen as 'emptiness' (*suññatā*) (*Pati*.I.92), in that it is empty of attachment, hatred and delusion, being known in this aspect by deep insight into phenomena as 'empty' of a substantial self (*M*.I.297–9).

Positive descriptions of *Nibbāna* are generally of a poetic, suggestive nature. Thus it is said to be: the 'further shore' (beyond this 'shore' of life and its inherent suffering); the 'island amidst the flood' (a refuge from danger and suffering); the '(cool) cave of shelter' (a powerful image of peace and rest in the hot Indian climate); the marvellous. Certain positive descriptions give a less poetic indication of its nature. It is the 'calming (*samatha*) of all constructing activities' (*Vin*.I.5), peace, truth, and purity (*S*.IV.369–72). It is the 'highest bliss', the very opposite of *dukkha* (*M*.I.508). It is 'stable' (*S*.IV.370) and 'timeless' (*A*.I.158), for it is beyond time (*Miln*.323), and so is permanent and eternal (*Kvu*.121). Though it is approached and attained by the Holy Eightfold Path, it is not caused by it, being unconditioned. It is related to the Path as a mountain is related to a path which leads up to it (*Miln*.269). In general, Buddhism sees it as more appropriate to describe this Path than to try and precisely describe its goal.

Nevertheless, certain passages in the *Suttas* hint that *Nibbāna* may be a radically transformed state of consciousness (*viññāṇa*):

> The consciousness in which nothing can be made manifest (like
> space), endless, accessible from all sides (or: wholly radiant):
> *Here* it is that solidity, cohesion, heat and motion have no footing,
> Here long and short, coarse and fine, foul and lovely (have no
> footing),
> Here it is that mind (*nāma*) and body (*rūpa*) stop without remainder:
> By the stopping of consciousness, (all) this stops here. (*D*.I.223)

Like *Ud*.80, above, this describes a state beyond the four physical elements, where mind-and-body are transcended. As the heart of Conditioned Arising is the mutual conditioning of consciousness and mind-and-body, this state is where this interaction ceases: from the stopping of consciousness, mind-and-body stops. Consciousness is not non-existent when it stops, however; for it is said to be non-manifestive and endless. One passage on the stopping (*nirodha*) of the *nidāna* of consciousness (*S*.III.54–5) says that a monk abandons attachment for each of the five *khandhas*, such that there is no longer any object (*ārammaṇa*) or support (*patiṭṭhā*) for consciousness; consciousness is thus 'unsupported' (*apatiṭṭhita*) and free of constructing activities, so that it is released, steadfast, content, undisturbed, and attains *Nibbāna*. This description, of a 'stopped' consciousness which is unsupported by any mental object, where mind-and-body are transcended, seems to accord well with the *Ud*.80 description of *Nibbāna* itself.

To say that *Nibbāna* is unconditioned, objectless consciousness indicates something of its nature, but does not penetrate far into its mystery. For it seems impossible to imagine what awareness devoid of any object would be like. As regards the 'stopping' of mind-and-body, as a state occurring during life, this is perhaps to be understood as one where all mental processes (including ordinary consciousness) temporarily cease, and the matter of the body is seen as so ephemeral as not to signify a 'body'. A passage at *M*.I.329–30 which parallels *D*.I.223 says that the non-manifestive consciousness 'is not reached by the solidness of solidity, by the cohesiveness of cohesion...'. The analysis of *Nibbāna* as objectless consciousness, though, is the author's own interpretation. Theravādin tradition sees *Nibbāna* as 'objectless' (*Dhs*.1408), but regards 'consciousness' as *always* having an object. *D*.I.223 is thus interpreted as concerning *Nibbāna* as to-be-known-by-consciousness: *Nibbāna* is itself the object of the *Arahat's* consciousness (*Pati*.II.143–5).

The *Arahat*

Some further light is shed on *Nibbāna* during life by examining the nature of the *Arahat*, one who has attained the Nibbanic experience and been radically transformed by it. In *Nibbāna*, attachment, hatred and delusion are forever destroyed. As a person becomes an *Arahat* in this experience (which is then immediately known by a reviewing knowledge), the destruction of these three defilements is given both as the definition of *Nibbāna* during life and of 'Arahatness' (*Arahatta*; *S*.IV.252).

The word *Arahat* means 'worthy', i.e. worthy of great respect. He or she is one who has fully completed spiritual training, is fully endowed with all factors of the Path, and has quenched the 'fires' of the defilements. He has overcome the 'disease' of *dukkha* and attained complete mental health (*A*.II.143). Such a perfected one is described as follows: 'Calm is his mind, calm is his speech, calm is his behaviour who, rightly knowing, is wholly freed, perfectly peaceful and equipoised' (*Dhp*.96). The calm actions of the *Arahat* are such that they no longer create karmic results leading to rebirths. They are just pure spontaneous actions without any future fruit. The balanced detachment of the *Arahat's* mind is such that, while he may experience physical pain (as a result of past karma), no mental anguish at this can arise

(*Miln*.44–5). This is because he does not identify with the pain as 'mine', but simply sees it as a not-self passing phenomenon. As is said in a late text (the *Avadāna-śataka*), 'the sky and the palm of his hand were the same to his mind'. Even faced with the threat of death, the *Arahat* is unruffled. In this situation, the *Arahat* Adhimutta disconcerted a potential assailant by fearlessly asking why he should be perturbed at the prospect of the end of the constituents of 'his' personality: he had no thought of an 'I' being here, but just saw a stream of changing phenomena (*Thag*. 715–16). This so impressed the robber threatening him that he became Adhimutta's disciple!

Though free of fear and craving, the *Arahat* should not be thought of as apathetic and emotionless. The uprooting of negative emotions eradicates restrictions on such qualities as mindful alertness, lovingkindness and compassion. *Arahats* are not all alike, either; for some were noted for specific abilities: in teaching, in psychic powers based on meditation, in explaining concisely-phrased teachings, or in living an ascetic lifestyle. While the *Arahat* is one who has seen through the delusion of a permanent self or I, he nevertheless has an empirical self, or character, which is very well developed: he is 'one of developed self' (*bhāvit-atta*, *It*.79), not a 'small' person. He has a strong mind, 'like a thunderbolt' (*A*.I.124), in which flashes of insight arise, and he has fully developed the 'seven factors of enlightenment' (the *bojjhanga*'s): mindfulness, investigation of *Dhamma*, vigour, joy, tranquillity, concentration and equanimity (*Thag*.161 with *D*.III.106). Even in 'his' well-developed empirical personality or self, though, he sees that there is no substantial 'I': he has no 'I am' conceit.

Nibbāna beyond death

At the death of an *Arahat* or Buddha, the 'grasped at' personality factors come to an end. This raises the problem of what happens to an enlightened person beyond death: does he still exist? The Buddha was often asked this question of the state of a *Tathāgata*, or Perfect One after death: could it be said that he 'is' (*hoti*), that he 'is not' (being annihilated), that he 'both is and is not', or that he 'neither is nor is not'? These were part of a set of 'undetermined questions' which the Buddha set aside without answering (*S*.IV.373–400). One reason for this was that he saw speculating over them as a timewasting sidetrack from spiritual practice. When one monk told him that he would leave the *Sangha* unless he was given answers to these questions, the Buddha gave a simile to show how foolish he was (*M*.I.426–31). The simile was that of a man shot by a poisoned arrow who refused to let a doctor cure him until he knew everything about who shot the arrow, and what the arrow was made of: such a man would soon die. The Buddha then said that he had clearly explained *dukkha* and the way beyond it, but that the undetermined questions were not connected with, nor conducive to, *Nibbāna*. This accords with his saying that he taught only what was both true and spiritually useful (*M*.I.395).

Besides these practical considerations, the Buddha also clearly saw the undetermined questions as having a misconception built into them. Like the innocent man who was asked 'have you stopped beating your wife?', he could not rightly reply either 'yes' or 'no' to them. The Buddha explained that the questions were always asked by people who saw a permanent self as somehow related to the five *khandhas* (see p.54), but that he did not answer the questions because he had no such view (*S*.IV.395). That is, his questioners were asking about the fate of an enlightened substantial *self* after death, and as no such thing could be found during life, it was meaningless to discuss its state after death.

Setting aside this misconception, how might one understand the state of the enlightened person beyond death? Is he to be seen as annihilated with the ending of the five *khandhas*? Such a view, equivalent to the second undetermined question, is seen as particularly pernicious, however; for it is emphasized that all that ends at death is *dukkha* (*S*.III.109–12). Some light is shed on the situation by a passage in which the Buddha discusses the undetermined questions on a Perfect One, equating these with questions on whether an enlightened monk 'arises' (i.e. is reborn), or not, etc. after death (*M*.I.486–7). Here he says that, while one would know whether a burning fire has gone out, one could not meaningfully ask what direction the quenched fire had gone in: east, west, south or north. He then stresses that a Perfect One (even in life) is 'deep, immeasurable, hard-to-fathom as is the great ocean'. While to a Western-educated person, an extinct fire goes nowhere because it does not exist, the Buddha's audience in ancient India would generally have thought of an extinguished fire as going back into a non-manifested state as latent heat (e.g. *A*.III.340–1). The simile of the extinct fire thus suggests that the state of an enlightened person after death is one which is beyond normal comprehension, not that it is a state of nothingness: 'There exists no measuring of one who has gone out (like a flame). That by which he could be referred to no longer exists for him. When all phenomena are removed, then all ways of describing have also been removed' (*Sn.*1076). Similarly, it is said that the questions on the Perfect One are set aside because, beyond his death, there are absolutely no grounds for saying that he is with or without a body, with or without cognition, or neither with nor without cognition (*S.*IV.402).

Having destroyed all causes of rebirth, a Perfect One cannot be reborn in any way, such as in the very refined and subtle 'sphere of neither-cognition-nor-non-cognition'. While he is not annihilated at death, it can't be said he 'is' any thing. 'His' indefinable state must be seen as 'beyond' rather than 'after' death, for it must be beyond existence in time. As to what that state is, all that it can be is: *Nibbāna*, the cessation of conditioned phenomena. The nearest hint at what this might be, beyond death, is a passage on Godhika, who had attained *Nibbāna* at the very point of death (*S.*I.121–2). Seeing a smokiness going in the four directions, the Buddha said that this was Māra seeking out where Godhika's consciousness was 'supported', i.e. where he was reborn. The Buddha affirmed that Māra's quest was in vain, however, for 'with an unsupported consciousness, the clansman Godhika has attained *Nibbāna*'. As an 'unsupported' consciousness is no longer conditioned by constructing activities or any objects (as argued above), it must be unconditioned and beyond *dukkha*, no longer a *khandha*. As all that ends at death are the 'grasped at' *khandhas*, equivalent to *dukkha*, there seems to be no reason why such a mysterious consciousness should end at death too.

However one interprets the situation, the Theravāda tradition emphasizes that the Buddha, since his death, is beyond contact with the world and cannot respond to prayer or worship (cf. *Miln.* 95–101). Nevertheless, something of his *power* is seen to remain in the world, to be drawn on through his teaching (*Dhamma*) and even the bodily relics which remained after his cremation. One commentary says that 5,000 years after the *parinibbāna* (passing into *Nibbāna* at death) of the Buddha, the practice of Buddhism will have disappeared, such that the period of Gotama Buddha's influence will have ended. All his relics will then travel to the foot of the tree under which he attained enlightenment, and disappear in a flash of light (*Vibh.A.*433)! This is known as the *parinibbāna* of the relics.

While both aspects of *Nibbāna* proper pertain to the *Arahat*, the Stream-enterer and other lesser grades of saint also have knowledge of *Nibbāna*. At stream-entry, a person gains his first 'glimpse' of *Nibbāna*, for he gains the *Dhamma*-eye and 'sees' the *Dhamma* which is *Nibbāna* (see p.28). The *Nibbāna* which he sees must be none other than the timeless, unconditioned realm which the *Arahat* finally 'enters' at death, and which he also fully experiences during life. *Nibbāna*, indeed, is seen as existing whether or not anyone attains it, as is shown by the assertion that, if it were not for the existence of the unborn, unconditioned, it would not be possible to leave behind born, conditioned, *dukkha* phenomena (*It.*37). One could perhaps say that the *Arahat's* experience of *Nibbāna* during life is one of 'participating in' that unborn, unconditioned blissful reality.

THE FOURTH HOLY TRUTH: THE PATH

The Holy Eightfold Path (*Magga*) is the Middle Way of practice that leads to the cessation of *dukkha*. As later chapters will deal with the details of Buddhist practice, this section will be confined to a general outline of the Path and its dynamics, and the stages of sanctity reached by it.

The Path has eight factors, each described as right or perfect (*sammā*): (1) right view or understanding, (2) right directed thought, (3) right speech, (4) right action, (5) right livelihood, (6) right effort, (7) right mindfulness, and (8) right concentration. These factors are also grouped into three sections (*M.*I.301). Factors 3–5 pertain to *sīla*, moral virtue; factors 6–8 pertain to *samādhi*, meditative cultivation of the heart/mind (*citta*); factors 1–2 pertain to *paññā*, or wisdom (*sīla*, *samādhi*, and *paññā* are always given in this order). The eight factors exist at two basic levels, the ordinary, and the transcendent or Holy (see p. 46), so that there is both an ordinary and a Holy Eightfold Path (*M.*III.71–8). Most Buddhists seek to practise the ordinary Path, which is perfected only in those who are approaching the lead up to stream-entry. At stream-entry, a person gains a first glimpse of *Nibbāna* and the 'stream' which leads there, and enters this, the Holy Eightfold Path.

Each Path-factor conditions skilful states, and progressively wears away its opposite 'wrong' factor, until all unskilful states are destroyed. The form of the Path which immediately leads up to becoming an *Arahat* has two extra factors, right knowledge and right freedom, making it tenfold.

Ordinary 'right understanding' (*sammā-diṭṭhi*) relates mainly to such matters as karma and rebirth, making a person take full responsibility for his actions. It also covers intellectual, and partial experiential, understanding of the Four Holy Truths. Holy right understanding is true wisdom, knowledge which penetrates into the nature of reality in flashes of profound insight, direct seeing. It is not based on the concepts of 'existence' or 'non-existence', as are speculative view-points, but on insight into the Middle Way of Conditioned Arising. This gives a right understanding which sees: (i) how the world arises according to conditions, so that 'non-existence' does not apply to it; and (ii), how the world ceases from the cessation of conditions, so that it does not have substantial, eternal 'existence' either (*S*.II.16–17). Holy right understanding, then, directly knows the world as a constant flux of conditioned phenomena.

Right directed thought concerns the emotions, with thought rightly channelled towards peaceful freedom from sensuality, and away from ill-will and cruelty to lovingkindness and compassion. At the transcendent level, it is the focussed applied thought of one practising the Holy Path. Right speech, at the ordinary level, is the well-established abstaining from lying, back-biting, harsh speech, and empty gossip. At the transcendent level, each of the three factors relating to 'virtue' is a person's spontaneous restraint from wrong speech, action, or livelihood. Right action is abstaining from wrong bodily behaviour: onslaught on living beings, taking what is not given, and wrong conduct with regard to sense-pleasures. Right livelihood is avoiding ways of making a living which cause suffering to others: those based on trickery and greed (*M*.III.75), or on trade in weapons, living beings, meat, alcoholic drink, or poison (*A*.III.208).

The three last factors of the Path are of the Holy level when they are accompanied by other factors at this level (*M*.III.71). Right effort is directed at developing the mind in a wholesome way. The first effort is to avoid the arising of unskilful states of mind which express attachment, hatred or delusion. The second seeks to overcome or undermine unskilful states which nevertheless arise. The third is directed at the meditative development of skilful states of mind, while the fourth is the effort to maintain and stabilize skilful qualities of mind which have been generated. Right mindfulness (*sati*) is a crucial aspect of any Buddhist meditation, and is a state of keen awareness of mental and physical phenomena as they arise within and around one. Right concentration (*samādhi*) refers to various levels of deep calm known as *jhānas*: states of inner collectedness arising from attention closely focussed on a meditation object.

The order of the eight Path-factors is seen as that of a natural progression, with one factor following on from the one before it. Right understanding comes first because it knows the right and wrong form of each of the eight factors; it also counteracts spiritual ignorance, the first factor in Conditioned Arising. From the cold knowing of right understanding blossoms a right way of thinking, which has a balancing warmth. From this, a person's speech becomes improved, and thus his action. Once he is working on right action, it becomes natural to incline towards a virtuous livelihood. With this as basis, there can be progress in right effort. This facilitates the development of right mindfulness, whose clarity then allows the development of the calm of meditative concentration. Neither the ordinary nor the Holy Path is to be understood as a single progression from the first to eighth factor, however. Right effort and mindfulness work with right understanding to support the development of all the Path-factors: the Path-factors mutually support each other to allow a gradual deepening of the way in which the Path is trodden. In terms of the division of the Path into morality, meditation and wisdom, the Path can be seen to develop as follows. Influenced by good examples, a person's first commitment will be to develop virtue, a generous and self-controlled way of life for the benefit of self and others. To motivate this, he or she will have some degree of preliminary wisdom, in the form of some acquaintance with the Buddhist outlook and an aspiration to apply it, expressed as *saddhā*, trustful confidence or faith. With virtue as the indispensable basis for further progress, some meditation may be attempted. With appropriate application, this will lead to the mind becoming calmer, stronger and clearer. This will allow experiential understanding of the *Dhamma* to develop, so that deeper wisdom arises. From this, virtue is strengthened, becoming a basis for further progress in meditation and wisdom. With each more refined development of the virtue–meditation–wisdom sequence, the Path spirals up to a higher level, until the crucial transition of stream-entry is reached. The *Holy* Path then spirals up to Arahatship.

Any person not yet on the Holy Path is known as a *puthujjana*, an 'ordinary person'. Such people are seen as, so to speak 'deranged' (*Vibh*.A.186), as they lack the mental balance of those on the Holy Path, the eight kinds of 'Holy (*ariya*) persons'. These comprise the Holy *Sangha*, which with the Buddha and *Dhamma* are 'three refuges' of a Buddhist. The first Holy person is someone who, by strong insight into the 'three marks' (see p. 50), is one 'practising for the realization of the fruit which is stream-entry' (*A*.IV.293). He goes on to become a Stream-enterer, the second kind of Holy person, who is free from rebirths as a hell-being, animal, ghost or *asura*, as he has completely destroyed the first three of ten spiritual 'fetters' (*S*.V.357). He is sure to become an *Arahat* within seven lives (*A*.I.235). The first fetter is 'views on the existing group' (see p. 54), destroyed by deep insight into the Four Holy Truths and Conditioned Arising. The second is vacillation in commitment to the three refuges and the worth of morality. The Stream-enterer thus has unwavering confidence in the refuges and unblemished morality (*S*.II.69–70). This is because he has 'seen' and 'plunged into' the *Dhamma* (*M*.I.380), giving him trust in *Dhamma* and in the '*Dhamma*-become' Buddha (see p. 28), and is himself now a member of the Holy *Sangha*, whether or not he is a monk. The third fetter destroyed is grasping at precepts and vows, for although his morality is naturally pure, he knows that this alone is insufficient to attain *Nibbāna*.

By deepening his insight, a person may become one practising for the realization of once-returning, and then a Once-returner. A Once-returner can only be reborn once in the sense-desire world, as a human or lower god. Any other rebirths will be in the higher heavens. This is because he has destroyed the gross forms of the next two fetters, sensual desire and ill-will. The next Holy persons are the one practising for the realization of non-returning, and the Non-returner. The Non-returner has destroyed even subtle sensuous desire and ill-will, so that great equanimity is the tone of his experience, and he cannot be reborn in the sense-desire world. His insight is not quite sufficient for him to become an *Arahat*, and if he does not manage to become one later in life, he is reborn in the first of the five 'pure abodes', the most refined heavens in the pure form world, where only Non-returners can be reborn. In these he matures his insight till he becomes a long-lived *Arahat*-god. The final two Holy persons are the one practising for the realization of Arahatness, and the *Arahat* himself. The *Arahat* destroys all the five remaining fetters: attachment to the pure form or formless worlds, the 'I am' conceit, perhaps now in the form of lingering spiritual pride, restlessness, and spiritual ignorance. These are destroyed by the Tenfold Path, which brings *dukkha* and all rebirths to an end in the blissful experience of *Nibbāna*.

4

EARLY DEVELOPMENTS IN BUDDHISM

THE EARLY *SANGHA*

The *Sangha*, in the sense of the 'Community' of monks and nuns with the Buddha as its teacher, originated as one of the groups of *Samaṇas*. These suspended their wandering existence during the three months of the rainy season, and for the Buddhist *Samaṇas* this 'rains' (*Vassa*) period became a time of intensified religious practice, with greater contact with the public at large. They also tended to return to the same places at *Vassa*, such as parks donated by wealthy lay patrons, and these locations then became the basis for a more settled communal way of life. In this way, the Buddhists invented monastic life, which was a middle way between the life of the solitary Jain renouncers, and that of the Brahmin householders.

The monastic discipline (*Vinaya*) developed by the Buddha was designed to shape the *Sangha* as an ideal community, with the optimum conditions for spiritual growth. Its sustaining power is shown by the fact that no other human institution has had such a long-lasting continuous existence, along with such a wide diffusion, as the Buddhist *Sangha*. The Buddha advocated frequent meetings of each local *Sangha*, with the aim of reaching a unanimous consensus in matters of common concern (*D*.II.76–7). If necessary, there was also provision for voting and majority rule (*Vin*.II.84).

Just after the Buddha's passing away (*c*. 400 BC), a 'communal recitation' (council) of *Arahats* was held at Rājagaha (*Vin*.II.284–7) to agree the contents of the *Dhamma* and *Vinaya* which the Buddha had left as 'teacher'. Ānanda, the Buddha's faithful attendant monk, recited the *Suttas*, such that each begins: 'Thus have I heard'. The monk Upāli recited the *Vinaya*. The claim that the whole of the present *Vinaya* and *Sutta* sections of scripture were recited then is probably an exaggeration.

Perhaps seventy years after the first 'communal recitation', a second was held at Vesālī (*Vin*.II.294–307), this being to censure certain monks whose conduct was seen as lax on ten points, such as their accepting money. If these points were not already against the formal *Vinaya*, they were made so then. Sixteen or more years later, perhaps at a further council, at Pāṭaliputta, the first schism in the previously unified *Sangha* occurred; other such schisms followed. The causes of these were generally disagreements over monastic discipline, though the points of *Vinaya* which separated the early monastic fraternities (*nikāya*'s) often arose from variant developments in geographically separated communities, rather than from actual disagreements. Discussion of points of doctrine also led to the development of different interpretative schools of thought (*vāda*'s). Originally, these could not be a cause of schism, as the only *opinion* a monk could be condemned for was the persistent claim that there is nothing wrong with sensual pleasure (*Vin*.IV.134–5). Early on, it seems that adherents of a particular school of thought could be found among members of various monastic fraternities, but perhaps by the second century BC monastic fraternities started to become known for the specific doctrinal interpretations common among their members. By around 100 AD at least, schisms could occur over points of doctrine, and the distinction between a 'fraternity' and a 'school' faded. While members of different monastic fraternities could not take part in official *Sangha* business together, they often shared the same monasteries, and studied each other's doctrines. The laity was probably not very concerned about the differences between the schools.

The cause of the first schism is not agreed. The Theravāda tradition says that the schism was caused by the defeated party at the council of Vesālī. It cannot have been over the ten lax practices, however, as both of the fraternities which emerged from the schism agreed in condemning these. Other traditions say that the cause was doctrinal, concerning five points put forward by the monk Mahādeva. This dispute was probably a later one, however, and became projected back as the cause of the first schism. Recent scholarship shows that the probable cause of the schism was an attempt to slightly expand the number of monastic rules. Concern for monastic rigour and unity may have caused one section of the *Sangha* to incorporate some new rules in the section of the *Vinaya* on deportment, dress, and behaviour in public of the monks. This may have been to turn previous *de facto* practices into *de jure* rules, so as to properly train new members of the *Sangha*. As the reformists seem to have been based in western regions of India, where Buddhism was spreading, this would have been important to them. The reformist section could not win over the more conservative majority, so that agreement could not be reached, and a schism ensued. The reformists called themselves the *Sthavira-vāda*, the 'Ancient/primordial Teaching' fraternity. The majority called themselves the *Mahāsānghika*, or those 'Belonging to the Universal *Sangha*'.

EMPEROR ASOKA AND BUDDHISM

During the reign of the emperor Asoka (*c.* 268–239 BC), Buddhism spread more widely, reaching most of the Indian sub-continent, and also beyond, thus becoming a 'world religion'. The Magadhan empire which Asoka inherited included most of modern India except the far south: the largest in the sub-continent until its conquest by the British. Asoka adopted the social ethic of Buddhism as the guiding principle of his rule, and has been seen by Buddhists as the model of a compassionate Buddhist ruler. The most important sources for our knowledge of him are his numerous edicts, as promulgated on rocks and stone pillars in a variety of languages.

The Buddha seems to have had a liking for the semi-democratic republics of his day, but he was aware of the rising power of kingdoms. His ideals of kingship came from (i) his view that the first king in human society was elected by his people so as to preserve social harmony (p. 37), and (ii) his ideas on compassionate *Cakkavatti* rulers of the past, who ruled with great concern for *Dhamma*, in the sense of morality and social justice (e.g. *D*.III.58–9). At the start of his reign, Asoka seems to have been content to carry on the policy of his forebears, which saw it as the duty of a ruler to expand his realm by force, according to a 'might is right' philosophy. While Asoka had already become a nominal Buddhist in around 260 BC, the full implications of his new faith do not seem to have hit home till after his bloody conquest of the Kalinga region, in the following year. In an edict after this episode, he evinced great remorse at the carnage he had caused, and expressed the desire to govern, please and protect his subjects according to *Dhamma*. He now felt that it was his duty to improve the quality of his subjects' lives, so as to provide a sound framework for their following a moral and religious way of life, Buddhist or otherwise. He inaugurated public works, such as wells and rest-houses for travellers, supported medical aid for humans and animals, and gave aid for the fostering of such measures in regions beyond his empire. *Dhamma*-officials were appointed to encourage virtue, look after old people and orphans, and ensure equal judicial standards throughout the empire. While Asoka retained some judicial beatings, he abolished torture and, perhaps, the death penalty. Released prisoners were given some short-term financial help, and encouraged to make 'merit' for their future lives.

Asoka's concern for the moral improvement of his people was partly expressed in legislation, but more often in attempts to persuade people to live a better life. A prime value encouraged in his edicts was *ahiṃsā*, or 'non-injury': a key emphasis of both Buddhism and other Indian traditions. While he kept his army as a deterrent to invasion, Asoka gave up conquest. Hunting trips, the sport of kings, were replaced by pilgrimages to sites associated with the Buddha. In time, the large royal household became completely vegetarian. Brahmanical animal sacrifice was banned in the capital, and a wide range of non-food animals, birds and fishes were protected. Generosity towards *Samaṇas*, Brahmins and the aged was urged. Respect for these and parents, good behaviour towards friends and relatives, and good treatment of servants was praised. Mercy, truthfulness, sexual purity, gentleness, and contentment were recommended. The lay-orientation of Asoka's values is shown by the fact that the edicts refer to a harmonious society and heavenly rebirth as the goal of a good life lived according to *Dhamma*, making no mention of *Nibbāna*.

Asoka gave Buddhism a central place in his empire, just as the Roman emperor Constantine did for Christianity. Nevertheless, he supported not only Buddhist monks and nuns, but also Brahmins, Jain wanderers, and Ājīvaka ascetics, in accordance with a pattern that later Buddhist and Hindu rulers also followed. At a time when different religions were in competition for converts, he urged mutual respect and tolerance. He saw all religious traditions as contributing in some way to spiritual development, and his twelfth rock edict holds that a common basis for religions is that praising one's own tradition and criticizing others should be held in check: for religious wrangling brings harm both to one's own and others' religions, while mutual respect strengthens both. Though the Theravāda and Sarvāstivāda schools both claim a special association with Asoka, he was probably not partial to any one Buddhist school, and he discouraged schism. He was, however, interested in the purity of the *Sangha*, and may have assisted in the purging of lax monks.

In his pilgrimages to Buddhist sites, Asoka erected shrines and memorial pillars. According to later legendary accounts, he also opened up the original ten *Stūpas* and distributed their relics in many new ones throughout India, thus helping to popularize the cult of devotion at *Stūpas*. During his reign, Buddhist missionary activity was considerable. Theravādin sources record that the monk Tissa Moggaliputta sent out parties of monks to a number of 'border areas'. Asokan edicts also record that the emperor sent out embassies to a number of foreign lands; for he wished to spread the ideals he followed: a 'conquest by *Dhamma*' rather than a military conquest. To the north-west, embassies were sent as far as Syria, Egypt and Macedonia, though there is no record of their having arrived there. To the east, they went to 'Suvaṇṇa-bhūmi', probably the Mon country of lower Burma or central Thailand. To the south, they went to south Indian kingdoms and also to the island of Ceylon (now known, as a country, as Sri Lanka). The relationship between the missions and the embassies is not clear, but monks could well have accompanied the embassies, and there was clearly co-operation in the case of Sri Lanka. Here, in around 250 BC, a mission headed by Asoka's own son, the *Arahat* monk Mahinda, was very successful in implanting what was to become known as the Theravāda form of Buddhism.

DEVOTION AND SYMBOLISM IN EARLY BUDDHISM

Asoka's espousal of Buddhism helped it to develop as a popular religion. Prior to the popularization of the *Stūpa*-cult, it is probable that the main focus of devotion was the tree under which the Buddha attained enlightenment, and others grown from its cuttings or seeds. These became known as *Bodhi*, or 'Enlightenment' trees, and were greatly revered both as reminders of the Buddha's enlightenment, and as tangible links with his great spiritual powers. Building on pre-

Buddhist tree-worship, devotion at such a tree was expressed by making offerings such as flowers at an altar at its base, by tying pennants to it, and watering it. Clockwise circumambulation was also performed, an act which signified that what was walked around symbolized something ideally at the centre of a person's life.

The Buddhist *Stūpa* probably developed from pre-Buddhist burial mounds for kings, heroes and saints, which go back into pre-history in many cultures. They became important in Buddhism due to the holy relics they contained, their symbolizing the Buddha and his *parinibbāna*, and in some cases their location at significant sites. Relics placed in *Stūpas* are said to have been those of Gotama, *Arahats*, and even of past Buddhas. Having been part of the body of an enlightened being, they were considered to have been infused with something of the power-for-goodness of an enlightened mind, and to bring blessings to those who expressed devotion in their vicinity. Where funerary relics could not be found, hair or possessions of holy beings, copies of bodily relics or possessions, or Buddhist texts came to be used in their place.

The best-preserved ancient Buddhist *Stūpa*, dating from the first century AD in its present form, is at Sāñcī in central India. It was built over one dating from the third century BC, which may have been built or embellished by Asoka. The four gateways, or *toraṇa*'s place the *Stūpa* symbolically at a cross-roads, as the Buddha had specified, perhaps to indicate the openness and universality of the *Dhamma*. Carved reliefs on the gateways depict stories ascribed in *Jātaka* tales to previous lives of Gotama, along with symbolic indications of previous Buddhas and events in Gotama's final life. The circular *vedikā*, or railing, marks off the site dedicated to the *Stūpa*, and encloses the first of two paths for circumambulation (*pradakṣiṇā-patha*'s). The *Stūpa* dome, referred to in early texts as the *kumbha* or 'pot', is the outermost container of the relics. It is associated with an Indian symbol known as the 'vase of plenty', and symbolically acts as a reminder of an enlightened being as 'full' of uplifting *Dhamma*.

On top of the Sāñcī *Stūpa* is a pole and discs, which represent ceremonial parasols. As parasols were used as insignia of royalty in India, their inclusion on *Stūpas* can be seen as a way of symbolizing the spiritual sovereignty of the Buddha. The kingly connection probably derives from the ancient custom of rulers sitting under a sacred tree at

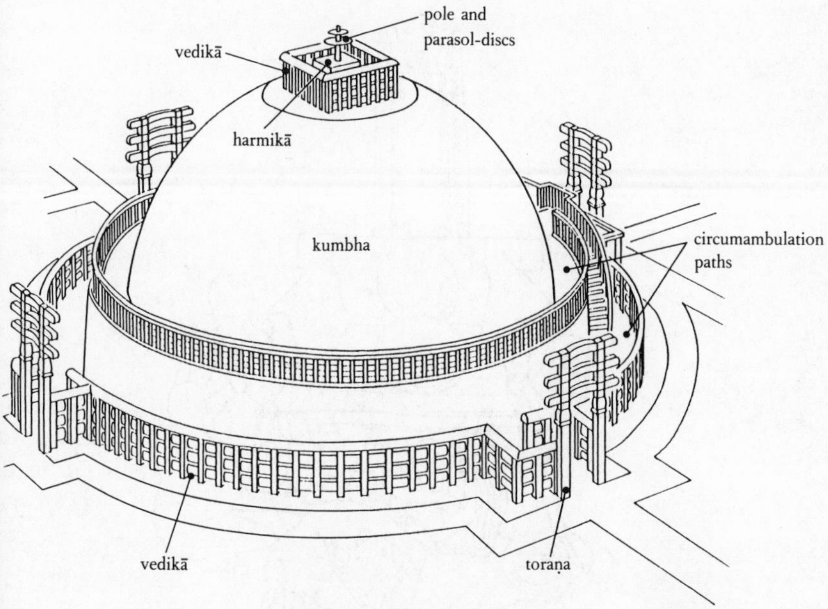

Figure 1 Sāñcī *Stūpa*.

the centre of a community to administer justice, with mobile parasols later replacing such shading trees. The parasol-structure on *Stūpas* also seems to have symbolized the Buddhist sacred tree, which in turn symbolized enlightenment. This is suggested by a second century BC stone relief of a *Stūpa* which shows it surmounted by a tree with parasol-shaped leaves. The structure at the base of the pole and discs has also been found, on a number of *Stūpas*, to have resembled the design of *Bodhi*-tree enclosures.

In later *Stūpas*, the top part fused into a spire, and several platforms were often added under the dome to elevate it in an honorific way. It then became possible to see each layer of the structure as symbolizing a particular set of spiritual qualities, such as the 'four right efforts' (see pp. 69ff.), with the spire symbolizing the powers and knowledge of a Buddha. *Stūpas* are now often known by the term 'Pagoda', probably a corruption of *Dagaba* ('relic-container'), the term used in Sri Lanka.

A notable feature of early representations of Gotama, even before his enlightenment, is that he is only shown by symbols. This must have

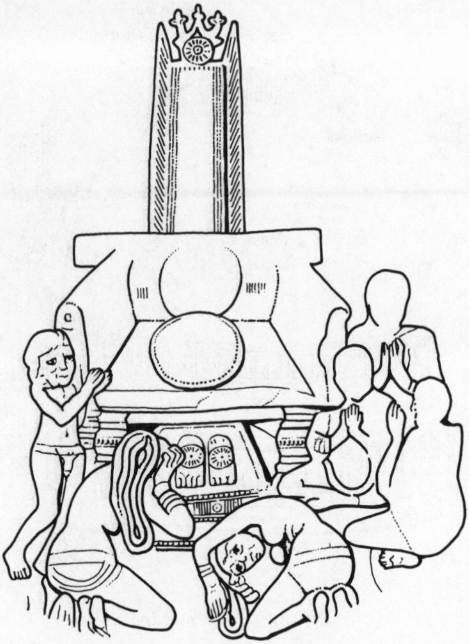

Figure 2 Gotama's former wife presenting his son to him, from a second century AD carved relief.

been due to the feeling that the profound nature of one nearing or attained to Buddhahood could not be adequately represented by a human form. Even contemporary Brahmanism only portrayed minor gods in non-symbolic ways. In Figure 2, the Buddha is indicated by footprints and a throne with *Dhamma*-wheel embellishments (see p. 23). The uncluttered space at the centre of the scene suggests the calm and stillness of the Buddha's mind, and the nature of *Nibbāna*, said to be as indescribable as empty space.

In time, the absence of the long-dead Buddha was keenly felt, and there arose a need for a representation of him in human form to act as a more personalized focus of devotion. The development of Buddha-images, in the second century AD, was probably preceded by the practice of visualizing the Buddha's form in the mind's eye. The period was also one in which a change in mood was affecting all Indian religions, leading to the portrayal of the founder of Jainism, and of major Hindu gods, as focuses of *bhakti*, or warm 'loving devotion'. In Buddhism, this change had also led to the compositions of more thorough sacred biographies of the Buddha, and contributed to the origin of the Mahāyāna.

The craftsmen who made the first Buddha-images drew on the tradition that Gotama had been born with the 'thirty-two characteristics of a Great Man', which indicated that he would become either a Buddha or a *Cakkavatti*. These bodily features are described as karmic results of specific spiritual perfections built up in past lives (*D*.III.142–78). The most obvious one shown on Buddha-images is Gotama's 'turbanned-head', meaning that he had a head shaped like a royal turban, or that one with spiritual vision could see a royal turban on his head. However interpreted, artistic portrayals first hid it under a top-knot of hair, and then showed it as a protuberance on the top of the head. The *Suttas* see it as a result of previous moral and spiritual prominence; later texts see it as a kind of 'wisdom bump' to accommodate a Buddha's supreme wisdom. A feature of Buddha-images not among the 'characteristics' is the elongated ear-lobes. These signify Gotama's royal upbringing, when he wore heavy gold ear-rings, and thus his renunciation of the option of political greatness. They may also be seen as a common symbol for nobility of character, or indicative of the Buddha's 'divine ear', a meditation-based psychic ability.

Buddha-images seem to have been first produced within the empire of Kaniṣka I, which was in the region of modern Afghanistan, Pakistan and north-west India. This occurred at about the same time in Gandhāra, a western region in which the images were influenced by Hellenistic Greek art, and in the Indian city of Mathurā. While the early images were somewhat faltering as spiritual statements, in time the craftsmen were able to express many spiritual qualities in stone. A fine example of the classical Buddha-image which developed during the Gupta period (AD 320–540) is shown in Plate 2. It has life, vigour and grace, and its features suggest joy, compassion, wisdom, serenity and meditative concentration. It expresses qualities attained by someone at the goal of Buddhism, and was intended to help stimulate the growth of such qualities in one who contemplated it.

Plate 2 An image from Sārnāth, showing the Buddha making the gesture of 'Setting in motion of the *Dhamma*-wheel', symbolizing his first sermon (fifth or sixth century AD).

THE *ABHIDHAMMA*

The faith-orientated developments described above were a complement to the wisdom-orientation expressed in the works of *Abhidhamma* (Skt *Abhidharma*). In the third century BC, a few schools added these to their canons of teachings, developing them from *Mātikā*'s, or tabulated summaries of topics, which may have originated with the Buddha. The *Abhidhammas* of the different schools differed appreciably in details, but all aimed to present the teachings of the *Suttas* systematically, along with interpretations which drew out their implications. Other schools in time expressed their views in extra-canonical treatises. The *Abhidhamma* literature sought to avoid some of the inexactitudes of colloquial conventional language, as is sometimes found in the *Suttas*, and state everything in psycho-philosophically exact language, expressing 'ultimate' (*paramattha*) teachings. The *Abhidhamma* performs two main tasks. On the one hand, it refines the *khandha* analysis so as to give a fine-grained enumeration and characterization of all the *dhamma*'s (Skt *dharma*'s), basic patterns or basic processes, which are experienced as making up the flow of mental and physical phenomena. Among these are included various sets of spiritual qualities. On the other hand, it refines the doctrine of Conditioned Arising by showing how the basic patterns condition each other in a web of complex ways. The first task is carried out in, for example, the first three books of the Theravādin *Abhidhamma*, the *Dhamma-saṅgaṇī* ('Enumeration of *Dhammas*'), the *Vibhaṅga* ('(Book of) Analysis') and *Dhātu-kathā* ('Discourse on Elements'). The second is carried out in its seventh, and probably latest book, the six-volume *Paṭṭhāna* ('Conditional Relations'), which goes into great detail on how particular *dhammas* are interrelated by one or more of twenty-four kinds of conditional relationships. The fourth book, the *Puggala-paññatti* ('Concept of Persons'), discusses various character-types and levels of spiritual development. While this literature has sometimes been seen as dry and scholastic, it is a spiritual psychology with a very practical purpose. It gives a detailed knowledge of the working of the mind, and thus can guide a person in meditative development, and it facilitates the proper understanding of personality as an interaction of impermanent, unsatisfactory, ownerless and insubstantial events.

The *Abhidhamma*, except in discussing character-types, analyses 'persons' and 'things' down into a number of *dhammas* that, as viewed in the light of the Buddha's teaching, or *Dhamma*, are basic facts of experience: interdependent basic patterns within the overall Basic Pattern (*Dhamma*) of the nature of reality. Each *dhamma* (other than *Nibbāna*, which is beyond change) is seen as a patterned process consisting of a stream of momentary events of a particular kind. The term '*dhamma*' is used both for such a process and the events it comprises. By the early centuries AD, existence came to be seen as consisting of the interaction of a limited number of such basic patterned processes: seventy-two according to the Theravāda school, and seventy-five in the Sarvāstivāda. Some attention is given to the types of physical processes: the four basic elements (see p. 49) and matter such as the sensitive part of sense-organs or the visible aspect of objects. However, most attention is focussed on the mind. In the Theravādin *Abhidhamma*, this is said to consist, at any micro-moment, of some form of the *dhamma* 'consciousness' or 'mind' (*citta*) along with various 'mental states' (*cetasika*'s), these being some form of feeling and cognition, and some of fifty constructing activities. *Citta* is of many types according to whether it is, for example, ethically skilful, unskilful, or the result of previous ethically active states. The precise cluster of 'mental states' accompanying a moment of *citta* determines (and is determined by) its nature. At each instant in time, another cluster of *citta*-with-*cetasikas* arises, thus accounting for the subtle moment-to-moment changes in a person's experience. The *Paṭṭhāna*, along with the *Milindapañha* (p. 299–300), also develops the idea of *bhavanga*, a type of *citta* which is seen as the resting state of consciousness, as exists in dreamless sleep. Equivalent to the 'brightly shining mind' (see p. 56), this level of mental functioning is seen as being constantly flicked in and out of during waking consciousness. Following a few moments of *bhavanga*, other types of *citta* follow, which turn towards some sense object, such as a visual shape, come to know it, and then give some skilful or unskilful response. The mind then flicks back into the *bhavanga* level before turning towards the same or another sense object, such as a sound. Thus one does not see and hear strictly simultaneously, but the mind rapidly dances between *bhavanga* and the senses and mind-organ, building up a picture of the world like that built up by the moving dot on a television screen.

THE EARLY SCHOOLS AND THEIR DOCTRINES

Within the monastic fraternities originating from the Sthaviravāda of the first schism, three systematic schools of thought (*vādas*) developed during the third century BC: the Puggalavāda (Skt Pudgalavāda), Sarvāstivāda (Pali Sabbatthivāda), and Vibhajjavāda (Skt Vibhajyavāda). The fraternities originating from the Mahāsānghikas were more doctrinally open, and so drew on ideas from these *vādas*, and later took to Mahāyāna ideas more readily.

The Puggalavādins, or 'Personalists', were dissatisfied with the doctrinal non-acceptance of any kind of substantial self. While other schools saw *Sutta* references to the 'person' as merely a conventional way of referring to the collection of *khandhas*, they saw the 'person' as being just as real as the *khandhas*: a kind of subtle self which, being an organic whole which included them, was neither the same as nor distinct from them. Over time, it was neither identical nor different, neither eternal nor non-eternal. Though criticized by all other Buddhist schools, the Puggalavādins were quite successful, and in the seventh century AD, under the patronage of the emperor Harṣa, a quarter of Indian monks belonged to their school. Other than in critiques by their opponents, however, their views have only survived in the Chinese translations of three short texts and the *Saṃmitīya-nikāya-śāstra*, a treatise (*Śāstra*) of one of their offshoots.

The Sarvāstivādins, or 'Pan-realists', became the dominant non-Mahāyāna school in north India, especially in the north-west under the patronage of Kaniṣka I, who ruled in the late first or early second century AD. From here, they became influential in Central Asia, on the route to China. Their canonical *Abhidharma* survives in Chinese translation. They became known for their view that not only present *dharmas* exist, but also past and future ones. They argued that knowledge of past and future must have objects which exist as realities, and that the past must exist in order to explain how past karma affects the present. Their opponents argued that only the present exists, and that the effect-producing impetus of past karma continues in the present. The Sarvāstivādin also reified *dharmas*, seeing them as the indivisible constituents of reality. Each was seen as having an 'own-nature' (Skt *svabhāva*), a unique inherent nature, and they were seen as bound together in a 'person' by a *dharma* known as *prāpti*, or 'possession'.

Dissenters from the Sarvāstivādin view split off to form the Sautrāntika school. This looked to the *Suttas* as alone authoritative, and argued that many of the *dharmas* of the Sarvāstivādins were not separate ultimate realities. Its adherents developed theories of their own, but regarded these as provisional explanatory devices, rather than as descriptions of the ultimate nature of things. One such notion was that, while there was no ultimate reality, 'possession', the fact that individuals had or lacked certain dispositions could be explained by saying that their body-mind complex contained certain 'seeds', or tendencies.

Due to different interpretations of *Abhidharma* points, a Sarvāstivādin council was held in around AD 100, under Kaniṣka I. This later resulted in the production of the *Mahā-vibhāṣā* which, in the form of a commentary on the first book of their *Abhidharma*, the *Jñāna-prasthāna*, discussed different interpretations. In general, it supported the views of Vasumitra, who held that conditioned *dharmas* simply move from a 'future' state, to a momentary manifestation in the 'present', when they are active, to a 'past' state. In all this, their inner nature does not change. The orthodox Sarvāstivādins took their stand on the *Mahā-vibhāṣā*, and so were often known as Vaibhāṣika's. In the fourth century, a masterly survey of their thought was elaborated by Vasubandhu in his *Abhidharma-kośa*. He then produced a commentary on this, the *Abhidharma-kośa-bhāṣya*, which offered an incisive critique of it from a largely Sautrāntika viewpoint. His initial work, however, remained the classic statement of *Abhidharma* in north India. Included in it were certain speculations on the meaning of a Buddha's '*Dharma*-body' (see p. 28), seeing it as a term for both the powers, abilities and perfections developed by a Buddha, and his purified inner nature.

While the Sarvāstivādins were not much represented in south India, this was an area where the Vibhajjavādins, or 'Distinctionists', were strong. The fraternity which became established in Sri Lanka, which called itself the Theravāda (Pali equivalent of Sanskrit Sthaviravāda) followed this school of thought. Theravāda survived in the south till the seventeenth century, and then withdrew to its stronghold in Sri Lanka. All other pre-Mahāyāna schools of thought eventually died out in India, though certain ones were studied by some of the Mahāyānists of Northern and Eastern Buddhism. In Japan, the small Kusha school still exists, based on study of the *Abhidharma-kośa*.

The Theravāda tradition holds that a council was held at Asoka's capital Pāṭaliputta in around 250 BC, at the end of which Tissa Moggaliputta composed the *Kathāvatthu*, a 'Book of Discourses' arguing against the views of other schools. This work, the fifth book of the Vibhajjavāda/Theravāda *Abhidhamma*, was probably added to in the subsequent two centuries. The Vibhajjavādins distinguished between the existence of present *dhammas*, and past or future ones, and largely resisted the tendency to reify *dhammas*, retaining the older, more experiential understanding of their nature. They insisted on the uniqueness of *Nibbāna* as the sole unconditioned *dhamma*. The Sarvāstivādins also included space in this category, and somewhat devalued *Nibbāna* by making it simply one among many metaphysical realities. The Vibhajjavādin view (e.g. at *Kvu*.VI.1–6, XIX.3–5) is that, as the unconditioned is beyond space and time, it cannot have any divisions within it. Another of their characteristic doctrines is that, at stream-entry, insight into the Four Holy Truths does not come gradually, in a series of separate thought-moments (as the Sarvāstivādins held), but simultaneously, in one thought moment (*Kvu*.II.9, *Paṭi*.II.105–6). As the first Truth is *dukkha*, and the third is the stopping of *dukkha*, or *Nibbāna*, this view seems to imply that the conditioned world of *dukkha* is not ultimately different from unconditioned *Nibbāna*. As unconditioned, *Nibbāna* can have no spatial or temporal relationship to *anything*, even by negation: no place or time can be nearer to or further from it. It is not separate from the conditioned world, but is, as it were, always available to be experienced. As it is also the stopping of conditioned *dhammas*, this seems to imply that, ultimately, these are not real. The notion of 'own-nature' does occur in the Theravāda as well as Sarvāstivāda tradition, but in a different sense than there. Buddhaghosa, the fifth century AD commentator, explains *dhammas* thus: 'They are *dhammas* because they uphold their own own-nature. They are *dhammas* because they are upheld by conditions or they are upheld according to their own-nature' (*Asl*.39). Here 'own-nature' would appear to mean a characteristic nature, which is not something inherent in a *dhamma* as a separate ultimate reality, but arises due to the supporting conditions both of other *dhammas* and previous occurrences of that *dhamma*. This is of significance as it makes the Mahāyāna critique of the Sarvāstivādin's notion of own-nature largely irrelevant to the Theravāda.

The Vibhajjavādins argued against the view, held by the Sarvāstivādins and Puggalavādins, that some *Arahats* could regress from their state after temporarily attaining it (*Kvu*.I.2). For the Vibhajjavādins, such a person was not yet a true *Arahat*. They also argued against related points which became known as the 'five points of Mahādeva', the earliest reference to which is in their *Kathāvatthu* (II.1–5). The first point is that, even though all *Arahats* are free of sensual desire, a Māra god can cause the bodies of some *Arahats* to emit semen; those with full mastery of meditative accomplishments are immune from this. The second point is that, as an *Arahat* may be ignorant of matters such as a person's name, he may lack a certain kind of *ñāṇa*, or insight. In their original form, in which the present fifth point was probably replaced by the idea that some *Arahats* could regress, the 'five points' were probably *Abhidhamma* debating points, used to sharpen up people's understanding of certain issues and distinctions. They may well originally have been propounded by the Sarvāstivāda school.

The monastic traditions of all surviving forms of Buddhism go back to the Sthaviravāda fraternities, which means that much less is known of the Mahāsāṅghika ones. The doctrines ascribed to them by others are described in relatively late texts, of the early centuries AD. These broadly differentiate a northern and southern branch, the Ekavyavahārika and Caitīy fraternities (which perhaps divided in the second century BC). Whoever originated the 'five points of Mahādeva', they became associated with the 'Mahāsāṅghikas', or more specifically with the Caitra branch. This may have been originated by the monk Mahādeva, who seems to have propounded a new formulation of the points. Some scholars have held that Mahādeva's points imply a 'downgrading' of an *Arahat* relative to a perfect Buddha. This seems to be incorrect, however. Only a slight 'downgrading' is implied, and this applies to one kind of *Arahat* relative to another. The first has only a limited attainment of the meditative state of *jhāna*, and lacks the higher knowledges which can be developed using these as a basis. The second has these higher knowledges, and can use them so as to be 'skilled in the states of others': he knows the inner states and needs of others, and can use this knowledge in compassionately helping them. Mahādeva's points are thus associated with an increased emphasis on altruistic action.

As regards actual Mahāsāṅghika texts, some of their *Sutta* collection and all of their *Vinaya* survive in Chinese translation. In a language approximating to Sanskrit, there survives a text known as the *Mahāvastu*, which also purports to be a *Vinaya* work. It describes itself as a work of the Lokottaravāda, or 'Transcendentalist' school, which is probably the same as the Ekavyavahārikas or 'One-utterancers'. The latter held that *all* the utterances of the Buddha were concerned with what was transcendent. The *Mahāvastu* grew over a number of centuries, perhaps beginning in the late second century BC. While its outlook has often been seen as foreshadowing certain Mahāyāna ideas, it has itself been shown to incorporate whole passages from early Mahāyāna scriptures, and may have been influenced by Mahāyāna concepts up to as late as the fifth century AD. It sees Gotama as 'transcendental' even before his Buddhahood. He leaves the Tusita heaven in a mind-created body to bestow his blessings on the world (see p. 16), and though highly spiritually developed, he pretends to start from the beginning, making 'mistakes' such as asceticism (*Mvs*.I.169–70). As a Buddha, he is an omniscient being who is ever in meditation. No dust sticks to his feet, and he is never tired. He eats out of mere conformity with the world, and so as to give others a chance to make much 'merit' by giving him alms food. For such a world-transcending being, it was felt that all incidents in his life must have occurred for a special reason. The *Mahāvastu* thus gives much attention to the Buddha's biography, and also includes many *Jātaka* tales. In examining his development to Buddhahood, a series of ten stages of the *Bodhisattva* (Pali *Bodhisatta*) career were outlined. This idea was also important in the Mahāyāna, though the details are different. Unlike the Mahāyāna, the Transcendentalists still saw the goal for most people as Arahatship, the way of the *Bodhisattva* being for extraordinary individuals.

THE RISE OF THE MAHĀYĀNA

The movement which became known as the Mahāyāna arose some time between 150 BC and AD 100, as the culmination of various earlier developments. Its origin is not associated with any named individual, nor was it uniquely linked to any early school or fraternity. It may well have arisen at around the same time in the south, north-west and east. It had three main ingredients. Firstly, a wholehearted adoption of the *Bodhisattva*-path, which various early schools had outlined. Secondly, a new cosmology arising from visualization practices devoutly directed at the Buddha as a glorified, transcendent being. Thirdly, a new perspective on *Abhidharma*, which derived from meditative insight into the deep 'emptiness' of phenomena (see p. 50), and led to a new philosophical outlook. There developed a new orientation to traditional Buddhist teachings and an upsurge of novel interpretations, whose gradual systematization established the Mahāyāna as a movement with an identity of its own.

The Mahāyāna emerges into history as a loose confederation of groups, each associated with one or more of a number of new *Sūtra*s (Pali *Sutta*s). These attained a written form, in Middle Indian dialects, very soon after they were composed. Scribal amendations then gradually transformed them into 'Buddhist Hybrid Sanskrit', which approximated to classical Sanskrit, the prestige language of India. Anyone accepting the new literature as genuine *Sūtras* – authoritative teachings of the Buddha – thereby belonged to the new movement. This did not necessitate monks and nuns abandoning their old fraternities, as they continued to follow the monastic discipline of the fraternities in which they had been ordained. The Mahāyānists remained a minority among Indian Buddhists for some time; though, in the seventh century, perhaps half of the 200,000 or more monks counted by the Chinese pilgrim Hsuan-tsang were Mahāyānist.

Traditionalists denied that the new literature was 'the word of the Buddha' (*Buddha-vacana*), like the early *Suttas*. This early material did include teachings and inspired utterances of the Buddha's major disciples, but these were accepted as 'the word of the Buddha' as he had agreed with the teachings, or because of his general praise for such disciples. Even after these were all dead, some remembered material was added to the *Suttas* if it harmonized well with the existing corpus in style and content. The new *Sūtras* were very different in style and tone, but were defended as 'the word of the Buddha' through various devices. Firstly, they were seen as inspired utterances coming from the still-existing Buddha, through meditative visions and vivid dreams. Secondly, they were seen as the products of the same kind of perfect wisdom which was the basis of the Buddha's own teaching of *Dharma* (Pali *Dhamma*) (*Asta*. 4). Thirdly, in later Mahāyāna, they were seen as teachings hidden by the Buddha in the world of serpent-deities (*nāga*'s), till there were humans capable of seeing the deeper implications of his message, who would recover the teachings by means of meditative powers. Each explanation saw the *Sūtras* as arising from meditative experiences. Nevertheless, they take the form of dialogues between the 'historical' Buddha and his disciples and gods.

The new *Sūtras* were regarded as the second 'turning of the *Dharma*-wheel' (see p. 23), a deeper level of teaching than the early *Suttas*, with the Buddha's *Bodhisattva* disciples portrayed as wiser than his *Arhat* (Pali *Arahat*) disciples. Because of the liberating truth the *Sūtras* were seen to contain, there was said to be a huge amount of 'merit' in copying them out, and disseminating, reciting, expounding, understanding, practising, and even ritually venerating them. Such claims suggest defensiveness on the part of a new, small movement trying to establish itself. The Mahāyāna *Sūtras* were probably produced by the new breed of charismatic *Dharma*-preachers who championed them. These monks, and some lay-people, directed their preaching both within and beyond the existing Buddhist community, to win converts. This they did by extolling the virtues of perfect Buddhahood, so as to elicit a conversion experience of profound psychological effect. This was the 'arising of the thought of enlightenment (*bodhi-citta*)', the heart-felt aspiration to strive for full Buddhahood, by means of the *Bodhisattva*-path.

The new perspective on scriptural legitimacy led to the Mahāyāna having an open, ongoing 'revelation', which produced a huge outpouring of new *Sūtras* in India in the period up to around AD 650. These were composed anonymously, often by a number of authors elaborating a basic text, to produce works frequently running to hundreds of pages in length. In contrast, the early *Suttas* are ninety-five printed pages long at most, and often only run to a page or two. In certain early *Suttas* such as the *Mahā-samaya* (*D*.II.253–62), the Buddha is a glorious spiritual being surrounded by countless gods and hundreds of disciples. The Mahāyāna *Sūtras* developed this style. In them, the Buddha uses hyperbolic language and paradox, and makes known many heavenly Buddhas and high-level heavenly *Bodhisattvas*, existing in many regions of the universe. A number of these saviour beings, Buddhas and in time *Bodhisattvas*, became objects of devotion and prayer, and greatly added to the appeal and missionary success of the Mahāyāna.

The nature of the Mahāyāna and its attitude to earlier schools

At first, the new movement was called the *Bodhisattva-yāna*, or '(spiritual) vehicle of the *Bodhisattva*'. This was in contradistinction to the 'vehicle of the Disciple' (*Śrāvaka-yāna*), followed by disciples of the Buddha's earlier teachings, who sought Arhatship rather than perfect Buddhahood. It was also contrasted to the 'vehicle of the solitary Buddha' (*Pratyeka-buddha-yāna*), a term used to cover the practice of certain solitary ascetics, mainly of a past age, who were seen to have attained Buddhahood, but who were unable to teach others as a perfect Buddha did. As the new movement responded to criticisms from those who did not accept the new *Sūtras*, it increasingly stressed the superiority of the *Bodhisattva-yāna*, and referred to it as the 'Great vehicle', the *Mahā-yāna*. The other 'vehicles' were disparaged as being the 'Inferior vehicle', or *Hīna-yāna*. The 'greatness' of the new vehicle was seen to lie in three areas: its compassionate motivation, directed at the salvation of countless beings; the profundity of the wisdom it cultivated; and its superior goal, omniscient Buddhahood.

Around AD 200, the *Sūtra* known as the *Saddharma-puṇḍarīka*, or 'Lotus of the True *Dharma*' ('Lotus' for short) developed a perspective which, while hostile to the 'Hīnayāna', sought to portray it as incorporated in and completed by the Mahāyāna. Chapter 2 of the *Sūtra* achieves this accommodation by what was to become a central Mahāyāna concept, that of skilful (*kauśalya*) means (*upāya*). This built on the old idea that the Buddha had adapted the particular contents of his teaching to the temperament and level of understanding of his audience. This was by simply selecting his specific teaching from a harmonious body of teachings. Now he was seen as having given different levels of teaching which might actually appear as conflicting, for the 'higher' level required the undoing of certain over-simplified lessons of the 'lower' level. While the Buddha's ultimate message was that *all* can become omniscient Buddhas, this would have been too unbelievable and confusing to give as a preliminary teaching. For the 'ignorant with low dispositions', he therefore began by teaching the Four Holy Truths, setting out the goal as attaining *Nirvāṇa* by becoming an *Arhat*. The *Arhat* was seen as still having a subtle pride, and as lacking in compassion in his hope of escaping the round of rebirths, thus leaving unenlightened beings to fend for themselves. For those who were prepared to listen further, the Buddha then taught that the true *Nirvāṇa* was attained at Buddhahood, and that all could attain this, even the *Arhats*, who currently thought that they had already reached the goal. The Buddha has just 'one vehicle' (*eka-yāna*), the all-inclusive Buddha-vehicle, but he uses his 'skilful means' to show this by means of three: the vehicles of the Disciple, solitary Buddha, and *Bodhisattva*. He holds out to people whichever of them corresponds to their inclinations and aspirations, but once he has got them to develop spiritually, he gives them all the supreme Buddha-vehicle. As the *Bodhisattva*-path leads to Buddhahood, it seems hard to differentiate the *Bodhisattva* and Buddha-vehicles. Not all Mahāyāna texts follow this 'one vehicle' perspective; for some follow a 'three vehicle' one in which *Arhats* cannot develop further, but have attained a *Nirvāṇa* which is inferior to Buddhahood.

According to the standards of Arhatship preserved by schools such as the Theravāda, the charge that the *Arhat* is proud and selfish is absurd. By definition, he or she is one who has finally destroyed the 'I am' conceit, the root of all egoism and selfishness. He is also described as imbued with lovingkindness and as compassionately teaching others. The Theravāda still acknowledges that the long path to Buddhahood, over many many lives, is the loftiest practice, as it aims at the salvation of countless beings (*Vism.*13). Nevertheless, while this *Bodhisattva*-path has been and is practised by a few Theravādins (often laypeople), it is seen as a way for the heroic few only. Most have gratefully made use of Gotama Buddha's teachings so as to move towards Arhatship, whether this be attained in the present life or a future one.

The peculiarity of the Mahāyāna was that it urged all 'sons and daughters of good family' to tread the *Bodhisattva*-path. Even so, the stereotype of the Mahāyāna as being more open to lay aspirations does not seem straightforwardly applicable to the early Mahāyāna. In early Chinese translations of Mahāyāna texts, the lay *Bodhisattva* is expected to live a life free of attachment to family, and to aim to ordain as soon as possible. In much of this, he is akin to the ideal devout lay disciple in the Pali *Suttas* (e.g. *A.*IV.208–21). He might reach an advanced spiritual stage, but so might a layperson in the Theravāda tradition, say. Nevertheless, lay practitioners do play a prominent part in several important Mahāyāna *Sūtras*, such as the *Vimalakīrti-nirdeśa*. The call to the *Bodhisattva*-path was inspired by the vision that the huge universe will always be in need of perfect Buddhas. The person entering this path aspired to be a compassionate, self-sacrificing hero. His path would be long, as he would need to build up moral and spiritual perfections not only for his own exalted state of Buddhahood, but also so as to be able altruistically to aid others by teaching, good deeds, 'merit' transference, and offering response to prayers. While compassion had always been an important part of the Buddhist path (see p. 69), it was now more strongly emphasized, as the motivating factor for the whole *Bodhisattva*-path.

Over the centuries, many monks studied and practised according to both the Śrāvakayāna and Mahāyāna; not infrequently, both were present in the same monastery. The Chinese, in fact, did not come to clearly differentiate the Mahāyāna as a separate movement till late in the fourth century. Moreover, in Eastern and Northern Buddhism, the term 'Hīnayāna' came to be mostly used to refer to the lower level of spiritual motivation and practice which prepared for the Mahāyāna level. In fact, it is a mistake to equate the 'Hīnayāna' with the Theravāda school, both because the term is a disparaging one not accepted by the school, and also because it was used to refer to all schools which did not accept the Mahāyāna *Sūtras* as authoritative. Moreover, these schools also included a *Bodhisattva*-path, so it is incorrect to see them as purely Śrāvakayāna in nature.

5

MAHĀYĀNA PHILOSOPHY

The Mahāyāna perspective is expressed both in *Sūtras* and a number of *Śāstras*, 'treatises' written by named authors. These systematically present the outlook of particular Mahāyāna schools, based on the *Sūtras*, logic, and meditational experience. Each school is associated with a particular group of *Sūtras*, whose meaning it sees as fully explicit; other *Sūtras* may be regarded as in need of interpretation. In India, the Mahāyāna developed two main philosophical schools: the Madhyamaka, and later the Yogācāra. Both have had a major influence on Northern and Eastern Buddhism.

THE PERFECTION OF WISDOM LITERATURE AND THE MADHYAMAKA SCHOOL

Sources and writers

The Madhyamaka school was also known as the Śūnyatā-vāda, the 'Emptiness Teaching', for its key concept is that of 'emptiness', also central to the *Prajñā-pāramitā*, or 'Perfection of Wisdom' *Sūtras*. Among these is the oldest extant Mahāyāna text, the *Aṣṭasāhasrikā*, or '8,000 Lines' Perfection of Wisdom *Sūtra*. Originating in the first centuries BC and AD, its contents were expanded, in the period to AD 300, to form works of varying sizes up to 100,000 lines. In the following century, two short versions were composed, the *Vajracchedikā*, or 'Diamond-cutter', and the one-page *Hṛdaya*, or 'Heart', Perfection of Wisdom *Sūtras*.

The Madhyamaka school, an adherent of which is known as a Mādhyamika, was founded by Nāgārjuna (*c.* AD 150–250), a south Indian monk, philosopher and mystic. The school's foundation-document is his *(Mūla)-madhyamaka-kārikā*, 'Verses on the (Fundamentals of) the Middle Way'. This argues for what Nāgārjuna sees as the true 'Middle Way' of the Buddha (see p. 69), seeking to convince those who did not accept the Mahāyāna *Sūtras* that a proper understanding of the early scriptures leads inevitably to seeing everything as 'empty'. Many other works are attributed to Nāgārjuna, though several were probably by later writers of the same name. Among the more reliable attributions is the *Vigraha-vyāvartanī*, 'Averting the Arguments', which seeks to overcome objections to his ideas. While his outlook seems close to that of the Perfection of Wisdom *Sūtras*, he does not in fact quote from these, or even refer to the 'Mahāyāna' or '*Bodhisattva*' in the *Madhyamaka-kārikā*. It was left to his other works, if authentic, or his key disciples, Āryadeva and Nāga, to make such explicit connections.

In the fifth century, Buddhapālita and then Bhāvaviveka built up the popularity of the school. The latter improved its logical methods and, around AD 500, developed a new interpretation of Nāgārjuna's ideas, thus forming the Svātantrika-Madhyamaka school. Its interpretation was then disputed by Candrakīrti (late sixth century), who built on the work of Buddhapālita to found the Prāsangika-Madhyamaka school as a definitive statement of Madhyamaka. Candrakīrti's ideas are expressed in such works as his commentary on the *Madhyamaka-kārikā*, the *Prasannapadā*, or 'Clear-worded'. In the eighth century, Śāntarakṣita and his pupil Kamalaśīla added some Yogācāra ideas to those of the Svātantrika-Madhyamaka, thus forming the Yogācāra-Madhyamaka school.

The Śūnyatāvādin orientation

The Perfection of Wisdom literature extols the wisdom (*prajñā*) which is *pāramitā*, literally 'gone beyond' (to *Nirvāṇa*), and also the other 'perfections' involved in the *Bodhisattva*-path. While it and Nāgārjuna's works were clearly for intellectuals, they re-emphasized the Buddha's rejection of all speculative 'views', claiming that *Abhidharma* analytical thinking could lead to a subtle form of intellectual grasping: the idea that one had 'grasped' the true nature of reality in a neat set of concepts. In later Zen, such an endeavour was seen as like trying to catch a slippery catfish in a equally slippery gourd. The new literature also saw the *Abhidharma's* contrasting *Nirvāṇa* with the conditioned *dharmas* making up a 'person', as the basis of a subtle form of spiritual self-seeking: the desire to 'attain' *Nirvāṇa* for oneself, to *get* something one did not already have. The new texts sought to re-emphasize that the goal was to be attained by totally 'letting go', so as to produce a thought transcending any sensory or mental object as support (*Vc.* sec. 10c; cf. p. 63).

Empty *dharmas* and Conditioned Arising

A key Perfection of Wisdom criticism of *Abhidharma* thought – primarily Sarvāstivādin – was that it did not go far enough in understanding that everything is not-self (Skt *anātman*), or 'empty' (*śūnya*) of self. It understood the 'non-selfness of persons' (*pudgala-nairātmya*), the absence of a permanent substantial self in a person. Nevertheless, it analysed 'persons' down into *dharmas*, each with an inherent 'own-nature', so it was seen not to have understood the 'non-selfness of *dharmas*' (*dharma-nairātmya*). That is, seeing a *dharma* as an ultimate building-block of reality, with an inherent nature of its 'own', is to hold that it can be identified without reference to other *dharmas* on which it depends. This implies that it can *exist* independently, making it a virtual self. Thus *dharma*-analysis, developed as a means to undercut self-centred attachment, was seen as having fallen short of its mark.

Nāgārjuna's critique of the notion of own-nature (*Mk.* ch. 15) argues that anything which arises according to conditions, as all phenomena do, can have no inherent nature, for what it is depends on what conditions it. Moreover, if there is nothing with own-nature, there can be nothing with 'other-nature' (*para-bhāva*), i.e. something which is dependent for its existence and nature on something *else* which has own-nature. Furthermore, if there is neither own-nature nor other-nature, there cannot be anything with a true, substantially existent nature (*bhāva*). If there is no true existent, then there can be no non-existent (*abhāva*); for Nāgārjuna takes this as simply a correlative term denoting that a true existent has gone out of existence. Like Nāgārjuna, the Perfection of Wisdom literature therefore regards all *dharmas* as like a dream or magical illusion (*māyā*). There is something there in experience, and one can describe it well in terms of *dharmas*, so it is wrong to deny these exist; yet they don't have substantial existence either. What we experience does not exist in an absolute sense, but only in a relative way, as a passing phenomenon. The nature of *dharmas* lies in between absolute 'non-existence' and substantial 'existence', in accordance with an early *Sutta* passage quoted by Nāgārjuna (*S*.II.16–17; see p. 69). This is what Nāgārjuna means by the 'Middle Way'.

The Madhyamaka interpretation of Conditioned Arising sees it as meaning that phenomena are not only mutually dependent for their 'arising' in time, but are so in their very nature. Thus they cannot really be spoken of as separate entities which interact. By 'itself', a thing is nothing. It is what it is only in relation to other things, and they are what they are in relation to it and yet other things. In his examination of the process of seeing (*Mk*. ch. 3), Nāgārjuna argues that there is no activity of vision which is presently not seeing. Therefore, one cannot say that there is something, 'vision', which may then go on to perform the separate action 'seeing': 'vision' and 'seeing' are mutually dependent, and cannot be separately identified. As the Perfection of Wisdom literature would paradoxically put it, vision is 'empty of' vision. There is, then, no real activity 'vision' which 'sees'. But if vision does not see, then non-vision certainly does not see, so how can one identify a 'seer' who is characterized by his 'seeing'? Without a seer, how can there be anything seen? All such concepts, and the more general ones of subject and object, are meaningful only in relationship to each other. Similarly, what is short depends on what is long; for long and short are correlative concepts. Light is light in relation to darkness; for it is its absence. By such reasoning, Nāgārjuna even says that the 'unconditioned' (traditionally a term for *Nirvāṇa* and, in Sarvāstivādin *Abhidharma*, space) is conceptually dependent on the conditioned, its opposite (*Mk*. ch. 7, v. 33).

Conventional truth and language

The Madhyamaka school holds that confusion over the nature of phenomena arises because people do not understand how the Buddha taught according to two levels of truth: 'conventional truth' (*saṃvṛti-satya*) and profound 'ultimate truth' (*paramārtha-satya*) (*Mk*. ch. 24, vv. 8–9). The concept of two levels of truth already existed in *Abhidharma*. There, 'conventional truths' were those expressed using terms such as 'person' and 'thing'; 'ultimate truth' referred to more exact statements, expressed in terms of *dharmas*. For the Mādhyamika writers, however, talk of *dharmas* is just another kind of provisional, conventional truth, which ultimate truth transcends.

For the Mādhyamikas, true statements at the conventional level are 'true' because humans agree to use concepts in certain ways; because of linguistic conventions. 'Ice is cold' is true because 'ice' is a term used to describe a form of 'water' which is experienced as 'cold'. The terms of language arise because, from the continuous flux of experience, discriminating conceptualization (*prapañca*) abstracts various segments and takes them to be separate entities or qualities, with fixed natures. These then become focuses of attachment. The language-constructs (*prajñapti*) which are labels for them are inter-related in many ways. They gain their meaning from how they are used, in relationship to other concepts, not by referring to objective referents existing outside language. Yet while language determines how we experience the world, it does not bring things into existence; it too is a dependent, empty phenomenon. A particular 'thing' enters the human world by being discriminated through a name or concept, but this exists in relation to a 'something' to which it is applied: both exist in relationship to each other (*Mk*. ch. 5).

Emptiness

In the Śūnyatāvādin perspective, each phenomenon lacks an inherent nature, and so all are said to share an empty 'non-nature' as their 'nature'. Thus one *dharma* cannot ultimately be distinguished from another: the notion of the 'sameness' of *dharmas*. Their shared 'nature' is 'emptiness' (*śūnyatā*). As the Heart *Sūtra* says, 'whatsoever is material shape, that is emptiness, and whatsoever is emptiness, that is material shape' (and similarly for the other four factors of personality). 'Emptiness', though, is not some ultimate basis and substance of the world, like the *Brahman* of the *Upaniṣads*. It implies that no such self-existent substance exists: the world is a web of fluxing, inter-dependent, baseless phenomena. Nāgārjuna, in fact, equates emptiness with the principle of Conditioned Arising; for this logically leads to it (*Mk*. ch. 24, v. 18). Emptiness, then, is an adjectival quality of '*dharmas*', not a substance which composes them. It is neither a thing nor is it nothingness; rather it refers to reality as incapable of ultimately being pinned down in concepts.

Some physicists have seen modern physics as containing parallels to this perspective. When the 'solid' objects of common-sense reality were first analysed, they were seen to consist of empty space and protons, neutrons and electrons. Classical physics saw these as hard, indivisible particles, the ultimate building blocks of matter; but further analysis showed them to consist of a whole range of odd particles such as 'quarks', whose nature is bound up with the forces through which they interact. Matter turns out to be a mysterious field of interaction, with 'particles' not being real separate entities, but provisional conceptual designations.

Critics from the early schools saw the emptiness-teaching as implying that the Four Holy Truths were themselves empty, thus subverting the Buddha's teaching. In reply, Nāgārjuna argued that it is the notion of *dharmas*-with-inherent-nature which subverts the Four Truths (*Mk*. ch. 24). If suffering had own-nature, it would be causeless and eternal, and could never be brought to an end. If the Path had own-nature, it could never be gradually developed in a person; for he or she would either have it or not have it. In a world of entities with own-nature, all change and activity would be impossible; everything would be static and eternal. It is because everything is empty that there can be activity, including spiritual development. An analogy, here, is that the decimal number system would collapse without the quantity zero (a concept which derives from India).

Skilful means and the transcending of views

Nāgārjuna emphasizes that ultimate truth, indicated by talk of emptiness, completes rather than subverts conventional truth. Indeed, it can be understood only if the conventional Four Holy Truths have been understood (*Mk*. ch. 24, v. 10). This relates to the concept of 'skilful means', which in the Śūnyatāvādin perspective is developed to mean that *all* Buddhist teachings – including Śūnyatāvādin ones – should be regarded as provisional devices. The teachings, especially on Conditioned Arising, are simply to induce people into a skilful frame of mind: one in which there can be insight into inexpressible ultimate truth, transcending all such teachings.

Nāgārjuna's method in the *Madhyamaka-kārikā* is to criticize all views and theories about ultimate entities or principles. This he does by showing that their necessary consequences (*prasanga*'s) contradict either the views themselves, which are thus reduced to absurdity, or experience. Moreover, he seeks to show that *all* logically possible views on specific topics are untenable. In this, he uses his method of 'four-cornered (*catuṣkoti*) negation', the device of examining and refuting all the four logically possible alternatives on a topic: x is y, x is non-y, x is both y and non-y, x is neither y nor non-y.

In chapter 1, he examines theories on causality. The first logical possibility is 'self-production': that an effect arises from a cause ultimately identical with itself, part of the same underlying substance (as in the Hindu Sāṃkhya school). This would lead to pointless self-duplication, however, and if a thing reproduced itself, there would be nothing to stop it continuing to do so for ever. The world is not observed to be like this. If the same substance is said to manifest itself differently only when conditions are appropriate, '*self*-production' has already been given up.

The second possibility, 'other-production', is that, ultimately, an effect arises from a cause that is inherently 'other' than it, with a different 'own-nature'. Here, Nāgārjuna argues that, if really distinct entities existed, all would be equally 'different', so anything could 'cause' anything. To say that a cause and its (different) effect always occur together is to *explain* nothing about how causality works. What is inherently 'other' than something cannot be its cause. A 'cause' is not a 'cause' in itself, then, but only in relation to its 'effect' (v. 5).

The third theory is that causality involves both 'self-production' and 'other-production'. If this means that parts of the cause and effect are the same, and part different, the problems of the first two views apply. If it means that all of the cause is both the same as and different from all of the effect, this is impossible. The final possibility is that things originate by neither 'self-production' nor 'other-production': spontaneously, without a cause. But if this were true, everything would be an unpredictable chaos, which it is not. This final view, note, is not that of Nāgārjuna. His 'position' seems to be that at the conventional, phenomenal level, causality can be observed, with 'one' thing causing 'another' to originate; yet none of the logically possible theories of causality can explain how it 'works'. This is because, at the ultimate level, no real 'things' can be found which 'originate'. Nāgārjuna also analyses such concepts as motion and time (chs. 2 and 19), and purports to show that our notions of them are inherently self-contradictory.

The Mādhyamikas' talk of emptiness, then, is intended as the antidote to *all* theories: 'Emptiness is proclaimed by the victorious ones (Buddhas) as the refutation of all views; but those who hold "emptiness" as a view are called incurable' (*Mk.* ch. 13, v. 8). Nāgārjuna examines the views of others as a form of spiritual therapy, to help liberate them from all constricting viewpoints. In doing this, he claims not to have any presuppositions of his own, but to work with those of his opponents, and conventional logic, performing a kind of logical judo. The insights which this produces are also to be deepened by meditative contemplation of phenomena.

The Svātantrika-Madhyamaka school held that logic itself is not empty, but has an autonomous existence (*svatantra*), such that valid positive statements can be made from a Madhyamaka perspective. The inferences made at the conventional level are a real bridge to at least some aspects of ultimate truth. The Prāsangika school, on the other hand, emphasized that the Madhyamaka contained only a negative dialectic, to disprove the views of others, and that ultimate truth completely transcends all logic, words and concepts. This seems to accord with the Perfection of Wisdom *Sūtras*, which certainly sought to avoid setting up any views, or indeed to 'say' anything: 'There is nothing at all to understand. For nothing in particular has been indicated, nothing in particular has been explained' (*Asta.* 38).

Ultimate truth and thusness

At the ultimate level, even talk of 'emptiness' is to be finally given up: as the things which are said to be empty do not ultimately exist, one cannot even say that 'they' are 'empty' (*Mk.* ch. 22, v. 11): 'the emptiness of all *dharmas* is empty of that emptiness' (*Panca.*196). The ultimate truth, then, is that reality is inconceivable and inexpressible: 'When the domain of thought ceases, that which can be stated ceases' (*Mk.* ch. 18, v. 7). The Perfection of Wisdom literature contains an elusive series of subtle allusions to that which lies beyond words. An indicator which it uses for this is the notion of *tathatā*: 'thusness' or 'suchness'. The thusness of something, equivalent to its emptiness, is its very as-it-is-ness, what it is such as it is, without conceptually adding anything to it or taking anything away from it: it is simply 'thus'. Thusness is 'immutable and unchangeable, undiscriminated, undifferentiated', it belongs to nowhere, is neither past, present nor future, and the same thusness is found in all *dharmas* (*Asta*.307). 'True reality' (*tattva*) is 'not conditioned by something else, peaceful, not elaborated by conceptual proliferation (*prapañca*)' (*Mk*. ch. 18, v. 9). Ultimate truth is known when spiritual ignorance is transcended and the limitations of language are totally seen-through, with no further generation of, or attachment to, dream-like linguistic constructs, just perfect evenmindedness. Empty, conditioned phenomena are seen as worthless and are thus no longer constructed, so that insight into ultimate truth is attaining the bliss of *Nirvāṇa* (*Mk*. ch. 24, vv. 10 and 24).

Nirvāṇa and *saṃsāra*

In Śūnyatāvādin thought, the *Nirvāṇa* which is thus attained is not seen as a *dharma* different from conditioned *dharmas* of *saṃsāra*, 'there is not the slightest bit of difference between the two' (*Mk*. ch. 25, v. 20). How can this be? The very fact of the 'unconditioned' *Nirvāṇa* being contrasted, at the conventional level, to *saṃsāra*, makes it exist only *in relationship* to it, and thus empty. *Nirvāṇa*, indeed, was held to be emptiness (Pali *suññatā*) even by the early schools of Buddhism; for it was seen as empty of defilements and beyond conceptualization in any positive terms. The conditioned and the unconditioned cannot, then, be differentiated because 'both' are found to 'be' emptiness. What is more, while *Nirvāṇa* is seen by all schools of Buddhism as 'unborn', 'deathless' and not impermanent, in the Śūnyatāvādin perspective, conditioned *dharmas* can be similarly described. This is because, if they lack own-nature, and do not exist as such, they cannot be said to 'originate' or 'cease'. Consequently, they cannot be said to be impermanent (not that they are permanent): they remain 'unoriginated' (the Heart *Sūtra*), 'unborn', and without differentiation from *Nirvāṇa*. Thus *Nirvāṇa* is not attained by the eradication of anything real, namely defilements, but by the non-construction of the conditioned world of *saṃsāra*: for 'all *dharmas* are nirvanic from the very beginning'. *Nirvāṇa* and *saṃsāra* are not two separate realities, but the field of emptiness, seen by either spiritual ignorance or true knowledge.

The idea that *Nirvāṇa* and *saṃsāra* are non-different plays a central role in the Perfection of Wisdom perspective. Once 'established', there followed other conclusions with consequences for the whole of Mahāyāna thought. Most importantly, the *Bodhisattva* need not seek to escape *saṃsāra* to attain *Nirvāṇa*. He can tirelessly work to aid 'suffering beings', sustained by the idea that *Nirvāṇa* is something already present in *saṃsāra*. As an advanced *Bodhisattva*, he directly experiences this non-duality of *saṃsāra* and *Nirvāṇa*, this realization being fully matured when Buddhahood – *Nirvāṇa* in the highest sense – is reached. The nature of Buddhahood, 'Buddhaness' (*buddhatā*), is of course emptiness, as is the nature of everything. Because of this, all beings are seen to have a nature which is non-different from Buddhaness. Without this, how could ordinary frail beings eventually become omniscient Buddhas? The task of beings, then, is not to 'attain' something that they do not already possess, but to *uncover* and know their Buddhaness. The task of the *Bodhisattva* is to skilfully help them in this.

THE YOGĀCĀRA SCHOOL

Sources and writers

The Yogācāra school is rooted in the ideas of certain *Sūtras* which began to appear in the third century AD. The most important is the *Saṃdhinirmocana* ('Freeing the Underlying Meaning'), which sees itself as a 'third turning of the *Dharma*-wheel', surpassing the first two 'turnings': the teachings on the Four Holy Truths, and the Perfection of Wisdom *Sūtras*. The *Mahāyāna-abhidharma Sūtra* is another. The influential *Lankāvatāra* ('Descent into Lankā') *Sūtra*, which gradually developed from around AD 300, also contains many Yogācāra ideas in its unsystematic summary of Mahāyāna teachings. The Yogācāra was founded as a separate school by Asanga (fourth or fifth century), seen by tradition as a monk ordained in the Sthaviravādin Mahīśāsaka fraternity. His 'teacher' was one Maitreyanātha, or Maitreya, who may have been a human teacher, or the heavenly *Bodhisattva* Maitreya. In time, Asanga converted his half-brother Vasubandhu to the Mahāyāna. The scholarly debate as to whether the brother was the same 'Vasubandhu' who composed the Sarvāstivādin *Abhidharma-kośa* is as yet unresolved.

Asanga's works include the *Mahāyāna-saṃgraha* ('Compendium of the Mahāyāna'), the *Abhidharma-samuccaya* ('Collection of *Abhidharma*'), this being a Yogācāra version of the *Abhidharma*, and a commentary on the *Saṃdhinirmocana Sūtra*. Several other works associated with Asanga are attributed by either Chinese or Tibetan tradition to 'Maitreya', in the sense that this *Bodhisattva* inspired Asanga to write them. The most philosophically important of these is the *Madhyānta-vibhāga* ('Discrimination between the Middle and Extremes'). Vasubandhu's most important works are: the *Triṃśatikā-kārikā* ('Thirty Verses'); the *Viṃśatikā-kārikā* ('Twenty Verses') and his commentary on this, the *Viṃśatikā-vṛtti*; the *Tri-svabhāva-nirdeśa* ('Exposition of the Three Natures'), and his commentary on the *Madhyānta-vibhāga*, the *Madhyānta-vibhāga-kārikā-bhāṣya*.

The Yogācāra orientation

Asanga and Vasubandhu not only developed the characteristic ideas of the Yogācāra school, but also sought to systematize and synthesize all the strands of the Mahāyāna, and some Śrāvakayāna ideas. While Vasubandhu was primarily a theoretician, and gave the school its classical form, Asanga's writings were deeply rooted in the practice *dhyāna* (Pali *jhāna*), or meditative trance. Accordingly, 'Yogācāra' means the 'Practice of Yoga', referring to the *Bodhisattva's* path of meditative development. While the Mādhyamikas and Yogācārins had their philosophical differences, they both had Buddhahood as their goal, and can be seen as being complementary in their approaches. The Mādhyamikas had an analytical, dialectic approach to reality, emphasizing *prajñā* (wisdom); the Yogācārins emphasized *samādhi* (meditative concentration) and the withdrawal of the mind from sensory phenomena. Just as the early Buddhists sought to transcend limiting attachment by seeing phenomena as impermanent, unsatisfactory and not-self, so the Mādhyamikas sought this by seeing them as 'empty', and the Yogācārins sought it by seeing perceived phenomena as mental constructions.

The Mādhyamikas regarded the normal experience of the world as a product of conceptual constructions, but had not concerned themselves with the psychological details of this process. The Yogācārins addressed this question and related ones. For example, how are memories and the effects of past karma transmitted over time, if a being is composed of a stream of momentary events, as described in the *Abhidharma*? Here, the Yogācārin answer built on those of earlier schools, such as the Sautrāntikas, who had posited a series of momentary karmic 'seeds' reproducing themselves over time, and the Vibhajjavādins, who had posited *bhavanga* consciousness, which gave continuity to personality even through dreamless sleep. In continuing to wrestle with such questions, the Yogācārins developed a new *Abhidharma* literature set within a Mahāyāna framework.

Central to the Yogācāra is an emphasis on consciousness; indeed an alternative later name for the school was Vijñāna-vāda, the 'Consciousness Teaching'. In early Buddhism (see ch. 3), the flux of consciousness is seen as the crucial link between rebirths, and a transformed state of consciousness is associated with *Nibbāna*. The perceiving mind is also that which interprets experience so as to construct a 'world', and can be the basis for experiencing the world-transcending *Nibbāna*. In the Yogācāra, the role of the mind in constructing the world is so emphasized that all concepts of an external physical reality are rejected: the perceived world is seen as 'representation-only' (*vijñapti-mātra*) or 'thought-only' (*citta-mātra*). In this, the Yogācārins went one step beyond the Sautrāntikas' theory, in which objects were seen as real, but were only known by inference from the representations that they caused in the mind.

The Yogācāra and the Madhyamaka

Both the Mādhyamikas and the Yogācārins saw themselves as preserving the Buddhist Middle Way between the extremes of nihilism (everything is unreal) and substantialism (substantial entities exist). The Yogācārins criticized the Mādhyamikas for tending towards nihilism, while the Mādhyamikas criticized the Yogācārins for tending towards substantialism, setting up mind as an ultimate entity when all was equally 'empty'. The Madhyamaka assessment is reflected in a fifth century schema, later used in Tibet, which grades the key schools according to their grasp of the truth: (i) Vaibhāṣika Sarvāstivāda, (ii) Sautrāntika, (iii) Citta-mātra (Yogācāra), (iv) Madhyamaka. To reach the Madhyamaka level, however, the other schools had to be progressively studied. Moreover, the Yogācāra-Madhyamaka later developed as a powerful syncretistic school. The 'substantialism' of the Yogācārins is in fact more apparent than real, as their theories on mind are essentially tentative devices, 'skilful means' to be used in conjunction with a series of meditations in leading the practitioner beyond all mental constructions, including all theories, to a direct experience of ultimate reality.

For them, one who cannot get beyond words and theories is like someone who mistakes a finger-tip for the thing that it is pointing at (*Lanka*.196).

The Yogācārin view of the role and nature of consciousness

In early Buddhism, the personality factor of consciousness (Pali *viññāṇa*, Skt *vijñāna*) was referred to equally as *viññāṇa*, *citta* (thought) or *mano* (mind-organ; Skt *manas*), and was seen to be of six types: eye-, ear-, nose-, tongue-, body- and mind-consciousness, each related to a particular sense-organ. In the Yogācāra, however, two more types of consciousness or *citta* are added, making a total of eight. As in earlier *Abhidharma*, each *citta* is seen as consisting of a series of momentary events, accompanied by an appropriate collection of 'mental states' (*Trims*. v. 3–8).

The first addition is made by treating *manas* as a separate type of consciousness, a process of subliminal thought. This organizes data from the six consciousnesses into the experience of a meaningful world, according to set categories. It contains the basis both for correct judgements and misperception of reality, and for both skilful and unskilful karma, which are generated by volitions accompanying the six consciousnesses (*Trims*. vv. 6–8).

Manas and the six consciousnesses represent only the surface of the mind, which is active and oriented towards 'objects'. There is, though, an eighth form of consciousness, which is the *āśraya*, or 'basis' of the rest; it is their fundamental root. Devoid of purposive activity and unaware of objects, it is an underlying unconscious level of mind known as *ālaya-vijñāna*, the 'storehouse consciousness'. Asanga equates it with what the *Mahāyāna-abhidharma Sūtra* calls the 'Realm (*dhātu*) without beginning in time, which is the common basis of all *dharmas*' (*Ms*. ch. 2).

When a person performs actions, or karmas, traces are left on his unconscious: 'seeds' of future karmic effects sink into the *ālaya*, a receptacle which actively stores them. The *ālaya* consists of a series of *cittas*, accompanied by both karmic 'seeds' and the 'seeds' of potential defilements and memories. These all reproduce themselves over time, thus accounting for the continuity of personality through death and periods of unconsciousness, when the seven active consciousnesses are absent (*Trims*. v. 16).

The *ālaya* is also said to contain some intrinsically pure 'seeds', the source of religious striving. They arise from the profound depths of the *ālaya*, the *param-ālaya* or '*ālaya* which is beyond' (*Lanka*.272). In the She-lun school, the earliest Chinese version of the Yogācāra, this is designated as a ninth, 'taintless', consciousness. This depth-aspect of *ālaya* is seen to be beyond the dualisms of subject and object, existence and non-existence, and is known as the *Dharma-dhātu*, the '*Dharma*-realm', or as 'thusness', equivalent to emptiness and *Nirvāṇa*. It is a 'level' of *ālaya* which goes beyond the individual unconscious, and can be seen as a universal reality which lies 'within' all beings. The *Lankāvatāra Sūtra* (pp. 46–7, 38–9) sees the seven active consciousnesses as related to the *ālaya* as waves are related to the ocean: they are not really separate from it, but are simply perturbations in it. These perturbations do not affect the ever-still depths of the ocean-like *ālaya*, though.

Ālaya acts as the basis of the active consciousnesses by actually projecting them out of itself. The Yogācāra, then, regards a person's perception of the world as a product of the unconscious mind. This notion is related to the observation that, in any situation, we only really notice what our mind is attuned to perceive, be this something that interests us, threatens us, excites us, or disgusts us. We only ever get 'edited highlights' of the possible field of perception. What we perceive is clearly related to our nature, which is the product, among other things, of our previous actions (cf. pp. 40 and 57). The Yogācārins emphasized this to such an extent that perception is regarded as essentially a process of imagining, in which the mind generates mental constructions that are perceived as a world.

The Yogācāra philosophy explains the 'mechanics' of the process of construction as follows. Within the *ālaya*, the karmic 'seeds' are matured by the subtle influence of *vāsanā*'s or perfuming 'impressions' generated by ingrained attachment to mental constructions. The 'seeds' then ripen in the form of the flow of experiences which consists of *manas* and the six consciousnesses, each oriented to its own type of 'object', of which it is a 'representation' (*vijñapti*) (*Lanka*.44, and *Trims*.v.2). *Manas* splits the seamless flow of experience into an experiencing 'subject' and an experienced 'object', or 'grasper' and the 'graspable'. Building on this, it then generates other forms of delusory discrimination (*vikalpa*). In this process, language plays a large role. It is suffused with the subject/object distinction and provides concepts under which 'significant' forms can be separated out from the flow of experience and named, as supposedly fixed entities (*Lanka*.226).

While all that is actually experienced is consciousness and its mental concomitants, then, discrimination produces the fiction that these are experiences undergone by an 'inner' subject, and are of a separate 'external' world, along with 'inner' feelings and emotions. For the Yogācārin, the flow of experiences is actually neither 'internal' nor 'external' – it just is. A rough analogy is afforded by the situation of watching a two-dimensional television picture (cf. p. 84), where the mind perceives in it a three-dimensional world and may also identify with one of the characters depicted. The analogy is, of course, imperfect. It still contains a watcher of the television, whereas in the Yogācāra view the watcher 'himself' is like the television picture! *Manas* takes the supposed 'subject' as a real permanent self or I, partly due to a confused awareness of the *ālaya* which is its basis. This I-delusion is then the source of cravings related to 'objects', and of a variety of volitions which generate karmic 'seeds' – to be stored in the *ālaya* till they ripen into the future flow of experience. Thus the cycle of life and lives continues, with *ālaya* and *manas* mutually conditioning each other.

The world as 'thought-only'

The Yogācāra view has been generally taken as a form of philosophical idealism, which denies the reality of the material world and asserts that reality is mental. It can certainly sound idealist: 'Visible entities are not found, the external world is merely thought (*citta*) seen as a multiplicity (of objects); body, property and environment – these I call thought-only (*citta-mātra*)' (*Lanka*.154). The intention of the school, though, is not to propound a mere philosophical viewpoint, but to develop a perspective which will facilitate enlightenment. In doing this, it develops many tentative theories which aim to articulate what is immediately experienced, and rejects theories which go beyond this to discuss a 'material world'. If an extra-mental reality exists, we never experience it. Our actual 'world' is merely 'thought' or a 'representation' produced by consciousness. Conscious experience may contain some shadowy reflection of extra-mental existences, but is so massively conditioned by mental constructs that it is these that must be the focus of analysis and spiritual change.

To support this view, meditative experience is appealed to. In this, concentration on an object can generate a mental image such as a coloured disc of light, which in time becomes more vivid and clear than objects seen with the open eyes. Asanga argues that, however real such images appear, they are clearly nothing apart from thought. If this applies to experiences had in a calm, less deluded state, how much more does it apply to ordinary experience? He also argues that, as some advanced meditators can change earth into water, then these are not really outside the mind. Moreover, dreams show that one can have pleasant and unpleasant impressions when there is no real object to cause them (*Ms.* ch. 2, vv. 6–8, 4, and 27).

This perspective is not taken to mean that we all inhabit totally private worlds. The similarity in people's karmic 'seeds' means that our 'worlds' have much in common, and what one being does can help or harm another. Vasubandhu asserts that this is not through the action of material bodies and external speech, but by one being's mental 'representations' causing an effect in those of another. While beings are only streams of mental phenomena, these do interact (*Vims.* vv. 18–20).

The three natures

While the Mādhyamikas talk in terms of 'two levels of truth', a central Yogācārin concept is that of three apparent 'natures' – the three *svabhāva*'s. Each is a perspective on experience which concerns both a type of real or supposed knowledge, and a degree of reality that this knowledge relates to. As in the Madhyamaka, the intention is to move from one's ordinary, vitiated experience to that of the highest degree of truth or reality. For the Yogācārins, there is also an intermediary level of reality, though the Mādhyamikas regarded this as an impossible mix of reality and unreality.

The first of the three 'natures' is the *parikalpita*, the '(mentally) constructed' or 'imagined'. This is what is structured by the subject/object discrimination: the commonsense world of self, people and things, and 'objects' of thought such as mental and physical *dharmas*, all wrongly seen as having real permanent essences ('own-nature'). Its 'degree' of reality is zero: it is just an illusory appearance. As a kind of 'knowledge', it is taken in by the illusion, engrossed in its general forms and details (*Lanka*.67).

The second 'nature' is the *paratantra*, the 'other-dependent'. This is the level of relative reality, in the form of the flow of changing mental phenomena (i.e. *dharmas* properly understood), arising dependent on one another as in the system of eight forms of *citta* and accompanying mental states (*Mv*. ch. 1, vv. 9–10). It also refers to the relative knowledge which comprehends these phenomena as mutually dependent and impermanent. It is not the highest level of reality, however, for it is the very process which generates the subject/object duality and so projects the 'constructed' nature: it is the 'construction of the unreal' (*Tsn*. v. 4).

The third and highest 'nature' is the *pariniṣpanna*, the 'absolutely accomplished'. This is the absolutely real level, devoid of the subject/object duality, in which knowledge is perfected due to directly knowing the world as 'representation only'. While the 'constructed' is like the water in a mirage, and the 'other-dependent' is like the mirage itself, the 'absolutely accomplished' is like the complete lack of real water in the mirage. Or the first is like the illusory hairs seen by a person with cataracts, the second is like that which produces these illusions, and the third is like the unconfused objects seen by one with sound eyes.

Because it knows that the imaginary 'constructed' is empty of a real 'nature', and that the inter-dependent phenomena of the 'other-dependent' level are also empty of a real inherent 'nature' (as in Madhyamaka thought), the 'absolutely accomplished' is knowledge of the very empty 'nature' of all phenomena: emptiness. This 'nature' is also known as thusness, the inconceivable as-it-is-ness of reality. As the knowledge which knows it has totally transcended the subject/object illusion, it *is* the very thusness which it knows. Thusness is the very nature of reality and the three 'natures' are just three different perspectives on it, of varying degrees of adequacy (*Tsn*. vv. 18–21).

While the Mādhyamikas see 'emptiness' as simply indicating the absence of inherent nature in phenomena, the Yogācārins see it as itself positively existing – in the form of the non-dual nature of 'construction of the unreal'. Reality, understood according to the true Middle Way, is empty of duality but not empty of existence. 'Construction of the unreal', the 'other dependent' is not totally unreal, but exists 'within' emptiness, being neither separate from nor identical to it, just as impermanent things are not separate from nor identical to impermanence (*Mvkb*. ch. 1, vv. 3 and 14). It has an 'ineffable nature' known only by Buddhas (*Vṛtti*. v. 10).

The Yogācāra path and goal

The first two natures are the basis of defilements and thus of suffering. The Yogācāra path therefore aims to understand the dualistic 'constructed' so as to undermine the 'other-dependent', its basis, till this is finally cleansed away from the 'absolutely accomplished'. In deep meditative calm, the mind gradually overcomes the tendency to interpret experiences as indicating external 'objects'. As this tendency wanes, consciousness is still grasped at as a real 'subject', more real than 'objects'. Finally, the full realization of 'representation-only' comes when the utter transcending of any 'object' leads to the collapse of any notion of 'subject', which is merely its dualistic contrast (*Tsn*. v. 36). Thus arises the experience of transcendent knowledge, which is an undifferentiated unity, beyond the subject/object duality and concepts of any kind, even 'thought'. It is thought which is no longer what is usually meant by 'thought', as it is without object, contentless (*Trims*. vv. 28–9 and commentary; cf. p.63). This is the realization of the 'absolutely accomplished', and is said to be perception of the 'unlimitedness' of the *Dharma*-realm, enlightenment (*bodhi*) (*Tsn*. vv. 37–8).

The path to *Nirvāṇa* is a gradual development of virtue, meditative concentration, and insight into the emptiness of 'other-dependent' phenomena. The final attainment comes suddenly, however, as a momentous spiritual transition, a shattering upheaval which takes place at the root of the mind – in *ālaya* in its form as *manas*. This event is known as the 'reversal of the basis' (*āśraya-parāvṛtti*). It is where the usual flow of the worldly mind suddenly stops, so that the six sensory consciousnesses no longer present information. Having stopped discriminating 'objects' in the flow of the six consciousnesses, *manas* 'turns round' from these and attains direct intuitive knowledge of *ālaya* as its basis. Due to this, *ālaya* is no longer capable of carrying karmic 'seeds', the source of the consciousness of 'objects', as its deluding nature is seen through. The intuition thus penetrates to the non-dual depths of *ālaya*, the *Dharma*-realm which is ultimate reality, so that everything is seen as 'thought-only' in the highest sense. In the mirror of *manas*, the unknowing *ālaya* has gained knowledge of its inner nature, so that *Nirvāṇa* is 'the *ālaya*-consciousness which is realized inwardly, after a reversal has taken place' (*Lanka*.62). *Nirvāṇa*, then, is the transfiguration of *saṃsāra*, not its abolition: as in the Madhyamaka, 'there is no difference between *saṃsāra* and *Nirvāṇa*' (*Lanka*.61).

An advanced *Bodhisattva* who has experienced *Nirvāṇa* does not rest content with this. He turns again to *saṃsāra* in the service of others, which the *Mahāyāna-saṃgraha* calls his *Nirvāṇa* 'without standstill' (*apratiṣṭhita*). He does this by meditatively sending forth a seemingly physical 'mind-made body' (*Lanka*.136, *Ms*. ch. 2, v. 27), in which he tunes into and perceives the apparent 'world' of those he is seeking to aid.

Purity and defilement

The Yogācārins reflected much on the relationship between a 'pure' ultimate reality and a defiled, impure *saṃsāra* found 'within' it. 'Reversal' does not bring about a change in ultimate reality; for what is changeable is impermanent. Its purity is intrinsic to it: 'As is pure gold, water free from dirt, the sky without a cloud, so it is pure when detached from imagination' (*Lanka*.131). Emptiness is seen as undefiled due to its very nature, the brightly shining state of the transcendental *citta*, but this purity is hidden by arriving defilements (*Mv*. ch. 1, v. 23, cf. p. 56). Vasubandhu comments that the existence of these alien defilements (at the 'other-dependent' level) explain why people do not attain liberation without effort, while the shining nature of ultimate reality explains why the effort to attain purity will not be fruitless. He also comments (on *Mv*. ch. 5, v. 21): 'The *Dharma*-realm, being like space, is pure by nature, and the duality "pure" and "impure" is only adventitious, arriving later'. That is, only in contrast to 'impure' defilements is the ultimate reality 'pure'; in itself it is beyond all such dualities.

TATHĀGATA-GARBHA THOUGHT

According to the Chinese tradition, Indian Mahāyāna thought consisted of the Madhyamaka, Yogācāra and 'Tathāgata-garbha' schools. The Indian and Tibetan traditions did not count the latter strand of thought as a separate philosophical school, though, as it originated in the period between the origin of the Madhyamaka and Yogācāra, its ideas were in some ways intermediary between theirs, and they both drew on these ideas. Moreover, there were no great Indian teachers associated with this strand of thought. This was probably because it was not intended as a well worked-out system, but arose among those seeking to articulate and support aspects of religious practice. Nevertheless, it made an important contribution to Mahāyāna thought.

Tathāgata-garbha sources

The earliest known Tathāgata-garbha text was the *Tathāgata-garbha Sūtra*, composed *c.* 200–250 AD. The most important one, however, is the *Śrīmālā-devī Siṃhanāda Sūtra*, the '*Sūtra* on the Lion's Roar of Queen Śrīmālā', composed some time between 250 and 350 AD. Also important is the single extant Sanskrit treatise on the *Tathāgata-garbha*. This is known as the *Ratnagotra-vibhāga*, 'An Analysis of the Jewels and Lineages', or *Uttara-tantra*, 'The Treatise on the Supreme'. The Chinese tradition attributes this to a Sthiramati/Sāramati; the Tibetan tradition less plausibly attributes it to the *Bodhisattva* Maitreya, via Asanga. This text, which quotes liberally from the *Śrīmālā-devī Siṃhanāda Sūtra*, was probably composed soon after it. The *Lankāvatāra Sūtra* also assimilates Tathāgata-garbha thought to the Yogācāra viewpoint, and this assimilation is developed further in a text which was a widely-used summary of the Mahāyāna in China. This is the *Ta-ch'eng ch'i-hsin lun*, 'The Treatise on the Awakening of Faith in the Mahāyāna', composed, or possibly translated, in 550 AD.

The *Tathāgata-garbha*

The first word in the term *Tathāgata-garbha* means 'Perfect One' or buddha, while the second basically means either an embryo, or a womb or other container. Tibetan translations are based on the first meaning of *garbha*, while Chinese ones are based on the second. *Tathāgata-garbha* thus means something like 'embryonic Perfect One' or 'matrix of the Perfect One'. The former meaning seems to be the original one. This 'embryo' is seen as existing within all living beings, indicating that, however deluded or defiled they are, they can mature into Buddhas. The *Tathāgata-garbha*, then, represents the 'Buddha-potential' within all beings. In the *Tathāgata-garbha Sūtra* it is said to be equivalent to the 'Buddha-nature' (from Chinese, Skt *Buddha-dhātu?*), and is affirmed by the Buddha to be 'complete with virtues and not different from myself' (p. 457c). It is an emptiness which is itself full of possibilities; it is resplendent with the qualities of Buddhahood, beginningless, unchanging and permanent (*Rv.* vv. 51, 84). It is beyond duality, having the nature of thought and the intrinsic purity of a jewel, space or water (*Rv.* vv. 28, 30, 49). It is brightly shining with lucid clarity (*Rv.* v. 170) and is 'by nature brightly shining and pure' (*Lanka*.77). Beings are seen as ignorant of this great inner treasure, but the Buddha reveals it to them so as to encourage them in spiritual development. Moreover, it is the *Tathāgata-garbha* which responds to spiritual teachings and aspires for *Nirvāṇa* (*Srim.* ch. 13).

The *Tathāgata-garbha* and the defilements

In the *Tathāgata-garbha Sūtra* and *Ratnagotra-vibhāga* (vv. 96–8), a number of metaphors are used to illustrate the relationship between the intrinsically pure *Tathāgata-garbha* and the 'stains of adventitious defilements' – greed, hatred, delusion, etc. – which are said to obscure it. It is both like a Buddha-image wrapped in tattered rags, which suggests an unchanging perfection which has simply to be uncovered, and also like the shoots of a great tree piercing through the fruit from which it grows, suggesting that it is a potential in need of cultivation. Indeed it is to be seen as both 'since beginningless time naturally present' and 'perfected through proper cultivation' (*Rv.* v. 149). It is already present, 'the immaculate true nature to which nothing need be added and from which nothing need be taken' (*Rv.* v. 113). Yet it has to be separated from accompanying impurities, just as gold-ore has to be refined so as to bring out and manifest the intrinsic purity of gold. In *Bodhisattvas*, it is partly purified, and in Buddhas, it is wholly purified (*Rv.* v. 47).

If the *Tathāgata-garbha* is the pure basis of successful spiritual striving, it is necessary to account for the existence of the alien defilements which hold living beings back from enlightenment. How do they co-exist in a being? The *Ratnagotra-vibhāga* sees the defilements as a 'shell' as beginningless as the 'stainless nature of mind' that it covers (v. 129). The *Śrīmālā-devī Siṃhanāda Sūtra* says that defilements are ultimately rooted in beginningless ignorance, but that only a Buddha can comprehend how the mind, whose inner nature is the intrinsically pure *Tathāgata-garbha*, can be in *any way* associated with defilements. Here, in fact, one can see a Buddhist version of the problem of evil: from where does evil originate? Buddhism avoids the 'theological' problem of evil (see p. 37), but a similar problem arises here. This is because the *Tathāgata-garbha* is seen as the eternal foundation and support of both the unconditioned, including 'inconceivable Buddha-qualities' (*Srim.* ch. 13), and the conditioned world of *saṃsāra*. Quoting from the *Mahāyāna-abhidharma Sūtra*, the *Ratnagotra-vibhāga* (pp. 72–3) equates the *Tathāgata-garbha* with the 'Realm' (*dhātu*), or *Dharma*-realm, which is described thus (cf. p. 107):

> The Realm is without beginning in time,
> It is the common basis (*āśraya*) of all *dharmas*.
> Because it exists, there also exist
> All places of rebirth and full attainment of *Nirvāṇa*.

Making the *Tathāgata-garbha* the basis of all clearly implies that it is also the basis of the defilements and ignorance. The *Ratnagotra-vibhāga* supports this implication by saying that karma and the defilements are based on unsystematic attention (which perceives the conditioned world as permanent and substantial); that this is based on 'the mind's purity', but that this 'true nature of mind' is itself without any further basis (*Rv.* vv. 56–7). The *Lankāvatāra Sūtra* actually says that the *Tathāgata-garbha* 'holds within it the cause for both good and evil, and by it all forms of existence are produced. Like an actor it takes on a variety of forms...' (p. 220). In the final analysis, though, the Tathāgata-garbha texts seek to avoid any notion that genuine evil comes from the pure *Tathāgata-garbha*. Thus the defilements are seen as insubstantial, unreal, but as imagined by the deluded mind. This is seen by the fact that the true *Nirvāṇa*, Buddhahood, is not regarded as the extinction of anything (the defilements), but as the '*Dharma*-body' or *Tathāgata* (*Srim.* chs. 5 and 8). This already exists, for, 'covered' by defilements, it is the *Tathāgata-garbha*. As in the Madhyamaka and Yogācāra, enlightenment is not realized by destroying real defilements, but simply by not originating illusory ones, and the illusory suffering to which they lead. Why these illusions should be imagined is still not explained, however: only a Buddha can know.

Tathāgata-garbha thought in relation to the Madhyamaka and Yogācāra

Both the Tathāgata-garbha writers and the Yogācārins hold to a more positive interpretation of emptiness than is (explicitly) found in classical Madhyamaka. The *Tathāgata-garbha* is equated with emptiness, and is said to be empty of and separate from all defilements, but not empty of or separate from 'the inconceivable Buddha-qualities, more numerous than the sands of the Ganges' (*Srim.* ch. 9). This sets up a dichotomy between unreal defilements, and the truly real Buddha-qualities. This perspective differs from the Yogācāra one, where there are *three* levels of reality, the three *svabhāvas*. Thus the Tathāgata-garbha writers hold there to be two levels of reality, like the Mādhyamikas, but hold a more substantivist view of the highest reality than the Mādhyamikas.

In both the Madhyamaka/Perfection-of-Wisdom and the Yogācāra is found the notion of the 'brightly shining *citta*', which ultimately derives from an early *Sutta* (see p. 56) and is a key Tathāgata-garbha concept. In the Perfection of Wisdom literature, it is said of the 'thought of enlightenment' (*bodhi-citta*), 'That thought is no thought, since by nature it is brightly shining', and that it is a state of 'no-mindedness' (*acittatā*) which is beyond existence and non-existence (*Asta*.5–6). This equates the brightly shining *citta* with the *bodhi-citta*, which Tathāgata-garbha literature sees as arising when a person becomes aware of the *Tathāgata-garbha* within. Nevertheless, the Perfection of Wisdom passage sees the brightly shining mind as empty of the own-nature of mind, and does not set it up as the basis of the world. In both Tathāgata-garbha thought and the Yogācāra, an aspect of mind *is* set up as the basis for both the conditioned world and attainment of the unconditioned. For the Tathāgata-garbha writers, this basis was the shining *Tathāgata-garbha*, while for the Yogācārins it was the depths of the *ālaya-vijñāna*.

It is notable that the *Ratnagotra-vibhāga* quotes from the *Mahāyāna-abhidharma Sūtra*, a Yogācārin text, and that another early Yogācārin text, the *Mahāyāna-sūtrālaṃkāra* emphasizes the brightly shining mind, which it says is the nature of the *Tathāgata* and a *garbha* that all beings have. These facts suggest a particular affinity between Tathāgata-garbha and Yogācāra thought. It may well be that they developed in similar circles. While the Tathāgata-garbha writers retained an emphasis on the intrinsic purity of the mind, the Yogācārins moved on to explain the arising and working of defiled, empirical consciousness. In this, the origin of defilement, termed 'the construction of the unreal', was accorded a greater reality than in Tathāgata-garbha thought. In the *Lankāvatāra Sūtra*, the two strands of thought are united, for it is actually said that the *ālaya-vijñāna* is also known as the *Tathāgata-garbha* (p. 221).

A final problem is that the *Lankāvatāra Sūtra* describes the *Tathāgata-garbha* as 'hidden in the body of every being like a gem of great value... it is eternal, permanent' (p. 77–8). Given this description, how then does it differ from a permanent Self (Pali *atta*, Skt *ātman*), which Buddhism had never accepted? The texts seem somewhat ambivalent on this. On the one hand, the *Dharma*-body, the fully mature *Tathāgata-garbha*, is the perfection of permanence and of Self (*Srim*. ch. 12). On the other, while the *Tathāgata-garbha* may seem like either a Self or eternal creator to the ignorant, it is not so, for it is the same as emptiness (*Lanka*.78). It may be Self-like, but is not a true Self, in the sense of an 'I': 'The Buddha is neither a Self nor the conditioned personality factors, he is knowledge free from evil cankers' (*Lanka*.358).

THE *AVATAṂSAKA SŪTRA* AND THE HUA-YEN SCHOOL

While Tathāgata-garbha thought was perceived by the Chinese as a third school of Indian Mahāyāna philosophy, the Chinese themselves developed the Hua-yen school, based on the *Avataṃsaka*, or 'Flower Ornament' *Sūtra* (Ch. *Hua-yen Ching*). This is a huge work, many of whose chapters circulated as separate *Sūtras*. Some were translated into Chinese in the second century AD, but the whole was translated in the seventh century. A translation also exists in Tibetan. The notion of emptiness recurs, and the idea of all worlds depending on the *ālaya-vijñāna* is also found. The most important books, both surviving in Sanskrit, are the *Daśa-bhūmika Sūtra*, on the 'Ten Stages' of the *Bodhisattva*-path, and the *Gaṇḍavyūha*, or 'Array of Flowers' *Sūtra*, which comprises more than a quarter of the whole *Avataṃsaka*.

The *Gaṇḍavyūha* is a literary masterpiece whose 'grand intuitions' are considered by D. T. Suzuki to be 'the most imposing monument erected by the Indian mind to the spiritual life of all mankind' (*Essays*, III, 69). It deals with the spiritual pilgrimage of the youth Sudhana, who is sent on a journey to fifty-two teachers to learn the secrets of the *Bodhisattva*-path. Near his journey's end, he comes to the *Bodhisattva* Maitreya, who shows him the huge tower of the Buddha Vairocana ('The Resplendent One'). This is described as the abode of all *Bodhisattvas*, meaning that it represents the universe as seen by their wisdom and compassion. Sudhana enters the tower, where he finds a wondrous world, as vast as space, full of countless paths, palaces, banners and trees, all made of jewels, along with countless mirrors, burning lamps, and singing birds. Moreover, the tower is also found to contain countless other towers, each as vast as itself, yet these do not interfere with each other in any way, but harmoniously intermingle and preserve their separate identities. All are contained in one and one in all; and in each Sudhana sees himself, so that he feels as if his body and mind had melted away. In an especially large tower, of exquisite beauty, Sudhana sees all the worlds of the universe, with Buddhas active in each. In jewel-walls surrounding each tower, he sees reflections of the past *Bodhisattva*-actions of Maitreya. After this visionary experience, which arises because of Maitreya's power and Sudhana's own knowledge, Maitreya explains, 'such is the own-nature of things, which is not complete in itself, being like a dream, a vision, a reflection' (*Essays*, III, 144–5). Sudhana then returns to the *Bodhisattva* Mañjuśrī, who sent him on his pilgrimage, and completes his development as a *Bodhisattva*, knowing that a *Bodhisattva* is not separate from the beings he seeks to help.

The visionary world described in this *Sūtra* is in some ways reminiscent of the mythological city of a *Cakkavatti* emperor described in an early *Sutta*, the *Mahā-sudassana* (*D*.II.169–98). It is not intended as a mere play of the imagination, but is an attempt to convey, through a series of images for contemplation, an insight into the 'unthinkable' (*acintya*) nature of reality. The heart of this insight is the notion of the 'interpenetration' of all existences. This grows out of the notion of emptiness, that things are what they are because of their relationship to other things, in a web of interdependence. It is also an expression of the consequent 'sameness' (*samatā*) of things. The *Sūtra* depicts a world of light and jewels; for jewels are such that light passes through them and reflects from them; each ray of light, which does not interfere with other rays of light, represents a line of dependence between inter-dependent existences which lack own-nature (are 'transparent'). The Hua-yen master Fa-tsang thus illustrated the interpenetration of all things by an image drawn from the *Avataṃsaka Sūtra*: the jewel-net of the god Indra, wherein each jewel in the net reflects every other one, including their reflections of each jewel, and so on to infinity. The world of Vairocana's Tower is the transcendental *Dharma*-realm, the realm where insight penetrates into the mutual interfusion of everything, seeing into the thusness of things. It is the abode of all those who 'make one *dharma* enter into all *dharmas* and all *dharmas* into one *dharma* and yet without each being annihilated' (*Essays*, III, p. 121). The *Dharma*-realm is not different from the *loka-dhātu*, the worldly-realm of 'separate' phenomena, but is immanent in it, interpenetrating it. The *Dharma*-realm is the totality of the interpenetrating web of existence. In each part of this whole, the whole is present, and in the whole, each part is a necessary ingredient. Just as any part of a three-dimensional holographic image of a thing contains the whole image, each part of the *Dharma*-realm, each item of existence, reflects and includes each and every other part; for all are inter-dependent. And yet each item of existence remains what it is, without obstruction from the other items – indeed it cannot be what it is without its relationship with them. Here is a holistic, organic vision of things, in which the entire universe of space and time is present in a particle of dust: 'Every living being and every minute thing is significant, since even the tiniest thing contains the whole mystery.'

The Chinese Hua-yen masters utilized certain Yogācāra notions such as the three natures, and the centrality of mind, in systematizing the *Sūtra's* message. The *Dharma*-realm is seen as emptiness, thusness, the *Tathāgata-garbha*, and the one Mind of reality, pure, perfect and bright. It is true reality (Ch. *li*) which interpenetrates phenomena (*shih*) as they do each other. Phenomena are empty, but are not unreal; for they are no different from *li*. Emptiness is seen, not just as the antidote to all views, but as the ground for a positive appreciation of the concrete realities of nature, as part of a harmonious organic unity. In tune with the Chinese love of harmony and nature, every item of existence is seen as worthy of respect and honour; for all is the 'body' of Vairocana Buddha.

6

MAHĀYĀNA HOLY BEINGS

THE PATH OF THE *BODHISATTVA*

Wisdom, compassion and skilful means

The Mahāyāna is focussed on the *Bodhisattva*, one on the path to perfect Buddhahood, whose task is to compassionately help beings while maturing his or her own wisdom. In his wisdom (*prajñā*), he knows that there are no 'beings', just fluxes of empty '*dharmas*', but his 'skilful means' enables him to reconcile this wisdom with his compassion (*karuṇā*). This urges him to work for the salvation of all beings, for such empty fluxes do experience 'themselves' as 'suffering beings' (*Vc*. sec. 3).

Wisdom itself aids compassion in a number of ways. Ultimately, it leads to becoming an omniscient Buddha, who can teach and aid beings in countless ways. It also ensures that compassionate action is appropriate, effective, and not covertly self-seeking. Moreover, it strengthens the feeling of solidarity with others, by insight into the 'sameness of beings': 'self' and 'others' being equally empty, there is no ultimate difference between them. The *Bodhisattva* can also rub shoulders with wrong-doers, in an effort to 'reach' them, as he knows that their bad characteristics are not inherent realities. Any potential pride at the good he does is tempered by the reflection that his 'merit' is also 'empty' (*Vc*. sec. 8).

Compassion also aids wisdom's undercutting of self-centredness, by motivating a life of self-sacrifice and active service for others. The *Śikṣā-samuccaya* of Śāntideva (seventh century) asserts that the *Bodhisattva* may even do a deed leading to hell, if this is a necessary part of helping someone else and giving them a more wholesome outlook on life. The great flexibility that the doctrine of skilful means gave the Mahāyāna, however, is guarded from becoming licence by its association with compassion, purifying meditations, and belief in the results of karma.

The perfections and stages of the *Bodhisattva*

The *Bodhisattva*-path begins with the arising of the *bodhi-citta*, the aspiration to strive for Buddhahood for its own sake, and for the sake of helping suffering beings. For this momentous event to occur, a person requires 'merit' and knowledge, generated by moral and spiritual practice in the present and past lives, combined with devotion and reflections on the sufferings of beings and the need for Buddhas. The power of the arising of the *bodhi-citta* is such that it generates much 'merit' and wears out much past bad karma.

After the arising of the *bodhi-citta*, a person takes various *Bodhisattva* vows (*praṇidhāna*'s) in the presence of others who live by them, or with all Buddhas and *Bodhisattvas* as witness. Some are general vows: to overcome innumerable defilements, attain incomparable Buddhahood, and to save all beings; others may be to help beings in more specific ways. The vow to save all beings is made more credible and less overly ambitious by the notion that beings already have 'Buddhaness', or the *Tathāgata-garbha*, and non-egoistic by the notion that beings are not ultimately different from the *Bodhisattva*. Such vows are not taken lightly, however. They become a powerful autonomous force within the psyche and lead to great 'demerit' if broken. In general, they are seen to take from three to thirty-three 'incalculable eons' to fulfil (see p. 33). Such a hugely long *Bodhisattva*-path may not have been envisaged by the early Perfection of Wisdom literature, but be the product of later glorification and scholasticism.

The *Bodhisattva*-path is practised by developing a number of 'perfections' (*pāramitā*'s) and progressing through the ten *Bodhisattva* 'stages' (*bhūmi*'s). Six 'perfections' are described in the Perfection of Wisdom literature, though another four were later added to co-ordinate with the last four of the 'stages'. The stages are described in such works as the *Bodhisattva-bhūmi*, possibly by Asanga, and the *Daśa-bhūmika Sūtra*. They pertain to the Holy (*Ārya*) *Bodhisattva*, though just as the ordinary Eightfold Path leads to the Holy Eightfold Path, so the *Bodhisattva* practises the perfections at an ordinary level before becoming a Holy person. This transition, akin to stream-entry (see p. 68), occurs on the attainment of the 'Path of Seeing', a level of spiritual progress where meditative insight leads to the first full experience of emptiness.

In the first stage, the Holy *Bodhisattva* is full of joy and faith, and concentrates on developing the perfection of generosity (*dāna*) to a high degree. This is done by giving away wealth, teachings, life, limb, and even spouse and family, for the benefit of others. The 'merit' from such acts is dedicated to the future Buddhahood of himself and others. Śāntideva praises the transfer (*pariṇāmanā*) of 'merit' in the final chapter of his *Bodhi-caryāvatāra*. He prays that, by the 'merit' generated by his writing this poem, humans and other beings should be free from various afflictions and be endowed with morality, faith, wisdom and compassion. In one verse, he even prays that the sufferings of the world should ripen in him: that he should take on the bad karma of others, not just give them his 'merit'.

In the second stage, the *Bodhisattva* concentrates on the perfection of moral virtue (*śīla*) till his conduct becomes spontaneously pure. He also urges others to avoid immorality, as it leads to unfortunate rebirths. His meditative development allows him to see and worship many heavenly Buddhas. In the third stage, he concentrates on the perfection of patience (*kṣānti*), aided by meditations on lovingkindness and compassion. He develops great forbearance in adversity, avoids anger, and patiently perseveres in seeking to fathom the profound *Dharma*. In the fourth stage, the perfection of vigour (*vīrya*) is developed, due to increasing aspiration and compassion. Mindful alertness is emphasized, and the stage is particularly appropriate for practising the discipline of a monk or nun. In the fifth stage, the focus is on the perfection of meditation (*dhyāna*). Meditative trances are mastered, but the heavenly rebirths that they can lead to are not accepted. The Four Holy Truths are comprehended and the ability to move between conventional and ultimate truth is developed. Abilities in such fields as maths, medicine and poetry are cultivated, as ways to help others and teach the *Dharma*.

In the sixth stage, the perfection of wisdom is attained. The *Bodhisattva* gains full insight into Conditioned Arising, not-self and emptiness, and thus reaches a level of development parallel to that of the *Arhat*. At death, he *could* leave the round of rebirths and enter *Nirvāṇa*, but his Mahāyāna 'great compassion' prevents him from doing so. By the perfection of wisdom, the five previously emphasized perfections become transcendent, attaining completeness and full perfection. Their most difficult acts are carried out totally free of self-consciousness or ulterior motive. For example, in giving, he does not perceive either 'giver', 'gift', 'recipient' or 'result'; for all dissolve in emptiness (*Texts*.131).

At the seventh stage, the *Bodhisattva* goes beyond being reborn according to karma, and becomes a 'Great Being' (*Mahā-sattva*), a heavenly saviour being who, by his perfection of skilful means, magically projects himself into many worlds so as to teach and help beings in appropriate ways. Knowing that *saṃsāra* is not ultimately different from *Nirvāṇa*, he attains '*Nirvāṇa* without standstill' (see p. 113). At the eighth stage, he reaches a non-relapsing level, such that he is now certain to attain Buddhahood. His knowledge enables him to appear anywhere in the universe at will, teaching beings while appearing just like them. He fully masters the transfer of 'merit' from his vast store, so that beings who pray to him receive it as a free spiritual uplift of grace. In the ninth stage, the *Bodhisattva* perfects his power (*bala*), using his tremendous insight into beings' characters to guide and teach them in the most precisely appropriate ways.

In the tenth stage, the *Bodhisattva* dwells in the Tuṣita heaven, as Maitreya does now (see p. 15). He has a resplendent body and is surrounded by a retinue of lesser *Bodhisattvas*. In the Diamond-like meditative concentration of omniscience, he has the perfection of knowledge (*jñāna*). Buddhas then come to consecrate him as ready for perfect Buddhahood, which he attains in the following *Tathāgata*-stage.

The attainment of Buddhahood is not seen as taking place on earth, but in the Akaniṣṭha heaven, the most refined of the pure form heavens (*Lanka*.361). In early Buddhism, this was seen as the highest of the five 'pure abodes', where only Non-returners are reborn and subsequently experience *Nirvāṇa* (see p. 72). The life-span of the 'Eldest' (Pali Akaniṭṭha) gods there was seen as 16,000 eons. In the Mahāyāna, it is where a *Bodhisattva* attains the definitive *Nirvāṇa*, namely Buddhahood. In some ways, the Great Beings can be seen as akin to the Non-returners of early teachings, as Non-returners' insight was often seen as close to that of *Arhats*, but they continued in heavenly rebirths before finally attaining *Nirvāṇa*. The Mahāyāna would stress, however, that Great Beings and Buddhas have greater wisdom than an *Arhat* or lesser grade of saint.

THE MAHĀYĀNA BUDDHOLOGY

The Mahāyāna developed a new perspective on the nature of the historical Buddha, whom it refers to as Śākyamuni. This is first expressed in the chapter on the 'Duration of the life of the *Tathāgata*' in the Lotus *Sūtra*, a work which reached its final form by around AD 200. Here, the Buddha explains that he became enlightened countless eons ago: more eons ago than there are atoms in fifty million myriads of world-systems. Since that time, he has been constantly teaching in this 'Sahā world-system' and countless others. Over the ages, he had already appeared on earth in the form of past Buddhas such as Dīpankara (see p. 15), and taught according to people's spiritual capacities. All such earthly Buddhas teach those of lesser understanding that Buddhas pass into final *Nirvāṇa*, beyond contact with living beings, when they die. This is only a skilful means, however, to ensure that people do not become overly dependent on Buddhas, but actually use the spiritual medicine that Buddhas give. In fact, the heavenly Buddha (also known as Śākyamuni), who appeared in the form of earthly Buddhas, will live on for twice the time that has passed since he became enlightened; only then will he pass into final *Nirvāṇa*. In this world, this compassionate 'protector of all creatures' has a presence on Vultures' Peak near where the first Council was held. Those who are virtuous and gentle may even now, with the eye of faith, see him preaching there.

This message of light and hope, then, sees Śākyamuni as a manifestation skilfully projected into earthly life by a long-enlightened transcendent being, who is still available to teach the faithful through visionary experiences. At the popular level, the message is taken to mean that the omniscient Buddha Śākyamuni is an omnipresent, eternal being, watching over the world and supremely worthy of worship. While he is seen as enlightened for a hugely long length of time, however, the idea is still expressed that he became a Buddha by practising the *Bodhisattva*-path, starting out as an ordinary being. He is, then, neither a recently enlightened human who has passed into *Nirvāṇa*, nor an eternal monotheistic God-type figure. As a Buddha, he does not exist forever, and is only 'eternal' in that he knows, and has become identical with, that which lies *beyond* time.

By around AD 300, the early Mahāyāna ideas on the nature of 6
Buddhas were systematized by the Yogācārins into what is known as the *Tri-kāya* or 'Three-body' doctrine. This central framework of

Mahāyāna belief sees Buddhahood as having three aspects, namely: (i) the *Nirmāṇa-kāya*, or 'Transformation-body', (ii) the *Sambhoga-kāya*, or 'Enjoyment-body', and (iii) the *Dharma-kāya*, or '*Dharma*-body'.

The 'Transformation-body' refers to earthly Buddhas, seen as teaching devices compassionately projected into the world to show people the path to Buddhahood. Some texts see them as actual beings of flesh and blood, while others, such as the *Suvarṇa-bhāsottama Sūtra*, see them as mere appearances. At death, they are generally withdrawn back into the heavenly Buddha, or even Great Being *Bodhisattva*, who manifested them. The term is also applied to other beings beside Buddhas. Some Mahāyānists, such as D. T. Suzuki, have even seen non-Buddhist religious teachers as Transformation-bodies manifested in a form appropriate to a particular culture.

An 'Enjoyment-body' is seen as a refulgent subtle body of limitless form, endowed with the 'thirty-two characteristics of a Great Man', which is the product of the 'merit' of a *Bodhisattva*'s training. It is adopted by a Buddha for the 'enjoyment' of Holy *Bodhisattvas*; for it is a form in which he can appear to and teach them through visionary experiences or, for the heavenly Great Beings, by a direct presence. The heavenly Buddha Śākyamuni is of the Enjoyment-body type, but there are many others, 'as numerous as there are grains of sand on the banks of the river Ganges', dwelling in various regions of the universe. Their form and wondrous powers vary slightly according to their past *Bodhisattva*-vows and 'merit'.

Each Enjoyment-body Buddha is seen as presiding over his own 'Buddha Land' (*Buddha-kṣetra*), the world-system where he finally attained Buddhahood in its Akaniṣṭha heaven. Many such Lands are said to be 'Pure Lands', mystical universes created by the appropriate Buddha. Buddhism had always accepted that karma is a dominant force in the world. Combining this with the Yogācāra notion of reality as thought-only, there developed the idea that a Buddha could draw on his immeasurable store of 'merit', and the power of his mind, to conjure up a world for the benefit of others. While these Pure Lands are described in paradisaical terms, they are primarily realms where it is easy to hear and practise the *Dharma*: conditions very conducive to attaining enlightenment. Pure Lands are outside the normal system of rebirth according to personal karma. To be reborn in one requires a transfer of some of the huge stock of 'merit' of a Land's presiding Buddha, stimulated by devout prayer. Once faith has led to rebirth in a Pure Land, either as a human-like being or god, a person can develop his wisdom and so become either an *Arhat* or a Great Being *Bodhisattva*. Besides the 'Pure' Buddha Lands, there are also 'impure' ones, normal world-systems like our own. At the centre of our world, though, resides Śākyamuni Buddha in the mini-Pure-Land realm of Vultures' Peak.

The term '*Dharma*-body' has a pre-Mahāyāna ancestry. In the early *Suttas*, the Buddha applies it to himself (see p. 28.), and the Sarvāstivādins later speculated on the nature of such a 'body'. In the Mahāyāna, it refers to the ultimate nature both of Buddhas and of reality in general, thus having two aspects. The first is the 'Knowledge-body' (*Jñāna-kāya*), the inner nature shared by all Buddhas, their Buddha-ness (*buddhatā*). It is the omniscient knowledge, perfect wisdom, and spiritual qualities through which a *Bodhisattva* becomes a Buddha, being for a Buddha's 'self-enjoyment'. It is regarded as having a very subtle, shining, limitless material form from which speech can come, due to the autonomous working of the *Bodhisattva* vows. In this respect, the *Dharma*-body is given a semi-personalized aspect, making it somewhat akin to the concept of God in other religions. The *Dharma*-body is thus sometimes personified as the Buddha Vairocana, the 'Resplendent One' referred to in the *Avataṃsaka Sūtra*. In the tenth century, the process of personification was carried further, in the concept of the *Ādi*, or 'Primordial', ever-enlightened Buddha.

The second aspect of the *Dharma*-body is the 'Self-existent-body (*Svabhāvika-kāya*)'. This is the ultimate nature of reality, thusness, emptiness: the non-nature which is the very nature of *dharmas*, their *dharma*-ness (*dharmatā*). It is the *Tathāgata-garbha* and *bodhi-citta* hidden within beings, and the transformed 'storehouse-consciousness'. It is what is known and realized on attaining Buddhahood, it is *Nirvāṇa*. Only for convenience of explanation are the Knowledge and Self-existent bodies described as different. A Buddha's knowledge is beyond the subject–object duality, so he cannot be distinguished from the thusness which is the 'object' of his knowledge: 'The thusness of the Thus-gone (*Tathāgata*) and the thusness of all *dharmas* are both one single thusness, not two, not divided' (*Asta*.307). As a Buddha's knowledge is also omniscient, he is non-different from *all* empty phenomena: he is the 'same' as everything. Buddha-ness is *dharma*-ness (*Asta*.513).

On the ultimate level, only the *Dharma*-body in its aspect as the Self-existent-body is real; the Transformation and Enjoyment bodies, known in the Śūnyatāvādin perspective and Tathāgata-garbha thought as 'form (*rūpa*)' bodies, are provisional ways of talking about and apprehending it. The real nature of a *Tathāgata* can only be seen in the *Dharma*-body (*Asta*.513). Transformation- and Enjoyment-body Buddhas, Pure Lands, and Great Beings, then, are not truly real: any more than the book you are now reading or the eyes with which you read it! In emptiness, nothing stands out with separate reality. At the conventional level of truth, however, such Buddhas, etc. are just as real as anything else. Indeed in popular Mahāyāna practice, the Enjoyment-body Buddhas and Great Beings are treated as wholly real, and rebirth in their Pure Lands is ardently sought through faith. The rather disconcerting feeling generated by switching between ultimate and conventional truth is nicely captured in an explanation given by a Chinese recluse to John Blofeld: 'Believe me, the *Bodhisattvas* are as real as earth and sky, and have infinite power to aid beings in distress, but they exist within our common mind, which, to speak the truth, is itself the *container* of earth and sky'.[1]

From the conventional perspective, the Great Beings and heavenly Buddhas are those who have heroically striven to be close to, or attained to, Buddhahood. From the ultimate perspective, they are the symbolic forms in which the 'minds' of empty 'beings' perceive the *Dharma*-body, the all-encompassing totality which is the *Dharma*-realm described in the *Avataṃsaka Sūtra*. As an analogy, the *Dharma*-body can be seen as a blinding blaze of light. Only a Buddha can see this in an unobstructed fashion. The obstructions remaining in the minds of Holy *Bodhisattvas* mean that the light is filtered and they see it as Enjoyment-body Buddhas. In ordinary beings, the light is even more filtered, so that they can only see it in the form of Transformation-bodies. Those with great insight, though, can see it in the thusness of any worldly object, for as the *Avataṃsaka Sūtra* says, the whole mystery is present in a grain of dust. To non-Buddhists such as Hindus, the *Dharma*-body is known in the form of Enjoyment-bodies which take the form of the gods of their religion (*Lanka*.192–3). In Buddhist Japan, indeed, the major *kami*'s, or deities, of the indigenous Shintō religion became identified with particular heavenly Buddhas or Great Beings.

THE MAHĀYĀNA PANTHEON

Of the 'countless' heavenly Buddhas and *Bodhisattvas*, some of the named ones became focuses of devotion as saviour beings, with specific Great Beings also symbolizing and exemplifying specific spiritual qualities.

Of the heavenly Buddhas, one of the earliest mentioned is Amitābha, who became of central importance in the Pure Land schools of Eastern Buddhism, where he is known as Amitā (China) or Amida (Japan). His cult is based on three key *Sūtras*, the first of which was composed by the late second century AD. These are the 'Larger' and 'Smaller' *Sukhāvatī-vyūha*, or 'Array of the Happy Land' *Sūtras*, and the *Amitāyur-dhyāna*, or 'Meditation on Amitāyus' *Sūtra*. The latter may have been composed in Central Asia or even China. The name 'Amitābha', or 'Infinite Radiance', is an expression of light symbolism. In early Buddhism, radiance was already associated with Brahmā gods, wisdom, and the 'brightly shining' level of mind (see p. 56). The alternative name of 'Amit-āyus' means 'Infinite Life', referring to the immeasurably long life of this Buddha.

The 'Larger' Happy Land *Sūtra* tells how, many eons ago, under a previous Buddha, the monk Dharmākara aspired to become a Buddha in a future time. After hearing of the Pure Lands of many Buddhas, he resolved that he would generate one combining the excellences of all of them. He then made forty-six *Bodhisattva* vows, describing these excellences, and affirming that he would only become a Buddha when his *Bodhisattva* course had been karmically potent enough to produce such a Pure Land. In it, beings would be in their final life, of immeasurable length, except for *Bodhisattvas* wishing to be reborn elsewhere to aid beings. Its inhabitants would have the highest 'perfections', memory of previous lives, and the ability to see myriads of other Buddha Lands. They would immediately hear whatever *Dharma* they wished, would have no idea of property, even with regard to their own bodies, and would have the same happiness of those in deep meditative trance. The Pure Land of Sukhāvatī would be a paradise full of 'jewel-trees', which would stimulate calm and contemplative states of mind, a realm where everything would be as beings wished, free from temptation and defilement. Most importantly, Dharmākara vowed that he would appear before any dying being who aspired to enlightenment and devoutly called him to mind, so as to conduct him to his Pure Land.

Dharmākara is seen as having become the Buddha Amitābha, who presides over the far-distant Happy Land (*Sukhāvatī*), in the 'western region of the universe'. To attain rebirth there, the 'Larger' Happy Land *Sūtra* says that a person needs to earnestly desire it, have faith in Amitābha, generate 'merit', and dedicate this towards such a rebirth. In the 'Smaller' *Sūtra*, there is only reference to repeating and remembering Amitābha's name for several nights before death. In the *Amitāyur-dhyāna Sūtra*, it is possible to scrape into the Happy Land on a bare minimum of personal worth, due to Amitābha's grace. Only someone who slanders or obstructs the *Dharma* cannot be reborn there. A person must nevertheless prepare himself before death by serenely reciting *Nāmo Amitābhāya Buddhāya*, 'Honour to Amitābha Buddha', ten times while continually thinking of Amitābha. In the Happy Land, however, an evil-doer will initially go through a kind of purgatory, being reborn in a 'lotus' which remains closed for many ages before he can benefit from the Pure Land. Others will be closer to enlightenment according to the extent of their faith, virtue, meditation and knowledge.

The notion of gaining rebirth in the Happy Land has long provided a hope to people struggling with existence, living less than perfect lives. If currently unable to behave like true *Bodhisattvas*, the environment of the Happy Land will enable them to do so, and the immeasurably long life-span there will encompass the hugely long *Bodhisattva*-path.

Another popular heavenly Buddha is Bhaiṣajya-guru, the 'Master of Healing', his Pure Land being in an 'eastern region of the universe'. His vows are such that faith in him and sincere repetition of his name will lead to the curing of illnesses and deformities, and give a person insight into his own bad karma, so that he will reform and aspire to Buddhahood. Calling on him at death may also enable a person to avoid an unfortunate rebirth that bad karma would otherwise lead to.

Of the heavenly *Bodhisattvas*, the earliest one referred to is Maitreya, 'The Kindly One', who is acknowledged even in the Southern tradition. In the Mahāyāna, it is said that, after attaining Buddhahood, he will send a Transformation-body to be the next Buddha to teach on earth. Sometimes Maitreya is shown, in anticipation, as a Buddha. In Eastern Buddhism, he is often portrayed in the form of one of his recognized manifestations, the tenth-century Pu-tai. This Ch'an monk was a jolly, pot-bellied, wandering teacher who carried presents for children in his cloth bag (*pu-tai*). In the West, images of Pu-tai are often known as 'Laughing Buddhas'.

By far the most popular of the Great Beings is Avalokiteśvara, a ninth stage *Bodhisattva* who is said to be one of the two helpers of Amitābha, along with Mahāsthāmaprāpta ('He of Great Power'). The latter represents Amitābha's wisdom, and acts on his behalf in opening people's eyes to the need for liberation. Avalokiteśvara enacts Amitābha's compassionate concern for the world, and is in fact seen as the very embodiment of compassion, the driving force of all *Bodhisattvas*. His vows are such that he will not become a Buddha until *all* beings are saved. As a Buddha, he would have a limited, though absolutely huge, lifespan, but as a *Bodhisattva* he can remain in contact with suffering beings, helping them till the end of time. The name Avalokiteśvara means 'The Lord Who Looks Down (with compassion)', while in China he is called Kuan-yin, 'Cry Regarder', or Kuan-shih-yin, 'Regarder of the Cries of the World', these names being based on a Sanskrit form 'Avalokitasvara'. In all Mahāyāna lands, he is the focus of devout worship, contemplation, and prayers for help.

An important text on him is the chapter in the Lotus *Sūtra* on the 'All-sided One', which originally circulated as a separate *Sūtra*, and is often still treated as such. His manifestations in many worlds are in forms which may include a Transformation-body Buddha, an *Arhat*, a Hindu god, a monk, nun, layman or laywoman. He even manifests himself in hells, and in the worlds of ghosts or animals. In one Chinese painting, he is shown appearing in the form of a bull, in order to convert a butcher from his wrong livelihood. His various manifestations may mysteriously disappear after they have appeared to help someone, or they may live out a full life, or even a series of them, as in the case of the Dalai Lamas of Tibet.

Like most other Great Beings, Avalokiteśvara is shown crowned and with royal garments, rather than the monastic robes of a Buddha. This is to show that *Bodhisattvas* are more in contact with the world than Buddhas, and more actively engaged in helping beings. In his crown, Avalokiteśvara has an image of Amitābha, the inspiration of his work. He holds a lotus bud, which symbolizes the pure beauty of his compassion, or the worldly minds of beings which he encourages in their efforts to 'bloom' into enlightenment. He is often shown with his

Plate 3 A *thang-ka*, or hanging scroll, depicting the *Bodhisattva* Mañjuśrī, at the Manjushri Institute, a Tibetan Buddhist college in the Lake District, England.

hands cupped together around a 'wish granting jewel' (*cintā-maṇi*). Originally a pre-Buddhist amulet against evil, this became an emblem of his willingness to grant righteous wishes. Its clarity also symbolizes the natural purity, hidden by coverings of spiritual defilements, in the minds of beings. These defilements are suggested by the cupping hands, also said to be like a lotus bud.

Another important Great Being is Mañjuśrī, 'Sweet Glory', who with Samantabhadra, 'The All-round Blissful One', is said to be the helper of the heavenly Buddha Śākyamuni. A tenth stage *Bodhisattva*, he is seen as the greatest embodiment of wisdom, and has the special task of destroying ignorance and awakening spiritual knowledge. Accordingly, he is shown holding a lotus on which rests a copy of a Perfection of Wisdom *Sūtra*, and wielding a flaming sword, symbolic of the wisdom with which he cuts away delusion. He is seen as the patron of scholars and a protector of *Dharma*-preachers. Those who devoutly recite his name, and meditate on his teachings and images, are said to be protected by him, to have many good rebirths, and to see him in dreams and meditative visions, in which he inspires and teaches them.

The Great Being Kṣitigarbha, or 'Earth-matrix', is also associated with Śākyamuni's Buddha Land, our world. In Japan, where he is known as Jizō, he is the second most popular *Bodhisattva*. His vows were to help humankind until the next Buddha appeared on earth. He acts as a guardian of travellers, those in trouble and women and children. He is regarded as continually working for the alleviation of those reborn in hells, and to be particularly concerned about the destiny of dead children. He is shown in a monastic robe, as a genial figure holding a staff with which he opens the doors of hells. In Japan, statues of him are often found at the side of country roads and mountain paths, and they are placed in graveyards as prayer-offerings for the good rebirth of dead children.

THE TANTRIC PERSPECTIVE

In late Indian Buddhism, a form of the Mahāyāna arose which saw itself as a new, more powerful 'vehicle' to salvation. This came to predominate in the lands of Northern Buddhism, while in Korea and Japan it exists alongside various other forms of the Mahāyāna.

The new 'vehicle' was based on a large body of texts called *Tantra*'s, which outline complex meditational 'systems' which incorporate ritual, magic and a rich symbolism. These concern advanced practices for those who have prepared themselves by prior Mahāyāna training. They aim to generate deep religious experiences which can lead to Buddhahood more quickly than the hugely long *Bodhisattva*-path, which they refer to as the *pāramitā-yāna*, or 'vehicle of the perfections'. Tantric texts did not appear as public documents till the sixth century; they continued being composed in India till around AD 1200. Nevertheless, they were said to have been taught by the historical Buddha, to a select band of disciples who had then passed them on. They are often expressed in a veiled kind of language that needs explaining by a *Guru*, a spiritual preceptor known in Tibet as a *bLama* (pron. *Lama*), or 'Superior One'. Such a person, whether a monk, nun or advanced lay practitioner, guides a small group of initiates in the use of the potent tantric methods.

The elements which led to the rise of the Tantra-yāna were various. Firstly, the development of ritual by lay Buddhists reached a point where it was transformed from being a preliminary to higher practices, into the basis of a new spiritual 'vehicle'. Secondly, complex ritual techniques were borrowed from Hinduism, especially the use of *mantras*. These were sacred words of power which were originally used in the *Vedas*, but further developed in Tantric Hinduism. Thirdly, the magical side of Buddhism was augmented by elements drawn from the beliefs and practices common in agricultural societies. Fourthly, female 'deities' and re-interpreted Hindu ones were admitted into the Buddhist pantheon of holy beings. Lastly, key Mahāyāna concepts were used to give a rationale for developing new methods for attaining spiritual realization. If the world was non-different from *Nirvāṇa*, *any* object or action could potentially be used as an entrance to ultimate reality, if the motive and method were right, using skilful means. Rites could be used to harness the unconscious forces of passion or hatred and 'magically' transmute them into their opposites. If all was 'thought-only', complex and vivid visualizations could be developed as a new, and transforming, world of experience.

Key masters of the new way were the eighty-four *Mahā-siddha*'s, or 'Great Accomplished Ones', who arose between the eighth and twelfth centuries. They were usually long-haired lay-people who lived unconventional wandering lives as crazy-sounding wizard-saints. They sought to inject a fresh dynamic spirit into the somewhat over-systematized Mahāyāna, and re-emphasize the role of the lay practitioner. The Tantric way fairly soon became absorbed into the mainstream of Indian Mahāyāna, being studied at monastic universities from the eighth century.

A common term for the new movement was the *Vajra-yāna*, the 'Thunderbolt' or 'Diamond' vehicle. In pre-Buddhist India, the *Vajra* was seen as the power-laden sceptre of Indra, ruler of the Vedic gods. In early Buddhism, the *Arhat* was said to have a mind like a *Vajra*, and in the Mahāyāna a tenth stage *Bodhisattva* is said to enter a *Vajra*-like meditative state. Tantric Buddhism saw the *Vajra* as a good symbol for its powerful methods and the enlightened mind. This was because it saw it as a substance which was: as irresistible as a thunderbolt, suggesting the overwhelming power of the enlightened mind to destroy spiritual obstacles; as hard as diamond, suggesting the indestructible nature of the enlightened mind; and as clear as empty space, suggesting the 'empty', void-like nature of such a mind. The *Vajra*, then, symbolized enlightenment, ultimate reality, and the *Dharma*-body, personified as Vajra-sattva, the *Vajra*-being. The aim of the Vajrayāna adept was to become conscious of the identity between Vajra-sattva and his 'own' empty 'nature', so as to 'become' such a 'being'. To do this was to gain enlightenment, or *siddhi*, 'success'.

The *Vajra*-sceptre became a symbolic ritual implement, as did the *Vajra*-bell. The centre of the sceptre symbolizes emptiness, and the three bulges represent the sense-desire, pure form, and formless worlds, which 'emerge' from emptiness. The axis and four (sometimes eight, as in Plate 4) prongs represent the five main Vajrayāna Buddhas, whose unity is suggested by the merging of the prongs at the end of the sceptre. The whole is thus a supreme image of the *Dharma*-body, from which the world and Buddhas emerge. The handle of the bell also represents the eternal *Dharma*-body, while the bell part, with its fading tone, represents the conditioned world of change. Together, they show that these two are inextricably linked. The sceptre and bell also symbolize skilful means and wisdom, a complementary pair whose perfect union is seen as sparking off enlightenment.

Another term used for Tantric Buddhism is the '*Mantra-yāna*', the 'vehicle of *mantras*'. From the third century, *Sūtras* contained *dhāraṇī*'s, short formulas 'preserving' or 'maintaining' the *Dharma* and aiding its followers. The pre-Mahāyāna *Sūtras* also contain *paritta*'s, or short

Plate 4 A *Vajra*-sceptre and *Vajra*-bell.

protective chants. Building on such a basis, *mantras* were adopted from Hinduism, these being 'mental instruments' used to contact gods, or as spells to gain a good harvest, health, children, or even to bewitch someone. In the Mantrayāna, they also became chanted in rites to aid visualizations, in which a particular holy being is conjured up out of emptiness, as a basis for developing the spiritual qualities that the being embodies.

The most famous *mantra* is that of Avalokiteśvara: *Oṃ maṇi padme hūṃ*. *Oṃ* and *hūṃ* are sacred sounds used in the *Vedas*, the first being seen as the basic sound of the universe. *Maṇi padme* literally means 'O jewelled-lotus lady'. In later exegesis, *maṇi* is seen as referring to the jewel that this *Bodhisattva* holds, while *padme* refers to his symbol, the lotus. A complex set of symbolic explanations is also given to this *mantra*. For example, its six syllables are associated with the six perfections, or the six realms of rebirth. As it is recited, rays of light may be visualized as streaming out to the beings in these realms.

Plate 5 An image of Tārā in the courtyard of a temple in Kathmandu, Nepal.

Among the female deities which Tantric Buddhism reveres, the most important came to be the *Bodhisattva* Tārā, the 'Saviouress'. She is seen as having various forms, but the 'Green' and 'White' forms are the most popular (see Plate 5). In Tibet, these came to be among the most well-loved deities, one becoming Tibet's patron goddess. They are seen as graceful, attractive and approachable, and as ever-ready to tenderly care for those in distress. Their compassionate nature, in responding to those who call on them, is reflected in the story that they were born from two tears shed by Avalokiteśvara when he saw the horrors of hell.

One strand of Tantrism included taboo- and convention-breaking practices to overcome attachments and aid insight into seeing everything as the *Dharma*-body. The *Hevajra Tantra* asserts that the world is bound by lust, and may also be released by lust. This referred to the practice of sexual yoga, in which the power of lust is harnessed, and transmuted into a power for liberation, by means of visualizing the flow of various mystical energies within the body. At a time when Buddhist influence had led to widespread vegetarianism, such rites might be carried out after eating meat and drinking wine, in a cemetery at night, the sexual partner being a low-caste girl visualized as a deity. The importance of the body, which the *Tantras* stress, goes back to the Buddha saying that *Nirvāṇa* is in 'this fathom-long carcase' (see p. 59), while cemeteries were often seen as good places in which to meditate on the nature of the body and death. The bizarre-sounding tantric rites were certainly an innovation, though!

The *Mahā-siddha* Saraha (ninth century?) also developed an iconoclastic, intuitionist approach which dispensed with *mantras* and complex rites as side-tracks. In his *Dohā-kośa*, he says that perfect knowledge may be developed without being a monk, but while married and enjoying sense-pleasures. He rigorously emphasizes the importance of spiritual practice, under a *Guru*, rather than dying of thirst 'in the desert of multitudinous treatises' (v.56). Such practice involved cultivating a state free from thought, a spontaneous, natural state akin to the innocence of a child. This '*Sahaja-yāna*' way would make manifest the 'Innate' (*Sahaja*), the profound, non-dual ultimate reality which could be seen in everything.

7

THE LATER HISTORY AND SPREAD OF BUDDHISM

BUDDHISM IN INDIA AND CENTRAL ASIA

During the Hindu Gupta dynasty (320–540), which ruled much of north India, Hinduism grew stronger. Buddhism generally continued to flourish, though, with the rulers patronizing both religions. During the century from around AD 450, the White Huns, originally from Central Asia, devastated monasteries in Afghanistan, northern Pakistan and areas of western India. By the seventh century, a slow recovery was being made in the north-west, with the Buddhism of southern Pakistan remaining strong. In western and some southern regions of India, though, it was losing out to Hinduism and Jainism. From AD 750, the mostly Buddhist Pāla dynasty ruled in the north-east, patronizing Buddhism and supporting five monastic universities, the major one being the internationally renowned Nālandā. In the eleventh century, Pāla rule weakened, and it was followed in 1118 by the Hindu Sen dynasty. From AD 986, the Muslim Turks started raiding north-west India from Afghanistan, plundering western India early in the eleventh century. Forced conversions to Islam were made, and Buddhist images smashed, due to the Islamic dislike of 'idolatry'. By 1192, the Turks established rule over north India from Delhi. The north-eastern stronghold of Buddhism then fell, with the destruction of Nālandā university in 1198. In the north-east, east, and Kashmir, Buddhism lingered on for another two centuries or so, with some royal patronage in the latter two areas. In Kashmir it was forcibly stamped out by the Muslims in the fifteenth century. Buddhist refugees fled to south India (where Hindu kings resisted Muslim power), South-east Asia, Nepal and Tibet. The Theravāda school flourished in the south until at least the seventeenth century, before it withdrew from the war-torn region to Ceylon. From the sixteenth century, however, it had been re-introduced from Burma to the north-eastern fringes of the Indian sub-continent.

North of Tibet, in the area known as Central Asia, was an international trade-route called the Silk Road, as silk was exported along it from China to north-west India, and even to the Mediterranean world. Among Indian merchants were many Buddhists, who, often accompanied by wandering monks, helped spread the religion in Central Asia. Buddhism was present in the region from the second century BC, and in the first century AD both Sarvāstivāda and Mahāyāna Buddhism flourished in several of the city states of the area. Central Asia remained Buddhist until the tenth or eleventh centuries, when the Turks brought conversions to Islam.

What factors contributed to the decline and virtual demise of Buddhism within the Indian sub-continent (excluding the Himālayan region and Ceylon)? One was a dilution of the distinctiveness of Buddhism relative to the rising power of Hinduism. Mahāyāna writers were quite critical of Hinduism, but the surface similarities of Hindu and Mahāyāna devotional cults and Tantrism may have led the laity to perceive the two religions as quite similar. Hinduism also borrowed elements from Buddhism. The devotees of the god Viṣṇu came to frown on animal sacrifices and to practise vegetarianism, while some Śaivites (followers of the god Śiva) viewed caste-distinctions as being of little relevance to religious practice. The great theologian Śankara (788–820) developed a monasticism paralleling the *Sangha*, and also used the Buddhist concept of 'two levels of truth', already borrowed by his predecessor Gauḍapāda (seventh century). Hinduism could not ignore the Buddha; so by around the sixth century, it recognized him as the ninth incarnation of Viṣṇu.

Hindu hostility also played a part. The Buddha incarnation was seen as a way to delude demons into denying the authority of the *Vedas*, so as to lead them to hell. Śankara described the Buddha as an enemy of the people, and sporadic persecution was directed at Buddhists from the sixth century. There is also evidence for social ostracism of Buddhists, probably due to their lack of enthusiasm for the caste system, which became particularly influential on society from around AD 600. While Buddhism sought to influence society from its monastic centres, Hinduism wove itself into the fabric of society through the caste system, with Brahmin priests having a certain authority over others within it. Unlike the more universal Buddhism, Hinduism came to be seen as the 'national' religion of India.

The Muslim invasions were the worst blow, however, for Buddhism had few royal defenders and, unlike Hinduism with its *Kṣatriya* warrior class, it lacked a soldierly spirit. The *Sangha*, whose survival is essential for the flourishing of Buddhism, was an easily identifiable and thus vulnerable institution. The devastation of agriculture due to the invasions also meant that the laity no longer had surpluses to support their monks. The *Sangha* thus died out in most areas, and could not be revived without existing monks to ordain new ones. Between the alien Muslims, with their doctrinal justification of a 'holy war' to spread the faith, and Hindus, closely identified with Indian culture and with a more entrenched social dimension, the Buddhists were squeezed out of existence. Lay Buddhists were left with a folk form of Buddhism, and gradually merged into Hinduism, or converted to Islam. Buddhism therefore died out in all but the fringes of its homeland, though it had long since spread beyond it.

SRI LANKA

The history of Ceylon and its Buddhism is chronicled in works such as the *Dīpavaṃsa*, *Mahāvaṃsa* and *Cūlavaṃsa*. The monks of Mahinda's mission of around 250 BC brought the Pali Canon in their memories, along with the developing commentaries. These continued to be orally transmitted till around 80 BC, when invasion and famine meant that parts of the Canon could be lost as monks died. A council was therefore held to see to the writing down of the Canon, in Pali, and the commentaries in the local Sinhala dialect of Indo-Aryan. Mahinda established an indigenous *Sangha* in Sri Lanka, and his sister, the nun Sanghamittā, brought a cutting from the original *Bodhi*-tree to plant in the capital Anurādhapura. She also brought relics of the Buddha, which were enshrined in the first of the many *Dagaba*'s (*Stūpas*) to be built on the island.

Since then, Buddhism has been the major religion. The *Sangha* taught and advised the kings, and at several times in the island's history it influenced the choice of ruler. The Sinhalese have long felt that civilized life is impossible without the presence of monks in society.

They required their kings to be Buddhist, and from the tenth century saw them as *Bodhisattas*. In general, the most devout kings have been the most active in social welfare: building irrigation works, supporting medical and veterinary services, and providing homes for the incurable. Education was supported via support for the monks, who became the educators of the people.

In the fifth century, the monk Buddhaghosa came to Sri Lanka, as he had heard that extensive commentaries on the scriptures existed there. He was allowed to translate these into Pali, edit them, and add certain thoughts of his own. To prove his suitability for this task, he first composed the *Visuddhimagga*, or 'Path of Purification', a masterly survey of meditation and doctrine which became the classic expression of Theravāda Buddhism. Sri Lanka and other Theravāda lands produced a thriving Pali literature: chronicles, commentaries and sub-commentaries, and works of devotion, doctrine and *Abhidhamma*. Of particular note is Anuruddha's *Abhidhammattha-sangaha* (eleventh century), a systematic compendium of *Abhidhamma*.

Three monastic fraternities developed, though all used the Pali Canon as scripture. The oldest was centred on the Mahā-vihāra, the 'Great Monastery' established by Mahinda. Then, around 98 BC, king Vaṭṭagāmaṇi donated the Abhayagiri monastery to a favoured monk. As this was not given to the community as a whole, the monk was expelled from the Mahā-vihāra fraternity, leading to a schism. Later, the Jetavana fraternity formed, again due to donation of a monastery to an individual monk, by king Mahāsena (AD 274–301). The monks of the Abhayagiri fraternity were more receptive to Mahāyāna ideas than the more conservative Mahā-vihāra monks, while the Jetavana monks vacillated. Mahāsena supported the Mahāyāna and destroyed the Great Monastery, but his successor rebuilt it. The Mahā-vihāra fraternity was later strengthened by the work of Buddhaghosa, though in the eighth and ninth centuries, there was a period of considerable Mahāyāna and Mantrayāna influence. From late tenth century, there was a decline in Buddhism and monastic discipline due to Tamil invasions and civil wars. In the early eleventh century, the monks' ordination line had to be re-imported from Burma, where it had recently been taken, but the nuns' Order died out. King Parakkama Bahu I (1153–86) halted the decline and purified the *Sangha*, also unifying it on the basis of the Mahā-vihāra fraternity. Around this period, Southern Buddhism entered its golden age in both Sri Lanka and South-east Asia, incorporating selected Mahāyāna/Mantrayāna practices and aspirations into its existing framework of *Sutta* teachings, Theravādin *Vinaya* and Vibhajjavādin *Abhidhamma*.

In time, Sri Lanka became a prized goal for Western colonial powers. The Catholic Portuguese (1505–1658), then the Calvinist Dutch (1658–1796) controlled certain lowland coastal regions. In the late sixteenth century, persecution by a Śaivite king led to a decline in which the ordination line for monks (but not novices) was again lost. Only in 1753 was it successfully re-introduced, from Thailand. The British finally brought an end to the highland kingdom of Kandy in 1815, so as to rule the whole island. While only the Portuguese had persecuted Buddhism, each colonial power tried to transmit its own brand of Christianity to the islanders.

SOUTH-EAST ASIA EXCLUDING VIETNAM

A small Buddhist community may have existed among the Mons of southern Burma/central Thailand since the time of Asoka. In any case, the tradition of Sri Lanka was probably introduced to the Mons in the early centuries AD. In northern Burma, Sarvāstivāda and Mahāyāna Buddhism, along with Hinduism, were present from the third century AD, with Tantric Buddhism arriving by the ninth century. A change came about when a northern king, Anawratā (1040–77), unified the country and gave his allegiance to the Theravāda of the Mons; for he was impressed by the simplicity of its doctrines. Since that time, Theravāda Buddhism has been the main religion of the Burmese, though Tantric elements have lingered on, and the gods of the pre-Buddhist nature religion have a place in Buddhist cosmology. Anawratā established contact with Sri Lanka, and, by the fifteenth century, a Theravāda ordination line from there was finally established as the orthodox one.

Merchants brought Brahmanism to the Khmers of Cambodia in the first century AD, and north-Indian Sanskritizing forms of Buddhism in the second century. From the sixth century, a mix of Hindu Śaivism and Mahāyāna was the religion of urban areas, though there was some royal persecution of Buddhism in the seventh century. From 802 to 1432, there was a powerful Khmer empire, with the king being seen as an incarnation of both Śiva and a great *Bodhisattva*. Tantrism also had an influence. From the twelfth century, Mon missions won over the lower classes and countryfolk, who preferred Theravāda to the complex religion of the court. In the fourteenth century, royalty turned to the Theravāda, and the tradition became well established in the country as a whole.

In the region of modern Thailand, a mix of Mahāyāna and Śaivism was present from the tenth century. In the thirteenth century, the Tai people, driven south from China by the Mongolians, entered the area and drove out its Khmer rulers. Theravāda missions, sent from Burma from the eleventh century, found a response from the ruler of the Tais, once followers of Chinese Mahāyāna Buddhism. Theravāda then became the dominant religious tradition. Like Burma, Thailand had links with the Buddhism of Sri Lanka over the centuries. The Tai people also settled in Laos. Early in the fourteenth century, the Cambodian wife of a ruler helped convert the royal court and people to Theravāda Buddhism, so that it became the official religion in around 1350. In the fifteenth century, Theravāda also spread to the Dai, another branch of the Tai people in what is now China.

Buddhism was present in the Malay peninsular from the fourth century, with a Buddhist state existing in the north in the fifth century. From this time, Śaivism and Mahāyāna Buddhism were influential in the peninsular and on the Indonesian islands of Java and Sumatra. In the seventh century, the Sarvāstivādins also became well established on Sumatra, and Tantric Buddhism became popular in the region in the eighth century. In around 800, a huge *Stūpa*, still the largest monument in the southern hemisphere, was built at Borobuḍur, Java. From the eleventh century, the dominant religion of the region increasingly became a mix of the Tantric forms of Buddhism and Śaivism. In the fourteenth century, Islam was brought by merchants, and in the fifteenth century it rapidly spread to become the dominant religion. The Hindu-Buddhist syncretism still exists on the small island of Bali, however, and Buddhism is also found among the Chinese community in the region.

THE LANDS OF NORTHERN BUDDHISM

Nepal shared in the developments of north Indian Buddhism and Hinduism, and by the thirteenth century, Hinduism had become the dominant religion, favoured by rulers. By the fifteenth century, monks were increasingly abandoning celibacy and forming an hereditary caste, and scholarship was declining. Buddhism has been found mainly among the Newars of the Kathmandu valley. Since 1786, when the Gurkhas conquered the country, they have held out against rulers' attempts to fully Hinduize this area.

Buddhism did not reach Tibet, the heartland of Northern Buddhism, till relatively late, the country being isolated and mountainous. Its indigenous religion, Bon, is centred on a cult of dead kings, spirit-possession, magic, and exorcism of demons and vampires, though it shares a belief in rebirth with Buddhism. The first real Buddhist influence in Tibet came under king Srong-bstan-sgam-po (pron. Songtsen Gampo; AD 616–50), who was converted by two wives, from Nepal and China. A minister visited India for texts, and then invented the first Tibetan script, for writing down translations. After the king's death, the impetus for Buddhism ran out, though many Tibetans studied it in Nepal. In the following century, Buddhist influences came from India, China and Central Asia, and king Khri-srong-lde-brstan (pron. Trhisong Detsen; 755–97?) tried to establish the first monastery in the country. Tradition says, however, that his efforts were frustrated by earthquakes and disease, seen as coming from the hostility of the Bon deities. The problems continued even after the Mahāyāna teacher Śāntarakṣita, of Nālandā university, was brought to bless the site. The latter advised the king that Tantric Buddhism would have most appeal for the Tibetans, with their love of magic, and suggested that Padmasambhava, one of the *Mahā-siddhas*, be invited to Tibet. When he came, he successfully exorcized the site in around 775, and converted many people. He is also said to have converted many of the native deities, so that they became protectors of Buddhism, which was recognized as the state religion in 779. The Buddhism which took root was a mixture of monastically-based Mahāyāna, represented by Śāntarakṣita, and tantric mysticism and ritual, represented by the revered Padmasambhava: a mix which became typical for Tibet. Translations were carried out in earnest, and in the period up to around AD 1000, many Tibetans studied in India and Indian teachers visited Tibet.

The school which looks back to Padmasambhava as its founder is the rNying-ma (pron. Nyingma), the school (*pa*) of those who are

'Adherents of the Old (*Tantras*)'. It has a strong emphasis on Tantrism and magic, and has been influenced by Bon, which by the eleventh century itself became much influenced by Buddhism. Bon hostility led to king gLang-dar-ma (pron. Langdarma; 838–42) persecuting Buddhism. Though he was then assassinated by a Buddhist monk, the period of political turmoil following did not favour the spread of Buddhism. In this time, political power was held by regional kings and even some large monasteries.

In the eleventh century, a renaissance of Buddhism led to its firm establishment throughout Tibet. At the invitation of a regional king, the ageing monk-professor Atīśa came from India on a missionary tour in 1042. He helped purify the *Sangha*, emphasizing celibacy, and improved Tibet's understanding of Buddhist doctrine, as based on a mix of Madhyamaka and the *Tantras*. His reforms led his main disciple to establish the bKa'-gdams-pa (pron. Kadam-pa), or 'Bound by Command (of monastic discipline) School', and also influenced two other new schools of the period. The first was the bKa'brgyud-pa (pron. Kagyu-pa), the 'Whispered Transmission School'. Its founder was Mar-pa (1012–96), a married layman who had studied with tantric Gurus in India, and translated many texts. He emphasized a complex system of yoga and secret instructions whispered from master to disciple. His chief pupil was the great poet-hermit-saint Mi-la-ras-pa (pron. Milarepa; 1040–1123), whose own pupil sGam-po-pa (pron. Gampopa) first established bKa'brgyud-pa monasteries. The other new school was the Sa-skya-pa (pron. Sakya-pa), founded in 1073 at the Sa-skya monastery. It is noted for its scholarship and is close to the bKa'brgyud-pa in most matters.

The powerful Mongols had designs on disunified Tibet and, in 1244, their ruler summoned the head Sa-skya *bLama* to his court. In return for the submission of Tibet, the *bLama* was made regent over it. He also spread (Sa-skya) Buddhism to Mongolia and regions of northern China within the Mongolian empire. His successor 'Phags-pa (pron. Phakpa; 1235–80) was the spiritual adviser to Khubilai Khan, who became Mongol emperor of China. Sa-skya power was resisted by the other schools and their soldiers, and came to an end in 1336. A line of kings followed from 1358 to 1635.

By the fourteenth century, the Tibetan Canon of scriptures, based on careful and often literal translations, was complete. Tibet's Buddhism is the direct heir of late north Indian Buddhism, and as the Muslims had destroyed libraries in India, the Tibetan Canon is the best, if incomplete, indication of the nature of this.

The last major school of Tibetan Buddhism was founded by the reformer Tsong-kha-pa (1357–1410), on the basis of the bKa'-gdams school and Atīśa's arrangement of teachings in a series of levels, with a purified Tantrism at the top. He founded the dGe-lugs-pa (pron. Geluk-pa), or 'Virtuous School', whose monks are distinguished from others by the yellow colour of their ceremonial hats. Tsong-kha-pa emphasized the study of Madhyamaka, and the following of monastic discipline. He cut down on magical practices and eliminated sexual yoga for monks. The three main dGe-lugs monasteries, near the capital Lhasa, were modelled on the monastic universities of India, and became great centres of Buddhist scholarship, logic and debate. In the sixteenth century, the head of the dGe-lugs school reintroduced Buddhism to the Mongols, who had lapsed from it. One of the Mongol rulers, Altan Khan, therefore gave him the Mongolian title of *Dalai*, 'Ocean (of Wisdom)', *bLama* (pron. *Lama*). He was regarded as the second reincarnation of a former dGe-lugs leader, Tsong-kha-pa's nephew, so that the latter was seen, retrospectively, as the first Dalai Lama. Each Dalai Lama was also seen as a re-manifested Transformation-body (Tib. *sprul-sku*, pron. *trulku*) of Avalokiteśvara, one among the 300 or so recognized *sprul-skus* in Tibet. *Sprul-skus* are recognized as children, based on predictions of their predecessors and the ability to pick out their possessions from similar looking ones. This practice became the basis for a system of succession to leadership of monasteries, and the political power that sometimes attended this.

In 1641, the Mongolians invaded Tibet and established the fifth Dalai Lama as ruler of the country. From then, the dGe-lugs school became the 'established church'. Some of the bKa'brgyud-pa monks and *bLamas* who were unhappy with this moved to Sikkim and Bhutan, thus spreading Buddhism there. In Mongolia, Buddhism became well established and popular, pacifying a once war-like people. In the eighteenth century, it spread northwards to the nomads of what are now the Buryat and Tuva Soviet republics. A branch of the Mongolian people also migrated westwards to the Kalmyk Soviet republic, by the Caspian sea. A community in the Baltic states of the USSR also claims a long Buddhist heritage, from Mongol roots.

CHINA

Early history

As the religion of foreign merchants arriving from Central Asia, Buddhism was present in China by around AD 50. By the middle of the next century, Chinese interest led to texts being translated: firstly Śrāvakayāna works on meditation and *Abhidharma*, then also Perfection of Wisdom *Sūtras* and works on the Pure Lands of Amitābha and Bhaiṣajya-guru, and the heaven of Maitreya.

Unlike most other lands where Buddhism spread, China already had an ancient literate civilization, yet Buddhism managed to bridge the wide cultural chasm between the Indian and Chinese worlds. The dominant ideology of society was Confucianism, a social philosophy going back to K'ung Fu-tzu (Confucius; 551–497 BC). K'ung stressed the importance of the family and correct, harmonious social relationships, particularly filial piety, or respect for parents. This extended to respectful worship of ancestors, in line with long-standing Chinese practice. Man was seen as part of a triangle of forces: Earth, Man and an impersonally conceived Heaven (*T'ien*). K'ung's ideal was the scholar-gentleman, who studied the ancient classics that he had edited, and cultivated a life of human-ness and proper, respectful social relationships. In the Han dynasty (206 BC–AD 220), such scholar-gentlemen ran the bureaucracy of the huge Chinese empire on behalf of the emperor, who was seen as the mediator of the forces of Earth, Man and Heaven, and as worthy of worship.

The other strand of Chinese thought was Taoism, a religio-philosophical system founded by the semi-mythical Lao-tzu ('Old Sage'), said to have been born in 604 BC. To him is attributed the *Tao-Te-Ching*, 'The Standard Work on the Way (*Tao*) and its Power'. This sees the mysterious, indescribable *Tao* as a force flowing through and generating all things in nature. The Taoist sage is one who tries to be like the *Tao* in acting effortlessly, spontaneously and naturally. Thus Taoism dislikes the formality engendered by Confucianism, though it shares its love of harmony. The sage should be humble, compassionate, and seek to become one with the *Tao* by meditatively contemplating it. From the second century AD, a form of Taoism developed which was based on worship of many gods, and the quest for longevity, or physical 'immortality', using alchemy, diet and meditation.

In Buddhism's transmission to China, some of the problems it faced related to its monasticism. Celibacy was seen as undermining the Chinese stress on continuing the family line, so as not to deprive the ancestors of worship. The 'unfilial' monks also lived a life which was not based on home and family, the centre of Chinese life. Moreover, the Chinese expected all but the scholar-gentleman to be engaged in productive work, but the monks lived off alms. When monasteries in time became wealthy, through the donation of both land and precious metals for images, Buddhism was attacked as being an economic drain on the country. The *Sangha* was also regarded with some suspicion; for it was an autonomous group, which needed to be regulated before it could fit into the totalitarian structure of Chinese society. A symbol of this autonomy was the fact that, initially, monks would not bow in worship to the emperor; for monks should not bow to even the most senior layperson.

Though the Chinese loved foreign exotica, the nationalistic Confucian literati came to criticize the growing religion as suitable only for foreign barbarians. Buddhist thought tended to see class differences as unimportant, while social hierarchy was important in Confucianism. The metaphysical, other-worldly aspects of Buddhist thought were also in tension with Chinese pragmatism and focus on this world. To Confucian rationalists, there was no evidence for rebirth, there was nothing wrong with killing animals, and the fate of individuals and kingdoms depended on the will of Heaven, not individual karma.

How was it, then, that Buddhism came to be for a long time the major religion of all classes in China, with Taoism as the second religion, and Confucianism remaining as the main influence on social ethics? A key event was the decline and break-up of the Han dynasty, which led to a crisis of values due to the apparent failure of Confucianism. In this situation of uncertainty, Buddhism stepped in to fill a vacuum and put down its roots. In some ways, this has parallels with the origins of Buddhism in India, which was also at a time of social change, anxiety, and the seeking of new values.

Buddhism had *both* a developed ethic, as Confucianism had, *and* a developed philosophy, as Taoism had. It was more popularly orientated than Confucianism, and had a more systematic philosophy of man than Taoism. Particularly popular was the concept of all people having the Buddha-nature, an equal potential for enlightenment, which introduced to China the notion of the equal worth of all people. The compassionate assistance of heavenly Buddhas and Great Beings brought hope and solace in sorrow; the karma-rebirth doctrines came to be seen as a good support for morality, and the 'alien' faith proved to be adaptable and tolerant. Adaptations were facilitated by the notion of skilful means. Ancestors could be cared for by transferring 'merit' to them, so that Buddhist monks came to be much called on for rites for the dead. Dead abbots were worshipped as the 'ancestors' of a monastery, and a novice monk was expected to behave in a respectful, filial way towards the monk assigned to watch over him. Moreover, schools of Buddhism developed which had a more this-worldly, pragmatic emphasis.

Following the Han dynasty, China was split into a northern part, controlled by non-Chinese 'barbarians' such as the Huns, and a southern part, governed by a series of weak Chinese dynasties. In the north, missionary monks had a reputation for meditation-based psychic powers, and so were sought out by the magic-loving people to teach meditation, seen as a means of protection in the war-torn period. The rulers sought out the 'psychic' monks as advisers on political and military matters, and the monks then gradually civilized them, tempered their excesses, and converted them into protectors of Buddhism: a good example of skilful means at work. As a non-Chinese religion, Buddhism found favour with the powerful rulers, and also became the religion of the people. The practical side of Buddhism was stressed, in the form of devotion, meditation and good works, with more than 30,000 temples being constructed in the north by the sixth century. Many translations were also made, especially by the large translation-bureau run by the Central Asian monk Kumārajīva from AD 402 to 413. Brief Taoist- and Confucian-inspired suppressions in 446–52 and 574–78 were ineffective in stemming the growth of Buddhism.

In the south, Buddhism at first allied itself with Taoism; for it was seen as a form of Taoism that Lao-tzu had taught to foreigners in the west. Taoists looked to Buddhism for solutions to certain problems in Taoist philosophy and, till the fourth century, Buddhist terms were frequently translated by Taoist ones. Emphasis in the south was not on religious practice but on intellectual discussion among the nobility and literati, particularly on the Perfection of Wisdom literature. Once Buddhism began to flourish in its own right, Taoism looked on it as a rival, while being influenced by some of its forms such as a Canon of scriptures and an ecclesiastical structure. When the Sui dynasty

(589–617) re-unified China, Buddhism was consolidated in Chinese culture, as it was seen as a unifying force that also encouraged peace.

The schools of Chinese Buddhism

From the fifth century, a number of different schools of Buddhism emerged, each being known as a *tsung*: a 'clan' which traced its lineage back to a certain founder or patriarch. Each school specialized in a particular aspect of Buddhist teaching or practice, and monks or nuns often studied or practised according to several of them.

Some of the schools were straight imports from India. The first was the San-lun, or 'Three Treatise' school, which was the Chinese form of the Madhyamaka. This was introduced by the translator Kumārajīva, and was based on three key texts. The second was the Fa-hsiang, or 'Characteristics of *Dharmas*' school, a form of the Yogācāra introduced by the pilgrim-translator Hsuan-tsang (596–664). An earlier form of the Yogācāra known as She-lun, introduced in the sixth century by the translator Paramārtha, died out. Paramārtha also introduced the Chu-she, a form of the Sarvāstivāda based on the study of the *Abhidharma-kośa*. It was then organized by Hsuan-tsang. These schools lost their separate identity after a time, but as subjects of study they influenced others. A late import, arriving in the eighth century, was the Chen-yen, the '*Mantra*' or 'Efficacious Word' school. While it died out in China in a ninth-century persecution of Buddhism, this form of the Mantrayāna had considerable success in Korea and Japan.

Two important schools which originated in China were ones which, stimulated by the Chinese love of harmony, produced a philosophical synthesis of the teachings of different texts. They emphasized that the Buddha taught according to skilful means, and categorized the various Śrāvakayāna and Mahāyāna *Sūtras* as belonging to one or other of several levels of teaching, given at different periods in his life. At the highest level, the schools placed a chosen *Sūtra* as representing supreme truth. The T'ien-t'ai school was named after Mount 'Heavenly Terrace', where its headquarters was located. Founded by Chih-i (539–97), it placed the Lotus *Sūtra* and the Mahāyāna *Parinirvāṇa Sūtra* at the pinnacle of its teaching, and stressed both study and meditation. It emphasized the notion of the Buddha-nature as present in all things, and that the world is non-different from absolute Mind, thusness, emptiness or *Nirvāna*. The Hua-yen school put the *Avataṃsaka Sūtra* in pride of place (see pp. 118ff.). Founded by the meditation-master Tu-shun (557–640), it was philosophically systematized by its third patriarch Fa-tsang (643–712), and came to be influential on the Ch'an school. Both the synthesizing schools flourished in the T'ang dynasty (618–907). Influenced by Chinese ways of thought, they emphasized ultimate reality as immanent in the world, like the *Tao*, and as fathomable by penetration into the thusness of any natural phenomenon.

In seeking to be all-inclusive, T'ien-t'ai and Hua-yen diffused much energy on long hours of study and a range of practices. The remaining schools studied only a few selected texts, and focussed their energy on a limited number of practices. The smallest was the Lu, or 'Vinaya' school, introduced around AD 650. Based on the Śrāvakayāna Dharmaguptaka school, it emphasized the study of monastic discipline, and had high standards for ordination and monastic life. In these respects it influenced the practice of other schools, especially Ch'an. The two other practice-orientated schools became the most successful: Ch'ing-t'u and Ch'an.

The Pure Land school

The Ch'ing-t'u, or 'Pure Land' school became the most popular form of Buddhism in China, particularly among the laity. It is based on the three main *Sūtras* related to Amitābha, and the *Sukhāvatī-vyūhopadeśa* ('Instruction on the Array of the Happy Land'), a work attributed to Vasubandhu which systematizes the ideas of the Larger *Sukhāvatī-vyūha Sūtra*. At the start of the fifth century, Hui-yuan organized a society for meditation on Amitābha's Pure Land, but T'an-luan (476–542) was the first to properly organize the school, and is regarded as its first patriarch. He was a learned former Taoist, inspired by a missionary monk to see true immortality as gaining immeasurable life in Sukhāvatī (the 'Happy Land'). While his writings drew on Madhyamaka and Yogācāra ideas, he stressed faith in the power of Amitābha's vows, which could save even an evil doer. His ideal was establishing a pure, firm and uninterrupted faith throughout life. This would ensure the ability, as death approached, to call on Amitābha for ten consecutive moments of genuine faith: the minimum requirement for rebirth in Sukhāvatī. The main practice he advocated was one called *nien-fo* (Jap. *nembutsu*), a term which translated *Buddhānusmṛti*, 'recollection of the Buddha'. He explained it to mean both 'recollection' and 'calling on' Amitābha, this being done by repeatedly reciting the Chinese translation of the short formula of praise to Amitābha (see pp. 130 and 187).

The second patriarch, Tao-ch'o (562–645) emphasized the idea that, from AD 549, the world was in the degenerate age of the 'latter-day *Dharma*' (Ch. *ma-fa*, Jap. *mappō*). This was because the Chinese thought that 549 was 1,500 years after the Buddha's death, thus being the beginning of an age of decline in Buddhism and morality predicted by the Lotus *Sūtra*. In such a situation, most people could not follow the difficult 'path of the saints', based on their own virtue and meditation, but must rely on the 'easy path' of devotion to Amitābha. 'Self-power' must be replaced by 'other-power'. The third patriarch, Shan-tao (613–681) gave the school its classical form and did much to popularize it. From the ninth century, the school was so widely diffused that it no longer needed special patriarchs as leaders.

The Ch'an school

The name of the Ch'an, or 'Meditation' school (Jap. Zen) is an abbreviated transliteration of the Sanskrit *dhyāna*, referring to the state of deep meditation (Pali *jhāna*). In time, Ch'an became the most popular school among monks, artists and intellectuals. Like Tantric Buddhism in India, it developed powerful new methods of practice. In its terminology and spontaneous style, it was influenced by Taoism. Its expression of Buddhist ideas in direct, down-to-earth form was also in keeping with the Chinese temper. Meditation (*ch'an*) had existed in Chinese Buddhism from its earliest days, but Ch'an specialized in it. Its founding genius was seen as the semi-legendary Indian monk Bodhidharma, who may have been active in China in the period AD 470 to 520, and appears to have been a great meditation master and champion of the *Lankāvatāra Sūtra*. One of the legends about him was that he spent nine years in meditation gazing at a wall, until his legs fell off! This illustrates the Ch'an single-minded emphasis on meditation as *the* method for attaining enlightenment. Another legend is that he told the pious emperor Wu that the latter had earned 'no merit at all' by his many good works. This shocking saying probably meant that 'merit', like everything else, is empty of inherent existence, and that more important than good works is insight into reality. Though good works, devotion and study play their part in Ch'an, they should not become hindering focuses of attachment. Ch'an therefore has an iconoclastic streak, such that certain accomplished masters have burnt Buddha-images or torn up *Sūtras* as a means of undercutting someone's attachment. This has sometimes been misunderstood by Western students of Ch'an/Zen. When one such student, after a few days in a Japanese monastery, remarked that the old masters used to burn or spit on Buddha-images, not bow to them, the master simply replied 'you spits, I bow'.

A late saying attributed to Bodhidharma is:

> A special transmission outside the scriptures;
> Without depending on words and letters;
> Pointing directly to the human mind;
> Seeing the innate nature, one becomes a Buddha.

This expresses the secondary importance of study in Ch'an, and the idea that insight arises by direct mind-to-mind transmission from master to pupil. Indeed, Ch'an is said to have originated in a supposed incident in the Buddha's life, when he held up a flower. Mahākaśyapa smiled in understanding at this silent sermon, and so received the 'seal of *Dharma*' to pass on the teaching. The 'innate nature' within the mind is the Buddha-nature. Various levels of awakening (Ch. *wu*, Jap. *satori*) are attained by gaining direct insight into this. The highest realization is when this potentiality is fully actualized, and a person becomes a Buddha, one who truly knows that his mind had never been separate from Buddhahood. Other people and their teachings cannot really make a person see their Buddha-nature. This must come as a direct intuition, when he totally stops looking outside himself for the truth. The Ch'an master, then, can only try to stimulate the arising of this realization from *within* his pupil.

In the eighth century, there was controversy among some groups of Ch'an practitioners. A Southern school emphasized that, for the wise, enlightenment comes suddenly, and attributed to the flourishing Northern school the view that it is arrived at in stages, by a gradual process of purification. The Southern school took Hui-neng (638–713) as the 'sixth patriarch', while the Northern one took Shen-hsiu (600–706) as this. The bitter squabbles between the schools was due to the earnestness with which their followers sought enlightenment, and the importance which had come to be attached to the genuine 'mind-to-mind' transmission of truth. The matter was settled at a council in 796, when an emperor chose in favour of the Southern school. Subsequently, the various groups of Ch'an practitioners were assembled under the umbrella of this school. Its ascendancy was due to the campaigning of Shen-hui (668–760), who championed its cause by building up Hui-neng into a legendary figure regarded as the second founder of Ch'an. The tradition came to accept an account of his life and teachings given in the *Liu-tzu T'an-ching*, 'The Platform *Sūtra* of the Sixth Patriarch', composed around AD 820. This relates that Hui-neng, as an illiterate boy, had an awakening when he heard a monk reciting from the Diamond-cutter Perfection of Wisdom *Sūtra*. As a young man, he went to join the monastic community of the 'fifth patriarch', Hung-jen (601–74), and was put to work in the kitchens, without being ordained. Eight months later, the patriarch was due to name his successor, whom everyone expected to be the community's chief monk, Shen-hsiu. Nevertheless, the patriarch decided to choose his successor on the basis of the insight expressed in a verse. Shen-hsiu wrote on the monastery wall:

> The body is the Enlightenment (*Bodhi*) tree;
> The mind is like a clear mirror.
> At all times we must strive to polish it,
> And must not let the dust collect. (*Plat.* sec. 6)

This was judged to express only partial understanding and was surpassed by two verses which Hui-neng had a friend write on the wall. One was:

> Enlightenment originally has no tree;
> The mirror also has no stand
> Buddha-nature is always clear and pure;
> Where is there room for dust? (*Plat.* sec. 8)

Here, the ultimate level of truth is expressed: all phenomena, however exalted, are empty. To be like a mirror clearly reflecting reality, the mind has no need of gradual purification – it is already the pristine Buddha-nature. One does not need to purify oneself to Buddhahood, but to realize one's innate purity, the *Dharma*-body or true thusness. Hung-jen then called Hui-neng to his room at midnight, deepened his wisdom by teaching the Diamond-cutter *Sūtra*, and made him the sixth patriarch. Hui-neng secretly left the community, lest jealousy over a mere kitchen helper becoming patriarch should cause difficulties. For sixteen years he lived in the mountains as a layman, and then in 676 he ordained and came to gather many pupils.

The methods developed by Ch'an were aimed at enabling a person to directly intuit his true nature. To do this, the mind must be free of old habits, prejudices, restrictive thought-processes, and even ordinary conceptual thought. The basis for doing this, especially in the monasteries, was a disciplined life-style, which limited the expression of ego-desires so that a person could cultivate a naturalness and spontaneity which came from deep within: from the pure depths of the store-house consciousness. While a layperson could practise Ch'an, as it did not require long hours of study, monastic life was seen as providing a more conducive atmosphere for meditation, and gave closer access to the all-important meditation master. As he would have many pupils, private interviews with him were precious and long-awaited. In such an interview, the master would diagnose the specific spiritual problem that a pupil was currently subject to, and treat it accordingly. This might be by advice or explanation, or even by provocation, sudden actions, blows or shouts: whatever was appropriate to the pupil's state of mind, so as to help trigger an awakening. An awakening was said to depend on the right moment, the pupil's own Buddha-nature, and the master's direct pointing at this. The fierce methods used by some is reflected by this description of Ma-tsu (707–786): 'He strode along like a bull, and glared about him like a tiger.' The master would sometimes engage his pupil in a rapid dialogue which compressed different levels of understanding, and was intended to prod the pupil into himself finding and expressing the ultimate level of truth. In this, Ch'an was influenced by the Perfection of Wisdom paradoxical style of dialogue, Madhyamaka dialectic, and a probing style of questioning found in the *Śūrangama Sūtra*. A simple example is:

Monk: How can silence be expressed?
Master: I will not express it here.
Monk: Where will you express it?
Master: Last night at midnight, I lost three pennies by my bed.[2]

Here, the 'thusness' of silence is conveyed, not by describing it, but by conjuring up the picture of groping in the darkness and silence of night for some coins.

Records of some of these question-and-answer sessions, and of the spontaneous acts of masters, provided important paradigms for Ch'an practice. Such a record was known as a *kung-an* (Jap. *kōan*), or 'public record'. These were used as themes for one type of meditation, and as discussion points in private interviews. They were used increasingly from the eighth century, and by the twelfth century there were large anthologies of them. These were used as the basis of a system in which practitioners would have to wrestle with a series of enigmatic questions, such as 'what was my original face before my mother and father were born?', that is: what is my true nature, beyond existence in time and space? This was a way to educate people the 'hard way'.

Of the different Ch'an lineages, two survived the vicissitudes of history, and came to dominate after the eleventh century. The first is the Lin-chi (Jap. Rinzai) school, founded by Lin-chi (died 867). It emphasizes the use of *kung-ans*, harsh methods in interviews, and that awakenings come suddenly. The second is the Ts'ao-tung (Jap. Sōtō) school, founded by *Ts'ao*-shan (840–901) and *Tung*-shan (807–869). This emphasizes a form of sitting meditation, and came to see awakenings as gradually unfolding. While the Japanese forms of these two schools have remained separate, they merged in China during the Ming dynasty (1368–1644).

By the sixteenth century, the pervasive Pure Land practice of *nien-fo* came to be part of the daily liturgy of Ch'an monasteries. In this context, however, it became more of a Ch'an 'self-power' exercise than a Pure Land 'other-power' one. This was because, in addition to the recitation, a common topic of meditation was 'who recites the name of the Buddha?', that is, what is one's true nature? A syncretism between Pure Land and Ch'an also developed, in which the Buddha-nature 'within' and Amitābha Buddha 'without' were seen as different ways of looking at the same reality.

Later history

Buddhism flourished in the T'ang dynasty (618–907), when monasteries were large, well-endowed institutions which fostered artistic creativity, cared for the sick, old and orphans, and ran community development projects. Buddhism's influence and the wealth accumulated by its monasteries, however, led to machinations by rival Taoists. The government was in need of money after a civil war, and looked to the precious metals used in Buddhist images, temple lands, and the tax-exemption enjoyed by monks and the laity working in the monasteries. In 842, the emperor confiscated land belonging to lax monks and nuns, and in 845 he had all but a few temple-monasteries destroyed, laicized many monks and nuns, and took much of the *Sangha's* land. The persecution was short, but it devastated Buddhist institutions throughout China. The emperor died in 846, and his policy was reversed, but most schools did not recover and went into decline. T'ien-t'ai retained some of its power, but the main surviving schools were Ch'an and Pure Land. Ch'an survived because it was less dependent on libraries and images, etc., its monks had come to grow their own food, and many of its centres were geographically isolated. Pure Land survived because it was mainly a lay movement. Buddhism in China was now past its peak.

During the Sung dynasty (960–1279), though, the entire Canon of Buddhist scriptures was printed, using over 130,000 wooden printing blocks (972–83). In time, however, Buddhism came to lose out to the rising power of Neo-Confucianism, which reached its classic form in the twelfth century. Drawing elements from Buddhist philosophy, this was an all-embracing ideology and metaphysic which became the basis of competitive civil-service exams. Under its influence, Buddhism was increasingly seen as fit only for the masses. The decline of Buddhism under this reformulated expression of indigenous Chinese beliefs is in some way akin to its decline in India under Hinduism, a reformulated Brahmanism. In both cases, a religion or philosophy closely tied to a national culture came to overshadow a universal religion from which it borrowed. In time, however, it became quite common for people's practice to draw on Confucianism, Taoism and Buddhism.

In the Mongolian Yuan dynasty (1280–1368), state patronage increased again, though it was mainly for Northern Buddhism. Early in the Ming dynasty (1368–1644), Buddhism had a small revival due to initial state encouragement, but then the control of education by Confucian scholars, and the prevention of Buddhists being state officials, led to a decline in Buddhist scholarship. Popular Buddhism still thrived, however, though it became increasingly mingled with Taoism and folk religion. In the Ch'ing, or Manchu dynasty (1644–1911), Buddhism continued to be criticized by Neo-Confucian propaganda, but in the seventeenth century it was spread to the island of Taiwan by Chinese immigrants.

VIETNAM AND KOREA

Śrāvakayāna and Mahāyāna Buddhism had reached north Vietnam, from both China and India, by the third century AD. The Pure Land school was influential at the popular level from the ninth century, and Thien (Ch. Ch'an) became the most influential school in the monasteries. From the tenth century, Buddhism flourished among all classes of people, and state patronage began, with Thien monks being the learned cultural elite.

In the south, Hinduism and Śrāvakayāna and Mahāyāna Buddhism reached the kingdom of Champā by the third century AD. By around 900 AD, a mix of the Mahāyāna and Śaivism was patronized by the rulers. In the fifteenth century, an invasion from the north led to the subsequent dominance of the Chinese-based form of the Mahāyāna over all of Vietnam, though Theravāda continued to exist in the south near to Cambodia. A revival of Confucianism as the state ideology led to a gradual decline in Buddhism, however, and from the late sixteenth century, Catholic Christianity, spread by Spanish then French missionaries, had some success in the south. In the eighteenth century, Buddhism had something of a revival.

The indigenous religion of Korea is a form of shamanism, as in many cultures, and this continues to this day. By the late fourth century, Buddhism had reached the north and south-east, and by the sixth century it had penetrated the whole of the Korean peninsula, bringing much of Chinese culture with it. In the sixth and seventh centuries, Korean monks studying in China brought back most of the schools of Chinese Buddhism. Buddhism became the religion of the elite, with its Pure Land form having some success among the common people. Confucianism was the philosophy of the lower aristocracy, however. During the Silla period (688–935), Buddhism became a dominant force in society, with Son (Ch. Ch'an) becoming a major school from the ninth century. In the Koryo period (935–1392), Buddhism was very influential, being a popular as well as aristocratic religion from the twelfth century. There was considerable state patronage, and Buddhist monks succeeded, in 1036, in getting the death penalty abolished. The entire Chinese Canon was printed in the twelfth century and a new edition was printed in the thirteenth century, using 81,258 wooden printing blocks (which are still in existence). In the fourteenth century, Buddhism dominated cultural life.

The unconventional monk-cum-layman Won Hyo (617–86) wrote extensive commentaries on the doctrines and *Sūtras* emphasized by all the competing schools, seeking to harmonize them around the idea of the 'One Mind'. His writings were influential in China, and in Korea he was the first to develop the syncretistic trend which was to become common. After the introduction of Son in the ninth century, however, there was considerable rivalry between it, emphasizing mind-to-mind oral teaching, and the other, *Sūtra*-based schools, particularly Hwaom (Ch. Hua-yen). Son also argued for a 'sudden' approach to realization, rather than a gradualist one. Uich'on (1055–1101) was the first to attempt a reconciliation between what he saw as one-sided approaches emphasizing study or meditation, instead of a balance of the two. His *rapprochement* was based on a revival of the Ch'ont'ae (Ch. T'ien-t'ai) school, but after his death this just became another contending school. The person most responsible for the harmonizing trend of Korean Buddhism was the Son monk Chinul (1158–1210), who also established a truly Korean form of Son. Unusually, he used the *Sūtras* to guide his Son practice, and so came to teach the usefulness of scriptural study. As in traditional Son, he accepted the central importance of sudden insights into one's Buddha-nature. He also accepted, however, that many people needed to mature such insights by gradual cultivation of wholesome states, while seeing that these and defilements were 'empty'. He drew on the practices of several schools in a pragmatic way, according to the needs of people of different capacities. Essentially, however, he developed a synthesis of Son with the philosophy and practices of Hwaom. In the fourteenth century, the Lin-chi *kung-an* method, which he had begun to experiment with, became the normative Son method.

Buddhism suffered a reversal in the Yi dynasty (1392–1910), when Neo-Confucianism from China came to be adopted as the state ideology. In the early fifteenth century, monastery lands were confiscated, monasteries were reduced to 242, then 88, and schools were reduced to seven, then to two umbrella organizations. These were the Son, or Meditation school, dominated by Son, but including Kyeyul (Ch. Lu), Ch'ont'ae and Milgyo (Ch. Chen-yen), and the Kyo, or Textual school, which included the remaining schools. Government anti-Buddhist measures were at their height in the early sixteenth century; monks were banned from entering the capital (1623), and aristocrats' children forbidden from ordaining. Buddhism therefore retreated to mountain monasteries, and ticked over as a religion of the masses, as in China, with a revival developing in the 1890s.

JAPAN

Early history

The indigenous religious tradition of Japan is Shintō, the 'Way of the Gods', which is based on worship of a range of divine beings, each known as a *kami*. Some are seen as personalized creative forces, many as impersonal forces present in notable natural objects and animals, and some as extraordinary humans: anything awe-inspiring or mysterious can be seen as a *kami*. The tradition did not have a strong ethical dimension, but it had a developed appreciation of natural beauty, and a concern for ritual purity.

Buddhism first officially reached Japan in AD 538, when a Korean king sent ambassadors with a Buddha-image, scriptures, and a group of monks. Subsequently, it brought much of Chinese civilization, including Confucianism and Taoism, to a country in the process of developing a centralized monarchy. Buddhism was at first adopted through the appeal of its art and ritual, the protective power offered by 'merit' making and magical rites, and the power of its ethic to encourage unity among rival clans. The pious and learned Regent, prince Shōtoku (573–622), firmly implanted Buddhism by making it the state religion, with responsibility for the welfare of Japan, and made Confucianism the state philosophy. From this early period onwards, Buddhism had links with the power of the state.

In the Nara period (710–84), the devout emperor Shōmu ordered the building of temples throughout the land. Monks acted as scribes, thus introducing writing, and helped open up a country-wide road system. Six schools of Chinese Buddhism were introduced, the most influential being the Kegon (Ch. Hua-yen). In Nara, the capital, Shōmu built a temple enshrining a 16-metre tall image of Vairocana: the central, *Dharma*-body Buddha according to the Kegon school. This image represented the centre of both spiritual and temporal power in the realm. Just as Kegon saw ultimate reality as interpenetrating phenomenal reality without these impeding each other, so the power of the emperor was seen as interpenetrating Japanese society. This notion fitted well with the blend of collectivism and individualism found in Japanese culture. A Nara *kami* was also recognized as a *Bodhisattva* and made the protector of the main temple.

Nara Buddhism was primarily for the elite. It attracted wealth and also politically ambitious monks, who had been ordered to ordain for the 'merit' of the ruler. Consequently it became corrupt and politically meddlesome. The capital was therefore moved to Kyoto at the start of the Heian period (794–1185). Japanese Buddhism now came of age.

The Japanese monk Saichō (767–822) introduced the Tendai (Ch. T'ien-t'ai) school from China in 805. Its head temple-monastery was set up on Mount Hiei, near Kyoto, where Saichō established a twelve-year training regime of study, meditation and monastic discipline. This became the most important temple in the land, and housed 30,000 monks in its heyday. The Japanese monk Kūkai (774–835) brought the Mantrayāna Shingon school from China in 816, establishing its central temple on Mount Kōya, fifty miles from the capital. He helped develop the present written form of Japanese, had a notable impact on the arts, and popularized many protective rites and liturgies. Shingon's colourful and complex rites came to supplant Tendai influence at the royal court, and the school also had some influence on Tendai itself. Shingon practitioners aimed to establish contact with various holy powers, and realize their identity with Vairocana Buddha.

While the Tendai and Shingon schools flourished at the court, devotion to Amitābha and Avalokiteśvara was being spread among the people. Shintō remained strong in the countryside, though it came to be synthesized with Buddhism in a form known as Ryōbu, or 'Dual aspect', Shintō. In this, the Shingon and Tendai schools taught that major *kamis* were manifestations of heavenly Buddhas and *Bodhisattvas*, the sun-goddess Amaterasu being a form of Vairocana. In Shintō shrines, images of the corresponding Buddhist holy beings were set up, and Shintō borrowed heavily from Buddhism, as well as Confucianism and Taoism, to systematize and strengthen itself.

In late Heian times, the Tendai and Shingon schools became decadent and a period of social, political and religious chaos occurred, such that the 'period of the latter-day *Dharma*' (*mappō*) was seen to have started in 1052. During the troubled Kamakura period (1192–1333), rule was by military Shōguns and the samurai, or warrior-knight, class. The latter helped Buddhism spread to the people, however, and thus put down deep roots. Five new schools began, as there was a move towards simpler forms of Buddhism which saw themselves as more practical than the long, complex Tendai path, and more open than esoteric Shingon ritual. All were founded by monks who had gone through the Tendai training on Mount Hiei, but felt it to have become corrupt. In their different ways, all attached importance to the quality of faith. Japanese Buddhist schools had harder edges than in other Buddhist lands, and became more like separate sects, with their own specific lay followers. They also tended to split into many sub-sects over time.

The Pure Land schools

Aspects of Pure Land practice existed in the Tendai synthesis, and during the tenth century various unorthodox Tendai monks had begun to spread devotion to Amida (Skt Amitābha) among the people. The school did not take off until the Kamakura era, though, under the leadership of Hōnen (1133–1212) and Shinran (1173–1263). Hōnen was a scholar-monk who, at forty-three, came to view the Tendai path as too difficult a means to enlightenment in the degenerate *mappō* age. He therefore humbly turned to the 'easy path' of reliance on Amida and his 'original vow' to save all. Leaving Mount Hiei, he popularized the practice of *nembutsu* in Kyoto for many years, and wrote a work emphasizing a sincere and simple faith in Amida. He was disrobed and banished from Kyoto, however, as the Tendai authorities did not like him going against orthodoxy. The aged Hōnen, however, just took this as an opportunity to preach in the countryside, feeling concern lest the divine powers which he saw as protecting him would punish those opposing his message. He did not himself found a new school (*shū*), but one developed from his followers. These comprised the first Japanese Buddhist group independent of state power, uniting people of different classes. Harassment strengthened their unity, so that they eventually split off from Tendai to become the Jōdo-shū, or 'Pure Land School'.

Shinran left Mount Hiei to follow Hōnen, going into exile with him and then travelling widely to popularize Amida-devotion among the poor and the samurai. He felt incapable of attaining enlightenment by his own efforts, so his last resort was faith in Amida – though he did not know whether the *nembutsu* would lead to the Pure Land or hell.

He felt that humans were helpless sinners, full of passion and depravity, ignorant of what is truly good or evil. His interpretation of Hōnen's message made it simpler and more extreme. People must give up any hopeless attempt at 'self-power' and should beware lest the deliberate cultivation of virtue or wisdom leads to pride and lack of faith in Amida. Hōnen taught that, as even wicked people could be reborn in Sukhāvatī, then good ones certainly could be; Shinran taught that, as even good people could be reborn there, 'wicked' ones stood an even better chance: an idea paralleling the Christian concept of the 'salvation of sinners'. Salvation comes from gratefully accepting Amida's saving grace, not by any good works. Even a person's faith comes from grace, for the all-pervading power of Amida can be found within one, prompting the Buddha-nature to overcome arrogance and sin.

For Hōnen, *nembutsu* recitation was the central religious act, but worship of other Buddhas and *Bodhisattvas* was still accepted. One should seek to improve oneself and practise frequent repetitions of the *nembutsu* to make salvation more certain. Only one's attitude could make this a form of 'self-power', not the number of recitations. Shinran taught, however, that one sincere recitation was sufficient; after this, recitations should be done simply to thank Amida for already having saved one. Repetition to aid salvation was a form of 'self-power'. As it is so easy to slip into the way of 'self-power', Shinran taught that 'other-power' was the difficult path, not the 'easy path' (see p. 153). While salvation by pure grace is very unlike the early Buddhist emphasis on self-reliance, it does share with it the ideal of 'letting go'. Early Buddhism advocated letting go of all conditioned phenomena so as to undermine the 'I am' conceit, while Shinran advocated letting go of 'self-power' into the saving power of Amida. Both aim to overcome egoism, but the early Buddhists saw this as possible by using and developing inner resources through practising the *Dhamma* made available by Gotama, while Shinran saw the resources as coming from Amida.

While most of Hōnen's monastic followers retained celibacy, Shinran abandoned it when he dreamt that Avalokiteśvara told him to marry. He regarded monasticism as unnecessary for salvation, and marriage as a realistic admission of human weakness. He thus initiated a kind of married hereditary clergy, and advocated the family as the centre of religious life. Though an aristocrat by birth, he humbly described himself as an 'ignorant baldhead', addressing his followers as 'fellow believers'. In time, these formed the Jōdo-shin-shū, or 'True Pure Land School', also known as the Shin-shū.

The Zen schools

Zen meditation had been included in Tendai, and Ch'an masters had visited from China, but Zen never caught on as a separate school until the Kamakura period. The monk Eisai (1141–1215) first introduced it from China, in its Rinzai (Ch. Lin-chi) form. He experienced opposition from Tendai monks when he said that Zen was the best form of practice, but his adaptability ensured that Zen took root, for he also gave Tendai, Shingon and Ritsu (Ch. Lu) teachings. When it was said that Zen would have a debilitating effect on people, he argued that it would strengthen them and protect the land. Indeed, Zen's meditational and ethical discipline, and indifference to death, appealed to the samurai, who were thereby better able to resist two attempted Mongolian invasions in 1274 and 1281. Eisai gained the protection of a Shōgun at the capital Kamakura, and established the long-lasting alliance between Rinzai and the samurai. This can be seen as an example of 'skilful means', in the form of an adaptation of Buddhism to the way of life of a particular group of people.

While Rinzai Zen was mainly successful among the samurai, Sōtō (Ch. Ts'ao-tung) Zen had a more popular appeal, becoming known as 'farmers' Zen'. It was introduced by Dōgen (1200–1253), perhaps the greatest figure in Japanese Buddhism. This religious genius, admired by all Japanese, gave Zen both an identity fully separate from Tendai, and a more Japanese form. As a Tendai monk, a problem which plagued him was: if people already have the Buddha-nature, why do they need to exert themselves in religious practice to attain Buddhahood? His quest for an answer took him to a Rinzai temple, and then to China. There he met a master who sparked off an awakening in him. In 1227, he returned to Japan, and though he did not want to found a new school, his single-minded advocation of Zen meant that one formed around him. He attracted many pupils, monastic and lay, male and female, and several times had to move to a bigger temple to accommodate his community. He emphasized a strict and simple life of monastic discipline and *zazen*, or 'sitting meditation', and preferred to have a few good pupils than a richly patronized monastery with many sham ones.

Dōgen left many writings and, like Eisai and Chinul, was critical of the late Ch'an neglect of the *Sūtras*, seeing these as in accord with the direct mind-to-mind transmission of truth. He was himself widely read in Śrāvakayāna and Mahāyāna *Sūtras*, and felt that study was acceptable provided it was done to support practice, and not for its own sake: 'It is you who gets lost in the *Sūtras*, not the *Sūtras* that lead you astray.'

In his reading, Dōgen was deeply impressed by the personal example of the historical Buddha, whom he saw as having lived a simple ascetic life of constant exertion for the benefit of others. For Zen, Śākyamuni became less of a glorious heavenly being, and returned to being more of a human-like teacher and example. In line with this, both Ch'an and Zen have had a liking for the early *Arhat* followers of the Buddha. For Dōgen, reading the *Sūtras* was seen as leading to faith in the Buddha and ultimate reality. Such faith was also roused by experience of impermanence and suffering – Dōgen's parents died when he was young – so that the *Dharma* was looked to as a way beyond these. Faith should lead to respect for any Buddhist object or practice, and should lead to trust in one's Zen teacher.

Dōgen advocated *zazen*, or 'sitting meditation', as a return to the true Buddhism of the Buddha, a natural and easy method open to all and encompassing all other practices. He criticized the Rinzai reliance on the *kōan* as one-sidedly mental, and stressed the importance of also training the body by correctly using the 'lotus' meditation posture of the Buddhas. *Zazen* is not seen as a 'method' to 'attain' enlightenment, but is itself enlightenment, a way of simply exhibiting one's innate Buddha-nature. Thus did Dōgen resolve the problem which set him on his spiritual quest. A person must sit in *zazen* with constant awareness, and with faith that he is already a Buddha. The process is one of self-forgetting in which the Buddha-nature gradually unfolds its infinite potential throughout one's life. As an aid to this, physical, mental, moral and intellectual discipline provides a fitting framework for a life of selfless action.

The Nichiren school

The Nichiren school is named after the monk Nichiren (1222–82). This fisherman's son aimed to reform Tendai by a single-minded advocacy of its chief scripture, the Lotus *Sūtra*, which he regarded as expressing the essence of Buddhism. He saw himself both as the successor to the founder of T'ien-t'ai, and as the incarnation of a *Bodhisattva* which the Lotus *Sūtra* said would protect its teachings in the *mappō* age. He was probably influenced by a kind of Tendai meditation which involved worship and recitation of the Lotus *Sūtra*, and circumambulation of a copy of it.

In 1253, he started a campaign to convert Japan to faith in the Lotus *Sūtra*. He saw a number of natural calamities as a product of national degeneracy, and predicted the attempted Mongol invasion of 1274. He was a patriot who had a mission to save Japan, saying that it would prosper when it revered true Buddhism, and would be the source from which this spread to the whole world, bringing about a golden age. He advocated a 'self-power' method that was easy for all to practise. This was to chant the formula *Na-mu myō-hō ren-ge-kyō*, 'Honour to the Lotus *Sūtra* of the True *Dharma*', and to contemplate a wooden plaque or scroll on which this invocation was written. This would activate the Buddha-nature, lead to the moral uplift of the individual and society, and to the attainment of Buddhahood. Nichiren castigated all other schools as wicked ruiners of the country, and said that the state should wipe them out. This was because they all neglected the Śākyamuni of the Lotus *Sūtra* in some way. The Pure Land schools worshipped the imaginary Amida, the Zen schools revered the earthly Śākyamuni, but not the heavenly one, and the Shingon worshipped Vairocana. If Shinran wondered if the *nembutsu* recitation would lead to hell, Nichiren was sure that it would! Such virulent denunciation is most uncharacteristic of Buddhism, and Nichiren cuts a figure more like an Old Testament prophet than a traditional Buddhist sage. His pronouncements meant that he was nearly executed, and was twice banished. He took all such sufferings in the spirit of a martyr, seeing them as the results of his karma and as helping to purify him. Moreover, his charismatic style of fierce evangelism and personal courage attracted many, who came to form the Nichiren school.

Later history

The Ashikaga period (1333–1573) was one of almost constant turmoil, with simultaneous rule by two emperors followed by rule by rival warring Shōguns. During this time, Rinzai Zen had great influence. Zen temples were havens of peace, culture, education and art, with Rinzai fostering developments in painting, calligraphy, sculpture, printing, gardening, architecture, literature, theatre and medicine.

In the Jōdo-shū, Ryōyo (1341–1420) developed the idea that the Pure

Land is in fact everywhere, and is to be entered by a changed attitude of mind during life, rather than at death. In the Jōdo-shin-shū, the 'second founder', Rennyo (1415–99), opposed a strand of thought which said that moral conduct was irrelevant to those with faith in Amida. He stressed that sincere faith implied a pure heart, and that a moral life expressed gratitude to Amida. He taught that other schools should not be criticized, but that Amida alone should be worshipped as the 'original Buddha' who includes all others. That is, Amida was the embodiment of the *Dharma*-body.

Jōdo-shin-shū became centred on fortified temples, with its armed followers acting to defend the faith. In the last century of the Ashikaga period, the sect organized and led peasant uprisings and became the ruling power in one region of Japan. Tendai and Shingon also maintained troops, some of them monks, and in the sixteenth century Nichiren Buddhists attacked the Shin and Tendai headquarters. Such unbuddhist behaviour can perhaps be seen as the product of violent times, where political power was up for grabs and ambition rose to the surface.

Two powerful Shōguns then put an end to military monasteries, leading up to the Tokugawa era (1603–1867), when the country was unified under a military dictatorship. During this time, Japan closed its doors to all but a few traders from the outside world. In the sixteenth century, the Portuguese had brought Christianity to Japan. Some rulers had favoured it as a foil to the power of Buddhist monasteries, and had propagated it with violence. Now, it was ruthlessly persecuted as being a possible conduit of foreign influence, and struggled on as the secret religion of a few.

In 1614, Buddhism was made the established Church and arm of the state, with all people having to register and periodically attend at their nearest temple. Buddhism was not short of financial support, but became too comfortable and moribund. The code of the influential samurai contained several unbuddhist elements, such as the obligation to revenge and a disregard for life. An increasing secularism also developed as people moved to growing cities. Nevertheless, Buddhist scholarship continued, primary schools were run, and the Rinzai master Hakuin (1685–1768) revitalized the use of the *kōan* and gave many popular sermons. The Zen layman Bashō (1644–94) also popularized the seventeen-syllable *Haiku* poem as a religious art-form.

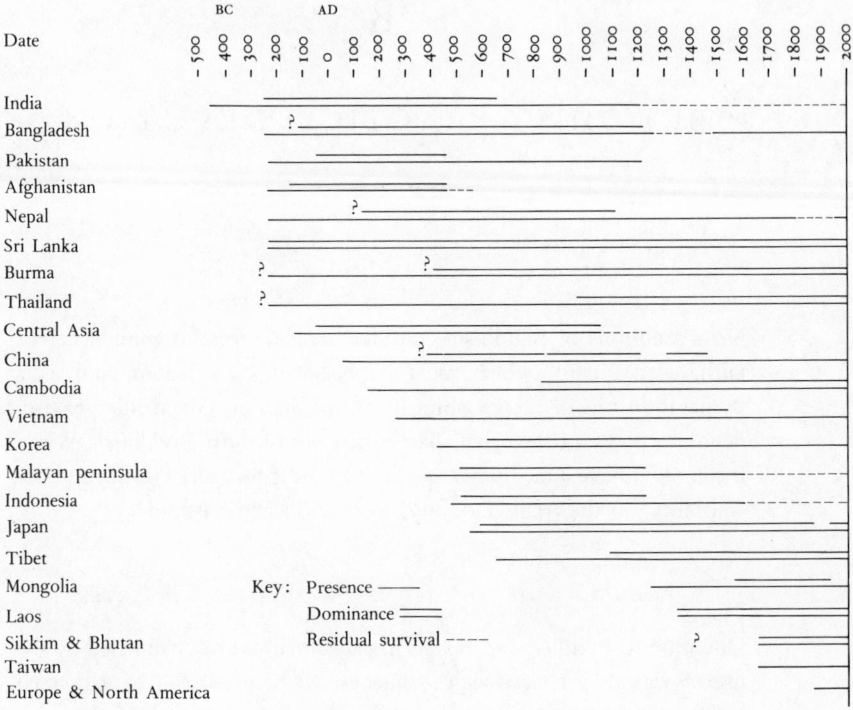

Figure 3 Chart showing the presence, dominance and residual survival of Buddhism in different lands.

Neo-Confucianism became increasingly influential as the state ideology, however, and from the eighteenth century a new form of Shintō began to be developed as the 'true religion' of the Japanese, a pure and spontaneous expression of religiosity unlike the 'artificialities' of foreign Buddhism and Confucianism. In 1868, this culminated in a *coup d'état* which ended the Tokugawa Shōgunate, who supported these foreign traditions. Power was restored to the emperor, seen as a *kami* who had descended from the sun goddess. Soon after, Japan opened its doors to Western influence.

8

BUDDHIST PRACTICE: DEVOTION

Most traditions of Buddhism consider *saddhā*, 'trustful confidence' or faith, as a quality which must be balanced by wisdom, and as a preparation for, or accompaniment of, meditation. Given this proviso, devotion plays an important part in the life of most Buddhists. While it can often have a meditative quality to it, it is formally classified under 'morality' in the triad 'morality, meditation and wisdom'.

FOCUSES AND LOCATIONS OF DEVOTIONAL ACTS

Devotion to Buddhas and *Bodhisattvas* is focussed or channelled by the use of various artefacts such as images. At home, it can be expressed before a home shrine, which may be as simple as a high shelf and a picture in a quiet corner. In temples, there will always be some kind of shrine-room or image-hall, where large images are housed: in Theravāda temples, these are of Gotama, sometimes flanked by his two chief *Arahat* disciples; in Mahāyāna ones, there is often a group of three heavenly Buddhas, or a Buddha and two *Bodhisattvas*, perhaps with images of sixteen or eighteen chief *Arahat* disciples along the walls of the hall. There will always be accommodation for monks and/or nuns, or, as in Japan, married clerics. Thus temples are in fact temple-monasteries, Theravāda ones often being known by the Pali term for a monastery, *vihāra*. There is frequently a *Stūpa* of some kind, including the multi-roofed form, known in the West as a Pagoda, which evolved in China. Most *Stūpas* are such that one cannot enter them, except for the East Asian multi-roofed form. They can be anything from a metre high, with some large ones being the major feature of a temple. The famous Shwe-dāgon *Stūpa* in Rangoon, capital of Burma, is 112 metres tall (see Plate 6). It is said to contain some hairs of Gotama, and

Plate 6 The Shwe-dāgon *Stūpa*, Rangoon, Burma, complete with scaffolding for re-gilding.

belongings of three previous Buddhas. Because of the sanctity of these, it has been encased in gold plate and gold leaf, and topped by an orb studded in diamonds. Temples may also have: a meeting/preaching hall; a separate meditation hall, as in Zen temples; a *Bodhi*-tree, as at many Theravāda temples; a library and administrative buildings, and finally shrines for one of more gods or nature spirits. Most temples are free-standing, but throughout the Buddhist world there are also natural and specially excavated caves, whose cool, calm, rather awesome interiors have been used as temples.

Devotional artefacts may be paid for by a community or an individual. In either case, the community can share in its embellishment: in South-east Asia, images are often gradually gilded with individual squares of gold-leaf. As giving generates 'merit', which can be shared, artefacts may be specially donated, perhaps for the benefit of a new-born child, someone who has recently died, success in a business venture, or an end to a war. In 1961 the Burmese government organized the making of 60,000 temporary sand *Stūpas* to avert a world calamity predicted by astrologers throughout Asia. The motive of generating 'merit' means that temples often have more images than are 'needed', and new *Stūpas* may be built beside crumbling old ones. This is because there is generally more joy in starting something new than in repairing something. Greater joy leaves a stronger wholesome 'imprint' on the mind, and so is seen as producing better quality karmic fruits. In Burma, '*Stūpa* Builder' is a title of respect, and 'merit' *Stūpas* are so popular that several can be seen in any landscape.

BOWING, OFFERINGS AND CHANTING

Most Buddhist devotional acts are not congregational in essence, though they are frequently occasions for coming together in a shared activity and experience. In the home, they are often carried out in the morning and/or evening. Temple-visits can be at any time, though they are most common at festivals, or at special 'observance days'. On visiting a temple, a person performs acts which amount to showing devotion to the 'three refuges'. The Buddha is represented by image, *Stūpa* and *Bodhi*-tree; the *Dhamma* is represented by a sermon, or informal teachings which the monks may give, and the *Sangha* is represented by the monks. Devotion at home or temple is expressed by *pūjā*: 'reverencing' or 'honouring' which involves bowing, making offerings, and chanting.

In Buddhist cultures, people bow on many occasions. Children bow to parents and teachers; adults bow to monks, nuns, *bLamas* and the elderly; and monks bow to those ordained for longer than themselves. Such lowering of the head acknowledges someone else as having more experience of life or of spiritual practice, and develops respect and humility. It is natural, then, to bow before sacred objects which point towards the highest reality, and also to locate a Buddha-image on the highest 'seat' in a room. Within a shrine-room or the compound surrounding a *Stūpa* or *Bodhi*-tree, humility is also shown by not wearing shoes; for in ancient times, wearing shoes was a sign of wealth and status.

Bowing before sacred objects is generally done three times, so as to show respect to the 'three refuges'. A person stands or kneels with palms joined in a gesture known as *namaskāra*. They are held at the chest and forehead or, in Northern Buddhism, at the head, lips and chest: symbolizing respect offered by mind, speech and body. From a kneeling position, a person then places the elbows, hands and head on the ground. In Northern Buddhism, a fuller form known as a 'grand prostration' involves laying full-length on the ground. Devotion is also shown by circumambulation of *Stūpas*, *Bodhi*-trees and temples, which in Northern Buddhism may be done by repeated prostrations. In Eastern Buddhism, too, an important practice is repeated bowing before an image in a spirit of repentance.

Offerings are usually accompanied by appropriate chanted verses. Together, these aim to arouse joyful and devout contemplation of the qualities of a holy being, and aspiration for spiritual progress. Such acts consequently generate 'merit'. The most common offerings are flowers. One Theravāda flower-offering verse says, in Pali

> This mass of flowers, fresh-hued, odorous and choice,
> I offer at the blessed lotus-like feet of the Lord of sages.
> With diverse flowers, the Buddha/*Dhamma*/*Saṅgha* I revere;
> And through this 'merit' may there be release.
> Just as this flower fades, so my body goes towards destruction.

This combines joyous reverence, aspiration, and reflection on the impermanence of human life. A Zen flower-offering verse aspires that the 'flowers of the mind' should 'bloom in the springtime of enlightenment'.

The pleasant odour of smouldering incense-sticks frequently greets a person on entering a Buddhist temple. A Pali incense-offering verse

Plate 7 A Thai Buddha-image and offerings, in the shrine-room of a meditation centre in Manchester, England

refers to the Buddha as 'He of fragrant body and fragrant face, fragrant with infinite virtues'. This reflects the idea that the Buddha had an 'odour of sanctity': a certain 'air' about him suggestive of his glorious character and virtues. Incense both reminds a person of this and also creates a sense of delight, which can then be focussed on the Buddha. Another common offering is the light of small lamps or candles, a reminder of Buddhas as 'Enlightened' or 'Awakened' beings who give light to the world through their teachings. A Theravāda offering verse thus describes the Buddha as 'the lamp of the three worlds, dispeller of darkness'.

In Northern Buddhism, butter-lamps of finely wrought silver often burn perpetually before images. It is also common for seven kinds of offerings to be set before an image. Water 'for the face' and 'for the feet' symbolize hospitality, while flowers, incense, lamps, perfume and food represent the five senses, ideally expressing a devotee's dedication of his whole being to spiritual development. The offerings are placed in seven bowls, or water and grain in these are visualized as being the offerings. The devotee also uses *mudrā*'s, ritual gestures representing offerings such as flowers, a lamp, or the whole world. He may additionally offer a white cotton or silk *kha-btags* (pron. *kuttha*), generally known as a 'scarf of felicity', to an image. These are normally used as a friendship-offering to put a relationship on a good footing. Here they are used to form a bond of friendship with a holy being.

In all schools of Buddhism, chanting is very common as a vehicle for devotion or other ceremonial acts. Its use derives from early Buddhism, when Indian society made little use of writing, and a learned person was 'much-heard' rather than 'well-read'. Chanting aided accurate memory of the Buddha's teachings, as it has a rhythm which encourages the mind to flow on from word to word, and lacks melody, which might demand that the sound of some words be distorted. It is also a public medium, so that errors of memory could be known and corrected. After the teachings were written down, it was still thought better that they be well memorized, and chanting had also become part of devotional life.

Buddhist chanting is neither singing nor a monotonous dirge. While being deep-toned and slightly solemn, it holds the interest with its small variations of pitch and rhythm. It is particularly impressive when a group of monks and/or nuns chant, for they may use different keys, all blending into a harmonious whole. The chants are usually in ancient languages, such as Pali or old Tibetan, thus giving them an added air of sanctity. This, plus their sound-quality and accompanying thoughts, generates a mixture of uplifting joy, often felt as a glow of warmth in the chest, and contemplative calm. Such states tend to arise even in those listening to a chant, if they do so with a relaxed but attentive mind. Thus monks and nuns can transmit something of the tranquillity of their way of life when chanting for the laity. Many monks know the full meaning of the chants, as they know the relevant language to some extent, and can explain them to the laity. Vernacular chants also exist.

In all traditions, the most common chants are short verbal formulas, which may be strung together or repeated to form longer continuous chants. A very common Southern Buddhist chant, honouring Gotama Buddha, is: *Namo tassa bhagavato, arahato, sammā-sambuddhassa*, 'Honour to the Lord, *Arahat*, perfectly and completely Enlightened One!' This is repeated three times and is usually followed by a chanted avowal of commitment to the 'three refuges' and five moral precepts.

In all traditions, rosaries can be used to count off repeated chants. In Southern Buddhism, a *mantra* may be used such as '*du sa ni ma*; *sa ni ma du*; *ni ma du sa*; *ma du sa ni*'. This is based on the initial letters of the words for the Four Holy Truths: *dukkha*, *samudaya*, *nirodha*, *magga*. It concentrates the mind, keeps it alert, and opens it to understanding. A devotional rosary-chant used in Southern Buddhism is '*Buddha*, *Dhamma*, *Sangha*'.

THE REFUGES

The key expression of commitment to Buddhism is 'taking the refuges'. The ancient formula for this, in its Pali form, begins: '*Buddhaṃ saraṇaṃ gacchāmi*, *Dhammaṃ saraṇaṃ gacchāmi*, *Sanghaṃ saraṇaṃ gacchāmi*.' This affirms that 'I go to the Buddha as refuge, I go to the *Dhamma* as refuge, I go to the *Sangha* as refuge.' Each affirmation is then repeated 'for the second time...' (*dutiyam pi*...) and 'for the third time...' (*tatiyam pi*...). The threefold repetition marks off the recitation from ordinary uses of speech, and ensures that the mind dwells on the meaning of each affirmation at least once. The notion of a 'refuge', here, is not that of a place to hide, but of something the thought of which purifies, uplifts and strengthens the heart. Orientation towards these three guides to a better way of living is experienced as a joyful haven of calm, a firm 'island amidst a flood', in contrast to the troubles of life. The 'refuges' remind the Buddhist of calm, wise, spiritual people and states of mind, and so help engender these states. Their value is denoted by the fact that they are also known as the *Ti-ratana* or 'three jewels': spiritual treasures of supreme worth.

The meaning of each refuge varies somewhat between different traditions. The Theravāda understanding is expressed in a frequently used chant drawn from the Pali Canon. On the Buddha, it affirms: 'Thus he is the Lord: because he is an *Arahat*, perfectly and completely Enlightened, endowed with knowledge and (good) conduct, Well-gone [to *Nibbāna*], knower of worlds, an incomparable charioteer for the training of persons, teacher of gods and humans, Buddha, Lord.' The 'Buddha' referred to here is primarily Gotama, who is regarded with reverence and gratitude as the rediscoverer and exemplifier of *Dhamma*, who also showed others how to live by and experience it. As benefits of living by *Dhamma* are experienced, this reverence and gratitude naturally develop greater depth. One recently popularized Sinhalese liturgy states, 'Thus infinite, possessing measureless qualities, unequalled, equal to the unequalled, god to the gods, to me the Lord, my own Buddha mother, my own Buddha father, the orb of dawn to the darkness of delusion...'[3] The Buddha refuge does not only refer to Gotama, but also to previous and future Buddhas, and to the principle of enlightenment as supremely worthy of attainment. In this respect, the first refuge can also be taken as a pointer to the faculty of wisdom developing within the practitioner.

The Pali chant on *Dhamma* is: 'Well-expounded by the Lord is *Dhamma*, visible here and now, timeless, inviting investigation, leading onward [to the stages of sanctity and finally *Nibbāna*], to be experienced within by the wise.' This emphasizes *Dhamma* as immediately accessible to all, and as of progressively greater benefit. As refuge, *Dhamma* is explained as the Holy Path (*Khp.A.*19). More generally, it refers to: (a) *pariyatti*, or the body of teachings, (b) *paṭipatti* or the 'practice' of the way, and (c) *paṭivedha*, or 'realization' of the stages of sanctity – in the highest sense, *Nibbāna* itself. *Dhamma*, then, is to be heard/read and understood, practised, and realized. It is the 'law-orderliness' inherent in nature, the 'Basic Pattern' in which phenomena occur according to the Conditioned Arising principle, from appropriate conditions.

The Pali chant on the *Sangha*, or Community is: 'Of good conduct is the

the Community of the disciples of the Lord; of upright conduct...; of wise conduct...; of proper conduct...; that is to say, the four pairs of persons, the eight kinds of individuals; this Community... is worthy of gifts, hospitality, offerings, and reverential salutation, an incomparable field of "merit" for the world.' Here, the 'four pairs of persons, the eight kinds of individuals' are the Stream-enterer, Once-returner, Non-returner, *Arahat*, and those established on the paths to these spiritual 'fruits'; that is, all who have attained *Nibbāna*, glimpsed it, or are on the brink of glimpsing it. This is the precious *ariya-Sangha*, the Community of 'Holy' persons, who may be found within the monastic *Sangha*, its symbolic representative, or among spiritually advanced laypeople or even gods. Being of exemplary conduct, its members are worthy of gifts and respect; the monastic *Sangha* seeks to emulate them in this. The concept of a 'field of "merit"', is that, just as a seed planted in better ground yields better fruit, so a gift given to a more virtuous person generates more 'merit'. This idea is partly based on the fact that, if one gives to someone of suspect character, one may regret the act somewhat; whereas in giving to a virtuous or holy person, one puts all one's heart into the act and can rejoice at it. Giving also sets up a bond of association. The Holy *Sangha* therefore benefits the world with the opportunity for generating abundant auspicious, purifying 'merit'.

In the Mahāyāna, the 'Three body' doctrine means that the Buddha refuge refers not only to Gotama and other Transformation-body Buddhas, but also, and more importantly, to the heavenly Enjoyment-body Buddhas. In the Pure Land schools, emphasis is primarily or exclusively on Amitābha. In Ch'an/Zen, the emphasis is on the historical Buddha as a heroic, stirring example, but more particularly on the idea of the Buddha-nature within: 'take refuge in the three treasures in your own natures. The Buddha is enlightenment, the *Dharma* is truth, the *Sangha* is purity... take refuge in the Buddha within yourselves... If you do not rely upon your own natures, there is nothing else on which to rely' (*Plat*. sec. 23). Transformation-body Buddhas are also figuratively seen as good and wise thoughts within one's mind, and refuge is taken in 'the future perfect Enjoyment-body in my own physical body' (*Plat*. sec. 20). In the Mahāyāna, the *Dharma* refuge, in its highest sense, refers to the *Dharma*-body, ultimate reality. Holy *Bodhisattvas* are included in the *Sangha* refuge, and taking refuge in them is allied to taking vows, often repeated on a daily basis, to become like them.

In the Mantrayāna of Northern Buddhism, extra refuges are taken. Prior to the three usual ones, a person takes refuge in his *bLama*, the source of his deepening knowledge of the other refuges and regarded as an embodiment of their virtues. After the usual refuges, an individual may then take refuge in his *yi-dam*, a holy being which is his tutelary deity. An adept preparing for training in meditative visualizations must also complete preliminary practices of a devotional and purificatory nature. Five or six such practices are generally given, each of which must be done 100,000 times. One is the 'grand prostration', which is done while holding wooden blocks, to prevent the hands being blistered by repeatedly sliding along the floor (or a special wooden board) to the fully prostrate position. As this is done, the devotee may say: 'I, so-and-so, on behalf of all sentient beings and freely offering my body, speech and mind, bow to the earth in adoration of the Guru and the Three Precious Ones.'[4] Accompanying this affirmation is the visualization of a 'refuge tree': a concourse of holy beings whose radiant light suffuses the devotee. After a period of struggle and pain, the practice is said to induce great joy. It also conduces to a balance of 'self-power' and 'other-power': relying on oneself and on the power of holy beings.

ATTITUDES TO IMAGES

Images always function as reminders of the spiritual qualities of holy beings, if in no other way. When a Theravādin, for example, expresses devotion before an image of Gotama Buddha, he is reminded of his struggle for enlightenment, his virtues, his teachings, and the ideal he represents. He joyfully recollects the Buddha, developing a warm heart and a pure mind. The spiritual qualities expressed by the form of a good image also help to stimulate the arising of such qualities in one who contemplates it.

In Northern and Eastern Buddhism, except perhaps in Ch'an/Zen, images function as more than reminders. Especially in Mantrayāna schools, they are seen as infused with the spirit and power of the being they represent. Moreover, as image and being 'meet' in both being ultimately 'thought-only' or emptiness, the image comes to be seen as an actual form of the being. For this, it must have the traditional form and symbolism and be consecrated. This is done by chanting prayers and *mantras* over it; by placing in it scriptures or relics, and even internal organs of clay, and by completing and wetting the eyes. This associates it with holy sounds and objects, giving it a power-for-good, and animates it, the wet eyes suggesting the response of a living gaze.

Even in Southern Buddhism, a temple image seems to act as more than a reminder; for it is generally thought that it must be consecrated before it can function as a focus for devotion. Consecration involves the placing of relics in the image, and a monk reciting some Pali verses over it. In Sri Lanka, these verses are the ones said to have been spoken by the Buddha immediately after his enlightenment. This harmonizes with the fact that the eyes are often completed at around 5 am., the time at which Gotama became fully enlightened. These two aspects seem to suggest that the consecrated image is seen as a representative of, rather than just a representation of, the Buddha. Other aspects of consecration reinforce this idea. In Sri Lanka, the lay craftsmen completing the eyes act as if this were connecting the image to a source of power which, like electricity, is dangerous if handled carelessly. They ritually prepare themselves for hours, and then only look at the eyes in a mirror while painting them in; until completed, their direct gaze is considered harmful. Some Westernized monks deny that there is any need to consecrate images.

In fact, in Southern Buddhism there is a widely held belief in a kind of 'Buddha-force' which will remain in the world for as long as Buddhism is practised (see p. 67). Indeed, a booklet produced by a Thai temple in London says of the Buddha: 'Although now his physical form no longer exists, his spiritual form, that is his benevolence and great compassion remains in the world.' This attitude is reflected in the way that Southern Buddhists regard relics and *Bodhi*-trees as having a protective power-for-good. The 'Buddha-force' which many believe in is particularly associated with images, especially ones used in devotion for centuries, suggesting that these are seen as having been thus 'charged up' with the Buddha's power. Less educated Southern Buddhists sometimes go so far as to regard the Buddha as still alive as an individual, and as somehow present in consecrated images of himself.

PROTECTIVE CHANTING

In all schools of Buddhism, chanting, or listening to it, is often used as a form of protection. In Southern Buddhism, chanted passages called *paritta*'s, or 'safety-runes' are used. Most are excerpts from the Pali scriptures, the most common one being that on the qualities of the three refuges, as translated above. Other popular ones include: the *Karaṇīya-metta Sutta*, which radiates feelings of lovingkindness to all living beings; the *Mangala Sutta*, which describes such 'blessings' as a good education, generosity, hearing the *Dhamma*, and attaining *Nibbāna*; and the *Ratana Sutta*, which calls down the protection of the gods and praises the 'three jewels' (see *Khp*.2–6 and 8–9). While most *parittas* are used as a general protection, some are used against particular dangers, such as one against death from snake-bite, said in the *Suttas* to have been given by the Buddha specifically as a '*paritta*' (*Khandha paritta*, *A*.II.72). *Parittas* are used, for example, for warding off wild animals, human attackers or ghosts, exorcizing people, curing illnesses, and averting dangers from accidents or natural disasters. They are also used to gain a good harvest, to help pass an exam, to bless a new building, or simple to make 'merit'. There are limits to their power, though. They are said to work only for a virtuous person with confidence in the 'three refuges', and cannot, for example, cure a person of an illness if it is due to his past karma (*Miln*.150–4). Within these limits, the working of *parittas* is seen as involving a number of factors.

Firstly, to chant or listen to a *paritta* is soothing and leads to self-confidence and a calm, pure mind, due to both its sound-quality and meaning. As the mind is in a healthier state, this may cure psychosomatic illnesses, or make a person more alert and better at avoiding the dangers of life. Secondly, chanting a *paritta*, especially one which expresses lovingkindness to all beings, is thought to calm down a hostile person, animal or ghost, making them more well-disposed towards the chanter and listeners. Thirdly, as well as making new 'merit', *paritta*-chanting is thought to stimulate past 'merit' into bringing some of its good results immediately. Fourthly, chanting or listening to a *paritta* is thought to please those gods who are devotees of the Buddha, so that they offer what protection and assistance it is in their power to give. Finally, the spiritual power of the Buddha, the 'greatly compassionate protector' (*Mahā-jayamangala Gāthā paritta*), and of the truth he expressed, seems to be seen as continuing in his words, with its beneficial influence being liberated when these are devoutly chanted. This partly relates to the concept, found in the early texts, of an 'asseveration of truth' (discussed at *Miln*. 119–22). By affirming some genuine virtue of oneself or someone else, or publicly admitting an embarrassing fault, a wonder-working power-for-good is liberated, to the benefit of oneself and others. Accordingly, a *Ratana Sutta* refrain, 'by this truth, may there be well-being!', is repeated after various excellences of the 'three jewels' have been enumerated.

While an ordinary layperson or specialist chanter can activate the power of the Buddha's words by chanting, it is more efficacious for monks to do so. This is because they try to live fully the way of life taught by the Buddha. When members of the monastic *Sangha* chant the *Dhamma*, as taught by the Buddha, there is a powerful combination, of benefit to listening laypeople. To symbolize the protective power passing from the monks, they hold a cord while chanting *paritta*. This is also tied to a Buddha-image, suggesting that the image is being impregnated with the *paritta*'s power, or, equally, that it is discharging some of its previously accumulated power to add to that of the *paritta*. Afterwards, pieces of the '*paritta*-cord' are tied to the laypeople's wrists as a reminder of, and a 'store' of, the *paritta*'s protective power. When the cord is tied on, a Pali verse is uttered which means: 'By the majesty of the power attained by all Buddhas, solitary Buddhas and *Arahats*, I tie on a complete protection.'

In Eastern and Northern traditions, including Ch'an/Zen, chanted formulas used in a similar way to *parittas* are *dhāraṇī*'s, utterances 'preserving' Buddhism and its followers. These are strings of Sanskrit words and syllables, originating as mnemonic formulas summarizing a *Sūtra* or teaching, which may be unintelligible without explanation. The Southern '*du, sa, ni, ma*...' rosary chant quoted above is akin to these.

DEVOTION TO AVALOKITEŚVARA

Devotion to Avalokiteśvara pervades Eastern and Northern Buddhism. A text much used in liturgies is the verse section of the *Avalokiteśvara Sūtra*, an extract from the Lotus *Sūtra*. Expressing profound devotion, this speaks of: 'True regard, serene regard, far-reaching wise regard, regard of pity, compassionate regard, ever longed for, ever looked for! Pure and serene in radiance, wisdom's sun destroying darkness... law of pity, thunder quivering, compassion wondrous as a great cloud, pouring spiritual rain like nectar, quenching the flames of distress!' Statues and paintings of Avalokiteśvara are found in abundance, depicting him in around 130 different ways, each aiming to express some aspect of his nature. In China, as Kuan-yin, 'he' gradually came to be portrayed as female. This may have been because the Chinese saw his compassion as a female quality; it may also have been partly due to the female reference in his *mantra* (see p. 136). Moreover, from the fifth century, some of 'his' popular incarnations were female, and 'he' may also have merged with a pre-Buddhist goddess thought to care for mariners. Kuan-yin thus became an all-compassionate 'mother-goddess', the most popular diety in all of China, being portrayed as a graceful, lotus-holding figure in a white robe (see Plate 8). An artistic form common in Tibet and Japan shows Avalokiteśvara with 'a thousand' arms (fewer, for practical reasons, in statues) and eleven heads (see Plate 9). Seven hands hold various emblems, while the rest represent his boundless skilful means. Each makes a *mudrā*, or 'gesture', denoting 'be fearless', and on its palm is an eye, representing his ever-watchful nature, ready to rush to the aid of beings. His eleven heads are explained by a story that, on seeing so many beings suffering in the hells, his horror and tears caused him momentarily to despair of fulfilling his vow to save all. His head then split into ten pieces, as he said it would if he ever abandoned his resolve. Amitābha Buddha then brought him back to life to renew his vow. Making each of the head-fragments into a new head, he assembled them on Avalokiteśvara's shoulders, and surmounted them with a replica of his own head, symbolizing that he would continue to inspire the *Bodhisattva* in his work. With eleven heads, Avalokiteśvara was now even better equipped to look for beings in need! From Avalokiteśvara's tears, moreover, two forms of Tārā had been born.

The *Avalokiteśvara Sutrā* says that Avalokiteśvara will instantly respond to those who 'with all their mind call upon his name'. 'By virtue of the power of that *Bodhisattva*'s majesty', they will be unburnt by a fire; saved at sea in a storm; the hearts of murdering foes will turn to kindness; as prisoners, guilty or innocent, they will be set free from their chains; merchants will be freed from the dangers of robbers; threatening wild beasts will flee; success will be attained in a court of law or battle, and a woman will have a virtuous child, of the sex of her choice. Devotees will also be freed from attachment, hatred and delusion by 'keeping in mind and remembering' Avalokiteśvara. Much of this is comparable to the power attributed to *paritta*-chanting. The wondrous help of Avalokiteśvara is understood both as a literal

Plate 8 A modern porcelain figure of Kuan-yin.

Plate 9 A *thang-ka* depicting Avalokiteśvara, with offering bowls in front of it.

intervention in the world, perhaps through the aid of a mysterious stranger, or a vision guiding someone through mists on a dangerous mountain, and as coming from the power of a devotee's faith. In the *Śūrangama Sūtra*, it is said that Avalokiteśvara aids beings by awakening them to their compassionate Buddha-nature, and in accordance with this, any act of great kindness may be seen as the 'help' of Avalokiteśvara.

Ch'an/Zen, for which 'To be compassionate is Kuan-yin' (*Plat.* sec. 35), generally understands his/her aid in purely internal spiritual terms: for a 'storm' is anger, 'fire' is desire, 'chains' are simply those of fear, a sense of oppression comes from lack of patience, and animals only threaten one who has ill-will. Accordingly, Ch'an/Zen devotion to Kuan-yin is thought of primarily in terms of 'developing the heart of Kuan-yin': growing the seed of great compassion so that one becomes ever-ready to help others.

In Northern Buddhism, the *Maṇi mantra* (see p. 136). is very popular in invoking the help of Avalokiteśvara and in developing compassion. Accompanied by the click of rosaries, it is frequently heard on the lips of all who have any degree of devotion to Buddhism. It may be uttered as a person goes about his or her business, either under the breath or as an audible rhythmic murmur called 'purring' by the Tibetans. The Tibetans also activate the power of this *mantra*, and generate 'merit', by use of the '*Maṇi* religion wheel', known in the West as a 'prayer wheel'. The formula is carved or painted on the outside of a shorter cylinder, and is written many times on a tightly rolled piece of paper inside. Each revolution of the cylinder is held to be equivalent to the repetition of all the formulas written on and in it, an idea related to that of the Buddha's first sermon as the 'setting in motion of the *Dhamma*-wheel'. '*Maṇi* religion wheels' are of various types. Hand-held ones have cylinders about 7 centimetres long, mounted on handles about 12 centimetres long; a small weight attached to the cylinder on a chain enables it to be spun on a spindle fixed in the handle. Wheels around 25 centimetres high are also fixed in rows along the sides of *Stūpas* or monasteries, so that people can turn them as they circumambulate these. The largest wheels, found at the entrance to temples, may be 4 metres high and 2 metres in diameter, and contain thousands of *Maṇi* formulas, along with scriptures and images. There are also wheels driven by streams or chimney smoke. The *Maṇi mantra* is also carved on stones deposited on hill-top cairns, on rock-faces by the side of paths, on long walls specially built at the approaches to towns, and is printed on 'prayer flags'. 'Merit' accrues to those who pay for any of these or produce them, to all who glance at them, thinking of Avalokiteśvara and his compassion, and even insects who come into contact with them.

DEVOTION TO AMITĀBHA

Devotion to Amitābha Buddha is found within most schools of the Mahāyāna, but is the essence of Pure Land practice, which centres on the 'Buddha invocation' (Ch. *nien-fo*, Jap. *nembutsu*). This is the repetition of '*Nan-mo A-mi-t'o* Fo' (Ch.) or '*Nama Amida Butsu*' (Jap.), translations of the Sanskrit '*Namo Amitābhāya Buddhāya*', meaning 'Hail to Amitābha Buddha'. In China, recitation is done in tune with the steady and natural breath, and may be repeated many times a day, as the practitioner never knows when he has done it the minimum necessary 'ten times' with 'unwavering concentration'. A byproduct of concentration, focussed on Amitābha and the enlightenment attainable in his Pure Land, is that the mind is purified of distracting passions. The *nembutsu* also has a certain *mantra*-like quality, in that it is seen as opening up a channel between a holy being and a devotee: in this case, the channel of grace. Furthermore, when the practice is done wholeheartedly, it becomes spontaneous, and can be seen as reciting itself in a mental space in which the ego has temporarily dissolved. Through association with *nembutsu*-practice, a person's rosary often comes to be a revered object; touching it may immediately start the recitation revolving in the mind, and bring on the associated mental states.

In China, Shan-tao (613–681) came to emphasize the invocation as the 'primary' Pure Land practice. 'Secondary' ones included: chanting the Pure Land *Sūtras*; visualization of Amitābha and his Pure Land; worship of various Buddhas; singing hymns of praise to Amitābha; resolving to be reborn in his land, and developing generosity and compassion by helping the needy, and through vegetarianism. In Japan, the Jōdo-shin school came to put single-minded emphasis on Amitābha Buddha, and on the *nembutsu* as including all other practices, though the secondary practices could be done as expressions of gratitude for

Plate 10 A small Japanese shrine depicting Amitābha and his two *Bodhisattva* helpers. Lacquered wood, with sandalwood Figures; c. 1920.

salvation. The sole aim of the *nembutsu* is to facilitate the awakening of faith; the moment when this truly occurs is seen as a transcendental, atemporal experience in which the devotee is at one with Amitābha in the form of the numinous *nembutsu*. After faith has arisen, any recitation is done solely as an expression of gratitude, often shown by merely wearing a rosary wrapped around the hand. This is also a reminder that 'sinful humans' are but a bundle of passions compared to Amitābha. Devotees express joyful adoration of Amitābha, and liken him to father and mother, so that he is commonly called *Oyasama*, 'The Parent'.

Plate 10 shows a small Japanese shrine which opens out to show Amitābha in meditation, with the meeting of his index fingers and thumbs indicating that devotees should give up 'self-power' and rely on 'other-power' for salvation. Amitābha appears as a serene and gentle being, who draws the devotee to him by his compassion. His radiant form, floating on a lotus, is flanked by his two *Bodhisattva* helpers: Avalokiteśvara (offering three wish-granting jewels on a lotus) to his left, and Mahāsthāmaprāpta to his right. The whole seeks to depict the central focus of Sukhāvatī, and to stimulate an uplifting spiritual experience, deepening the aspiration to be reborn in this Pure Land. Indeed, much Mahāyāna art has been inspired by visionary experiences and has helped to inspire further experiences of a similar kind.

DEVOTION TO BHAIṢAJYA-GURU

Devotion to Bhaiṣajya-guru Buddha, the 'Master of Healing', is important in both Northern and Eastern Buddhism. In Chinese temples, image-halls most commonly have images of him and Amitābha flanking one of Śākyamuni. He generally holds a bowl said to be made of lapis lazuli, an intensely blue gem-stone thought to have healing properties. His body is also said to be like lapis lazuli, and to blaze with light. In one Chinese healing rite, a person keeps eight vows for seven days, makes offerings to monks, worships Bhaiṣajya-guru, recites his *Sūtra* seventy-nine times, makes seven images of him, and then contemplates his image so that it comes alive with his spiritual force and healing energy. Tuning into this, the devotee then mentally merges with him.

DEVOTION TO THE LOTUS *SŪTRA*

Within the Japanese Nichiren school, the symbolically rich title of the 'Lotus *Sūtra* of the True *Dharma*', *Myōhō-renge-kyō*, is a revered focus of devotion. This is known as the *daimoku*, and is seen to represent ultimate reality in its intrinsic purity. It is contained in the seven-syllable invocatory formula, *Na-mu myō-hō ren-ge-kyō*, whose repetition, accompanied by drums, is the central practice. Chanting this with sincere faith in the power of the truths of the *Sūtra* is held to purify the mind, protect and benefit the chanter, and develop the *Bodhisattva* perfections. The title is also written or carved on a scroll or plaque known as the *gohonzon*, or 'main object of worship'. Down the centre of this is the invocation in bold Japanese characters; above, left and right, are the names of Prabhūtaratna Buddha, a past Buddha who re-manifests himself in an incident in the Lotus *Sūtra*, and *Śākyamuni*; at its sides are the names of the 'four great kings', guardian deities who live in the lowest heaven described in ancient Buddhist cosmology; in the remaining space are names of various holy beings mentioned in the *Sūtra* – including the *Bodhisattva* of whom Nichiren said he was an incarnation – and of certain Shintō *kamis*. The *gohonzon* is seen as representing the final truth, as revealed in the *Sūtra*, emphasising Śākyamuni Buddha as all-pervading reality and universal power. The *gohonzon* is thus the primary focus of worship and object of contemplation, prominently displayed in Nichiren temples between images of Śākyamuni and Prabhūtaratna. The sub-sect known as the Nichiren Shō-shū, however, has an image of Nichiren himself in a central position. A secondary Nichiren practice is to chant the sections of the Lotus *Sūtra* on skilful means and the 'eternal' life-span of Śākyamuni.

PILGRIMAGE

Pilgrimage is a fairly common practice in Buddhism, and may be done for a variety of reasons: to bring alive events from the life of holy beings and so strengthen spiritual aspirations; to make 'merit'; to be suffused by the power-for-good of relics and *Bodhi*-trees; to receive protection from deities at the sites; or to fulfil a vow that pilgrimage would be made if aid was received from a certain *Bodhisattva*. The most ancient sites are those of the Buddha's birth, first sermon, enlightenment and *parinibbāna*. The Buddha said these should be visited with thoughts of reverence, such that anyone dying on the journey would be reborn in a heaven (*D*.II.140–1). The most important is Bodh-Gayā, whose focus is an ancient *Bodhi*-tree directly descended from the one under which Gotama attained enlightenment. Its sagging boughs are reverently propped up, prayer flags flutter from its branches, and pilgrims treasure any leaves which fall from it.

In Sri Lanka, a cutting from the original *Bodhi*-tree grows at the ancient capital of Anurādhapura, and is a favourite pilgrimage site. Another is in Kandy, where the 'Temple of the Tooth' houses a tooth-relic of the Buddha. Pilgrims also visit Mount Siripāda, known in English as 'Adam's Peak', the most spectacular mountain in Sri Lanka. On its summit is a 1·7 metre long depression in the rock, held to be a footprint left by the Buddha when he used his meditative powers to fly to the island on a teaching trip. Such 'footprints' exist elsewhere in the Buddhist world, and are greatly valued as objects associated with Gotama. On Siripāda, devotion is expressed both at the 'footprint' and at the shrine of Saman, the Stream-enterer god who guards the peak. In a remarkably ecumenical spirit, Hindus revere the footprint as that of Śiva, and Moslems reverse it as Adam's.

In South-east Asia, pilgrimage sites such as the Shwe-dāgon *Stūpa* are revered for their relics, or as the site of a visit by Gotama in his final or previous lives. An important Tibetan site is the Potala palace, traditional home of the Dalai Lamas. In China, pilgrims visit four sacred mountains seen as this-worldly 'residences' of certain 'Great Beings'. In Japan, Avalokiteśvara is said to have manifested himself in one or other of his guises at thirty-three sites around Kyoto. Each has a temple or shrine, where the devout pilgrim may perform ascetic practices, such as bathing in a freezing cold waterfall or praying all night. The pilgrim gets stamps put in his 'pilgrimage book' or on a 'pilgrimage scroll', which are treasured as reminders of the pilgrimage and the devotion it expressed and aroused.

FESTIVALS

Buddhists enjoy and appreciate festivals as times for reaffirming devotion and commitment, making 'merit' for the individual and community, strengthening community ties and values, and merry-making. The Southern, Northern and Eastern traditions each have their major festivals, and there are also national variations on these, as well as local festivals, for example on the anniversary of the founding of a temple. Some festivals which Buddhists celebrate are not Buddhist, as such, but pertain to the agricultural cycle, national deities, or traditions such as Confucianism.

In Southern Buddhism, most major festivals occur at the time of a full moon. As in Northern Buddhism, the lunar cycle also marks off the sabbath-like *uposatha*'s, or 'observance days', at the full-moon, new-moon and, less importantly, two half-moon days. Except at times of major festivals, observance days are attended only by the more devout, who spend a day and night at their local monastery. The monks are solemnly offered food, commitment to certain ethical precepts is made, the monks chant for the laity, and sometimes a sermon is given: features also occurring at all Southern Buddhist festivals. The rest of the time is spent in expressing devotion, reading, talking to the monks, and perhaps in some meditation.

In the lands of Southern Buddhism, the festival year starts at the traditional New Year, celebrated at various times, for up to four days, in mid-April. On the first day, houses are thoroughly cleaned of the dirt of the old year. Water, sometimes scented, is ceremonially poured over Buddha-images and the hands of monks and elderly relatives, as a mark of respect. In South-east Asia, this is frequently followed by a good-humoured period when the laity throw water at all and sundry. On the second day, in Thailand, Cambodia and Laos, sand *Stūpas* are built in temple-compounds or on river banks. When the new year starts on the next day, the sand is spread out to form a new compound floor, or is washed away by the river. Its dispersal is seen as symbolically 'cleansing' a person of the past year's bad deeds, represented by the grains of sand. Reflecting on past misdeeds, people thus rededicate themselves to Buddhist values. Accordingly, the New Year is also a time for aiding living beings by releasing caged birds and rescuing fish from drying-out ponds and streams. Accompanying festivities may include boat races, kite fights, music, traditional dancing and plays.

At the full moon in the lunar month of Vesākha, usually in May, comes *Vesākha Pūjā*, celebrating the Buddha's birth, enlightenment and *parinibbāna*. In Sri Lanka, this is the most important festival, when houses are decorated with garlands and paper lanterns, and driveways and temple courtyards are illuminated. People wander between pavement pantomimes and pavilions displaying paintings of the Buddha's life, with food being given out from roadside alms-stalls. In Burma, *Bodhi*-trees are watered with scented water, while in Thailand, Cambodia and Laos, the monks lead the laity in a threefold circumambulation of a temple, *Stūpa* or Buddha-image. The sermon which follows, on the Buddha's life, sometimes lasts all night.

In Sri Lanka, the next full moon day marks the *Poson* festival, celebrating the spreading of Buddhism to the island by Mahinda. Paintings of him are paraded through the streets to the sound of drumming, and pilgrimages are made to Anurādhapura and nearby Mihintale, where he met and converted the king.

The next full moon marks *Āsālha Pūjā*, celebrating the Buddha's renunciation and first sermon, and marking the start of the three-month period of *Vassa* (the 'Rains'). During this, monks stay at their home monasteries, except for short absences, for concentration on study and meditation, and many young men in South-east Asia temporarily ordain. The laity also deepen their religious commitment. They tend to avoid festivities, especially secular ones such as marriages, and more people than usual observe *uposathas* at their local monasteries. Most ordinations take place in the time leading up to *Āsālha Pūjā*, with their 'merit'-potential seen as contributing to the timely start of the rains.

At the full-moon marking the end of *Vassa*, the monks hold the ceremony of *Pavāraṇā*. When they chant and meditate, wax drips into a bowl of water from a burning candle, and it is thought that something of the monks' 'merit', built up during *Vassa*, suffuses and sacralizes the water. This is then sprinkled on the laity as a blessing. In South-east Asia, especially Burma, the following day is the *Tāvatiṃsa*, festival, celebrating the time when the Buddha, after spending *Vassa* in the Tāvatiṃsa heaven teaching his mother, descended to earth. As the 'light' of the world was then accessible again, this is a festival of lights, which illuminate houses, monasteries and *Stūpas*, and may be floated on rivers in small leaf-boats. A special food-offering is also made to a procession of monks, headed by a layman holding a Buddha-image and alms-bowl, symbolizing the returning Buddha.

The following month is the season for *Kaṭhina* celebrations, at which new robes, useful goods and money are given to the monasteries. The focal act is the donation of patches of cloth which the monks dye and make into a special robe, during the same day, commemorating the robes made from sewn-together rags in early Buddhism. These highly auspicious ceremonies, held at most local *vihāras*, complete the annual round of the more important festivals in Southern Buddhism.

Other than in Nepal, several festivals in Northern Buddhism more or less coincide with corresponding Southern ones: the celebration of the enlightenment and *parinirvāṇa* of the Buddha (his birth being celebrated eight days earlier), the first sermon and the descent from a heaven (here seen as the Tuṣita heaven). The different schools also have festivals relating to their founders, with the death of Tsong-kha-pa (in November) being of general importance; monasteries also have festivals relating to their specific tutelary deity. An important and characteristic festival centres on the Tibetan New Year, in February. In the preceding two weeks, monks dressed in masks and brightly coloured robes perform impressive ritual dances before a large lay audience. Accompanied by booming alpine horns, drums, shrilling oboes and clashing cymbals, they act out a series of solemn but impressive movements, lasting several hours. These are seen as driving away evil powers, while other rituals seek to help beings to progress towards enlightenment. From the fourth to the twenty-fifth day of the first month, monks perform the ceremonies of *sMon lam* (pron. *Monlam*), the 'Great Vow', centred on a five-day celebration of the Buddha's 'marvel of the pairs' at Śrāvasti (Pali Sāvatthī; see p. 26). As an event in which rival teachers were confounded, this became an appropriate symbol for the overcoming of evil forces, and of Buddhism's past victory over Bon. On the thirteenth day, dances portray Tibetan Buddhism's fierce protector-deities in their struggle against demons and spiritual ignorance. These are represented by a small human effigy which is ritually killed, symbolizing victory over evil and the securing of a safe and prosperous new year. To raise people's energy levels for the new year, horse races and archery competitions are held around this period.

In the lands of Eastern Buddhism, the annual round of festivals have fewer Buddhist elements, and more from Confucianism, Shintō and folk traditions. In Communist China, festivals are now largely secularized and politicized, though they continue much as before in Taiwan and among expatriate Chinese. Among the Chinese, who determine festivals by a lunar calender, the birth of the Buddha is celebrated in May, as in Korea, while in Japan it is celebrated on 8 April. The principal rite recalls the story that the new-born Śākyamuni stood and was bathed by water sent down by gods: small standing images of the child are placed in bowls and scented water or tea is ladled over them. For Chinese Buddhists, the festival is also a popular time for the release of living beings into the water or air. In Korea, it is a time for illuminating temples with paper lanterns. In Japan the festival is known as *Hana matsuri*, the 'Flower Festival', and retains elements of a pre-Buddhist festival involving the gathering of wild mountain flowers so as to bring home deities to protect the rice-fields. The Buddhist connection is that Śākyamuni was born in a flower-laden grove, so that the infant-Buddha images are housed in floral shrines.

The other important Chinese Buddhist festivals are those of the 'birth', 'enlightenment' and 'death' of Kuan-yin, and especially *Ullambana*, which is also celebrated by non-Buddhists. This 'Festival of Hungry Ghosts', in August/September, is when ancestors reborn as ghosts are said to wander in the human world, as a potential source of danger. At the full moon, which ends the three-month 'Summer Retreat', monks transfer 'merit', put out food and chant *Sūtras* for them, so as to help them to a better rebirth. The laity sponsor the rites and participate by burning large paper boats which will help 'ferry across' hungry ghosts to a better world, thus showing filial regard for ancestors. A favourite story told at this time is that of Mu-lien (Pali Moggallāna), a key *Arhat* disciple of the Buddha who discovered that his mother was reborn as a hungry ghost or in a hell (there are two versions of the story). On the advice of the Buddha, he then helped her attain a better rebirth by transferring 'merit' to her. In Japan, *Ullambana* became *O-bon*, the 'Feast for the Dead', celebrated from 13 to 15 July. Graves are washed and tended, and an altar is set up in or near the home for offerings of fresh herbs and flowers. A fire and candles are lit to welcome ancestral spirits to partake of the offerings, and a Buddhist priest is invited to chant a *Sūtra* in each home in his parish.

9

BUDDHIST PRACTICE: ETHICS

THE ROLE AND BASIS OF ETHICS IN BUDDHISM

In Buddhism, moral virtue is the foundation of the spiritual path, though a fixed *attachment* to ethical precepts and vows is seen as a hindering 'fetter' (see p. 71). Virtue generates freedom from remorse, and this leads on through gladness and joy to meditative calm, insight and liberation (*A*.v.2). While this model of ethics as part of a 'path' predominates, it is modified in some Mahāyāna schools, particularly in Japan. Here, Sōtō Zen sees morality as the making manifest of one's innate Buddha-nature, while Jōdo-shin sees it as simply expressing gratitude to Amitābha for having saved one.

The overcoming of *dukkha*, both in oneself and others, is Buddhism's central preoccupation, towards which ethical action contributes. Buddhism says that, if one wants to attain prosperity, amicable social relationships or a good reputation, self-confidence or calm and joy, a good rebirth or progress towards *Nibbāna*, then act in such and such a way: for this is how such things are fostered. If one behaves otherwise, then one will suffer in this and subsequent lives, as a natural (karmic) result of unwholesome actions. It is in the nature of things that behaving ethically reduces suffering and increases happiness, for oneself and those one interacts with. A moral life is not a burdensome duty or set of 'oughts' but an uplifting source of happiness, in which the sacrifice of lesser pleasures facilitates the experiencing of more enriching and satisfying ones.

Having no real 'oughts', Buddhist ethics has levels of practice suiting different levels of commitment, rather than one set of universal obligations. Most importantly, monks and nuns make undertakings ruling out actions, such as sexual intercourse, which are acceptable for a layperson.

As a Buddhist comes to understand the extent of *dukkha* in his own life, a natural development is concern about others' suffering, and a deepening compassion. Indeed, the importance of 'comparing oneself with others' is stressed: 'Since the self of others is dear to each one, let him who loves himself not harm another' (*Ud*.47). The key basis for ethical action is the reflection that it is inappropriate to inflict on other beings what you yourself find unpleasant (*S*.v.353–4). They are just like oneself in desiring pleasure and disliking pain, so there is no good reason to add to the common lot of suffering. Moreover, the benefit of self and others are intertwined, so that concern to lessen one's own suffering goes hand-in-hand with lessening that of others. Helping others helps oneself (through karmic results and developing good qualities of mind), and helping oneself (by purifying one's character) enables one to help others better.

One implication of 'impermanence' is that people should always be respected as capable of change-for-the-better. The *Suttas* contain a famous example of this, when the Buddha visited the haunt of the murderous bandit Aṅguḷimāla, seeing that he needed only a little exhortation to change his ways, became a monk, and soon attain *Nibbāna* (*M*.II.97–105). Whatever a person is like on the surface, the depths of his mind are seen as 'brightly shining' and pure. This depth purity, known in the Mahāyāna as the *Tathāgata-garbha* or the Buddha-nature, represents the potential for ultimate transformation, and as such is a basis for respecting all beings.

The changes involved in the round of rebirths are also ethically relevant. Any suffering one now witnesses will have been undergone by oneself in some past life, and all beings will have been good to one at some time. Such considerations stimulate compassion, and positive regard for others, irrespective of their present roles, character and nature. Compassion is also appropriate towards someone who, being so evil as to have no apparent good points, will in future lives undergo great suffering as a karmic result of their actions (*Vism*.340).

The teaching on not-self, that no permanent self or I exists within a person, does not itself support a positive regard for persons as unique entities, as do Christian teachings. Rather, it supports ethics by undermining the very source of lack of respect, self-ishness. This is done by undercutting the notion that 'I' am a substantial, self-identical entity, one that should be gratified and be able to brush aside others if they get in 'my' way. It does not deny that each person has an individual history and character, but it emphasizes that these are compounds of universal factors. In particular, it means that 'your' suffering and 'my' suffering are not inherently different. They are just suffering, so the barrier which generally keeps us within our own 'self-interest' should be dissolved, or widened in its scope till it includes all beings. The non-self teaching also emphasizes that we are not as in control of ourselves as we would like to think: this adds a leavening of humility and a sense of humour to our attitude to the weaknesses of ourselves and others.

Besides such arguments for ethical action, Buddhism also encourages it through the popular *Jātaka* stories, on former lives and actions of Gotama.

GIVING

The primary ethical activity which a Buddhist learns to develop is giving, *dāna*, which forms a basis for further moral and spiritual development. In Southern Buddhism, it is the first of the ten 'auspicious actions' which produce 'merit': giving, keeping the precepts, meditation, sharing 'merit', rejoicing at the 'merit' of others, giving service, showing respect, teaching *Dhamma*, listening to *Dhamma*, and acting with right view. The key focus of giving is the monastic *Sangha*, which depends on the laity for such items as alms-food, robes, medicine, and accommodation. The monks and nuns, by teaching and example, return a greater gift, for 'The gift of *Dhamma* excels all gifts' (*Dhp*.354). Such acts of mutual giving thus form a key feature of the lay–monastic relationship: 'Thus, monks, this holy life is lived in mutual dependence, for ferrying across the flood [of *saṃsāra*], for the utter ending of *dukkha*' (*It*.111). The *Sangha*, moreover, is a potent 'field of "merit"', so gifts 'planted' in it are seen as providing a good harvest of 'merit' for the donors. As alms bestow long life, good appearance, happiness and strength on the recipient, then these, in a human or heavenly rebirth, are said to be the karmic results of alms-giving (*A*.IV.57). On the other hand, being stingy is said to lead to being poor (*M*.III.205). Generosity is not only practised towards the *Sangha*, but is a pervading value of Buddhist societies. Fielding Hall, a British official in nineteenth-century Burma, once asked for a bill at what he had taken to be a village restaurant, and found that he had been fed as a guest in a private house!

One fairly common practice is to contribute to the costs of printing

Buddhist books for free distribution. Buddhists are also keen to give their assistance, goods and money at an ordination, funeral, festival or illness, so as to make 'merit', and share it with others. Communities are bound together in acts of communal 'merit'-making, and obligations are fulfilled by contributing to a ceremony sponsored by someone who has previously helped one in this way. Some ceremonies can be expensive, and so a rich person may also help sponsor the ordination of a poorer person's son.

While any act of giving is seen as generating 'merit', this becomes more abundant as the motive becomes purer. Giving may initially be performed for the sake of material karmic results, but the joy and contentment that giving brings is then likely to provide the motive. The constant practice of giving also aids spiritual development by reducing possessiveness, cultivating an open-hearted and sensitive attitude towards others, and expressing non-attachment and renunciation, reflected in the practice of 'giving up' home and family life to become a monk or nun. Giving is also the first of the *Bodhisattva* 'perfections', according to all traditions.

KEEPING THE PRECEPTS

On a basis of developing *dāna*, the Buddhist cultivates *sīla* ('virtue') by observing ethical precepts, the most common of which are the 'five virtues' (*pañca-sīlāni*). The avowal of each of these begins 'I undertake the rule of training to abstain from...' The five abstentions are from: (i) 'harming living beings', (ii) 'taking what is not given', (iii) 'misconduct concerning sense-pleasures', (iv) 'false speech', and (v) 'unmindful states due to alcoholic drinks or drugs'. Each precept is a 'rule of training' – as is each item of the monastic code – which is a promise or vow to oneself. They are not 'commandments' from without, though their difference from these, in practice, can be exaggerated. In societies where Buddhism is the dominant religion, they become expected norms for people to seek to live by. Moreover, while the 'taking' of the precepts, by ritually chanting them, can be done by a layperson at any time, they are frequently 'taken' by chanting them after a monk, who fulfils the role of 'administering' them. In such a context, the resolve to keep the precepts has a greater psychological impact, and thus generates more 'merit'.

In Southern Buddhism, the five precepts are chanted at most

ceremonies, and often on a daily basis. People try to live up to them as best they can, according to their commitment and circumstances, but with particular care on observance or festival days. In East Asia, where Buddhism is only one ingredient in the religious situation, the precepts are only taken by those with a fairly strong commitment to Buddhism. In China, they are first taken, perhaps during a stay at a monastery, at a 'lay ordination' ceremony, which makes a person a recognized layman (*upāsaka*) or laywoman (*upāsikā*). The precepts are then regarded as quite weighty vows, so that a person may omit one if he feels he cannot live up to it (the first is never omitted, though). In Sōtō Zen, devout laypeople take the precepts at *Jūkai*, a week-long set of ceremonies held every spring while staying at a temple. First-timers also have a lay ordination ceremony. The precepts taken consist of the 'three pure precepts' and 'ten great precepts'. The former are 'Cease from evil, do only good, do good for others', the latter are equivalent to the first four of the five precepts, plus: (v) not taking or selling drugs or alcohol, (vi) not speaking against others, (vii) not praising oneself and abusing others, (viii) not being mean in giving *Dharma* or wealth, (ix) not being angry, and (x) not defaming the 'three jewels'.

Closely related to keeping the precepts is 'right livelihood'. This is making one's living in a way that does not involve the habitual breaking of the precepts by bringing harm to other beings, but which hopefully aids others and helps cultivate one's faculties and abilities (see p. 69).

Emphasis is sometimes laid on the need for a 'Middle Way' in keeping the precepts, avoiding the extremes of laxity and rigidity. In any case, Buddhism does not encourage the developing of strong guilt feelings if a precept is broken (though the Jōdo-shin school emphasizes the weak and sinful nature of man). Guilt is seen as part of the natural karmic result of unskilful action, and may therefore act as a deterrent. It should not be further indulged in, though, to produce self-dislike and mental turbulence, a spiritual hindrance. Regretting misdeeds is skilful, but only if this does not unnecessarily harp on past failings. Buddhism emphasizes a forward-looking morality of always seeking to do better in the future: taking the precepts as ideals to live up to in an increasingly complete way.

The role of 'conscience' is performed mainly by mindfulness, which makes a person aware of his actions and motives, and by *hiri* and *ottappa*: the two 'bright states which guard the world' and the immediate causes of virtue. *Hiri* is 'shame' at an action which lowers one's integrity, as it betrays one's self-respect. *Ottappa* is 'regard for consequences', being stimulated by concern over reproach and blame (whether from oneself or others), legal punishment, or the karmic results of an action (*Asl.* 124–7).

For an action to break a precept and incur 'demerit', it must be done with intention; this is not the case, for example, if one accidentally treads on an insect. Greater 'demerit' accrues, moreover, as the force of will behind an action increases; for this leaves a greater karmic 'trace' on the mind. Several things follow from this. Firstly, a state of diminished responsibility, due to madness or inflamed passion, reduces the karmic seriousness of an unwholesome action (*Miln.*221). Secondly, it is worse to pre-meditate an action. Thirdly, it is worse to do a wrong action if one does not regard it as wrong; for then it will be done in a deluded state without restraint or hesitation (*Miln.*84). Thus killing a human or animal without compunction is worse than doing so with trepidation. Finally, it is worse to kill a large animal than a small one, for the former involves a more sustained effort (*Script.* pp. 70–3). The gravity of an action also depends on the perversity of the intention. To harm a virtuous person, or a respect-worthy one such as a parent, is worse than harming others. Similarly, it is worse to harm a more highly developed form of life. While humans are seen as superior to animals, this is only a matter of degree; humans should show their superiority by using their freedom of choice to treat animals well, not by maltreating them.

The emphasis on the importance of volitional involvement can have certain unexpected results. For example in a valley of Kashmir bordering Tibet, Buddhists feel that they have to kill predatory wolves. This is done as indirectly as possible, though: after luring them into high-walled traps, large stones are thrown over the wall by a group of people, so that nobody knows for sure who kills the animals. In this way, people seek to distance themselves from a 'necessary' evil. In the West, a similar principle means that members of a firing squad often do not know whose bullets are live. There is no 'let out', however, in telling someone else to do a precept-breaking action for one: this is still a breach of the precept.

The Mahāyāna emphasis on 'skilful means' entails that this tradition has a greater tendency than Theravāda to flexibly adapt the precepts to circumstances. Asanga's *Bodhisattva-bhūmi* says that a *Bodhisattva* may kill a person about to murder his parents or a monk, so that the assailant avoids the evil karma of killing, which is experienced by himself instead. He may also lie to save others, and steal the booty of thieves and unjust rulers, so that they are hindered in their evil ways.

The first precept

The first precept, regarded as the most important, is the resolution not to kill or injure any human, animal, bird, fish or insect. While this has not meant that most Buddhists have been pacifists, pacifism has been the ideal. While the 'wrong livelihood' of 'trade in arms' refers to the arms-salesman and not the soldier, as such, a professional soldier who dies in battle is said to be reborn in a hell or as an animal (*S.*IV.308–9). It is emphasized that war is inconclusive and futile: 'Victory breeds hatred; the defeated live in pain; the peaceful live happily, giving up victory and defeat' (*Dhp.*201); 'The slayer gets a slayer in his turn, the conqueror gets one who conquers him' (*S.*I.85). Accordingly, Buddhism contributed to ending Asoka's violent expansion of his empire and tamed the warlike Tibetans and Mongolians; Chinese Buddhists were noted for 'shirking their military duties', and an early president of the United Nations was the devout Burmese Buddhist U Thant. Most lay Buddhists have been prepared to break the first precept in self-defence, though, and many have helped defend the community. In Thailand, the army is well respected for its role in serving and helping to run the country. In Korea, one response to a Japanese invasion in 1592 was that a leading monk actually raised a militia of 5,000 monks! The history of Buddhist countries has not been free of wars, and sometimes Buddhist sects have fought each other, as seen in chapter 7. The communal strife which erupted in Sri Lanka in 1983, pitting Tamils (mainly Hindu) against Sinhalese (mainly Buddhist), unfortunately shows that Buddhists are not immune from letting communalism make them forget some of their principles.

While Buddhism has no real objection to contraception, abortion is seen as breaking the first precept, as it cuts off a 'precious human rebirth', seen as beginning at conception. The bad karma from an abortion is said to vary according to the size of the foetus, and most Buddhists would accept abortion to save the mother's life. In secularizing, post-war Japan, abortion has been quite common, but many women have felt the need to atone for their deed by caring for the spirit of their aborted child through the cult of the *Bodhisattva* Jizō. Suicide again wastes a 'precious human rebirth', and the suffering instigating it is seen as probably set to continue unabated and intensified into the next, perhaps sub-human, rebirth. The case of someone compassionately 'giving' his life to help others is different, though. The *Jātaka* stories contain a number of examples of the *Bodhisattva* giving up his life to save another being, and there is a small tradition in Eastern Buddhism of 'religious suicides', as self-offerings to the Buddhas. During the Vietnam war, a number of Buddhists burned themselves to death to bring the world's attention to the plight of the South Vietnamese people under the Diem regime, their hope being that the 'merit' of the act of self-giving would help sustain Buddhism, and bring peace to Vietnam and the world.

While it is relatively easy to avoid killing humans, other forms of life can cause more problems in practice. There is generally a preference for removing pests to a safe distance and releasing them, though certain deadly and vicious snakes would be killed without hesitation. When Buddhists do kill pests, they may try to counteract the bad karmic results of doing so. In Thailand, farmers might only countenance the killing of a plague of crop-eating rats by arguing that some of the money thus saved can be used to make 'merit'. In Zen monasteries, rites are carried out to aid the destiny of vermin which have been killed.

Emperor Asoka made laws against killing animals on observance days, the castrating or branding of cattle, and indiscriminate burning of forests; some Theravāda kings have also prohibited or limited the slaughter of animals. Nevertheless, the first precept does not mean that most Buddhists are vegetarian, and the Buddha himself seems to have accepted meat in his alms-bowl. His emphasis was on avoiding intentional killing, so that it was worse to swat a fly than to eat a dead carcase. He allowed a monk to eat flesh if he had not seen, heard or suspected that the creature had been killed specifically for him, such food then being 'blameless' (*M*.II.368–71). As monks lived off alms, they should not pick and choose what food was acceptable, or deprive a donor of the opportunity of making 'merit' by refusing 'blameless' food. As regards laypeople, even killing so as to give meat as alms generates 'demerit', due to the distress felt by the animals while being brought to slaughter, and the pain when killed (*M*.I.371).

'Right livelihood' rules out 'trade in flesh', seen as including the butcher, hunter and fisherman: jobs which no committed Buddhist would carry out. In Buddhist societies, butchers are usually non-Buddhists, for example Muslims, and are seen as depraved or as outcastes. The position that meat is acceptable if someone else kills the animal is not necessarily an easy get-out clause. Buddhist countries lack the mass slaughter-houses of the West – which would be seen as hells on earth – so to get meat is more likely to involve *asking* a butcher to kill an animal, or killing it oneself. Indeed raising livestock for slaughter is generally seen as a breach of 'right livelihood' which Buddhists tend to steer clear of.

In Southern Buddhism, while only a few are vegetarian, this is universally admired, and most people have an uneasy conscience when they *think* about meat-eating. Some abstain on observance days, when they may also avoid farming, as it might harm worms and insects. A few monks are vegetarian and occasionally monks organize boycotts of butchers' shops in remote villages. In general, it is seen as worse to eat the flesh of an animal at a higher level of existence: it is worst to eat beef (in Burma, it was once a crime to kill a cow), less bad to eat goats or fowls, less bad again to eat eggs (usually seen as being fertilized), and least bad to eat fish, the most common form of flesh eaten. Many people catch their own fish, but those who make a living by fishing are looked down on in society.

In the Mahāyāna, the *Lankāvatāra Sūtra* (pp. 244–59) denies that the Buddha allowed 'blameless' meat for monks, and argues against meat-eating: all beings have been relatives in a past life; meat stinks; eating it hinders meditation and leads to bad health, arrogance and rebirth as a carnivorous animal or low-class human; if no meat is eaten, killing for consumption will cease. In China, the first precept (or at least the *Bodhisattva* vows) has been seen as entailing vegetarianism, so that monks, nuns and pious laypeople have avoided meat, and vegetarian feasts have been common at Buddhist celebrations. In Japanese tradition, no beef has been eaten and vegetarianism has existed, especially among Zen monks. Western influence has now decreased this, though. The Japanese preference for all kinds of food from the sea is probably due to Buddhist influence (fish are a low form of life), as well as the fact that Japan is an island. Unfortunately, whales also live in the sea, and more powerful boats and an increasing secularism means that Japan now catches many of these.

Most lands of Northern Buddhism have a harsh, cold climate, so that vegetarianism is seen as impractical. Nevertheless, among nomadic herdsmen, older, more pious members of families generally avoid killing livestock, and those who work as professional butchers are despised. In general, large animals are killed for food, in preference to killing many small ones for the same amount of meat. Nevertheless, Tibetans are noted for their kindness to animals; scruples are had even about eating honey, for this is seen as entailing both theft from and murder of bees.

The other precepts

The second precept is seen as ruling out any act of theft, but also fraud, cheating, borrowing without the intention to return, and taking more than is one's due. Often, gambling is also included. The precept clearly has relevance for the production and use of wealth. The ideal here is that one's wealth should be made in a moral way, which does not cheat or harm others; it should be used to give ease and pleasure to oneself, to share with others, and to make 'merit' with; and it should not be the object of one's greed and longing (*S*.IV.331–7). Miserliness and over-spending are both extremes to be avoided. If someone is well-off, this is generally seen as being aided by past 'merit', and the rich person is seen as having a greater opportunity to make 'merit' by giving liberally to the *Sangha* and the community. Combined with the idea that poverty tends to encourage theft and civil discontent (*D*.III.64–9, and *D*.I.135), this means that the Buddhist ideal is a society free from an imbalance of poverty and riches.

Buddhist countries are found at many different levels of economic development. At one extreme is Bhutan, now gradually emerging from a medieval life-style into the modern world. Here the people are poor, but seem generally contented, and the king has said that he is more interested in the 'Gross National Happiness' than the 'Gross National Product'. At the other extreme is Japan. Its rapid modernization has been aided by an emphasis on serving the group (rooted in traditional methods of agriculture, but reinforced by Confucianism), the samurai ethic of loyal service to feudal lord and state, and the Buddhist emphasis on selfless detachment, here in an active engaged mode. The Japanese seem now to have become attached to work almost for its own sake, though, and some have become concerned that too little time is being left for relaxation and spiritual matters.

The third precept primarily concerns avoiding causing suffering by one's sexual behaviour. This includes any enforced intercourse, intercourse with those married or engaged to another or under the protection of relatives, incest and adultery. What counts as 'adultery' varies according to the marriage patterns of different cultures, and Buddhism has been flexible in adapting to these. While monogamy is the preferred, and predominant pattern, it has also tolerated polygamy, and sometimes polyandry. Pre-marital sex has been regarded as a breach of the precept in some cultures, but not in others; flirting with a married woman may also be seen as a breach. Homosexual activity is seen as breaking the precept, and one born a homosexual is seen as unable to experience certain deep meditative states (*Vism.*177). Other socially taboo forms of sexuality have been seen as breaking the precept, doubtless due to the guilt feelings that they entail. Obsessive sexual activities also come within the precept, as do other sense-indulgences such as gorging oneself with food.

The first three precepts concern physical actions, and keeping them is the 'right action' factor of the Eightfold Path. The fourth precept, while it only specifically refers to 'false speech', is equivalent to all aspects of the Path-factor of 'right speech'. This precept is generally seen as the second most important one; for it is said that a person who has no shame at intentional lying is capable of any evil action (*M.*I.415). Moreover, in the Theravādin collection of *Jātaka* stories, though Gotama breaks several of the precepts in his past lives, he is never said to have lied. Any form of lying or deception, either for one's own benefit or that of another, is seen as a breach of the precept, though a small 'white lie' is, for example, much less serious than lying in a court of law. Lying is to be avoided not only because it often harms others, but because it goes against the Buddhist value of seeking the truth and seeing things 'as they really are'. The more a person deceives others, the more he is likely to deceive himself; thus his delusion and spiritual ignorance increase.

The other forms of 'right speech' are intended to further moderate speech-actions, so as to decrease unskilful mental states and increase skilful ones. They concern: avoiding words causing a listener to think less of some third party; harsh or angry words, and idle chatter. Right speech delights in speaking of people's *good* points, so as to spread harmony rather than discord; it is 'gentle, pleasing to the ear, affectionate, going to the heart, urbane, pleasant to the manyfolk'; it is spoken 'at the right time, in accordance with fact, about the goal, about *Dhamma*, about moral discipline', so as to be 'worth treasuring' (*M*.III.49). This description clearly shows a very comprehensive concern with verbal behaviour. The last item, dealing with chatter, is more emphasized in a meditative setting, but in general stresses the need to use one's words wisely: to inform, aid or express kindness to others, and not just for the sake of opening one's mouth. A list of 'ten skilful actions', comprised of the seven factors of right action and speech, plus avoiding covetousness, malevolence, and wrong views (*M*.III.45–50), seems to be the basis of Zen's 'ten great precepts'.

The fifth precept is not listed under the Path-factors of right action or right speech, but keeping it aids 'right mindfulness'. In intoxicated states lacking mental clarity or calm, one is also more likely to break all the other precepts. Certainly the wish to avoid life's sufferings by indulging in a false happiness is best avoided. In following this precept, some seek to avoid any intoxicating, or mind-altering substances, while others regard intoxication, and not the taking of a little drink, as a breach of the precept. Buddhism is not puritanical in such matters, and unlike some Muslim countries, no Buddhist country bans the sale or consumption of alcohol. Nevertheless, making a living by its sale is a 'wrong livelihood'.

The positive implications of the precepts

While each precept is expressed in negative wording, as an abstention, one who keeps these 'rules of training' increasingly comes to express positive virtues. As the roots of unskilful action are weakened, the natural depth-purity of the mind can manifest itself. Each precept thus has a positive counterpart, respectively: (i) kindness and compassion; (ii) generosity and renunciation; (iii) 'joyous satisfaction with one's own wife', contentment and fewness-of-wishes; (iv) loving truth by searching it out, recognizing falsity, and attaining precision of thought; and (v) mindfulness and awareness. Contentment is seen as the 'greatest of wealths' (*Dhp*.204), and the height of this virtue is shown by a remark of the eleventh-century Tibetan saint Mi-la-ras-pa who, living in threadbare cotton robes in a freezing Himālayan cave, said, 'to me, everything is comfortable'!

Taking extra precepts

Within Southern (and also Northern) Buddhism, a set of eight precepts may be taken by devout laypeople on 'observance' days. By taking extra precepts, they undertake a discipline which reduces stimulating sense-inputs that disturb calm and concentration, so that their conduct temporarily resembles that of monks. Regular attenders at observance days, who are usually aged over forty, are therefore known by the term for a devout male or female lay disciple, *upāsaka* and *upāsikā*. In daily life, these also observe the five precepts more faithfully than other people. The Northern and Eastern traditions continue the older practice of using the terms *upāsaka* or *upāsikā* (in translation) for anyone who observes the five precepts and takes the three refuges.

The difference between the eight and five precepts is firstly that the third precept is replaced by one on avoiding 'unchaste conduct': all sexual activity. After the usual fifth precept, three more are then taken, concerning abstention from: (vi) 'eating at an unseasonable time', (vii) 'dancing, singing, music and visiting shows; wearing garlands, perfumes and unguents, finery and adornment', and (viii) 'high or luxurious beds'. The sixth precept entails not eating any solid food after noon. The seventh means avoiding, or keeping one's distance from, entertainments, and avoiding make-up, perfume, jewellery and clothes other than plain white ones: disciplines also followed by those attending the Zen *Jūkai* festival. The eighth is intended to diminish slothfulness or feelings of grandeur, and entails sleeping and sitting on mats. In practice, however, this is how most laypeople sleep anyway.

There is also a set of ten precepts, the same as those observed by novice monks (*Khp.A*.22–37). Here, the seventh precept is split into two, and there is an additional undertaking to 'abstain from accepting gold and silver', precluding the actual handling of money. Unlike the eight precepts, the ten are only taken on a long-term basis. A few Theravāda men, usually elderly, permanently follow them and wear white or brown. A greater number of women do so. This is because, in the Southern (and Northern) tradition, the full order of nuns died out, and the greatest number of precepts that a woman can formally take is ten. More women than men also observe the eight precepts on observance days.

LOVINGKINDNESS AND COMPASSION

Lovingkindness (*mettā*) and compassion (*karunā*) are seen as part of the Path-factor of 'right directed thought', and as outgrowths from generosity, aids to deepening virtue, and factors undercutting the attachment to 'I'. They are also the first two of the four 'immeasurables' or 'divine abidings' (*brahma-vihāra*'s): qualities which, when developed to a high degree in meditation, are said to make the mind 'immeasurable' and like the mind of the loving god Brahmā. Lovingkindness is the heart-felt aspiration for the happiness of beings, and is the antidote to hatred and fear. Compassion is the aspiration that beings be free from suffering, and is the antidote to cruelty. Sympathetic joy (*muditā*) is joy at the joy of others, and is the antidote to jealousy and discontent. Equanimity (*upekkhā*) is an even-minded serenity towards beings, which balances concern for others with a realization that suffering is an inevitable part of being alive. It is the antidote the partiality and attachment.

Lovingkindness is stressed in such verses as, 'Conquer anger by lovingkindness; conquer evil by good; conquer the stingy by giving; conquer the liar by truth' (*Dhp*.223). Such benevolence and true friendliness is also the theme of the *Karaṇīya-metta Sutta*, a very popular *paritta* chant:

He who is skilled in good, and who wishes to attain that State of Peace [*Nibbāna*] should act thus: he should be able, upright, perfectly upright, of pleasant speech, gentle and humble, contented, easy to support [as a monk], unbusy, with sense controlled, discreet, modest, not greedily attached to families [for alms]. He should not commit any slight wrong on account of which other wise men might censure him. [Then he would think]: 'May all beings be happy and secure, may they be happy-minded! Whatever living beings there are – feeble or strong, long, stout or medium, short, small or large, seen or unseen [i.e. ghosts, gods and hell-beings], those dwelling far or near, those who are born or those who await rebirth – may all beings, without exception, be happy-minded! Let none deceive another nor despise any person whatever in any place; in anger or ill-will let them not wish any suffering to each other. Just as a mother would protect her only child at the risk of her own life, even so, let him cultivate a boundless heart towards all beings. Let his thoughts of boundless lovingkindness pervade the whole world: above, below and across, without obstruction, without any hatred, without any enmity. Whether he stands, walks, sits or lies down, as long as he is awake, he should develop this mindfulness. This, they say, is divine abiding here. Not falling into wrong views, virtuous and endowed with insight, he gives up attachment for sense-desires. He will surely not come again to any womb [i.e. rebirth]. (*Khp*.8–9)

Thus lovingkindness is ideally to be radiated to all beings, in the same strength as a mother's love for her child; though without the sentimentality and possessiveness that this may include. The height of this ideal is expressed thus: 'Monks, as low-down thieves might carve one limb from limb with a double-handed saw, yet even then whoever entertained hate in his heart on that account would not be one who carried out my teaching' (*M*.I.129). Lovingkindness can be practised in daily life by kindly actions, and chanting the above *Sutta* with full awareness of its meaning is one of the most common forms of meditation in Southern Buddhism. A more sustained meditation on lovingkindness is also practised (see chapter 11).

To help overcome ill-will for someone, a person developing lovingkindness may reflect on the harm brought to himself by entertaining anger and hostility: 'Whatever harm a foe may do to a foe, or a hater to a hater, an ill-directed mind can do one far greater harm' (*Dhp*.42). Getting angry at provocation is actually to co-operate in making oneself suffer (*Vism*.300). Other recommendations are to remember that all beings have once been good to one, or to reflect that the mind is ever-changing, so that 'the person who annoyed me' is no longer precisely the same person (*Vism*.301).

Compassion, as the root-motivation of the *Bodhisattva*, is much emphasized. In Eastern and Northern Buddhism, the taking of the *Bodhisattva* vows, often done after taking the precepts, is a solemn commitment which expresses the compassionate urge to aid all beings. This is to be done by constant practice of the 'perfections': generosity, virtue, patience, vigour, meditation and wisdom. In Southern Buddhism, there is a set of ten perfections (Pali *pāramī*'s), seen as noble qualities of aid in compassionately benefiting others: generosity, virtue, non-sensuality, wisdom, vigour, patience, truthfulness, determination, lovingkindness and equanimity. Though a *Bodhisatta* develops these to the highest degree, they are also seen as appropriate for all aspiring for *Nibbāna*.

The Buddha taught that 'whoever wishes to take care of me should take care of the sick' (*Vin.*I.301–2), and in his 'Precious Garland of Advice for the King', Nāgārjuna advised, 'Cause the blind, the sick, the lowly, the protectorless, the wretched and the crippled equally to attain food and drink without interruption.' A good example of this compassionate ideal at work was in T'ang China (618–907), where Buddhist monasteries, and lay religious societies set up by monks, ran hospitals, dispensaries, orphanages, homes for the elderly and rest-houses for pilgrims; they fed beggars, did famine relief work, built roads and bridges and sank wells. In the lands of Southern Buddhism, charitable works other than running orphanages have usually been left in the hands of wealthy laymen or rulers. Monasteries have, however, informally carried out a number of welfare roles. Today, lay Buddhist welfare work includes famine relief work, running organ-banks, and the Gandhian-influenced 'Sarvodaya Śramadāna' rural development movement in Sri Lanka.

The ideal of caring for animals is nicely expressed in a *Jātaka* story (no. 124), which tells of the *Bodhisatta* as a hermit who brought water to wild animals during a drought; as he was so intent on doing this, he had no time to get himself food, but the animals gathered it for him. In accord with this ideal, large Chinese monasteries have had a pool for fish rescued from the fishmonger, and livestock were released into their care, perhaps with contributions for their upkeep. Burma has 'retirement homes' for cows. Buddhism also has a tradition of providing veterinary care. In this, a badly afflicted animal would not normally be 'put out of its misery', but be cared for. Killing it would be seen as not much different from killing an afflicted human.

CARE FOR THE DYING AND THE DEAD

Compassionate help for others is no less important in death than in life, according to Buddhism. As death approaches, it is the duty of relatives and friends to help a person have a 'good death'; for in a rebirth perspective, death is the most important and problematical 'life-crisis'. The ideal is to die in a calm, aware state, joyfully recollecting previous good deeds, rather than regretting them, so that the best possible rebirth is obtained, within the limits set by previous karma (*M.*III.214).

In Southern Buddhism, monks are fed on behalf of a dying person, who is also calmed by the monks' chanting, and reminded of his good deeds. Funerals (by cremation) may have an almost festival atmosphere, and grief is seldom shown unless the death was especially untimely or tragic. 'Merit' is shared with the deceased, as it is at subsequent memorial services. At these, water is poured into a bowl till it overflows, and monks chant a verse which says that, just as water flows downwards, 'so may what is given here reach the departed' (*Khp*.6).

In Northern Buddhism, a dying and recently dead person will have the *Bar-do Thos-grol* (pron. *Parto Thotrol*; commonly known as 'The Tibetan Book of the Dead') read to him. This is to guide him through the experiences of the forty-nine days between lives, so as to help him overcome lingering attachment to his body and family, or even gain liberating insight. At the time of death, all people are said to experience the blissful brightly-shining Clear Light of emptiness, thusness or pure Mind. An advanced yogin may be able to attain enlightenment at this time. Most people, though, turn away in incomprehension, and go on to undergo the normal intermediary existence. In this, a person can travel at will, has powers such as telepathy, and meets the 'Innate Spirit' – representing his conscience – which outlines the details of his past life's karma. Visions of the various rebirth realms, and of a series of heavenly Buddhas and *Bodhisattvas* ensue. One who does not understand the nature of these visions is drawn forward to a new rebirth, according to his karma. One with understanding, however, may accelerate his development on the *Bodhisattva*-path, or may be able to gain rebirth in a Pure Land. After a death, the corpse is usually cremated. Sometimes, though, it is dismembered so that vultures can benefit by eating it.

In Eastern Buddhism, a dying person may hold strings attached to the hands in a painting of Amitābha. This is to help him to die peacefully, with the thought of being drawn to Amitābha's Pure Land. Chinese Buddhists have monks carry out rites for the dead a number of times during the forty-nine day between-lives period, and memorial rites are subsequently performed. The monks chant the name of the Buddha, or *Sūtras* to instruct the dead, and the 'merit' of the chanting and donations is transferred to them; requests are also made for the heavenly *Bodhisattvas* and Buddhas to transfer 'merit' to the dead.

THE ETHICS OF SOCIAL RELATIONSHIPS

Buddhist ethics also include guidelines for good social relationships, though how these have been adopted in practice varies considerably from culture to culture. An important basic text in this area is the *Sigālovāda Sutta* (*D.*III.180–93), described by Asoka as the code of discipline (*Vinaya*) for the laity, paralleling that for monks and nuns. In it, the Buddha comes across Sigāla, worshipping the six directions in accordance with his father's dying wish. He advises that there is a better way to serve the 'six directions': by proper actions towards six types of persons, so as to produce harmony in the web of relationships centred on an individual. A person should 'minister' to his parents as the 'eastern quarter' (where the sun rises), his teachers to the 'south', his wife to the 'west', his friends to the 'north', servants and employees 'below', and monks and Brahmins 'above'. In return, each of these should 'act in sympathy with' the person in various ways.

Regarding his parents, a person should think, 'Once supported by them, I will now be their support; I will perform duties incumbent on them, keep up the lineage and tradition of my family, make myself worthy of my heritage, and give alms on their behalf when they are dead.' In return, his parents 'restrain him from vice, exhort him to virtue, train him to a profession, contract a suitable marriage for him, and in due time they hand over his inheritance'. Elsewhere, it is said that 'Aid for mother and father, and support for wife and children; spheres of work that bring no conflict: this is a supreme blessing' (*Khp.*3). The *Sutta* says that parents only win the honour and respect of children by their kindly help to them. The law of karma ensures that children get the parents they deserve, and parents get the children they deserve. Some people have 'bad' parents, but it is said that the only way to repay the debt owed to parents for their care during childhood, is to establish them in trustful confidence, virtue, generosity or wisdom (*A.*I.61). The *Sigālovāda Sutta* – except in one Chinese translation – does not give obedience to parents as a duty, though this is praised in several of Asoka's edicts. Another teaching on family life is that family harmony and unity gives strength, just as a tree can resist a gale better if it is part of a forest, not alone (*Jat.*I.329).

Other relationships are dealt with in the *Sigālovāda Sutta* as follows. The pupil should minister to his teachers, 'By rising [from his seat in salutation], waiting upon them, eagerness to learn, personal service, and by attention when receiving their teaching.' In return, his teachers 'train him well, cause him to learn well, thoroughly instruct him in the lore of every art, speak well of him among friends and companions, and provide for his safety in every quarter'. The husband should minister to his wife, 'By respect, courtesy, faithfulness, handing over authority to her [in the home], and providing her with adornment.' In return, she 'performs her duties well, shows hospitality to kin of both, is faithful, watches over the goods he brings, and shows skill and artistry in discharging all her business'. A friend should minister to friends, 'By generosity, courtesy and benevolence, treating them as one treats oneself, and by being as good as one's word.' In return, they 'protect one when one is off one's guard, and on such occasions guard one's property; they become a refuge in danger, do not forsake one in times of trouble, and show consideration for one's family'. A master should minister to servants and employees, 'By assigning them work according to their strength; by supplying them with food and wages, tending them in sickness, sharing with them unusual delicacies, and granting them leave at all appropriate times.' In return, they 'rise before him, lie down to rest after him, are content with what is given to them, do their work well, and carry about his praise and good reputation.' Lastly, a householder should minister to monks, 'By lovingkindness in acts of body, speech and mind, by keeping open house to them, and supplying their temporal needs.' In return, they 'restrain him from evil, exhort him to good, love him with kindly good thoughts, teach him what he has not heard, and correct and purify what he has heard'. Each party to these six relationships has five modes of conduct appropriate for mutual enrichment, but the monks also have an extra one: showing the layperson 'the way to a heavenly rebirth.'

As regards marriage, Buddhism's monastic emphasis means that it does not regard this as 'sacred', but as a contract of partnership. Marriage services are not conducted by monks, though these may be asked to bless a couple at or after their marriage. A Japanese Buddhist is married by Shintō rites, while a Thai one is married perhaps by a simple household ceremony in which the family ancestors are informed that the couple are married, so as not to become offended when they have intercourse. At the start of a more elaborate Thai ceremony, the couple are the first to offer food to monks, using a single spoon. In this way they share in an act of 'merit', so as to link some of their future moments of happiness. In connection with this, it is said that a husband and wife, if matched in trustful confidence, virtue, generosity and wisdom, will be reborn together if they wish (*A*.II.61–2).

While Buddhism has no objection to divorce, as such, social pressures mean that this is not common among Buddhists. Unlike some societies, ones whose social ethics have been Buddhist have regarded the role of the single woman (spinster, divorced or widowed) as a respected one. In Southern and Northern Buddhism, laws relating to the grounds for divorce and the division of property and children have been relatively equal with regard to the husband and wife. Writing in 1902, Fielding Hall also said that he found the Burmese wife to be very free compared with Western women of his day.[5] In the lands of Eastern Buddhism, however, the Confucian social ethic has placed the wife in a clearly inferior position to the husband.

In Thailand, women have traditionally had an influential role outside the home in both small and large trading. In agriculture, there is little differentiation of jobs along sexual lines, though men tend to do the heavier work and to take the more important decisions. No attention is paid if a man does a 'woman's' job, or vice-versa: a woman may plough and a man be a midwife. In Southern Buddhist lands, women were traditionally found in law and medicine, and the royal harem had a major political role. In Sri Lanka, Mrs Bandaranayake was the first woman prime minister in the world. In Northern Buddhism, women have enjoyed considerable equality regarding sexual freedom, property rights and acting on their own behalf. They often head a household, and are active in trade, if less directly active in politics. Nevertheless, today there are many women in positions of high authority among Tibetan exiles. There have also been many important female *bLamas*. In East Asia, where the discriminatory Confucian ethic prevailed, the Ch'an/Zen school in particular emphasized sexual equality, based on the idea of all having the Buddha-nature.

While Buddhism sees all people as having had past lives as males and as females, a female rebirth is seen as to some extent less favourable. This is because a woman undergoes certain sufferings that a man is free from: having to leave her family for her husband's; menstruation; pregnancy; childbirth; and having to wait upon a man (*S*.IV.239). The first and last points are not prescriptive, but just describe current practice in ancient India. Both men and women are seen as having their characteristic strengths and weaknesses; thus it is said to be impossible for a female (while being a female) to be either a Buddha or a Māra (*M*.III.65–6). The Buddha's equal concern for both sexes, though, is made clear in a passage where he says that he would not die until the monks and nuns, laymen and laywomen were well trained (*D*.II.104). The early texts refer to many *Arahat* nuns ('far more' than 500, at *M*.I.490), a number of whom gave important teachings. The *Therīgāthā* ('Verses of the Elder Nuns') records teachings and experiences of over a hundred. While the Mahāyāna never had the concept of a female Buddha, it gradually came to emphasize sexual equality, partly through saying that 'maleness' and 'femaleness' are 'empty' of inherent reality. The 'Perfection of Wisdom' was personified as a female *Bodhisattva* and, figuratively, as 'the mother of all the Buddhas'; Tantric Buddhism also introduced many female holy beings associated with wisdom.

10

BUDDHIST PRACTICE: THE *SANGHA*

This chapter deals with the 'conventional' *Sangha* of monks and nuns, and also with certain types of married clerics. The 'fourfold assembly (*parisā*)' consists of all monks, nuns *upāsakas* and *upāsikās*, any of whom may also belong to the revered 'Holy' *Sangha* (see p. 178). The Pali terms translated as 'monk' and 'nun' are *bhikkhu* (Skt *bhikṣu*) and *bhikkhunī* (Skt *bhikṣuṇī*), literally 'almsman' and 'almswoman'. The original mendicancy of these, still current to varying extents, symbolized renunciation of normal worldly activities and involvements; it was an aid to humility, and also ensured that they did not become isolated from the laity. The often close lay–monastic relationship makes *bhikkhus* unlike most Christian 'monks'. They also differ from these in that their undertakings are not in principle taken for life, and in that they take no vow of obedience. The Buddha valued self-reliance, and left the *Sangha* as a community of individuals sharing a life under the guidance of *Dhamma* and *Vinaya*. The job of its members is to strive for their own spiritual development, and use their knowledge and experience of *Dhamma* to guide others, when asked: not to act as an intermediary between God and humankind, or officiate at life-cycle rites. Nevertheless, in practice they have come to serve the laity in several priest-like ways.

THE ROLE OF MONASTICISM

Members of the *Sangha* have probably comprised the most numerous clergy in the world. Though the hostility of Communist governments has reduced their number from well over a million in the middle of this century, at least a quarter of this number still remain. Their life is not an 'escapist' or 'selfish' one, as is sometimes thought. A layperson can distract himself from the realities of life and personal weaknesses with such things as entertainments, pastimes, drink and sex. The simple monastic life, however, is designed to have few distractions, so that there is less opportunity to ignore greed, hatred and delusion, and thus more opportunity to work at diminishing them and to guide others in doing so. Most monks and nuns seek to do this, though a few do take to monastic life as a lazy way of making a living. As regards being 'selfish', the whole aim of monastic life is to help diminish attachment to self and its consequent desires and aversions.

The Buddha felt that the life of a householder was somewhat spiritually cramping, such that it was difficult for a layperson to perfect the 'holy-life' (see p. 17). As the monastic life of one 'gone forth from home into homelessness' lacks many of the attachments and limiting involvements found in lay life, it is seen as having fewer obstacles to, and more opportunities for, persistent and consistent spiritual practice. The early texts do refer to many lay Stream-enterers, more than 1,000 eight-precept lay Non-returners (*M*.I.490–1), and a few lay *Arahats* (*A*.III.450–1). Indeed, while the conditions of lay life pose more obstacles, those who make the effort in spite of them can attain good spiritual progress. Nevertheless, most Buddhist schools see monasticism as a superior way of life, one that all should respect and aspire to join in this or some future life. In the Theravāda, it is said that a lay Stream-enterer should even bow to a monk of lesser attainment, as a way of showing respect to his way of life (*Miln*.162–4). Moreover, a layperson who attains Arahatship must be ordained that day (if he is not to pass away), as the lofty nature of this state cannot be expressed in a lay context (*Miln*.264–6). The Theravādin respect for monks is reflected in the special honorific terms used to address them, and in the fact that in South-east Asia, a monk does not 'eat food', but 'glorifies alms-food'.

In the predominantly Mantrayāna tradition of Northern Buddhism, a *bLama* is generally a monk or nun of long standing or special charisma, but a layperson accomplished in meditation or tantric rituals may also be such a revered teacher. In the rNying-ma school, lay *bLamas* are particularly common; they live apart from their local temple, but gather there for certain rituals. Some schools also allow experienced monks to temporarily suspend their undertaking of sexual abstinence to perform tantric rites involving sexual yoga. Lay *bLamas* are broadly considered to belong to the conventional *Sangha*, as are other figures such as non-ordained meditator-hermits or professional scripture readers.

In Nepal, centuries of Hindu influence led to the extinction of a celibate *Sangha* among the Newari Buddhists (though it continues among minorities of Tibetan culture). The tantric priests who remain are the descendants of monks, and form a distinct caste in society. Most are called *bhikṣus*, literally 'monks', while the elite are called *vajrācārya*'s, '*vajra*-masters'. Both live with their families in or around their 'monasteries' and the *bhikṣus* are frequently workers in precious metals. They are 'ordained' as novices some time before they are seven, and beg for alms for four days before being released from their vows, now seen as being too difficult to follow. This ritual serves as an initiation. The *bhikṣus* also don monastic garb when performing religious duties, these being of a more limited nature than those of the *vajrācāryas*, who receive a higher initiation, are specialists in various rituals, and keep alive knowledge of the scriptures.

In Japan, the lay–monastic distinction gradually diminished in importance. In the ninth century, Saichō introduced a less strict monastic code for Tendai monks, and unconventional holy men known as *hijiri* started to leave off their monastic robes and ignore rules against meat-eating while spreading Buddhism among the common people. In the thirteenth century, Shinran introduced a married priesthood to the Jōdo-shin school, setting a precedent that monks of other schools sometimes followed. From this period, Japanese Buddhism also came to develop a more this-worldly orientation, which generally saw ultimate reality as pervading everyday activities. It was to be known by living within the secular world with the right attitude, be this a devout faith in Amitābha, a Nichiren-inspired urge to purify society, or a Zen approach of giving oneself wholly over to the task at hand. The role of the monk or nun thus became less central, with less charisma, and Buddhism became more lay-oriented, with devotion mainly focussed before a home altar, rather than at a temple. After the Meiji restoration of 1868, the government decreed that monks of all schools could marry, and this has been taken up to such an extent that genuine (celibate) monks are now mostly young men in training. The nuns remain celibate. Monastic training is now seen as a preparation for the role of the priest, who performs rituals such as funerals for the laity, and often hands on his temple to a son. In the post-war period, priests' wives have been allowed to take on some priestly roles, but popular urban lay movements known as 'New Religions' have little need for priests or monks.

In Korea also, some 'monks' were married, but this trend increased rapidly during the Japanese occupation (1904–45), due to attempts to Japanize Korean life. Since then, anti-Japanese feeling has led to a move to re-establish celibacy for all clerics, but a large proportion of the male clergy remain married.

PATTERNS OF ORDINATION

Entry into the monastic *Sangha* is by two stages. From the age of seven or eight, a child can take the lower ordination, or 'going forth' (*pabbajjā*), so as to become a *sāmaṇera* (female, *sāmaṇerī*): a 'little *samaṇa*' or novice. These undertake the ten precepts (see p. 208). When aged twenty (from conception), a person can take higher ordination or 'admission' (*upasampadā*) as a *bhikkhu* or *bhikkhunī*. Once ordained, even as a novice, head hair is shaved off, as a sign of renunciation of vanity. Chinese monks and nuns are also identified by small scars made by burning incense cones on the scalp as an offering to the Buddha. Monastic robes are also worn: orange, yellow or orangy-brown in Southern Buddhism; russet-red in Northern Buddhism; usually grey in China and Korea, and generally black in Japan. In Northern and Eastern Buddhism, additional robes of the original orange may be used during rituals and ceremonies, while in Japan, high-ranking monks (and priests) sometimes wear elaborate silk-brocade robes. Another outward sign of the monk, nun or novice is the alms-bowl, which is generally a deep rounded container with a cover. Monks and nuns also take religious names, such as Ānanda (name of the Buddha's attendant monk) Metteyya (Pali for 'friendly one', and name of the next Buddha).

A new novice or monk generally acts as attendant to a senior monk, his teacher and companion in the monastic life, in a relationship explicitly modelled on that of father and son (*Vin.*I.45). In South-east Asia, short-term noviciates, lasting at least a few days or weeks, are quite common. These are to make 'merit' for a parent or dead relative, or, in Burma, as a kind of *rite de passage* for boys near puberty. Some novices, of course, stay on until they become monks. In Tibetan, Korean, and to a lesser extent in Chinese tradition, people often join the monastery as children; in China, though, formal novice ordination is delayed until the age of nineteen.

Candidates for higher ordination should be free of impediments such as contagious disease, debt, or recent crime, and have the permission of parents, and usually of a spouse, if married. They may also need to be able to read, write and chant a few simple texts. To ordain a monk, a quorum of five validly ordained monks is required, whose authority to ordain is seen as flowing through the unbroken monastic tradition from the Buddha. At ordination, the candidate takes the lower ordination, if he has not already done so, and then commits himself to over 200 training rules; in the Northern and Eastern traditions, he also takes the *Bodhisattva* vows.

The Buddha discouraged monks from disrobing, and originally ordination was taken with the intention that it would be for life. However, the monastic status has never been irrevocable. In most Buddhist lands, a person is expected to be a monk/priest or nun for life, but a system of temporary ordination has evolved in the Theravāda lands of South-east Asia. Here, the tradition is that every male Buddhist should join the *Sangha* at some time for a limited period, usually a *Vassa* (when the number of monks may double). In practice about 50 per cent join, often several times during life. While the continuity of monastic life is kept up by a core of permanent monks, the system makes for a close lay–monastic relationship and a good level of lay religious knowledge and experience. Temporary monkhood is often seen as 'maturing' a young man prior to marriage, and as a way for old people to make 'merit' for the next life. Particularly in Thailand, monastic life can provide a good education, both religious and secular, so that if a monk disrobes, his position in lay society is higher than it previously was, and he is also respected as an ex-monk. In Sri Lanka, however, an ex-monk has some stigma attached to him, and there has even been controversy over a two-week adult noviciate which one Colombo monk introduced in 1982.

NUNS

In Indian society of the Buddha's day, there were a few women ascetics and free-lance debaters, but the ordination of women was a relative innovation. Indeed the Buddha had reservations on this, probably due to social pressures against putting women in a respected position, the potential vulnerability of women following a wandering life, and the possibility of accusations of sexual relationships between monks and nuns. He finally agreed to the pleading of his widowed foster mother when his faithful attendant monk Ānanda asked him if women were capable of becoming Stream-enterers and *Arahats* (*Vin*.II.254–5). On agreeing that they were, he instituted the *bhikkhunī* Community. This, though, was on condition that the nuns observed eight special rules, such as that a nun should always respectfully bow to a monk, however junior he be. As a junior monk who is enlightened should bow to a senior one who is not, order of bowing does not indicate intrinsic worth; it does, though, provide a clear structure for who bows to whom in a monastic context. Other rules made the nuns dependent on the monks for many of their ceremonies, including ordination, to ensure that their Community would develop as a sound spiritual community fully independent of lay society. To be a spiritual adviser to nuns, a monk had to be a wise senior of good character and reputation, and also a good speaker (*A*.IV.279–80).

The nuns' Community now survives only in Eastern Buddhism, where its success is partly due to its having provided a respite from the low status of women in society at large. In China, nuns usually lived in inaccessible nunneries, due to Confucian strictures on the behaviour of women. In 1930, China had 225,200 nuns and 513,000 monks. In Korea, Confucian influence for long discouraged many women from becoming nuns, but this has changed since the 1920s, and South Korea now has around 15,000 nuns to its 8,000 monks (excluding male married clerics). Korean nuns have both a stronger emphasis on the *Vinaya* than monks, and are more accessible to the laity: the services and chanting that they do means that they are the mainstay of day-to-day Buddhism. In Japan, nuns have had a low status, having been unable to live in proper temples (only hermitages), to conduct funerals in their own right, or be recognized as Zen masters.. These restrictions have been changed in the more liberal climate since 1945.

In Tibet, the nuns' ordination line was not introduced from India, though monks ordained nuns themselves from the twelfth century. An influential body of opinion, however, did not accept this as a valid form of ordination, so that 'nuns' now follow the ten precepts of a novice, plus twenty-five more, rather than the full discipline of a *bhikṣuṇī*.

In Southern Buddhism, the *bhikkhunī* ordination line died out in eleventh-century Sri Lanka after a disastrous invasion; in Burma, it existed till at least the thirteenth century. A Theravāda 'nun' is now a woman who permanently keeps the eight or ten precepts, being known as a *sil māṇiyō* (Sri Lanka), *thela-shin* (Burma) or *mae chi* (Thailand). As with a monk, the head is shaved, a Pali name is taken, and a robe is worn: white, brown, pinkish-brown or yellow. Ordination is usually permanent, though in Burma many young girls ordain for a few weeks prior to puberty. The number of Theravādin nuns has been increasing during this century. In Sri Lanka, there are now about 3,000 (to around 20,000 monks), and in Thailand, 70,000 (to around 250,000 monks, during *Vassa*).

In Thailand, nuns tend to do domestic chores around the monastery, with less time than monks for study. Their upkeep comes from some family help, savings, food grown by themselves, and perhaps surplus alms and support from a lay donor. In a few country areas they themselves go on an alms-round. While they do not have the social prestige accorded to monks, the work of The Foundation of Thai Nuns, established in 1969, has helped to heighten people's regard for them. Nuns are now increasingly studying *Dhamma* and Pali, and are also teaching in schools attached to monasteries, helping in hospitals, or working with delinquent girls. In the countryside, some gifted nuns have set up independent nunneries, and teach meditation to other nuns and visiting laywomen. In Burma, most nuns live in independent nunneries; they are often supported by lay donations, especially in the larger nunneries, and also receive food on alms-round. They spend several hours a day in study, and some are very experienced meditators. In Sri Lanka, traditionally the only permanent nuns were old women who kept the eight precepts and lived by begging or charity. In 1907, the institution of the ten precept nun spread from Burma, and gradually came to attract young women. Since around 1945, these nuns have increased their activity, giving public sermons and developing an organization increasingly like that of the monks. Their time is spent in study and meditation, and in serving the laity by conducting rituals and teaching *Dhamma* to adults and children. In return, the laity support them with alms, etc. Due to their simple life-style and practice of meditation, the laity often see them as living a more virtuous life than that of the city and village monks.

Some nuns hope that the Theravādin *bhikkhunī* Community can be re-established. *Bhikkhunī* ordination, however, requires a group of properly ordained *bhikkhunīs* as well as a group of monks, so it is necessary to find a community of Mahāyāna *bhikṣuṇīs* who come up to

Theravādin standards as regards ordination-line and discipline. It is possible this may be found in Taiwan, South Korea or America, as the Chinese ordination line for nuns partly derives from fifth-century AD Sri Lanka. Twelve Theravāda nuns were ordained as *bhikkhunīs* in America in 1988, but such a move has yet to be formally recognized. For the *bhikkhunī* Community to be formally restarted, the agreement of senior monks in all the Theravādin countries would be required, which may be difficult to attain. Also, many nuns prefer their present status, in which they are more independent of monks than they would be as *bhikkhunīs*. Tibetan nuns also hope to re-establish a full *bhikṣuṇī* ordination line. Such aspirations led to the convening of an international conference of Buddhist nuns in February 1987 at Bodh-Gayā.

THE MONASTIC CODE OF DISCIPLINE

Sangha life is regulated by the *Vinaya*, meaning 'that by which one is led out (from suffering)'. The main components of this section of scriptures are a code of training-rules (*sikkhāpada*'s) for *bhikkhus*, one for *bhikkhunīs*, and ordinances for the smooth running of communal life and ceremonies. Each code is known as a *pāṭimokkha* (Skt *prātimokṣa*), and is contained in the *Sutta-vibhanga*. This also describes the supposed situation which led the Buddha to promulgate each rule, and mitigating circumstances which nullify or reduce the usual consequences of digression from it. The regulations for communal life, known as *kamma-vācanā*'s, are contained in the *Khandhaka*.

The *pāṭimokkha* gradually evolved during the Buddha's life, and for perhaps a century after. According to one etymology, '*pāṭimokkha*' means a 'bond': something which is 'against scattering' of spiritual states and the purity of the *Sangha*. In some ways, the code can be likened to one of professional conduct. As an elaboration of the ten precepts, it drastically limits the indulgence of desires, and promotes a very self-controlled, calm way of life, of benefit to the monks and nuns themselves and an example which 'inspires confidence' among the laity (*Vism*.19). The rules are not so much prohibitions as aids to spiritual training that require those observing them to be ever mindful. By constantly coming up against limiting boundaries, they are made more aware of their 'greed, hatred and delusion', and so are better able to deal with them.

The *pāṭimokkha* is chanted at the observance days at the full and new moons. Originally, this ceremony was for public acknowledgement of any digression from a rule, but this soon came to be made privately by one monk to another prior to the ceremony. At this, the code is chanted by a leading monk, often now in an abbreviated form, and the silence of the others is taken as a sign that their conduct is pure, with any digressions acknowledged. In this way the ceremony serves as a vital liturgical expression of the communal purity of a particular local *Sangha*. Accordingly, every monk present within the formally established boundary (*sīmā*) of a monastery must attend each such ceremony, unless he is ill, when he must send notice of his purity.

The early monastic fraternities developed different versions of the original *pāṭimokkha* of perhaps 150 rules, though these codes agreed in substance and most of the details. Three are still in use. The Theravādin code of 227 rules for monks (311 for nuns) is the one used in Southern Buddhism, the Mūla-Sarvāstivādin code of 258 rules for monks (366 for nuns) is used in Northern Buddhism, while the Dharmaguptaka code of 250 rules for monks (348 for nuns) is used in Eastern Buddhism.

The rules are arranged in categories according to degrees of gravity. The first relates to *pārājika* actions, which 'entail defeat' in monastic life and permanent dismissal. For monks, these are strong breaches of four of the ten precepts: intentional sexual intercourse of any kind; theft of an object having some value; murder of a human being; and false claims, made to the laity, of having attained states such as *jhāna* or stream-entry (a possible way of attracting more alms). As serious karmic consequences are seen to follow from a monk breaking these rules, it is held to be better to become a layperson, who can at least indulge in sexual intercourse, than live as a monk who is in danger of breaking the rule against this. The importance of celibacy is that sexual activity expresses quite strong attachment, and uses energy which could otherwise be used more fruitfully. For nuns, there are four extra *pārājika* offences: (with sensual intent) touching a man or going to a rendezvous with him; not making known that another nun has broken a *pārājika* rule; and persistently imitating a monk suspended for bad behaviour. The remaining rules explained here are those of the monks' *pāṭimokkha*.

The second category of rules covers those requiring a formal meeting of the *Sangha* to deal with digressions from them. A digresser is put on probation, being treated as the most junior monk and excluded from official *Sangha* affairs for as many days as he has concealed the digression, plus six more. There are thirteen such rules for monks. Five concern actions of a sensual nature other than intercourse. Two relate to monastic residences, which should not be too large, nor should building them involve clearing away trees, which would harm living beings. Two deal with false accusations of an offence involving 'defeat'; two with causing or supporting a schism in the *Sangha*; one with a monk who is persistently difficult to admonish about his misdeeds, and the final one deals with a monk who 'corrupts families' by giving small gifts in the hope of receiving abundant alms in return.

The third category includes two rules excluding a monk from sitting alone with a woman in certain secluded places. This was both to protect the *Sangha*'s reputation, and to avoid unnecessary temptation for monks.

The fourth category, of thirty rules, deals with actions requiring expiation (by acknowledgement) and forfeiture of an article. Allowable possessions should only be possessed in a certain small quantity, except for a short period, and should not be exchanged unless worn out. Money should not be received, handled or used in transactions (this does not prevent the acceptance and use of money by a monastery's lay stewards).

Digressions from the fifth category of rules require only expiation. The ninety-two rules included here (ninety for the Northern and Eastern codes) deal with such matters as:

(i) harming living beings by directly killing them, digging the ground or destroying plants or trees;

(ii) sleeping in the same dwelling as a woman, or sitting in a private place with one;

(iii) various forms of wrong speech, unfriendly behaviour towards a fellow monk, and true claims to the laity of having attained higher states;

(iv) eating after noon, drinking alcohol, and consuming food or drink (except water) that has not been formally offered;

(v) unseemly, frivolous behaviour, and going to see an army fighting or on parade;

(vi) sleeping in the same place as a layman for more than three nights, or using a high, luxurious bed;

(vii) disparaging the lesser rules as vexing, pretended ignorance of a rule, or knowingly concealing a monk's digression from one of the first seventeen rules.

The sixth category of rules requires only acknowledgement for digressions. Four rules are found here, such as a monk not accepting food from a nun who is not a relation (as nuns found it more difficult to get alms, and so should not be expected to share their food with monks).

The seventh category of rules are also followed by novices, and have no penalty attached to them. These guidelines – seventy-five in the Theravādin code – seek to ensure that the monks are graceful and dignified in the way that they wear their robes, walk, move, and collect and eat alms-food. Such a calm deportment is much valued by the laity.

The final set of seven rules outline procedures for resolving legal questions on digressions. They mainly outline types of verdict, such as innocent, non-culpable due to insanity, and a majority verdict.

After the *pāṭimokkha* code was closed, sub-categories of the rules were developed to cover acts not quite amounting to full digressions, but counted, in decreasing order of gravity, as 'grave digressions', 'digressions of wrongdoing', or as 'digressions of improper speech'.

Besides the penalites referred to above, a Community can impose ones such as censuring or suspension. Suspension is imposed for not accepting that a digression has been made, not making amends for it, or not giving up a wrong view on sensual behaviour. It goes beyond probation in that, for example, other monks should not speak to the monk.

The extent to which the *pāṭimokkha* is followed varies somewhat in practice. In Southern Buddhism, while there is generally a high level of adherence, many adaptations to circumstances have been accepted, and different monastic fraternities or lines of pupillary succession differ in interpretation of *Vinaya*. In Thailand, for example, while most monks belong to the Mahā Nikāya, the 'Great Fraternity', a prestigious minority belong to the Dhammayuttika Nikāya, a reformist tradition founded in the nineteenth century. Besides stressing stricter adherence to *Vinaya*, this also puts more emphasis on textual understanding and meditation, and less on pastoral work among the laity, than the Mahā Nikāya.

In Sri Lanka, the fraternities differ primarily in the castes that they recruit from. This is unfortunate, as the Buddha emphasized that social differences were irrelevant within the *Sangha*. The caste system developed among Buddhists in Sri Lanka due to the proximity of India, and the presence of a sizable Hindu minority. In India there are the four major classes, plus the 'untouchables' and approximately 3,000 castes arranged within these classes. In Sri Lanka, though, there are only about two dozen castes; most people belong to the highest one (the rice cultivating *goyigama*), and there is only one small group akin to 'untouchables'. People mostly marry within their caste, and while the different castes mix socially to some extent, a lower caste person must act respectfully towards one of a higher caste, and the latter will not accept most food and drink from a lower caste person. Since a royal decree of 1765, which referred to unworthy people being ordained, only *goyigama* men have been allowed to ordain in the Siyam Nikāya, which is based on the ordination line that had been re-introduced in 1753 from Thailand (then known as Siam). Ordination lines were then introduced from Burma: in 1803, to form the lower-caste Amarapura Nikāya (which came to have three sub-divisions), and in 1865, to form the reformist Rāmañña Nikāya, which is officially casteless but tends to recruit from the mid-range castes. Laymen are reluctant to pay respects to a lower caste monk, but many of the monks are ashamed of the existence of caste in the *Sangha*, and modernist ones openly criticize it.

In areas of Tibetan culture, the dGe-lugs school is generally stricter in adherence to *Vinaya* than the others. Due to the central role that monasteries have played in society, though, even ex-monks find a place in them. While they cannot take part in monastic services, they often still wear monastic robes, and live within the monastic complex, perhaps holding a post in the monastery's administration.

In Eastern Buddhism, the small Lu (Ch.) or Ritsu (Jap.) school specializes in strict *Vinaya* observance, and has helped to improve the standards of other schools. In Ch'an, blows and fines were added to previous penalties. Chinese monks also followed a supplementary 'Mahāyāna' code consisting of the 'three pure precepts' (see p. 200), and a set of *Bodhisattva*-precepts outlined in the *Brahmajāla Sūtra*. These consist of the 'ten great precepts' (see p. 200) and forty-eight minor ones. Some of these are also found in the *prātimokṣa* code, but others have a more compassion-orientated flavour, requiring vegetarianism, preaching, caring for the sick and exhorting others to give up immoral behaviour. In Japan, Saichō, founder of Tendai, set aside the traditional *Vinaya* as too difficult to keep in a time approaching the age of the 'latter-day *Dharma*'. He retained only the supplementary code, which does not seem formally to require total chastity. Shinran, of course, set a precedent for monks to become married priests. Dōgen, founder of Sōtō Zen, stressed a simple but rigorous life-style. He emphasized the 'three pure' and 'ten great' precepts, but also developed a meticulously detailed code for *unsui*, or trainee monks. This outlines how juniors should behave respectfully in the presence of seniors (sixty-two rules), how trainees should behave when relaxing or studying together, how they should behave when eating, and even how they should wash and clean their teeth. In practice, these rules precluded any sexual activity. While Zen trainees and priests are mostly vegetarian, those of other Japanese schools are now known both to eat meat and drink alcohol.

THE ECONOMIC BASE OF THE MONASTIC LIFE

The original ideal of the *bhikkhu* and *bhikkhunī* was that of a person with a minimum of possessions living a simple life-style, supported by lay donations rather than by any gainful occupation. The formal list of a monk's personal 'requisites', treated as his property, comprises an upper-, lower- and over-robe, a belt, a bowl, a razor, a needle, a water-strainer, a staff, and a tooth-pick. In practice, a monk also has such articles as sandals, a towel, extra work robes, a shoulder bag, an umbrella, books, writing materials, a clock, and a picture of his teacher. In Southern and Northern Buddhism, there is a structural tension between the ascetic tendencies of the *Sangha* and the laity's desire to make more abundant 'merit' by giving to more abstemious and ascetic monks. Thus a town monk with a good reputation may be given a fridge or even the use of a car. If he lives up to his reputation, though, he will use these with detachment (he cannot drive himself), and let other monks benefit from them.

The *piṇḍapāta*, or alms-round is the archetypal symbol for the dependence of monks and nuns on the laity, though the extent of its practice came to vary considerably. Today, while the morning alms-round is infrequent in Sri Lanka, it is still the norm in Theravādin South-east Asia. The giving is a calm, dignified affair, in which monks and novices silently file into a town or village, are met by women and a few men outside their homes, and open their bowls for the offering. No thanks are given for the food, as the donors are making 'merit', but a response such as 'may you be happy' can be given. In Southern Buddhism, other means of giving alms are: inviting monks for a meal;

bringing food to, or cooking it at a monastery, and establishing a fund to buy food, which is cooked by novices or boys living at a monastery. In Northern Buddhism, monks and nuns are rarely supported by alms, except if they are on pilgrimage; though at certain festivals the laity may pay for the food of a monastery for several days. It is usual for a family to give at least one son or daughter to the monastic life, after which they often help support them by produce and income from a plot of land set aside for this purpose. In Eastern Buddhism monks on alms-round are a rare sight, except in the case of Zen trainees.

The laity also donate other goods, and their labour: for example helping to build or repair a temple. Lay stewards usually deal with cash donations. In Southern Buddhism, temple boys also deal with financial transactions if a monk is travelling or buying food at a market. In Sri Lanka, however, a small number of monks receive a salary, as school or college teachers, but this is clearly against the *Vinaya* and is not well thought of. Tibetan monks are also paid for their ritual services by the laity. State patronage has been a source of support for large temples in many countries, but this is now much rarer.

Land has been given to the *Sangha* since the time of the Buddha, when it was used to erect simple monastic dwellings on. *Vinaya* rules forbidding monks to dig the earth were partly intended to prevent them from becoming self-supporting, and thus isolated from the laity. In time, accumulated land-donations meant that temples became landlords in a number of countries, especially where governments granted land. Monastic landlordism developed to a notable extent in Sri Lanka, where, between the ninth and twelfth centuries, large temples owned vast estates, which included plantations, complex irrigation schemes, the villages that depended on them, and rights over some of the labour of the villagers. Nowadays, some temples in Sri Lanka might still, for example, receive half the rice grown on its land by tenant farmers. In general, the twentieth century has seen a considerable reduction in monastic land-ownership, due to confiscations by Communist governments or land-reforms.

In China, master Pai-chang (720–814) made an additional code for Ch'an monasteries, the *Pai-chang ch'ing-kuei*, which in practice became more important than the *prātimokṣa* and *Brahmajāla* codes. It was influenced by Confucian ideas on deportment and etiquette, but also required monks to do daily manual labour, not only around the monastery, but also in the fields and gardens: 'one day no work, one day no food'. This was partly to counter Confucian accusations that monks were social 'parasites'. Digging the earth, as a breach of traditional *Vinaya*, was seen as acceptable if done to benefit the 'three treasures', and not for personal gain. Moreover, it was more than a means of support: its physical exercise was a good complement to long hours of seated meditation; if done with awareness it could itself be a meditation, and it helped to develop a spirit of working together on an equal basis. In later times, though, daily manual labour came to be somewhat neglected.

Large monasteries have also engaged in commercial activities. In Sri Lanka, they bought land, sold produce, and invested in merchants' guilds. In T'ang China (618–907), they acted as pawnbrokers and lenders of grain and cloth, owned grain-mills and oil-presses, and ran large markets, which started as fairs selling incense and images. In Japan, Rinzai Zen temples ran fleets of trading ships to China. In Northern Buddhism, the *Vinaya* specifically allows the use of surplus donations for lending at interest, if this is of benefit to the *Dharma* and *Sangha*. In pre-Communist Tibet, the monasteries were key economic institutions at the centre of a web of trading and donation relationships with the two other main sectors of Tibetan society: nomadic herdsmen and agriculturalists. Individual monks invested in such things as herds and seed-grain, but most capital was received and administered at the level of the 'college', a sub-division of the monastery which inherited the possessions of its members. Its superintendent, monastic or lay, ensured its support by getting a good return from land worked by leaseholders or peasants attached to the monastery, from grazing, forest and water rights, college herds, trade with China and India, bartering with herdsmen, and from loans and investments.

STUDY AND MEDITATION

Monastic life can be broadly divided into personal, communal and pastoral activities. The first includes observing the monastic code, meditation and study, all as means to spiritual development and the preservation of the *Dhamma* for the benefit of all. In practice, monks and nuns have tended to emphasize either study or meditation. Such specialization seems to have existed to some extent even in early Buddhism (*A*.III.355–6).

In Southern Buddhism, a distinction developed, early in the Christian era, between 'book-duty' (*gantha-dhura*) monks, with the duty of study and teaching, and 'insight-duty' (*vipassanā-dhura*) ones, with the duty of meditation. The former tend to dwell in villages, towns and cities, studying and ministering to the laity, while the latter tend to live a more secluded, ascetic life-style in the forest. Some 'forest-dwelling' monks, however, simply belong to a section of the *Sangha* that once lived in the forest. When the teachings were first written down in first century BC Sri Lanka, it was decided that learning was more important than meditation, which would not be possible if the teachings were lost. In Sri Lanka, therefore, many more monks have specialized in study than in meditation, a situation strengthened in recent centuries by the common belief that it is no longer possible to attain Arahatship. In the 1940s and 1950s, however, reform movements revived the forest meditation tradition, so that now, 3 per cent of the island's monks are genuine forest dwellers, and in 1968 a new *nikāya* for them was recognized. In South-east Asia, a larger proportion, though still a minority, of monks have specialized in meditation. Theravāda nuns generally practise meditation (often, but not always of a devotional nature) more than monks, though they study less. Specialization is not always a permanent thing, for a monk might study and then turn to meditation to experientially explore what he has learnt, or return from a forest monastery to a busier town monastery. In any case, a 'study' monk meditating for an hour a day may have fewer expectations and not try to force results, and thus achieve better meditation levels than most forest monks. Quality, not quantity counts. Some monks meditate or study little, though, and are more involved in running a monastery or pastoral activities. All monks chant, however, and this has a meditative quality.

In Northern Buddhism, the dGe-lugs school is noted for its emphasis on study, while others such as the bKa'brgyud emphasize meditation more. Monks of all schools, though, usually start by spending five years in study. This is followed by further study, by learning meditation and practising it in a hermitage, or simply by helping around the monastery.

In Eastern Buddhism, schools such as Hua-yen/Kegon include a scholarly emphasis, Pure Land emphasizes devotion, and Ch'an/Zen emphasizes meditation. Such relative specialization meant that Chinese monks sometimes developed different aspects of their practice by moving between different schools. Few have been proficient scholars, though, due to the difficulty of mastering written Chinese. Scholar-monks tended to reside in larger monasteries, from which they would go on lecture-tours, while the majority were semi-literate and lived in small temples ministering to the laity. In Korea, a novice monk or nun chooses to study (for about six years) or train in meditation. Recently, the trend has been to study then meditate.

Study

The extensive scriptures have been lovingly studied by generations of monks and nuns, who have produced many commentaries and treatises based on them. The need to preserve and disseminate the teachings has spread literate culture to many lands, ensured a generally high degree of literacy among Buddhists, and been responsible for the invention of printing and several written scripts. Buddhist monks and nuns have often been among the intellectual, cultural and artistic elite of their societies.

In Southern Buddhism, monks and novices begin by studying *Vinaya*, basic doctrines, *Jātaka* tales for use in sermons, and common chants. Some go further at monastic schools, colleges and universities. The basis of study beyond the preliminary level is a knowledge of Pali. Some Sanskrit may also be studied, as a key to knowledge of certain non-Theravādin texts. National languages have been used for many treatises and translations of key texts. Traditionally, the texts were inscribed on collections of oblong strips of dried palm-leaves, which are more long-lasting than paper in tropical climates. The first complete printing of the Pali Canon was in 1893, under king Chulalongkorn of Thailand, though the version printed in roman characters by the Pāli Text Society of London, since 1881, has become a widely used printed version. The 'Sixth Council', held in Burma from 1954 to 1956, cross-checked and revised the manuscript tradition and produced a printed Canon known as the *Chaṭṭa Saṅghāyana* (Sixth Council) version. Monks also keep alive the oral tradition, with some memorizing large sections of texts – a few even know the whole Canon! In Thailand, the institution of graded examination systems in Pali, Buddhism and some secular subjects, has both improved the general level of monastic education and produced a tendency to a stereotyped interpretation of scriptures. The study of subjects such as psychology, philosophy, and basic science is seen by traditionalists as leading monks to be worldly and more prone to disrobe, while modernists hold that monks need knowledge of them to be efficient communicators of Buddhism to an increasingly well-educated laity.

In China, Buddhism met a well-developed literate culture, so the entire corpus of texts in Sanskrit and other Indian and Central Asian languages was gradually translated: a vast task which is probably the greatest translation-project the world has seen. The Chinese Canon was also used in Korea, Vietnam and Japan, and was only translated into Japanese early this century. Besides translating genuine *Sūtras* from their Sanskrit originals, the Chinese also composed many themselves, listed as 'spurious *Sūtras*' in their *Sūtra* catalogues. These included texts arising from creative inspiration, but also over-simplified abbreviations of *Sūtras*, and attempts to palm off folk-beliefs as Buddhism, or to take advantage of it for some purpose. The value attached to the Platform *Sūtra*, however, meant that this Chinese text was counted as a 'genuine' *Sūtra* (*Ching*). The Chinese invented printing in the eighth century, using carved wooden blocks, to reproduce Buddhist images and chants. Soon after, texts were printed. The world's oldest extant printed book is in fact a copy of the Diamond-cutter Perfection of Wisdom *Sūtra*, printed in AD 868. The entire Canon was printed from 972 to 983, while the eleventh century saw the invention of movable wooden type. The largest and most definitive edition of the Chinese Canon is now the *Taishō Daizōkyō*, produced from 1924 to 1934 in Japan.

In Northern Buddhism, texts are collections of oblong strips of paper printed by wood-blocks. Traditional study was based on daily lectures on selected texts, followed by memorization and study of them. After the minimum five years, some monks would then spend at least seven years in a Tantric college in which mystical tantric texts would be studied and then used as a basis for meditations. The dGe-lugs have emphasized logic as a basic formative discipline, a student's doctrinal understanding being tested by public dialectical debates. Their full course of study could last up to twenty-five years, leading to the title of first or second class *dge-bshes* (pron. *geshe*), or Doctor of Buddhology. Traditional study also included medicine, astrology, astronomy, grammar, calligraphy, and religious painting. Since the destruction of many monasteries in Tibet by the Communist Chinese, traditional monastic learning has been continued by refugee monks in India and elsewhere.

The meditative life

In Southern Buddhism, a forest monastery usually consists of a simple wooden meeting-hall/shrine-room and huts or even caves as dwellings. It is usual for monks specializing in meditation to adhere to *Vinaya* more strictly, and they may also undertake, at least temporarily, some of the thirteen *dhutanga*'s, or 'austere practices', intended to cultivate non-attachment and vigour. Those more commonly practised include: living only off alms-food; eating only one meal a day, at around 10 a.m.; eating food only from the alms-bowl, and living at least half a mile from a village. The more hardy might undertake to live at the foot of a tree, or sleep in the sitting position. In Thailand, the *dhutangas* are often practised by monks walking on pilgrimage, sleeping under large umbrellas equipped with mosquito-nets. Paradoxically, while such wandering monks are conventionally admired, as approximating to the wandering life of the early *Sangha*, Thais have an ambivalent attitude towards them, as they are not properly integrated within the institutionalized monastic community.

In Northern Buddhism, many monasteries have caves or huts for intensive meditation or scholarship. Seclusion in such hermitages might be for a short period or, in the bKa'brgyud and rNying-ma schools, for perhaps three years, three months and three days. During this time the meditator is alone, with food and water being silently passed in through a small opening. Such seclusion is, of course, voluntary, and is only entered after an exhaustive preparation. It is used as a time to wholeheartedly develop meditation by drawing on both previous practice and innate mental resources.

In Eastern Buddhism, isolated retreats have also been practised, but the Ch'an/Zen school developed the institution of the 'meditation hall' (Jap. *zendō*) as the focus of life in larger, well-run monasteries. On a raised platform at the edge of the hall, the monks and nuns or trainees meditate, sleep and (in Japan) eat, with their few possessions neatly packed in a small box above or behind them. In Chinese tradition, monks sign up for six-month periods in the meditation hall, while others perform devotions, study, run the monastery and come to the hall for evening meditation. In Japan, a trainee's day includes both meditation and manual labour.

COMMUNAL LIFE

While monks and nuns may spend some time in solitary meditation, the monastic life is nurtured and supported by a communal life-style. In having shared values and ideals, the *Sangha* supports the spiritual development of its members by solidarity, example, teaching, mutual acknowledgement of digressions, an ordered life-style, communal discipline and minimal privacy. The ideal is that possessions should be shared, even down to the contents of an alms-bowl (*M*.II.251). Dōgen, the founder of Sōtō Zen, held that most actions of monks should be done in an identical manner, the correct ordering of daily life being the heart of Buddhism.

The section of *Vinaya* called the *Khandhaka* can be seen as the *Sangha's* constitution. It regulates communal life according to the legal devices set out in the *kamma-vācanās*, or 'announcements of action', which are dealt with by a quorum of monks democratically reaching a consensus on a proposal. This then becomes a valid 'action of the *Sangha*'. The *Khandhaka* deals with both procedures and rules. The procedures regulate such matters as *Vassa*, ordination, the *pāṭimokkha* ceremony, disciplinary issues, disputes and schisms. The specific discipline of *Vassa* (see p. 193) is generally observed quite well in Southern Buddhism, less so in Northern Buddhism, and not much in Eastern Buddhism, where it is known as the 'Summer Retreat'. The *Khandhaka* rules regulate, for example, the use of leather objects, the size and type of robes, and foods, drinks and medicines allowable to monks, especially after the last meal at noon.

Within the original *Sangha*, there was an order of precedence according to length of time as a monk, apportioning of duties to officials according to their abilities (which gave them no authority over others), equality in decision-making, and no hierarchy. The extent to which these features survive varies, but the basic equality of the monks has been preserved in all places except perhaps Japan. In Southern Buddhism, seniority is recognized by such titles as *Thera* (Elder) and *Mahā-thera* (Great Elder), conferred after ten and twenty years, respectively, as a monk. Mild hierarchies exist within each monastic fraternity in Sri Lanka, while in Thailand, the government has developed a strong national administrative hierarchy in the present century. Headed by a '*Sangha-rājā*' (appointed by the king) and a monastic council, it deals with such matters as discipline, supervision of *Sangha* property, registration of monks, and organization of ecclesiastical examinations. National hierarchies once existed in Sri Lanka, Burma, Cambodia and Laos, but lapsed when colonization or Communist governments brought an end to the monarchies on which they depended. In Burma, each monastery or small group of them thus became an independent unit, though the government re-instituted a national hierarchy in 1980. Theravāda abbots are usually appointed with the consent of other monks and leading laity, though in Sri Lanka they are either the eldest disciple of the previous abbot or his nephew. Their responsibilities are mainly administrative and their individual power is that of their charisma, if any, and their 'inviting' monks to do certain things (though it would be bad form to refuse).

In Chinese Buddhism, there has been no national hierarchy in recent centuries, though the nationwide Chinese Buddhist Association was formed in 1929 as part of a revival of Buddhism. Before the Communist era, most monasteries were independent institutions, except in the case of some which were branch monasteries of larger ones. There were around 100,000 small 'hereditary temples', each owned by the monks who lived there, and passed on to those whom they ordained as novices, so as to become the monastic 'sons' of the head monk. Higher ordination was only conferred at around 300 large 'public monasteries', which avoided ordaining novices so as not to become 'hereditary' in this sense. The population of hereditary temples was small, from one to thirty monks and novices, though 95 per cent of monks lived in them. Public monasteries had from twenty up to a thousand residents. Public monasteries were often located in inaccessible places, especially near to or on mountains, and were dedicated to meditation, devotion, study, and strict discipline. Their size necessitated efficient organization, headed by an abbot. Under him would come a variety of officials who were appointed every six months, being chosen from monks of the appropriate level of seniority, of which there were a number of ranks.

South Korea now has a national hierarchy, headed by monks and nuns but also including married clerics. In Japan, though, each sub-sect has had its own hierarchy. In 1970, there were 162 sub-sects: 20 Tendai, 48 Shingon, 25 Pure Land, 23 Zen, 37 Nichiren, 7 Nara (e.g. Kegon) and 2 'other'.

In Tibetan Buddhism, each of the schools has its hierarchy, with key positions being taken by *sprul-sku bLamas*. Traditionally, each large monastery had its own resident *sprul-sku* (sometimes, but not always, the abbot), who was the focus of much of its ritual life. In key dGe-lugs monasteries, the abbots were usually eminent *dge-bshes*'s. In Tibet as in Sri Lanka, some monasteries stayed under the control of one family by the abbotship going from uncle to nephew. Within the monasteries, there were a variety of officials in charge of such matters as property, revenue, discipline, tantric initiations, music and chanting. Offices were usually held for a specific term, and candidates for them were short-listed by the community before being selected by the school's hierarchy.

As in all traditions, the monastic day in Southern Buddhism starts early, around 5 a.m. A typical routine in a Thai town or village monastery begins with study or meditation, with breakfast being taken at around 7 a.m., after the alms-round. Communal chanting then follows for about an hour, though some senior monks might chant at the house of a layperson who has invited them for their meal. From around 9 to 10.30 a.m., seniors teach juniors and novices; the last meal of the day is then eaten so as to finish before noon. After a siesta, classes continue from 1.30 to 5 p.m. Alternatively, there might be an ordination, *pāṭimokkha* ceremony, or chanting at the laity's request. Around 5 p.m., cool fruit drinks, or milkless tea or coffee are served. After chores or free time, chanting takes place from around 7 to 8 p.m. The evening is then spent in administrative work, seeing lay visitors, study, and some meditation or chanting. In Thai forest monasteries, morning and sometimes evening chanting is omitted, and monks usually eat only morning alms-food. The siesta lasts from around 10 a.m. to 3 p.m., to recoup energy after meditating for much of the night. There is little if any study, this generally being replaced by work. In the evening the abbot may give a long experience-based discourse, then personal meditation guidance.

In Northern Buddhism, monastic life is regulated by obligatory attendance at daily and periodic rituals. These include *Sūtra*-recitation, worship and visualization of holy beings, exorcizing of evil powers, and generating 'merit' for self, the dead, evil-doers, and the monastic and lay communities. In these complex rituals, the monks may wear special hats symbolizing the holy beings they are seeking to invoke, and accompany their deep-throated liturgy with ritual hand-gestures, the manipulation of ritual instruments, and the sounds of drums and horns.

Communal rituals in the early morning and evening may last around two hours. The first and last hours of the day might be spent in private meditation. In larger monasteries, student monks receive a sermon and learned discussion of a text in the morning and spend from 2 to 4 p.m. and 6 to 10 p.m. in private study. The duty of a few monks is to worship the monastery's specific protector 'Lord' for twenty hours a day in the most sacred shrine in the monastery. As in Eastern Buddhism, the rule against meals after noon is not generally observed, though these are referred to as 'medicine'.

In Chinese Buddhism, while life in hereditary temples was a fairly relaxed one of devotion, some study, and rituals for the laity, the regime of public monasteries was usually rigorous and closely regulated. The monastery buildings such as meditation hall, Buddha-recitation hall, shrine hall, *Dharma* hall, wandering monks' hall, ancestors' hall, refectory and business office were all laid out in a very orderly fashion within a wall-enclosed rectangle. The key building was the meditation hall, or sometimes the Buddha-recitation hall, where invocation of Amitābha and *Sūtra*-recitations were performed. The schedule of meditation, meals, devotion, etc., and the series of phases within these, was mostly regulated by a signal-system of bells, drums and sounding boards. For those signed up in the meditation hall, around nine hours per day would be spent there, alternating between meditation and circumambulation of an image. In weeks of intensive practice, this could rise to fourteen hours. Much of this discipline is still found in South Korea, Taiwan and the Japanese Zen training temple. The Zen monks sometimes rise as early as 3 a.m. for meditation. Verses are recited before or after shaving, cleaning the teeth, using the lavatory, and bathing. One mealtime verse is:

> The first bite is to discard evil; the second bite is so that we may train in perfection; the third bite is to help all beings; we pray that all may be enlightened. We must think deeply of the ways and means by which this food has come. We must consider our merit when accepting it. We must protect ourselves from error by excluding greed from our minds. We will eat lest we become lean and die. We accept this food so that we may become enlightened.[6]

Before eating, some grains of rice are set aside for the 'hungry ghosts'.

While monks are often helped around their monasteries by novices, lay administrators and workers and, in Southern Buddhism, boys serving at the monastery in return for their keep, they also have work to do, especially the more junior ones. In all traditions, work includes such tasks as washing and mending robes, repairing or erecting buildings, fuel gathering, preparing articles for ritual use, and keeping the monastery tidy. Common to most traditions is the careful sweeping of paths and courtyards. This is not only for cleanliness and exercise, but is praised by the *Vinaya* as an opportunity for calm, mindful action and serving others (*Vin*.VI.129–30). In Southern Buddhism, the forest monks particularly value work due to its developing vigour, a good complement to the calm of meditation. In Eastern Buddhism, the Ch'an/Zen tradition praises work and extends it to include gardening, food-growing and cooking. The positions of head cook and head gardener are indeed important ones in Zen monasteries. The Ch'an/Zen attitude that enlightenment can be discovered in ordinary everyday activities, done with full presence of mind, is well expressed in a saying of the eighth-century Ch'an master Pang Wen: 'How wondrously supernatural, and how miraculous this! I draw water, and I carry fuel!' In all Buddhist traditions, monks may also be involved in producing religious art.

RELATIONS WITH THE LAITY

Over the centuries, and in many lands, Buddhist monks and nuns have acted as 'good friends' to the laity in a variety of ways, starting with being good examples and thus fruitful 'fields of "merit"'. The ethos of the *Sangha* has thus been radiated out into society, and the lay world has received various benefits from the 'world-renouncing' *Sangha* that it supports.

In the twentieth century, the actions of unsympathetic Communist governments, or increasing secularization, has in many lands reduced the role of the *Sangha* in people's lives. In any case, this was less in East Asia, due to the influence of Confucianism, or, as in Japan, the existence of a more lay-centred tradition. It is thus in the non-Communist lands of Southern Buddhism that the widest spectrum of lay–monastic relationships has continued into, and developed within, the modern world. Here, each village has at least one monastery which, though it is physically outside it, for quietness, is the focus of its life. The abbot is usually the most respected and influential man in the village and is sought out for advice on many matters, such as the arbitration of disputes, so as to act somewhat like a village parson. In South-east Asia, the monastery has offered a number of 'services', such as free accommodation. The old may use it as a retirement home by becoming monks or nuns; the homeless or chronically sick may be offered its shelter; temple boys from poor families are supported by it in return for their help with chores; boys studying away from home in a town may use it as a hostel; and travellers may use it as a rest-house. The monastery houses the village library, was the centre from which news from beyond the village traditionally radiated, and is the place where most gatherings of any size take place. It also serves in a limited way as a redistributor of property, for land donated by a wealthy patron may be let out for a nominal rent to farmers. Surplus donations of money may also be used by an abbot to help fund the building of a new school.

In Southern Buddhism, monks give sermons to the laity within the monastery, at funerals, at memorial services in the home, and at blessing ceremonies for some new venture. The themes are most frequently ethical, and often draw on the *Jātaka* stories. Teaching of a less formal nature is given to those who come to ask for advice on personal problems and with questions on *Dhamma*: visitors are always welcome. In the twentieth century, teaching meditation to the laity has increased in South-east Asia, and has been revived in Sri Lanka. In Northern Buddhism, one way in which the monks have communicated with the laity is through the performance of open-air mystery plays at certain festivals. In Chinese Buddhism, while the more learned laity might attend scholarly expositions of *Sūtras* at monasteries, traditionally the *Dharma* was spread among the often illiterate masses by peripatetic preachers, who held their audience's attention by amusing and entertaining stories, and dramatic elaborations of episodes from *Sūtras*.

While Buddhist monks were originally wandering world-renouncers, they came in time to serve as literate ceremonial specialists to the laity, particularly at funerals. A key ritual function has been to act as the conveyers of blessings and protections. In Southern Buddhism, monks might be invited to chant *paritta* at the opening of a new house or public building, the start of a new business venture, before or after a wedding, to aid an ill or disturbed person, or at a funeral. In Northern Buddhism, people have sought the services of monks, *bLamas* and lay ritual specialists at times of birth, illness, danger and death. The safety and health of the whole community has been seen as being ensured by the virtuous living and rituals of the *Sangha*. In Eastern Buddhism, monks have chanted *Sūtras* or invocations of Amitābha Buddha for the benefit of ill or deceased persons. In periods when Buddhism played a central role in national life, as in T'ang China (618–907), 'national monasteries' were supported by the state so as to promote the welfare of China and its emperor. In Southern, Northern and Eastern Buddhism, monks have responded to lay requests for the blessing of protective amulets, such as small Buddha-images.

The *Sangha* has also been active in education. In the lands of Southern and Northern Buddhism, monasteries were the major, or sole, source of education until modern times. This is reflected in the fact that the most common Burmese term for a monastery, *kyaung*, means 'school'. The education offered by monasteries was of an elementary nature, covering such matters as reading, writing, basic religious knowledge, arithmetic, and cultural traditions. It ensured, though, that the literacy rate in these lands has been high by Asian standards. In Tibet, the Communist Chinese have ended the educational role of the monastery. In Southern Buddhism, it was mainly boys who were educated at the monastery schools, but they passed on something of their education to their sisters and wives, and there were also some purely lay schools organized for girls. Today, education in Sri Lanka, Burma and Thailand is primarily in state schools, so that the monks have mostly lost their traditional role as school-teachers. Some monastery schools are recognized and supported by the state as primary schools, however, and some monks with modern educational qualifications also function in the state system as teachers and lecturers. This has generated much criticism, though, for many see it as depriving the monk of any specifically religious role.

The *Vinaya* does not allow a monk to make a living from any profession, including being a doctor, and the Buddha advised monks to use any medical knowledge they had to help only other monks/nuns or close relatives, so as to avoid accusations if the medicines did not work. Nevertheless, it was inevitable that, in societies where monks were the literate elite, they should come to respond to lay requests for medical help. In Southern Buddhism, some are noted for expertise with herbal cures, massage, or therapy using coloured lights. In Northern Buddhism, some study in the monasteries to be doctors; in Eastern Buddhism, monks have also practised medicine to some extent. The

Sangha has also served the laity in the area of social welfare and community development, as seen in the last chapter. Modern developments in this area will also be discussed in chapter 12.

In both the Southern and Northern traditions, some monks use their knowledge of astrology to analyse people's characters and guide them through the ups and downs that their karma has in store for them. In Eastern Buddhism, popular demand led temples to dispense divination slips: small pieces of bamboo or paper on which is written some prediction.

Monastic involvement in politics is a type of interaction with the lay world perhaps most at odds with the archetype of the monk as a non-involved world-renouncer. Nevertheless, as Buddhism spread literate culture into many societies in the process of political unification and organization, it is not surprising that the *Sangha* came to wield political influence, or even political power, in a number of countries.

The political power of the *Sangha* reached its height in pre-Communist Tibet, whose ruler was the Dalai Lama. At times of its ascendancy in China, Buddhism had considerable influence over the ruling secular elite, and Japan has had a long history of close contacts between *Sangha* and state. In the lands of Southern Buddhism, also, monks could have considerable political influence, and they have been politically active in twentieth-century Sri Lanka and Burma.

11

BUDDHIST PRACTICE: MEDITATION AND THE DEVELOPMENT OF WISDOM

THE APPROACH TO MEDITATION

In nearly all schools of Buddhism, the final goal can only be achieved by cultivating wisdom (Pali *paññā*, Skt *prajñā*), which directly sees things 'as they really are'. While such wisdom can be initiated by reflection on teachings from scriptures and living spiritual teachers, to mature fully it needs nourishing by meditative 'development' (*bhāvanā*) of the Path.

Wherever Buddhism has been healthy, those who have practised meditation have been not only monks, nuns, and married *bLamas*, but also the more committed lay people. There are also meditative aspects to the devotional practices carried out by most lay people. In the West, a relatively high proportion of those who have turned to Buddhism practise meditation.

Any type of meditation is done under the guidance of a meditation teacher, known in Theravāda tradition as one's 'good friend' (*kalyāṇa-mitta*). The Buddha saw having such a teacher as the most powerful external factor in aiding purification of the heart (*A*.I.14), and as the 'whole of the holy life', rather than merely half of it (*S*.V.2). Meditation requires personal guidance, as it is a subtle skill which cannot be properly conveyed by standardized written teachings. The teacher gets to know his pupil, guides him or her through difficulties as they occur, and guards against inappropriate use of the powerful means of self-change that meditation provides (*Vism*.97–110). In return, the pupil must apply himself well to the practice and be open to where it leads.

Learning meditation is a skill akin to learning to play a musical instrument: it is learning how to 'tune' and 'play' the mind, and regular, patient practice is the means to this. Progress will not occur if one is lax, but it cannot be forced. For this reason, meditation practice is also like gardening: one cannot force plants to grow, but one can assiduously provide them with the right conditions, so that they develop naturally. For meditation, the 'right conditions' are the appropriate application of mind and of the specific technique being used.

Most meditations are done with the legs crossed in the half- or full-lotus position, seated on a cushion if necessary, with the hands together in the lap, and the back straight but not stiff. Once a person is accustomed to this position, it is a stable one which can be used as a good basis for stilling the mind. The body itself remains still, with the extremities folded in, just as the attention is being centred. The general effects of meditation are a gradual increase in calm and awareness. A person becomes more patient, better able to deal with the ups and downs of life, clearer headed and more energetic. He becomes both more open in his dealings with others, and more self-confident and able to stand his own ground. These effects are sometimes quite well established after about nine months of practice, starting with five minutes a day and progressing to about forty minutes a day. The long-term effects go deeper, and are indicated below.

To develop a good basis for meditation, certain reflections may be recommended. In the Northern tradition, these begin by pondering, in turn: the rarity and opportunity of having attained a 'precious human rebirth'; the uncertainty of when this human life will end; the fact that one will then be reborn according to one's karma; that suffering is involved in every realm of rebirth; that such suffering can only be transcended by attaining *Nirvāṇa*; and finally that one needs a spiritual guide to aid one on the path to this. This method rouses motivation for a *Śrāvakayāna* level of practice, as it concerns one's own needs. Next, there are reflections concerning the needs of others, so as to develop the Mahāyāna motivation. This is done by developing the four 'immeasurable' meditations (see pp. 209 ff.), starting with equanimity, then going on to lovingkindness, compassion and sympathetic joy. In this, the meditator cultivates lovingkindness by reflecting on the great kindnesses his mother has shown him, then moving on to reflect that all beings have been his mothers in one or other of his many past lives. He then develops compassion by visualizing a suffering person or animal, and reflects that all his 'mothers' have experienced many such sufferings. Thus arises the aspiration to lead all beings from suffering:

the 'great compassion' (*mahā-karuṇā*). The constant dwelling on this leads to the *bodhi-citta* arising, in the form of the aspiration to work for the attainment of Buddhahood so that the task of saving others may be accomplished. All Mahāyāna practice presupposes this *Bodhisattva* motivation.

THE PRACTICE OF CALM MEDITATION IN SOUTHERN BUDDHISM

Theravāda meditation builds on a foundation of moral virtue to use right effort, right mindfulness and right concentration as mental 'tools' to cultivate the mind and thus develop wisdom. Right effort serves to enable the meditator to develop and sustain the specific kind of activity that meditation is: for it is not a passive thing. It also serves to undermine unskilful states of mind which intrude on the process of meditation. To prevent such states arising, the meditator practises 'guarding the sense-doors': being circumspect about how he relates to sense-objects, so that they do not trigger habitual responses of desire, aversion or confusion.

Mindfulness (*sati*) is the process of bearing something in mind, be it remembered or present before the senses or mind, with clear awareness. It is defined as 'not floating away' (*Asl.*121), that is, an awareness which does not drift along the surface of things, but is a thorough observation. One can be mindful of the passing sensations involved in the action of lifting an arm, or of changing feelings as they pass through the mind. Either way, mindfulness observes without judgement, without habitual reaction, but clearly acknowledges what is actually there in the flow of experience, noting its nature. It has been described as a kind of 'bare attention' which sees things as if for the first time. It is by mindfulness, for example, that one clearly remembers a dream, without confusion and without elaborating the dream further. Mindfulness is crucial to the process of meditation because, without its careful observation, one cannot see things 'as they really are'.

People's normal experience of 'concentration' usually varies from a half-hearted paying attention, to becoming absorbed in a good book, when most extraneous chatter subsides in the mind. Buddhist meditation, in common with many other forms of meditation such as Hindu yoga, aims to cultivate the power of concentration till it can become truly 'one-pointed', with 100 per cent of the attention focussed on a chosen calming object. In such a state of *samādhi* ('concentration' or 'collectedness'), the mind becomes free from all distraction and wavering, in a unified state of inner stillness.

In order for meditation to develop appropriately, the tools must be used in the right way. If a person attempted to develop strong concentration on an object, but without proper vigour or effort, he would become sleepy. If he vigorously developed concentration without also using mindfulness of the object, he could become obsessed or fixated on the object, this being 'wrong concentration'. Concentration, then, if developed on the basis of right effort, in unison with right mindfulness, is 'right concentration'. The development of concentration and mindfulness to high degrees is in fact the basis of one of the two main types of meditation. This is known as *Samatha*, or 'Calm' meditation. An object is chosen, mindfulness is applied to it, and concentration is focussed on specific aspects of the object. As concentration develops, mindfulness is developed as an adjunct which cultivates full presence of mind. Thus arises a state of tranquil, focussed alertness.

Buddhaghosa's *Visuddhimagga*, the classic meditation manual of Southern Buddhism, describes forty possible objects of Calm meditation (listed at *Vism.* 110–11). Some are of a devotional nature, such as reflecting on the qualities of the Buddha, *Dhamma* or *Sangha* (*Vism.* ch. 7). These enable people with a temperament rich in faith to develop a joyful state of relatively deep calm ('access' concentration). Devotional chanting is also used by many as a way of 'warming up' and purifying the mind before meditation practice. Some meditation objects are used mainly to counteract negative character traits. Thus a monk or nun who has trouble with lust might be assigned by a meditation teacher to meditate on the 'thirty-two parts of the body', which include hair, skin, bones, heart, entrails, sweat and snot: a sure way of developing disenchantment with the body!

Lovingkindness meditation

A very popular topic of meditation is lovingkindness (*mettā*), an 'immeasurable' which, when fully developed, expands the mind into an immeasurable field of benevolent concern (see pp. 209 ff.). While it can thus be used to develop a very deep level of calm and inner peace, it is generally used as a counteractive to ill-will. The practice consists of developing a friendliness which is warm, accepting, patient, and unsentimental. The meditator begins by focussing this on himself, for otherwise 'lovingkindness' for others is likely to be limited by an inability to like himself properly. Focussing lovingkindness on himself helps him get to know, and come to terms with, all aspects of himself, 'warts and all'. Once these are accepted – not in a complacent way – then other people, with all their faults, can become the objects of genuine lovingkindness: 'loving your neighbour as yourself', to use a Christian phrase, will then be of true benefit to others.

The meditator starts by saying to himself, for example, 'may I be well and happy, may I be free from difficulties and troubles', and tries to *feel* these words so as to generate a joyful and warm heart. After reviewing 'unlikeable' aspects of himself, he then goes on to focus lovingkindness on others. A common method (see *Vism.* ch. 9) is for the meditator to progressively focus on a greatly respected person, a friend, a person he is indifferent to, and a person he has some hostility towards (all being of the same sex as the meditator). Thus his mind becomes accustomed to spreading its circle of lovingkindness into increasingly difficult territory. If this is successful, he may then radiate lovingkindness to all sentient beings without exception, in all directions: in front, to the right, behind, to the left, below and above. The aim is to break down the barriers which make the mind friendly towards only a limited selection of beings; to cultivate an all-pervading kindness.

Mindfulness of breathing

Of the remaining topics of meditation, ten are certain devices known as *kasiṇa-maṇḍala*'s, or 'universal-circles': objects such as a blue disc, a circle of earth, or a bowl of water. A 'circle' is concentrated on until it can be seen clearly in the mind's eye as a mental image, representing such a 'universal' quality as blueness, earth or water (*Vism.*123–5, 177–84). The most common Calm meditation, however, is 'mindfulness of breathing' (*ānāpāna-sati*) (*Vism.*266–93). Its popularity arises because the breath is always present, and because it becomes more subtle, and thus more calming, as a person becomes calmer. According to one *Sutta*, it was by the method of Calm and then Insight (see below) based on the breath that the Buddha attained enlightenment.

Breathing meditation to induce calm is done with the eyes closed. It begins by some method of counting the in and out movements of the breath, so as to aid the mind in becoming accustomed to staying on it. After a time, the counting is dropped and the sensations arising from the breath going down into and out from the body are carefully followed; then the attention is focussed on the sensations at the nostrils. When a person begins meditation, the attention keeps wandering from the breath, but the method is to keep gently bringing it back. At first, it seems that the mind wanders more in meditation than at other times, but this is just due to a greater awareness of the fickle, shifting nature of thought. After some practice, the mind can remain on the breath for longer periods. At a certain stage, there arises a mental image, or 'sign' (*nimitta*), known as the 'acquired sign'. This can take various forms. It arises from there being good concentration and mindfulness focussed on the breath, just as attention to a 'universal circle' leads to a mental image. Once the image has arisen, in a state of deepening inner stillness, it becomes the focus of attention so as to stabilize it.

The five hindrances and access concentration

As the meditator learns to work with the mental image, he has to gradually suspend the 'five hindrances' which obstruct further progress. Each is a mental reaction to the process of developing sustained application to any task. The first is sensual desire, where the mind reaches out for something more alluring and interesting than the given object. The second is ill-will, where there is a reaction of aversion to the task at hand. The third is sloth and torpor, where there is lethargy and drowsiness. The fourth is restlessness and worry, where the mind alternates between over-sensitized excitedness at some success with the task, and unease over difficulties with it. The final hindrance is fear of commitment, where the mind vacillates and wavers, saying that the task is not worth performing. Overcoming the hindrances is likened both to the purification of gold-ore, which stands for the mind's potential (*S*.v.92), and to the training of a restless animal till it becomes still and tractable.

Once the hindrances are suspended, the image becomes the 'counterpart sign', which has a much brighter, clearer and subtler form. This is the stage of 'access concentration' (*upacāra-samādhi*), for it is the point of access to the full concentration of *jhāna* (*Vism*.125–37).

Working with this sign builds up the 'five factors of *jhāna*', which have been gradually developing all along, counteracting the hindrances. The first factor is 'applied thought', the process of projecting the mind onto the object. The second is 'examination', which leads to the mind remaining on the object. The third is 'joy', which starts in the form of warm tingles and culminates in a feeling of bliss pervading the entire body. This arises as other factors become developed in a balanced way. The fourth factor is 'happiness', a feeling of deep contentment which is more tranquil than joy, and which arises as the mind becomes harmonized and unagitated. The fifth *jhāna*-factor is 'one-pointedness of mind', that is, concentrated unification of the mind on the object. This arises once there is 'happiness', and the mind can contentedly stay with the object.

The *jhānas* and formless attainments

In access concentration, the *jhāna*-factors are still weak, like the legs of a toddler learning to walk. Once they are at full strength, and there is the state of 'absorption-concentration', then *jhāna* ('meditation'; Skt *dhyāna*) is attained (*Vism.*137–69). Here, the mind is blissfully absorbed in rapt concentration on the object, and is insensitive to sense-stimuli, so that *jhāna* can be seen as a sort of trance. This is not in the sense of a dull stupor with subsequent loss of memory of the state: due to the presence of a high degree of mindfulness, it is a lucid trance, and one in which wisdom is also present (*Dhs.* sec. 162). It has the deep, peaceful calm of sound sleep, but greater awareness than in waking consciousness. The mind has great clarity and tranquillity, so as to be like an unruffled, pellucid lake. Due to the radically different nature of this altered state of consciousness, it is classified as belonging to the 'realm of pure form', a level of existence in which the gods of the 'world of pure form' live (see pp. 34 ff.). It is a qualitatively different 'world' of experience, beyond the 'realm of sense-desire'. On emergence from it, there is a purifying afterglow, in which the compulsion to think is absent, and the urges to eat or sleep are weakened.

The state described above is the first of a set of four *jhānas*. Once it has been fully mastered, the meditator progressively develops the others, dropping certain *jhāna*-factors as relatively gross, cultivating deeper and more subtle degrees of calm, and channelling more and more energy into one-pointedness (*S.*IV.217). The fourth *jhāna* is a state of

Table 1 *States developed on the basis of Calm meditation*

States arising from Calm alone			*When combined with Insight*
THE FORMLESS REALM			
States present: one-pointedness, equanimity			
8	The sphere of neither-cognition-nor-non-cognition		→→→ ATTAINMENT OF CESSATION
7	The sphere of nothingness		
6	The sphere of infinite consciousness		
5	The sphere of infinite space		
THE REALM OF PURE FORM			
		States present	
4	Fourth *jhāna*–	One-pointedness equanimity	→→→ THE SIX HIGHER KNOWLEDGES Psychic powers Clairaudience Mind-reading Memory of previous lives Clairvoyance *Nibbāna*
3	Third *jhāna*–	One-pointedness, happiness, equanimity	
2	Second *jhāna*–	One-pointedness, happiness, joy	
1	First *jhāna*–	One-pointedness, happiness, joy, examination, applied thought	
THE SENSE-DESIRE REALM			
iii	Access concentration, based on 'counterpart sign'.		
ii	Work on 'acquired sign', so as to suspend the hindrances.		
i	Work on 'preliminary sign' (e.g. the breath or a *kasiṇa-maṇḍala*)		

profound stillness and peace, in which the mind rests with unshakeable one-pointedness and equanimity, and breathing has calmed to the point of stopping. The mind has a radiant purity, due to its 'brightly shining' depths having been uncovered and made manifest at the surface level. It is said to be very 'workable' and 'adaptable' like refined gold, which can be used to make all manner of precious and wonderful things. It is thus an ideal take-off point for various further developments. Indeed, it seems to have been the state from which the Buddha went on to attain enlightenment.

One possibility is simply to further deepen the process of calming by developing the four 'formless attainments' (*arūpa-samāpatti*'s; *Vism.* ch. 10), levels of mystical trance paralleling the 'formless' realms of rebirth (see Table 1). They are 'formless' as they have no shape or form as object, even the image that is the focus of the *jhānas*. In the first, the meditator expands the previous object to infinity, then focusses on the space it 'occupies'. Next, he focusses on the 'infinite consciousness' which had been aware of this space. Transcending this, he then focusses on the apparent nothingness that remains. Finally, even the extremely attenuated cognition which had been focussed on nothingness becomes the object of attention.

Cessation and the higher knowledges

The remaining states which can be developed on the basis of profound Calm require the addition of insight into the nature of things. From the highest formless state, a meditator can attain an anomalous state known as the 'cessation of cognition and feeling', or simply the 'attainment of cessation' (*nirodha-samāpatti*) (*Vism.*702–9). This is where the mind totally shuts down, devoid of even subtle cognition or feeling, due to turning away from even the very refined peace of the formless level. In this state, the heart stops, but a residual metabolism keeps the body alive for up to seven days. Here a person gains a sort of unconscious meeting with *Nibbāna*, for they are said to 'touch *Nibbāna* with their body'. Only someone who is already a Non-returner or *Arahat* can attain this state.

From fourth *jhāna*, the 'higher knowledges' (*abhiññā*'s) can also be fully developed (*Vism.* chs. 12–13). The last three of these comprise the 'threefold knowledge' (*tevijjā*), culminating in the (conscious) attainment of *Nibbāna* (see p. 21). The first three consist of various paranormal abilities. The first is a group of 'psychic powers' (*iddhi*'s): psychokinetic abilities such as walking on water, flying, diving into the earth, and being in several places at once. These are said to be developed by meditating on the elements of matter to gain control of them. The second 'higher knowledge' is clairaudience: the ability to hear sounds at great distance, including the speech of the gods. The third knowledge is that of reading the mental states of other people. Thus, based on the power and purity of fourth *jhāna*, many barriers can be overcome by the six higher knowledges, respectively those of physical laws, distance, the minds of others, time, death, and, highest of all, the barrier of conditioned existence as such.

THE PRACTICE OF INSIGHT MEDITATION IN SOUTHERN BUDDHISM

The other way to use the tools of meditation is to generate a high degree of mindfulness, based on right effort and a modicum of concentration. This is known as *Vipassanā*, or 'Insight' meditation. Calm meditation alone cannot lead to *Nibbāna*, for while it can temporarily suspend, and thus weaken, attachment, hatred and delusion, it cannot destroy them; only Insight combined with Calm can do this. Calm produces very valuable changes in a person, such as a deepening of morality. It also acts as an ideal preliminary to the practice of Insight: it gives the mind the clarity in which things can be seen 'as they really are'; it develops the ability to concentrate on an object for long enough to investigate it properly; it schools the mind in 'letting go', at least of objects other than the focus of meditation, and it makes the mind stable and strong, so that it is not agitated by the potentially disturbing insights into such matters as not-self. In these ways, then, Calm 'tunes' the mind, making it a more adequate instrument for knowledge and insight.

The most common way of developing meditation has thus been to practise 'Insight preceded by Calm', as described in such *Suttas* as the *Sāmañña-phala* (*D*.I.47–85). This method of training is known as the 'vehicle of Calm' (*Samatha-yāna*). In this, 'access concentration' or *jhāna(s)* are developed, and then Insight is cultivated and focussed on even these calm states, so as to overcome any attachment to them. A special case of this leads to the 'attainment of cessation'. The 'higher knowledges' are also developed by adding Insight to deep Calm. Another possible sequence, which has become popular in Burma in the twentieth century, is to practise 'Calm preceded by Insight': the 'vehicle of Insight' (*Vipassanā-yāna*). Here, the method is to develop powerful mindfulness, with just a little concentration on the breath to help keep the mind steady. From this, strong insight develops, and this naturally brings about stillness and calm due to strong momentary concentration and the detachment which insight brings. In a third way of practice, 'Calm-and-Insight-yoked together', the two are developed in unison: first one level of Calm, then Insight into it, then a deeper level of Calm, and Insight into this, etc. However meditation is developed, though, both Calm and Insight are necessary ingredients, for the breakthrough to the experience of *Nibbāna* occurs in an instant where there is both insight and at least the level of calm found in the first *jhāna*. At this level, *jhāna* is 'transcendent', and no longer 'ordinary' (see p. 68).

The four foundations of mindfulness

The basic framework for developing Insight practice is known as 'the four foundations of mindfulness', the *sati-paṭṭhāna*'s, which are described in such *Suttas* as the *Mahā-sati-paṭṭhāna* (*D*.II.290–315). Here, rather than focussing on one chosen object, as in Calm practice, the attention is opened out so that mindfulness carefully observes each passing sensory or mental object. The four 'foundations' are the spheres in which to develop mindfulness: body, feelings, states of mind, and *dhammas*, which comprise all aspects of personality, whether in oneself or others. As the body is more easily perceived, mindfulness takes this as its object first, so as to build up its power before observing the more fleeting mental processes. When not doing sitting meditation, the meditator may carefully observe the sensations involved in movements, such as bending and stretching the arms, eating, washing, and going to the toilet. 'Mindfulness of walking' is a specific kind of practice, also used by Calm practitioners to strengthen their mindfulness. In this, a person walks back and forth along a path with the mind focussed on the sensations in the feet and calf muscles, and the various phases of walking may be mentally noted with such terms as 'lifting', 'moving', and 'putting'. This develops a light, open feeling of spaciousness, and may even lead to the 'foot' disappearing into a flow of sensations.

During seated meditation, the breath is usually investigated, for it is through this rising and falling process that the body is kept alive. Such meditation is described in the *Ānāpāna-sati Sutta* (*M*.III.79–88). The mind does not remain solely on the breath, but also observes various physical sensations as they occur, such as itches and stomach rumbles. Insight meditation is more analytical and probing than Calm meditation, as it aims to investigate the nature of reality, rather than remaining fixed on one apparently stable object. Thus what might become a distraction within Calm meditation can become an object for Insight. Once mindfulness of the body is established, attention is turned to feelings. These are observed as they arise and pass away, noting simply whether they are pleasant, unpleasant or neutral, born of the body or of the mind. No 'significance' is attached to them, however: they are viewed simply as passing phenomena. Mindfulness then moves on to states of mind, noting moods and emotions as they arise and are allowed to pass. Finally, mindfulness investigates *dhammas* (cf. pp. 83 ff.), such as the five hindrances or the seven factors of enlightenment (see p. 65), noting when they are present, when they are absent, how they come to arise, and how they come to cease. Likewise, the five factors of personality and the Four Holy Truths are investigated, using the heightened awareness that mindfulness brings.

Investigation of the 'three marks'

While investigating the processes described above, the aim is to experientially recognize their shared features: the 'three marks' (see pp. 50ff.). Their constant arising and ceasing is seen to demonstrate their *impermanence*. Their *unsatisfactoriness* is seen in the fact that they are ephemeral, unstable, and limited: not the kind of thing that one can rely on. Their being *empty of self* is seen in the fact that they rise according to conditions, cannot be controlled at will, and thus do not 'belong' to anyone. Investigation shows that the appearance of 'oneself' and external 'things' as substantial self-identical entities is a misperception. These insights are not of a conceptual, intellectual nature, but arise as flashes of penetrative understanding, or wisdom. Once these have occurred during meditation, they may also arise in the course of the day, as things are observed with mindfulness. The arising of such wisdom gradually leads to disenchantment with the ephemeral phenomena of the world, so that the mind can come to turn away from them and perceive *Nibbāna*, the Deathless.

The seven stages of purification

The stages in the development of Insight are outlined in detail in the *Visuddhimagga*, which is structured round a scheme of seven purifications: two relating to morality and Calm, and five relating to Insight. In the third purification, no 'person' or 'being' is seen apart from changing mental and physical phenomena. In the fourth purification, insight into Conditioned Arising starts to develop, so that the tendency to think of a self-identical 'I' continuing over time starts to wane. Reality is seen to be rapidly renewed every moment as a stream of fluxing, unsatisfactory *dhammas*. Strong confidence in the three refuges now develops. In the fifth purification, clearer insight leads to the arising of ten 'defilements of insight', such as flashes of light and knowledge, great joy, and a subtle delighting attachment to these phenomena. These can lead the meditator to think, wrongly, that he has attained *Nibbāna*. Once this 'pseudo-*Nibbāna*' is recognized, the ten states can themselves be contemplated as having the three marks, so that attachment to them gradually passes.

In the sixth purification, a series of direct knowledges develop. These start by focussing on the cessation of each passing phenomenon, such that the world comes to be seen as constantly dissolving away, a terror-inspiring phantasmagoria which is unreliable and dangerous. A strong desire for deliverance from such worthless conditioned phenomena arises. They are seen as crumbling away, oppressive, and ownerless; then dread passes and sublime equanimity, clarity of mind and detachment arise. The conditioned world is simply observed as an empty and unsatisfactory flux which is not worth bothering with. Reviewing these insights, the meditator is endowed with intense faith, energy and mindfulness.

In the seventh purification, the mind finally lets go of conditioned phenomena so that a moment of 'Path-consciousness' occurs, which 'sees' the unconditioned, *Nibbāna*. This is perceived either as 'the signless' (devoid of signs indicative of anything graspable), as 'the undirected' (that which lies beyond goal-directedness concerning worthless phenomena) or as 'emptiness' (*suññatā*: void of any grounds for ego-feeling and incapable of being conceptualized in views). A few moments of blissful 'Fruition-consciousness' immediately follow. The first time these events take place, a person becomes a 'Stream-enterer' (see pp. 71 f.). The same path of seven purifications may subsequently be used to attain the three higher stages of sanctity, culminating in Arahatship, full liberation. Each attainment of 'Path-consciousness' is a profound cognitive shock, which destroys some of the hindrances and fetters and leads to great psychological and behavioural changes, so as to purify and perfect the practitioner.

THE CLASSICAL PATH OF CALM AND INSIGHT IN NORTHERN AND EASTERN BUDDHISM

In Northern and Eastern Buddhism, Calm (Skt *Śamatha*) and Insight (Skt *Vipaśyanā*) became modified by the Mahāyāna framework of belief and motivation. In Northern Buddhism, the classical practice of Calm and Insight is based on three works by the eighth-century Indian teacher Kamalaśīla, on *Bhāvanā-krama*, or 'Stages of Meditation'. It received perhaps its most thorough formulation in the *Lam-rim chen-mo*, or 'Graduated Path to Enlightenment' of Tsong-kha-pa, founder of the dGe-lugs school. In Eastern Buddhism, it received its most systematic working out by Chih-i, founder of T'ien-t'ai school, in his *Mo-ho Chih-Kuan* 'The Great Calm (*Chih*) and Insight (*Kuan*)'. The much-read 'Awakening of Faith in the Mahāyāna' also has a section (Part 4) devoted to Calm and Insight.

There is a broad similarity in these Northern and Eastern paths. Meditators begin with some combination of traditional Calm practices and the foundations of mindfulness (Skt *smṛtyupasthāna*'s), so as to attain access concentration (Skt *anāgamya*, 'arriving') and perhaps full *dhyāna* (Pali *jhāna*). Insight into the 'three marks' may then be cultivated. In T'ien-t'ai, Calm may subsequently be practised by special techniques in which the meditator seeks to become fully absorbed in such things as ritual preparation and purification of a meditation hall, bowing, circumambulation of images or a copy of the Lotus *Sūtra*, repentance, vows, recitation of *dhāraṇīs*, invocations of Amitābha's or another Buddha's name, and visualizations of the thirty-two characteristics of a Buddha. He then investigates the nature of the component phenomena of these rites, and of his mind. Alternatively, the mind may be the object of attention from the start. As in the Northern 'graduated path', phenomena are examined so as to see them as empty and thought-only. This leads up to the transcending of the subject/object duality, as in Yogācāra accounts of the path (see p. 112). Full realization only comes, however, when even knowledge of non-duality is seen as empty, and there is a liberating insight into emptiness. This is the 'Path of Seeing', which makes a person a Holy *Bodhisattva* (see p. 123). He must then integrate the vision of emptiness into his life, ensuring that it does not cause him to turn away from the suffering beings of the illusory conventional level of reality. According to T'ien-t'ai tradition, his Calm (of a transcendent level) enables him to constantly know emptiness/*Nirvāṇa*, but his Insight enables him to know that this is no different from the world of 'suffering beings'.

The Mahāyāna version of the classical path of Calm and Insight was seen as a way of cultivating the *Bodhisattva*-path over many lives. To accelerate progress in this, other techniques were also developed, cultivating Calm and Insight in relatively new ways which were seen as more powerful. These primarily involved either (i) techniques of visualization (related to the early *kasiṇa-maṇḍala* method), or (ii) cultivating spontaneous insight.

PURE LAND VISUALIZATIONS

While the emphasis in Pure Land practice is on devotion, it is not without its contemplative side. The *Sukhāvatī-vyūhopadeśa* (see p. 152) outlines five kinds of 'mindfulness' which are used to awaken absolute faith in Amitābha Buddha. The first three are counted as forms of purifying Calm. They use, respectively, actions of body, speech and mind: bowing to Amitābha while reflecting on his wondrous powers; praising him with the invocatory formula (see p. 187) while contemplating the meaning of his name; and arousing a single-minded determination to be reborn in his Pure Land.

The fourth mindfulness is a visualization. In a simple form, it can be done by contemplating an image of Amitābha/Amitāyus till it can be seen in great detail with the eyes closed. The most elaborate method, however, is outlined in the *Amitāyur-dhyāna Sūtra*, which describes a way of attaining *dhyāna* (accompanied by Insight) involving a series of sixteen meditations.

The first meditation is performed by the practitioner contemplating the setting sun (symbolic of the Buddha 'Infinite Radiance') until its image can be held clearly before the mind's eye. The next meditations begin by developing a mental image of water; this is then seen to turn to ice, and then into shimmering blue lapis lazuli surrounded by hundreds of shining jewels. From their light, a jewelled tower of ten million storeys (the Pure Land) is formed in the sky. This vision is then firmly established, till it remains throughout the day, with the eyes open or shut (as in *kasiṇa* practice). Next, visualizations of the details of the Pure Land are built up, for example jewel-trees 800 leagues high, and water in the form of soft jewels lapping over diamond sands. Next, the throne of Amitāyus/Amitābha is visualized as a huge iridescent lotus with 84,000 petals, each of which has 84,000 veins, from each of which come 84,000 rays of light, each of which is seen as clearly as one's face in a mirror! Amitāyus himself is then visualized, so that the mind, in contemplating the form in which the *Dharma*-body appears, has its own intrinsic Buddha-nature activated. Amitāyus's two *Bodhisattva* helpers are then visualized; all three give out rays of light which transmit their images throughout the jewels of the Pure Land, and the sound of *Dharma* being taught comes from light, streams and birds. Moving on, the details of the Buddha's huge body are visualized, for example an immeasurable radiance is emitted from his skin-pores, and in a halo as large as a hundred million universes are innumerable Buddhas. The attendant *Bodhisattvas* are then visualized in great detail. Next, the practitioner visualizes himself born in the Pure Land on a lotus, and then visualizes the Buddha and two *Bodhisattvas* together. The remaining meditations are on the way in which people of high, middling and low spiritual and moral abilities will be born in the Land, if they have faith.

Thus, through a series of visualizations of a radiant world, akin to that of the *Gaṇḍavyūha Sūtra* (see p. 119), the practitioner attains a foretaste of the Pure Land, thereby transforming his perception of the ordinary world by infusing it with his vision. He attains serene certainty of birth in Sukhāvatī, and reduction of the time he will be there before his 'lotus' opens and he can behold its glories. The *Sukhāvatī-vyūhopadeśa* sees visualization, in full mind-blowing detail, as a means to gaining an insight into the 'unthinkable' (cf. p. 119), the *Dharma*-body or pure Mind which lies beyond conceptual thought. It is thus counted as a form of Insight practice. The centre of the Pure Land, Amitābha's lotus throne, is the point at which the *Dharma*-body, the essence of all Buddhas, is manifested. The Pure Land, Amitābha and the

Bodhisattvas are said to form one organic entity, one *Dharma* which is the true object of Pure Land faith.

The *Sukhāvatī-vyūhopadeśa* regards the fifth 'mindfulness' as the activity of skilful means, which compassionately transfers the 'merit' of the previous practices to help all beings gain rebirth in the Pure Land.

TANTRIC VISUALIZATIONS

In Northern Buddhism, visualizations are a central feature of tantric meditations (they are also found in Milgyo and Shingon, the Korean and Japanese forms of Tantric Buddhism). In order to be guided through the complex and powerful meditations, a tantric practitioner must find a suitable *bLama* to act as his spiritual preceptor. Once he has found one with whom he has a personal affinity, he must prove his sincerity, purity and detachment before he will be accepted as a disciple; for his spiritual welfare will then be the responsibility of the *bLama*. In return, the disciple should implicitly obey all his *bLama's* instructions as a patient obeys the instructions of his doctor. He should also serve and have great devotion for his *bLama*.

After the practitioner has carried out a number of arduous preliminaries, to purify himself (see p. 179), his *bLama* will initiate him into the Mantrayāna, as he will also do to each new level of practice within it. An initiation (Skt *abhiṣeka*) is regarded as having several functions. Firstly, it helps remove spiritual obstructions in the practitioner. Secondly, it transmits a spiritual power from the *bLama*, seen as an 'empowerment' to practice in a certain way. Thirdly, it permits access to a body of written teachings and the oral instructions needed to understand and practise them properly. Lastly, it authorizes the practitioner to address himself in a particular way to a certain holy being or deity. At the initiation, the *bLama* selects a *mantra* and 'chosen deity' (Tib. *yi-dam*) appropriate to the practitioner's character type, and introduces him to the *maṇḍala*, or sacred diagram, of the *yi-dam*. The nature and role of *mantra*, *yi-dam* and *maṇḍala* are as follows.

Mantras

Mantras are sacred words of power, mostly meaningless syllables or strings of syllables, which give an arrangement of sound of great potency (see p. 136). When pronounced in the right way, with the right attitude of mind, the sound-arrangement of a *mantra* is seen as 'tuning in' the practitioner's mind to a being he wishes to visualize. This may perhaps be compared to the way in which certain musical chords naturally tend to evoke reactions of sadness or joy in people. In the case of *mantras*, they are seen as making the practitioner's mind so in tune with a particular holy being that it can appear to him in a visualized form. In the Yogācārin 'thought-only' perspective, the holy beings invoked can be seen as not 'external' to him, but as psychic forces or levels of consciousness latent within the practitioner's own mind. A *mantra* is seen as acting like a psychic key which enables a person to have power over 'physical' things, or enable him to visualize and communicate with a being/force whose *mantra* it is. Each holy being has its own *mantra*, which is seen to express its essence. For example that of the 'Saviouress' Tārā is *oṃ tāre, tuttāre ture svāha*! Each holy being also has a short 'seed' (Skt *bīja*) *mantra*: *trāṃ* in the case of the Buddha Ratnasambhava.

The *yi-dam*

A *yi-dam* is a particular holy being who is in harmony with the practitioner's nature, and who will act as his tutelary deity. By identifying with his *yi-dam*, a practitioner identifies with his own basic nature purged of faults. The *yi-dam* reveals aspects of his character which he persists in overlooking, for it visually represents them. Acting as a guide for his practice, the *yi-dam* enables the practitioner to magically transmute the energy of his characteristic fault into a parallel kind of wisdom, embodied by the *yi-dam*. For example, if Akṣobhya Buddha is taken as the *yi-dam*, the brilliance and power of hate and anger may be transmuted into the openness and precision of 'mirror-like wisdom'.

The *yi-dams* are grouped into five 'families', each associated with a particular fault and with one of the main Mantrayāna Buddhas: the five 'Conquerors (of delusion and death)' (Skt *Jina*'s). The first of these is the 'central' Buddha, seen as a personification of the *Dharma*-body: the ever-enlightened *Ādi*, or primordial, Buddha. As *Dharma*-body, he is seen as unifying and manifesting the other Buddhas. In different tantric systems, he is variously identified as Vairocana ('The Resplendent

One'), Vajrasattva ('Thunderbolt-being'), Vajradhāra ('Thunderbolt-holder'), Samantabhadra ('Universal Sage') or Akṣobhya ('The Imperturbable'). The other four *Jinas* are seen as dwelling in Pure Lands far to the east, south, west and north of the cosmos: respectively Akṣobhya, Ratnasambhava ('The Jewel-Born One'), Amitābha ('Infinite Radiance'), and Amoghasiddhi ('Infallible Success').

The *yi-dams* belonging to each of the five families may be of four different types, to correspond to further variations in human character. They may be male or female, and peaceful or wrathful in appearance. The male, peaceful ones are the five *Jinas* themselves and the ordinary *Bodhisattvas* of the Mahāyāna. The wrathful ones are for strong, unconventional people who are disgusted with the impermanent world and its dreary round of rebirths. The anger which the *yi-dam* shows is not that of a vengeful god, but, hate-free, it aims to open up the practitioner's heart by devastating his hesitations, doubts, confusions and ignorance. The male wrathful *yi-dams* are called *Heruka*'s and also *Vidyā-rājā*'s, 'Knowledge-kings'. Plate 11 shows a popular one called Yamāntaka, 'Conqueror of Death', the wrathful form of the *Bodhisattva* Mañjuśrī. By visualizing such a fearful form, which has the head of a raging bull, the practitioner can clearly see the danger in his own tendency to anger, and can transmute it into a wisdom. Yamāntaka is shown free and unbridled, like all wrathful *yi-dams*, trampling on corpses representing the 'I-am' conceit and its limiting, deadening influence. On his main head he wears as ornaments a crown of skulls, representing the five main human faults; the garland of heads hanging at his waist represent his triumph over many confused and neurotic ideas.

Plate 11 not only shows Yamāntaka, but also a wrathful female *yi-dam*. These are called *Ḍākiṇī*'s, which are seen as playful but tricky beings, often portrayed wielding a chopper and holding a skull-cup containing poison (human faults) transformed into the nectar of Deathlessness. The *Ḍākiṇīs* are the consorts of the *Herukas*, just as female peaceful *yi-dams* are seen as the consorts of the male peaceful ones. A consort is called the 'Wisdom' (Skt *Prajñā*) of her respective male partner, and represents the wise, passive power which makes possible the active and energetic skilful means of the male. Together, the two form a wisdom-energy, often represented, as in Plate 11, as *Yab*, 'Father', and *Yum*, 'Mother', in sexual union. This form symbolizes

Plate 11 A Tibetan image of the *Heruka* Yamāntaka and his female consort.

the idea that, just as sexual union leads to great pleasure, so the union of skilful means and wisdom leads to the bliss of enlightenment. Such sexual symbolism is minimized in East Asian Tantric Buddhism, as it offended against Confucian propriety.

A male peaceful *yi-dam* is called a *Bhagavat*, or 'Lord', while a female one is called a *Bhagavatī*, or 'Lady'. The most popular 'Ladies' are the Green and White forms of the *Bodhisattva* Tārā, the 'Saviouress' (see p. 137). Though some of her twenty-one forms are wrathful, the Green and White forms are the most popular of all *yi-dams*.

Maṇḍalas

A *maṇḍala* or '(sacred) circle' is a device developed in India between the seventh and twelfth centuries, possibly being derived from the *kasiṇa-maṇḍala*. Its basic function is to portray the luminous world, or Pure Land, of a specific holy being, with other holy beings particularly associated with it arrayed about it. A *maṇḍala* may be temporarily constructed, for a particular rite, out of coloured sands or dough and fragrant powders, using a raised horizontal platform as a base. In a more permanent form, it may be painted on a hanging scroll, or *thang-ka*, as in Plate 12.

Depending on the rite the *maṇḍala* is used in, the deities in it will vary, though the one portraying the five *Jinas* is the most important. By being introduced to his *yi-dam's maṇḍala*, a practitioner can familiarize himself with the deity's world and the holy beings associated with him or her. By vivid visualization of the deity and his or her world, he may master and integrate the psychic forces they represent, and achieve a wholeness in his life.

Depending on the materials of the *maṇḍala*, the deities may be represented by metal statues, painted images or seed-*mantras*. The pattern of a *maṇḍala* is based on that of a circular *Stūpa* with a square base oriented to the four directions. It can, in fact, be seen as a two-dimensional *Stūpa*-temple which contains the actual manifestations of the deities represented within it. Its form can also be related to the common belief in the magical efficacy of circles, and the Indian idea of each physical world as being a circular disc with a huge mountain (Sumeru), home of many gods, at its centre. The bands encircling the *maṇḍala* mark off its pure, sacred area from the profane area beyond, and also suggest the unfolding of spiritual vision gained by a practitioner when he visualizes himself enter the *maṇḍala*. Having crossed the threshold, he comes to the central citadel, representing the temple of his own heart. He enters by one of the four doors, over which there is a *Dharma*-wheel and two deer, representing the teachings of Buddhism. Passing one of the 'four great kings' – guardian gods

Plate 12 A *thang-ka* showing a maṇḍala surrounded by a number of Vajrayāna deities and spiritually realized beings.

accepted by all schools of Buddhism – he comes to the main *maṇḍala* deities. In the *maṇḍala* shown in Plate 12, the central deity is Akṣobhya Buddha, with Vairocana taking his usual place to the east (bottom); also shown are four *Bodhisattvas*.

Mudrās

Tantric rites may involve the use of ritual gestures which, like the gestures made by the hands of Buddha-images, are known as *mudrā*'s or 'signs'; as has been seen, these are also used in devotion. On Buddha-images, they are the 'signs' which characterize particular heavenly Buddhas, for example Akṣobhya is generally shown making the 'earth-witness' gesture (see plate 1). The much wider range of *mudrās* used in tantric ritual are seen as the 'signs' – and causes – of particular states of mind. What lies behind this idea is the observation that states of mind generally express themselves in a person's stance and gesture. Clenching a fist expresses anger, while holding up an open palm expresses the wish to calm down an argument. Ritual *mudrās* are seen as working on the reverse of this principle: by making various gestures, certain states of mind may be stimulated or enhanced. Thus the *mudrās* are used to amplify the efficacy of the *mantras* in evoking psychic forces and higher states of consciousness. These *mudrās* are often conjoined with the use of the *Vajra*-sceptre and *Vajra*-bell in certain rituals (see pp. 135 f.). The use of these implements symbolizes that the adept must come to develop both his/her 'male' skilful means (sceptre), and 'female' wisdom (bell).

Visualizations

Having been given a *yi-dam*, *mantra* and *maṇḍala*, the tantric practitioner can then go on to perform various meditations in the form of *sādhana*'s, or 'accomplishings'. *Sādhanas* involve the mind in vivid visualizations, the speech in chanting *mantras* and descriptions of holy beings, and the body in the use of *mudrās*. As visualization develops one-pointed concentration on a mental image, it has a 'Calm' aspect. It goes beyond the goals of ordinary Calm meditation, however, in that it is also a technique for developing insight. The vivid vision seems at least as real as 'external' physical objects, and so generation and reflection on it is a way of realizing that everything is 'thought-only', no more (or less) real than the vision.

The practice of a *sādhana* is performed in two stages. The first is that of Generation (Skt *Utpanna-krama*), which is the process of building up the visualization. The adept first familiarizes himself with the paintings and detailed textual description of the deity and his *maṇḍala*-world. He then gradually learns to build up a mental image of the deity till it is seen in full technicolour reality as a living, moving being.

When the visualization is fully established, the stage of Completion (Skt *Sampanna-krama*) is entered, where the adept draws on the energies and spiritual qualities of the archetypal visualized form. The most powerful way of doing this is at a level of tantric practice known as 'Supreme Union' (Skt *Anuttara-yoga*). Here, the adept first fully identifies himself with the *yi-dam*, thus overcoming all seeming duality between 'two' beings which are equally manifestations of Mind/emptiness/*Dharma*-body. This also has the effect of showing the arbitrary nature of ego-identification. The meditator visualizes himself as the *yi-dam*, both as regards his external appearance and the inner make-up of his mystical 'physiology', based on four or five psycho-physical centres known as *cakra*'s. He then sees around him the *maṇḍala* of the *yi-dam*, representing his Pure Land. By visualizing himself as the deity, the adept takes on some of its powers and virtues, which are symbolically expressed in many details of its appearance. Finally, the whole visualization is gradually dissolved into emptiness, so as to overcome any attachment to it. Visualizations and dissolutions are then repeated till mastery of the visualized world is attained. The Completion stage is then entered, where there is visualization and manipulation of the meditator/*yi-dam*'s energies and qualities. This takes great discipline and application, and is best done in a retreat setting. Here, the meditator draws on methods such as the 'Six yogas of Naropa', which are used particularly in the bKa'brgyud school. In these, the adept may: develop a great inner heat and an ego-transcending 'Great Bliss'; meditate on his reflection in a mirror; gain meditative control of dreams; retain awareness even in dreamless sleep; prepare himself to understand the intermediary period (Tib. *bar-do*) between rebirths, so as to accelerate spiritual progress then; and learn how to transfer his consciousness to Amitābha's Pure Land at death.

rNying-ma practice at the Supreme Union level may include yogic rites involving a (non-celibate) man and woman visualizing themselves as a *yi-dam* and his consort. This also involves sexual activity under very controlled meditative conditions, so that lust is directly confronted, and crushed, by transmuting its energy into a form of wisdom.

TANTRIC TECHNIQUES OF SPONTANEITY

Tantric practice also includes Zen-like techniques which are relatively unstructured and direct; which at a certain stage dispense with effort so as to allow a spontaneous state of freedom and openness to arise. These seem to be linked to the 'Innate vehicle' of Saraha (see p. 138). They include *Mahāmudrā*, a method of bKa'brgyud origin, and the rNying-ma practice of *Ati yoga*, also known as *rDzogs-chen* (pron. *Dzogchhen*; 'The Great Completion'). Both are based on the idea of beings as already having the Buddha-nature, so that it must simply be allowed to manifest itself. They are easier to master than complex visualizations, though they lack the power that these can have, and their relative simplicity means that there can be errors in assessing the level of progress made.

Mahāmudrā means 'Great Symbol', a term which is applied both to the method and the final state of realization it leads to. This is because the way of practice is itself seen as an expression of the reality it leads to. The technique involves cultivating Calm, then deepening this by a practice akin to developing the 'foundations of mindfulness', then developing Insight into this state. When not seated in meditation, the adept should keep his body loose and gentle by doing all activities in a smooth, relaxed and spontaneous way. He cultivates simplicity and directness of thought to facilitate carrying the awareness developed in meditation into his daily life. To develop Calm, the practitioner successively concentrates on a pebble, a vision of his *bLama* above his head, a Buddha-image, the seed-*mantra hūṃ*, and a shining dot. Breathing then becomes the focus of attention, in a series of phases culminating in holding the breath as an aid to stilling thoughts.

Thoughts still arise, however, and they themselves now become the object of mindfulness. They are seen to chase after various objects, taking them as real, so mindfulness is used to cut off each train of thought as it arises. When the ability to do this is well established, a stage of calm is reached where the fluxing stream of innumerable thought-moments is noticed to be like a tumbling waterfall, and is recognized as that which is to be transcended. Next, the mind is allowed to remain loose and natural, so that trains of thought are allowed to arise as they will. Observing them with equanimity, however, the meditator is unaffected by the thoughts. By this technique, the flow of thought-trains slows down, the state of calm deepens, and the mind becomes like a gently flowing river from which the 'sediments' of the defilements begin to settle out. Next, the mind is kept in an even tension by means of alternating tensing – cutting off thought-trains as they occur – and relaxation – allowing them to develop as they will. Next, even the thought of abandoning thoughts, and all effort and mindfulness in that direction, is left behind, so that the mind flows naturally and spontaneously. In this state, without thought-trains and with no feeling of the body, various visions arise out of emptiness, but these and the bliss or fear which accompany them are just allowed to pass by without attachment or rejection. In this state, the mind is firm and mindfulness occurs spontaneously. Thoughts arise, but are not seen as signifying any realities, they simply come and go without effect, like a pin pricking an elephant. There is awareness that the calm mind flickers, but in a way that does not disturb its steadiness.

Having reached and established this stage, Insight into it is then developed. By investigating both the steadiness and flickering of the mind, the meditator comes to see that they cannot be separated, and thus have no inherent nature of their own. Likewise, it comes to be seen that the awareness which watches all this is not separate from what it watches, thus overcoming the subject/object duality. This then allows full realization to be attained, when thought-moments are observed as thusness and emptiness, thereby transcending their delusion-making quality. Emptiness is therefore seen by a tantric transformation which changes hindering thoughts and passions into a basis for spiritual realization.

After this state, the adept is ever in a state of meditationless meditation, where there is a natural recognition of every event as empty and unproduced, a spontaneous expression of the innate *Dharma*-body, the crystal-clear, shining, blissful Mind. He lives in a spontaneous way, free from constructing thought, letting his natural 'ordinary mind' take its course, his actions being totally genuine, imbued with compassion for deluded beings.

rDzogs-chen practice is itself seen as a form of meditationless meditation. Its 'method' is akin to the phase of *Mahāmudrā* practice which uses mindfulness to still thoughts. At a certain point in this development, the flow suddenly stops, with the mind in a state of pure awareness of thusness. This is the attainment of the spontaneous perfection of the primordial Buddha Samantabhadra, personification of the *Dharma*-body.

ZEN MEDITATION

The techniques of Zen meditation are primarily those of developing high states of awareness, and wrestling with an enigmatic *kōan*. These techniques are emphasized, respectively, by the Sōtō (Ch. Ts'ao-tung) and Rinzai (Ch. Lin-chi) schools. They are regarded as 'patriarchal' meditation, in contrast to the traditional way of Calm and Insight, known as '*Tathāgata*' meditation. As will be seen, however, Sōtō practice is akin to the Theravāda *Vipassanā-yāna*, and Rinzai practice is akin to the *Samatha-yāna*.

Zazen, or 'sitting meditation' is used as the main basis for both awareness and *kōan* meditations, though the meditator is also encouraged to develop awareness, and work with his *kōan*, in any posture. Zen, particularly in its Sōtō form, attaches great importance to establishing correct posture in sitting meditation. The lower spine curves inwards, with the rest of the back straight and the abdomen completely relaxed. The area just below the navel, known as the *tanden*, becomes a focus of attention in much Zen meditation. From here, an energy develops which radiates throughout the body.

The initial task of the meditator is to learn to dampen down wandering thoughts by counting and following the breath. The eyes are lowered and are kept in focus, on the wall or floor one to three metres away, but the meditator does not look at anything in particular. If any mental images arise, such as glimmers of light or even visions of *Bodhisattvas*, these are dismissed as obstructing hallucinations, and dispelled by blinking.

Just Sitting

Once the meditator has learnt how to control his wandering thoughts to some extent, he may go on to develop high degrees of awareness while sitting, known as 'Just Sitting' (Jap. *Shikantaza*). Here, the meditator cultivates *nothing but* sitting, in full awareness of the here-and-now of sitting, in a method similar to the practice of the 'four foundations of mindfulness'. Thus Sōtō practice can be seen as akin to the *Vipassanā-yāna*, which develops Insight then Calm.

The attention in Just Sitting tends to rest on the movement of the respiratory muscles in the *tanden* area, but is not restricted to this. The meditator sets out to be in a state in which he is not trying to think, nor trying not to think; he just sits with no deliberate thought. When thoughts nevertheless arise, he just lets them pass by without comment, like watching traffic going over a bridge. He hears sounds, and notices any changes in his visual field, but does not react for or against them. If his mind begins 'mental chatter' on such a matter, he simply brings it back to sitting. The meditator sits with a bright, positive attitude, in full awareness of the body sitting and the flow of passing thoughts; ideally, he should have the taut alertness of a swordsman faced with potential death in a sudden duel.

To practise in this way, the meditator must keep his mind fully in the present, without any thought of what the practice might 'achieve'. Dōgen, the founder of Japanese Sōtō Zen, emphasized that one should not think that meditation is a way of *becoming* a Buddha, as this is like trying to polish a brick until it becomes a mirror. Rather, the meditator should sit in a purposeless, desireless stance, with deep faith in his pure Buddha-nature within: his original Buddhahood. Meditative training is thus not a means to an end, as in most other Buddhist meditation traditions. It is to be done for its own sake, for training and enlightenment are one: just sitting exhibits and gradually unfolds the innate Buddha-nature.

The practice of Just Sitting leads to an effortless watching, and the natural development of a strong one-pointed concentration. This develops Calm, in the state of 'self-mastery *samādhi*' (Jap. *jishu-zammai*), which seems equivalent to 'access' concentration. The meditator's body is so relaxed that he loses awareness of its position. As the mind becomes quieter, a deeper *samādhi* is then reached, where the mind is like the unruffled surface of a clear lake. Here 'body and mind are fallen off' in an experience of self-transcendence known as the 'great death'. The breath is so subtle that it seems not to exist; the meditator is unaware of time or space, but is in a condition of extreme wakefulness. These descriptions would seem to indicate a state akin to *jhāna*. It is known as the state of 'serene observation' (Jap. *moku shū*), a clear awareness in the tranquillity of a state where thought has stopped. Here there is the natural purity and calm of man's 'original nature' (*Plat.* sec. 19).

No-thought

The idea of transcending thought is much emphasized in Zen. The state in which this is attained is known in Japanese as *mu-nen* or *mu-shin*. *Mu-nen* is equivalent to Sanskrit *a-smṛti*, 'no-mindfulness', and is generally translated as 'no-thought', while *mu-shin* is equivalent to *a-citta*, 'no-mind' (cf. p. 117). The state referred to seems the same as the stage of *Mahāmudrā* meditation where even the effort to abandon thought-trains, and mindfulness so directed, is dropped. In Zen practice, when mindfulness reaches high intensity, it is seen as so taken up with its objects that it is not aware of itself, so it is 'no-mindfulness'. There is no separation of subject and object, and there is no awareness of the immediately prior moment of consciousness. Such a state may occasionally be experienced, for example, by a musician who is so absorbed in playing his instrument that he has no awareness of 'himself', his 'fingers', or the 'instrument'.

The experience of no-thought is not confined to the quiet of sitting meditation, but can be attained in the midst of daily activities. When the meditator is digging, he is *just* digging, not thinking; when walking, he is *just* walking; when he is thinking of something, he is fully thinking of that, and not of other things (cf. *Plat*. sec. 17). 'No-thought', then is not a state of dull thoughtlessness. When a person is in such a state, he is aware of his surroundings in a total, all-round way, without getting caught up and fixed on any particular. The mind does not pick and choose or reflect on itself, but is serenely free-flowing, innocent and direct, not encumbered with thought-forms. When the need arises, the 'mind of no-mind' can instantly react in an appropriate way.

Spontaneity and discipline

Partly influenced by the Taoist praise of natural and spontaneous action, Zen has valued this as a way of facilitating the attainment of free-flowing no-thought. Paradoxically, great discipline is necessary in cultivating spontaneity. Meditative discipline teaches a person how to go beyond the constraints of habitual, ego-centred thoughts and actions and thus allow spontaneous intuition to arise. In temporarily going beyond this feeling of 'I', a person's normal regulative, judging mind – the *manas* referred to by the Yogācāra school – is inactive, so that the underlying

'Buddha Mind' can act. The meditator allows his innate nature, the 'original mind', to function naturally and spontaneously in all activities.

The highest aim of Zen is to act in the world in a way which manifests the Buddha-nature and any measure of realization of it that the meditator has had. The meditator seeks to bring an inner stillness to all activities, performing them with mindfulness, perhaps to the point of no-thought. Thus the daily tasks of sweeping, polishing, cooking or digging are to be done with a beauty of spirit and a consideration for others which is expressed in little things like leaving slippers neat and tidy. The ideal of such an approach is to act with an uncomplicated mind free from attachments: 'straightforward mind at all times' (*Plat.* sec. 14).

Kōan meditation

In *kōan* meditation (see p. 157), the meditator contemplates the critical word or point in an enigmatic *kōan* story, known in Japanese as *watō*. In China, the most popular *kōan* centres on the question 'Who is it that recites the name of the Buddha?', that is, who recites the invocation to Amitābha Buddha in the daily devotional practice?: 'Who am I?' Here, the meditation focusses on the question 'Who?' By focussing on one thing, the practice thus begins by developing deep Calm. To 'answer' the question, though, Insight must then be developed. Thus Rinzai *kōan* meditation is akin to the *Samatha-yāna*, which develops Calm then Insight.

In China, only two other *kōans* are commonly used, one being that on one's 'original face' (see p. 157). The other centres on the reply of Chao Chou (778–897) when asked if a dog had the Buddha-nature. While, at the conventional level of truth, all beings have the Buddha-nature, his reply was '*Wu*' (Jap. *Mu*) meaning 'no', 'nothing'. This seems to allude to the 'emptiness' of everything. In Japanese Rinzai, the first *kōan* posed is either '*Mu*', or Hakuin's 'what is the sound of one hand clapping?' The meditator is then set to progress through a series of fifty or more *kōans*, with ones of an appropriate level being selected by the *Rōshi*, or Zen Master. The *kōans* are drawn from collections such as the 'Blue Cliff Records' (Jap. *Hekigan Roku*) and 'Gateless Gate' (Jap. *Mumonkan*), both compiled in China.

At first the meditator simply concentrates on the internally vocalized question, such as *Mu*, harmonizing this with watching the breath at the *tanden*. This dampens down wandering thoughts, and may be taken all the way to *dhyānic* 'serene observation'. The Rinzai tradition, however, says that the meditator will lose interest in 'solving' the *kōan* if he enters this state too soon, so he should not let his mind become quite so still, but keep it in a kind of active *samādhi* (akin to 'access' concentration) where he slowly recites the words of the question and watches it as a cat watches a mouse, trying to bore deeper and deeper into it, till he reaches the point from which it comes and intuits its meaning.

While practising thus, the meditator consults with the Master at least twice a day in *sanzen* interview, to offer 'answers' to the question. At first, he attempts intellectual answers, based on what he has read or heard, but these are useless and may be rejected with shouts or blows. He then tries to give 'Zennish' answers by bringing articles to the Master or doing some absurd action. These are also rejected, thus driving the student into a state of baffled perplexity, where the habit-structures and constructs of his mind are starting to be undermined. One record of a Zen interview with Master Ts'ao-shan (840–901), itself used as a *kōan*, goes:

Someone asked, 'With what sort of understanding should one be equipped to satisfactorily cope with the cross-examination of others?' The Master said, 'Don't use words and phrases.' 'Then what are you going to cross-examine about?' The Master said, 'Even the sword and the axe cannot pierce it through!' He said, 'What a fine cross-examination! But aren't there people who don't agree?' The Master said, 'There are.' 'Who?' he asked. The Master said, 'Me.' (*Trad.*, p. 235)

In *sanzen*, the role of the Master is crucial: only he can assess the answers of the pupil, and knock away his reliance on anything beyond his own intuition. By progressing through *kōans* over many years, the best pupils then become Masters themselves.

The meditator must 'solve' each enigmatic question by himself. Some *kōans* may be solved by relatively simple intuitions. Others require the meditator to struggle on with the question till he reaches the end of his tether. In a profound state of perplexity, he meets the 'doubt-sensation': a pure, contentless, existential 'great doubt'. The mind attains one-pointed concentration on this, with no distinction between doubter and doubt. The meditator is then in a stupefied, strangely ecstatic state, where he feels as if he is walking on air, not knowing if he is standing or walking. Nothing is what it seems to be, 'a mountain is not a mountain and water is not water', yet all is bright and suddenly complete.

In this condition, the meditator is said to be prone to a number of 'Zen sicknesses', whereby he will cling to some aspect of his experience, or take the lights or visions he may have as signs of revelation. These features seem akin to those of the 'pseudo-*Nibbāna*' on the Theravāda path. After the Master helps 'cure' him, the meditator can progress. Only when he pushes on and on, throwing himself into the abyss of doubt, will an 'answer' spontaneously arise from the depths of his mind. The deeper he goes into the doubt, the more thorough will be the 'great death' – the death of aspects of ego.

The breakthrough comes suddenly, perhaps after months of struggling. The stimulus may be a stone hitting a bamboo while the meditator is sweeping, or a timely prod from his Master. The conceptual, reasoning mind has reached its absolute dead-end, and the 'bottom' of the mind is broken through, so that the flow of thoughts suddenly stops, in a state of no-thought, and realization erupts from the depths. There is no longer anyone to ask or answer the question, but only a blissful, radiant emptiness beyond self and other, words or concepts. In this state of *dhyāna*, insight of various levels can be present.

Kenshō

The attainment of such a breakthrough is known in Chinese as *wu*, 'realization' and in Japanese as *satori*, 'catching on', or *kenshō*, 'seeing one's nature'. It is a blissful realization where a person's inner nature, the originally pure mind, is directly known as an illuminating emptiness, a thusness which is dynamic and immanent in the world. This vision of unity was hinted at by the Chinese monk Jo Hoshi (318–414): 'Heaven and earth and I are of the same root. All things and I are of the same substance.' When a *kenshō* passes, the meditator finds the conventional world is as it was, and yet somehow different: 'mountains are again mountains, and water is again water'.

Kenshōs may also be attained by an experienced practitioner of 'Just Sitting' when he emerges from deep inner stillness of the *samādhi* of no-thought, and starts to turn his mind outwards. In *samādhi*, there is an experience of the originally pure and shining mind uncovered by defilements. It is a state where the *Dharma*-body, thusness, or the Buddha-nature is regained, but there is not necessarily any recognition of it. When the mind emerges from its deep stillness, however, it is extremely alert and sensitive, and may be triggered into a *kenshō* experience, where it actually sees the 'original face'.

Kenshō is not a single experience, but refers to a whole series of realizations from a beginner's shallow glimpse of the nature of mind, up to a vision of emptiness equivalent to the 'Path of Seeing' (see p. 258), or to Buddhahood itself. In all of these, the same 'thing' is known, but in different degrees of clarity and profundity.

Sudden awakenings

While 'sudden awakenings' are usually associated with Zen, they are also referred to in other traditions. For example the Theravāda tradition cites the case of a nun who suddenly attained Arahatship when she extinguished a lamp (*Thig*.112–16). While Rinzai Zen emphasizes that *kenshōs* are sudden, it holds that to become attached to these as great attainments is to have the 'stink of Zen'. It also recognizes that they can only be attained after some degree of gradual practice. Moreover, their insights need to be gradually absorbed by the meditator if they are not to be lost. In this process of maturation, what has been realized, the *Dharma*-body, is increasingly identified with what is encountered in daily life.

In the Sōtō school, the meditator is discouraged from trying to achieve sudden *kenshōs*. Simply by 'Just Sitting', he authenticates and manifests his innate dignity and perfection, the Buddha-nature. The point of sitting in meditation is simply to develop the skill of showing one's original enlightenment. Even the beginner in meditation can do this, but such a showing needs to be endlessly repeated so as to permeate more and more of life's activities. Sōtō practice is often seen as a gradualist path, in contrast to the 'sudden' Rinzai practice; in fact, it is better seen as a series of sudden actualizations of the Buddha-nature, in contrast to Rinzai's sudden *seeings* of the Buddha-nature. In Sōtō, *kenshōs* are allowed to occur naturally, as a by-product of practice, or meditative training is seen as the unfolding of one great '*kenshō*'.

The meditative arts of Zen

The Zen emphasis on naturalness, spontaneity and manifesting the Buddha-nature in daily activities has meant that a whole variety of art forms came to be infused with the spirit of Zen, particularly in Japan. These include ink paintings of landscapes and Zen Masters, calligraphy, poetry, Nō theatre, landscape gardening, flower arrangement, and various activities not usually considered 'arts': archery, swordsmanship, and the 'Tea ceremony'.

Zen arts seek to express the true 'thusness' of a phenomenon or situation, its mysterious living 'spirit' as it is found as part of the ever-changing fabric of existence. This requires a free-flowing intuition arising from the state of no-thought. To accomplish the expression of thusness, the aspiring Zen artist must first have a long training to develop a perfect grasp of the technical skills of his art. He then calms his mind by giving attention to the breath, and seeks to develop intense one-pointedness on what he wishes to portray, ideally attaining the state of no-thought. He can then overcome all duality between 'himself' and his 'subject', so that he 'becomes' it, and can directly and spontaneously express it through the instruments of his art. Inspiration arises from deep within, from the ultimate Mind which is the inner nature of both himself and his subject, and he expresses its thusness from 'within' it, so to speak. 'Becoming' an object is also found in tantric visualizations, but while the related tantric art emphasizes the hidden richness and power of the pure empty Mind, Zen art emphasizes its participation in the simple things of ordinary life: in a stalk of bamboo rather than in a visualized *Bodhisattva*. When true Zen art is produced, it is seen as not so much a human artifice as nature spontaneously expressing itself through the artist. In Zen archery, for example, the release of the arrow should be like a ripe plum dropping from a tree, at a time when the archer has 'become' the target.

An example of Zen art is shown in plate 13. The artist avoids the use of colour, for he seeks to see past the details of surface appearance to capture the thusness of his subject: to re-create on paper its 'life's motion', its purposeless, free-flowing 'spirit'. Human life is shown harmoniously blending in with nature and its rhythms, in accordance with the Zen ideal. In the foreground, the asymmetric ruggedness of trees and rocks emphasizes naturalness, while in the mid-ground there

Plate 13 *Landscape with Pine Trees and Hut*, by Bunsei, fifteenth-century Japan.

is much empty space, suggesting the mysterious emptiness from which everything emerges.

Another example of a Zen art is the *Haiku*. This is a seventeen-syllable poem form popularized as a vehicle for Zen by the layman Matsuo Bashō (1644–94), Japan's most famous poet. His first real Zen *Haiku* occurred when talking to his meditation Master in a quiet garden. The Master asked him what reality was 'prior to the greenness of moss', that is, beyond the world of particulars. Hearing a noise, Bashō directly answered by expressing its thusness: 'A frog-jumps-in: plop!'. As a poet, he then made this into a *Haiku*:

An old pond, ah!
A-frog-jumps-in:
Plop!

This expresses a moment in which Bashō was the sound, and the sound was no longer a 'sound', but an indescribable expression of ultimate reality. A Zen *Haiku* seeks to *show*, rather than to describe such reality. Its form is brief, so as not to get in the way, and it simply evokes the thusness of a living moment, so that the reader's mind resonates with the poet's and 'tastes' the profound feeling of the moment of poetic expression.

12

THE MODERN HISTORY OF BUDDHISM IN ASIA

In the last 150 years, Buddhism has undergone a number of changes. In the twentieth century, many areas of Buddhist Asia have come under unsympathetic, and sometimes destructively aggressive Communist regimes. In other areas, cultural continuity has been better preserved and adapted to the modern world. In others, Buddhism has regained ground previously lost to it, while outside Asia, it has broken entirely new ground.

COMMUNIST ASIA: BUDDHISM UNDER A CLOUD

The People's Republic of China

After the devastation of many temples and monasteries during the Christian-inspired T'ai-p'ing rebellion (1850–64), there was a modest revival in Chinese Buddhism. In the Republican period (1912–49), there was also something of an intellectual renaissance, in an ideologically more open period free of Confucian dominance, and partly in response to well-organized Christian missionaries. There was a revitalization in a number of monasteries, and contact was made with other Buddhists in Asia and the West. Dozens of urban lay Buddhist societies developed in the 1930s, concerned with education, social welfare and devotion. Buddhism remained very strong in some provinces, but new political ideas meant that young people often saw it as being irrelevant to the needs of modern China.

The triumph of the Communists in 1949 brought suppression and manipulation. *Sangha* numbers were decimated as all 'hereditary temples', and many large 'public monasteries', closed down because their income-producing lands were confiscated. The monks had to support themselves by weaving, farming and running vegetarian restaurants. They were urged to see working in a Communist society as the true *Bodhisattva* way, and even to accept that killing the 'enemies of society' was compassionate. During the Cultural Revolution (1966–72), the Red Guards wrought great destruction, and all monasteries were closed, at least for a time. Since 1977, the general re-adjustment of policy in China has led to forty to fifty monasteries being re-opened, though some are wholly or partly used as museums for foreign tourists. As in the 1950s, Buddhism is seen as politically useful for making links with Buddhist countries, through the Chinese Buddhist Association. In 1980, ordination of monks (banned since 1957) was again permitted, and the state-funded Chinese Buddhist Academy was opened to provide training seminaries. The *Sangha* still suffers from not having any independent source of income, though. Little comes from the money from conducting rites for the dead that the monks have again been allowed to accept. In the current wholesale modernization of society, Chinese Buddhism is in a critical period. There are a number of good working monasteries, and lay activity is being renewed in certain regions, especially the provinces on the East coast. In 1986, it was estimated that there were 28,000 monks and nuns in China. In 1930, there had been 738,200. Those that remain are likely to be the more committed.

In Yunnan province, Southern Buddhism is still found in an isolated region bordering Laos and Burma, among the 840,000 Dai people. The main threat to their culture is their being swamped by an influx of Han Chinese. Northern Buddhism continues to some extent among Mongol people of Inner Mongolia (and in Mongolia proper, under Soviet influence since 1924), and also in western regions once belonging to Tibet. It remains strong in Tibet, now part of China.

In 1950, the Communist Chinese invaded Tibet, claiming that they were re-asserting a right over Chinese territory. The new Dalai Lama, enthroned not long before, continued to 'rule' in an uneasy co-existence with the Chinese until 1959, when an uprising against the Chinese was quashed, direct colonial rule was imposed, and the Dalai Lama fled to India. During the Red Guard period, around 6,000 monasteries were destroyed, along with their art and libraries, in an attempt to wipe out Tibet's rich and ancient Buddhist culture. The Dalai Lama estimates that one million Tibetans died: in the rebellion, from the famine arising from inappropriate agricultural policies, and in persecutions.

Since 1980, things have become easier, and around thirty monasteries have been rebuilt or repaired, though the number of monks is still only a fraction of the previous large number. The Tibetan Buddhist Canon is now being reprinted, much artistic restoration work is going ahead, and the people retain a strong devotion to Buddhism. Ordinations have continued since 1959, but the past disruption of study means that there is a severe shortage of learned Buddhist teachers.

Tibetan culture is being diluted by colonization by the Han Chinese, who now comprise a fifth of the population, by an alien education system, and by the consumerism that the Chinese have begun to introduce. Tourism has been permitted since 1984, and while this may in time prove corrosive of the culture, at present it allows Tibetans contact with the outside world so as to protest at Chinese occupation. Anti-Chinese riots occurred in 1987 and 1988, involving young monks as well as lay people. The Dalai Lama, who now lives in India, remains the focus of tremendous devotion. He supports demonstrations and civil disobedience if these are non-violent, and hopes that, if Tibet cannot be independent, it will be demilitarized and Han immigration will cease.

South-east Asia

From 1893, Vietnam, Cambodia and Laos were all colonies of France, forming the union of Indochina. They now share in having Soviet-backed Communist regimes dominated by the power of Vietnam. During the Vietnam War (1964–75), Vietnamese monks were active in welfare work, and in encouraging deserters from both armies, such that they were suspected by both sides. Since 1975 in Vietnam, a number of monasteries and temples have been closed, and Buddhism has been harassed, for example by political meetings being timed to clash with festivals.

In 1971, the Vietnam War spilled over into the once tranquil and gentle country of Cambodia. The devastation wrought by American bombing helped usher in the Khmer Rouge terror of 1975–8, when the fanatical Communist regime murdered many of the monks, and forced the rest to disrobe. Invasion by the Vietnamese established a more tolerant government. While the *Sangha* had been nearly destroyed, in 1981 it was estimated that around 600 monks had survived the holocaust.

In Laos, the Communist Pathet Lao came to power in 1975, after warring with the Royalist government. In this conflict, monks often joined the Pathet Lao as medics, porters and propaganda agents. Today, the *Sangha* has lost its once central place in society. Monks have been put to work by the government to support Communism, and been used as school teachers. Many have fled across the Mekong river to Thailand.

THE CONTINUING TRADITION AND ITS MODERN VARIETIES

Taiwan, Hong Kong and Singapore

On the island of Taiwan, the Nationalist Chinese government favours a revival of ancient Chinese culture, and Buddhism has benefited from this. New temples and monasteries have been built, Ch'an meditation is popular, there are Buddhist study groups in the universities, and many Buddhist Journals are published. There is a general stress on interpretations of Buddhism which see it as compatible with the modern outlook, and attempts to separate it from the 'superstitions' of popular folk religion. In Hong Kong and Singapore, a somewhat similar situation pertains.

Korea

In 1904, Japanese troops entered the country, and in the period 1910–45, Korea was a Japanese colony. Buddhism underwent a revival, but the Japanese wish to import and encourage its own forms of Buddhism caused tension, especially as regards an increase in the number of married clergy. Since the division of the country by the Korean War (1950–3), little is known of the fate of Buddhism in the harsh northern Communist regime.

In South Korea, Buddhism remains in a Westernized and rapidly modernizing society, along with Confucianism, Taoism and the native Shamanism. Christianity, present since the late seventeenth century, made many converts during the spiritual confusion of the post-war period, and is continuing to grow. The predominant ideology is Confucianism, while the fifteen million Buddhists are the biggest religious community, and the nine million Christians are very influential.

Free of the oppression of the Confucian Yi dynasty, and Japanese occupation, Korean Buddhism has undergone a definite revival. There are around 23,000 monks and nuns, and perhaps 20,000 married clerics. Young educated people continue to ordain, or go on meditation retreats to practise Son (Zen) meditation. A renewal in Buddhist scholarship has developed, with the Chinese Canon being translated into modern Korean, and there is a general increase in interest in Buddhist philosophy, in a modernized form. The Buddhist Youth Organization is active in both study and social work.

A new form of Buddhism, which dates from 1924 and has blossomed since 1953, is the Won, or 'Round' school. This is a reformed, simplified school whose sole focus of worship is a black circle representing the *Dharma*-body or emptiness. Western influence is apparent in its religious services, which include *Sūtra*-readings, prayers, hymns and a sermon. It seeks to balance inner quiet with selfless social service, which has lead to much charitable activity and the building of many schools. By 1973, it had 600,000 followers and 200 temples, mainly in the cities.

Japan

In 1853, Japan was rudely awakened from an inward-looking period of its history by the gun-boats of Admiral Perry, who demanded access for American traders. The Meiji restoration of 1868 led the country to end its feudal period, opening itself up to the outside world, and rapidly boosting its modernization. Shintō was separated from links with Buddhism, and a form of it known as 'State' or 'Shrine' Shintō was developed by the state as the natural expression of Japanese life. The end of state support, and attacks from Shintō, Christianity and Western science, stimulated a revival and modernization in some sections of Buddhism. Universities, schools and publishing houses were started, and monks and clergy visited Europe to study history and philosophy, and also the critical study of Indian Buddhism, Sanskrit and Pali.

State Shintō was increasingly used as a vehicle for nationalism and militarism. The Japanese fought the Russians, colonized Taiwan and Korea, and then attacked China and finally America. Defeat in the Second World War led to a discrediting of State Shintō, and American occupation initiated a new, even more culturally and religiously open period of rapid social change and spiritual crisis.

Traditional Buddhism, which lost much income due to post-war land reforms, was initially slow to address the new situation. Nevertheless, many 'New Religions' have flourished or arisen to respond to the needs of the people. These are lay-led movements which have their roots in Buddhism, Shintō, or even Christianity. Their followers are mostly urban members of the upper lower classes, who feel economically and socially frustrated, dislike the anonymity of the sprawling cities, and feel the need for a modernized spiritual tradition to guide them in a confusing secularized world. The New Religions promise that religious practice will lead to health, wealth, personal fulfilment and success. Their leaders are focuses of great faith, a feature which draws on the traditional Japanese value of group loyalty. The major Buddhist New Religions give members both a sense of belonging and a sense of personal importance. They are organized into small discussion groups, where personal and social problems are discussed in the light of religious faith, but the groups are also part of well-organized and successful movements. The impressive headquarters of many of the New Religions are large and elegant structures of concrete and steel, which artistically blend traditional and modern forms.

A number of the most successful New Religions are based on the Nichiren sect. This is probably because of Nichiren's emphasis on reforming society, which appealed in the post-war period. The Lotus *Sūtra* also holds out the promise of earthly happiness to those who revere it, and gives prominence to the lay *Bodhisattva*. The most successful New Religion has been the Sōka-gakkai ('Value Creating Society'), founded in 1930. The movement is formally a lay organization of the once small sub-sect Nichiren Shōshū ('True Nichiren Sect'). It sees the teachings of Nichiren and the Lotus *Sūtra* as representing absolute truth, with Nichiren as the supreme Buddha, but regards values as having to be positively created, drawing on faith in the Lotus *Sūtra*. Basic values include respect for the dignity of all life, and karma.

The central practice of the movement is morning and evening devout chanting of *Nam-Myō-hō Ren-ge-kyō* before the *gohonzon* (see p. 190), in which the presence of the 'Buddha Nichiren' is felt. Uttering *Nam* (adoration) is seen as summoning from within the revitalizing power of the universal law, or *Myō-hō* (True *Dharma*). *Ren-ge* (Lotus) is seen as the cause and effect of the emergence of the Buddha-nature in terms of benefit, happiness and fulfilment. *Kyō* (*Sūtra*, literally a thread) is seen as the thread of eternal truth which links all life. Chanting is regarded as a way of overcoming obstacles in life, such as poverty, domestic disharmony and ill health, and as a means to giving up drinking and smoking and to attaining happiness. It is seen as bringing out a person's

Buddha-nature, in the form of enhanced compassion, courage, wisdom and vital life force, so as to generate a 'human revolution'. Practitioners say that it makes them more patient, clear-thinking, energetic, confident and positive. At first, chanting is for personal goals, but it then moves on towards helping to solve national and even world problems, such as an end to all war. Daily discussion meetings relate faith to everyday life.

The Sōka-gakkai sees all other religions and forms of Buddhism as false, and its rapid growth in the 1950s was due to the 'compassionate' urge to convert people from such errors, using an aggressive technique known as 'breaking and subduing' (*shakubuku*). In this, persuasion was followed by barrages of propaganda from a number of converters. Rival objects of worship were destroyed; dire warnings were given of troubles to come if the 'true faith' was not accepted, and economic sanctions were applied. Adverse reactions to this method have since led to its being progressively toned down. Since 1975, action for conversion has also been directed beyond Japan, for Sōka-gakkai sees its message as the hope of the world and herald of a new humanism. The movement operates under the name 'Nichiren Shōshū' in Asia, North and South America, Europe and Africa, and claims a membership of 1·26 million outside Japan, in 114 countries. In 1988, it claimed ten million members in Japan.

In line with Nichiren's ideal of the union of politics and religion, the Sōka-gakkai developed a political wing in 1964. This is known as the Kōmei-tō, or 'Clean Government' Party, and has become the third or fourth largest in the Japanese Parliament. While it severed formal links with the movement in 1970, it remains influenced by it, and attracts a similar membership. It runs Citizens' Livelihood Discussion Centres which give free legal counselling, and act as a channel to government for grievances on such matters as housing, social security, education and pollution. Sōka-gakkai has also sponsored a labour union and student movement which seek to synthesize capitalist and socialist values.

The Risshō-kōseikai, founded in 1938, combines faith in the Lotus *Sūtra* and Śākyamuni Buddha, honouring of ancestors, and practice of ethical aspects of the Eightfold Path and *Bodhisattva* perfections. In group counselling sessions, members confess their failings and receive guidance on life's problems, based on the Lotus *Sūtra* and the Four Holy Truths.

The older Buddha sects, stimulated by the general atmosphere of modernization, have organized movements for the re-invigoration of lay practice. These include classes, lectures and discussions on Buddhism, organized pilgrimages, counselling services, kindergartens, Sunday Schools, youth societies, Boy Scout troops, and Zen meditation clubs. Many popular and scholarly Buddhist magazines and books exist, and there is much excellent scholarship on the historical and doctrinal roots of Buddhism. Nevertheless, the consumer-orientation of Japanese society has produced much secularization. Most priests wear Western suits, and many do non-religious jobs. Overall, there has been a decline in religious practice, though Buddhism remains much the most influential religion. A survey carried out in 1979, when the population of Japan was 115 million, showed that 33·6 per cent of people professed religious faith, 78·4 per cent of these saying that they were Buddhist and 3·3 per cent Shintō.[7] A year earlier, voluntarily reported membership figures of religious sects indicated that 76·4 per cent of people were Buddhist and 85·6 per cent Shintō (54·9 per cent and 89·4 per cent in 1954).[8] Such anomalous figures arise because people may be counted as members simply due to traditional family affiliation, may belong to two or more sects, and generally follow Shintō as well as Buddhism. In 1981, such figures gave a total Buddhist sect-membership of 111 million: 30 per cent Tendai, 30 per cent Nichiren, 18 per cent Pure Land, 11 per cent Shingon, 8 per cent Zen, and 4 per cent Nara sects.

Thailand

In the nineteenth century, Thailand skilfully avoided being colonized by European powers, and had two enlightened, modernizing rulers: king Mongkut (1851–68), inaccurately portrayed in the film 'The King and I', and his son king Chulalongkorn (1868–1910). In his time in the *Sangha* before being king, Mongkut established the reformist Dhammayuttika monastic fraternity, and sought to spread a purified, ethically oriented Buddhism to the people. Since 1932, the country has had a constitutional monarchy and been ruled mostly by a parliamentary government guided by the military. Royalty have continued to be much respected, and the country is the last, apart from Bhutan, to have a Buddhist king, with Buddhism as the state religion.

Since the 1960s, much economic development (and secularization) has taken place, though its unevenness has caused the government to ask the *Sangha* to co-operate with, encourage, and lead community development projects in poorer regions. Development workers always contact the local abbot before initiating a project, as this could not succeed without his approval; for the villagers tend to be suspicious of government officials. The abbot can provide useful practical information on the locality. He may also, at the end of a sermon, encourage villagers to participate in the project, such as building a road. Monks may then take part in or help organize this, which further motivates the villagers by legitimating the action as 'merit'-making. The *Sangha* has also initiated training programmes to help monks, particularly graduates, to participate more effectively in community development activities. Both leaders of the programmes and the government feel that the *Sangha* should help to ensure that material progress is not accompanied by moral and religious decline, or public disorder will ensue, and Communism will be more attractive to those in poorer regions. One of the activities of the monks is to seek to encourage the laity to widen their notion of what count as 'merit'-making activities. Historically, these have come to be identified with acts beneficial to the *Sangha*, though early texts also refer to activities such as planting medicinal plants and sinking wells as generating 'merit' (*S*.I.33). The training gives guidance in such matters as: effective leadership in the building of roads, bridges, clinics and wells; nutrition, first aid, sanitation, nature conservation, and mobilization of funds. The practical effects of such programmes have been reasonably encouraging, though the laity often need much persuasion to widen their notion of what makes 'merit', and there are limits to what the re-channelling of traditionally haphazard 'merit'-giving can achieve.

The involvement of monks in development work is not without its critics. Those who support greater social activism on the part of the *Sangha* argue that, through it, the monks can 're-assert their traditional role' as community leaders in a changing world, and thus retain respect. Opponents are those of a more cautious and traditional outlook, particularly among the laity. They argue that, if monks become too involved in the affairs of secular society, then they will compromise their unique exemplary role of being spiritual specialists, this being to the detriment of society. Some also criticize the government for making political use of the *Sangha* in work which is partly an anti-Communist strategy. Both sides have a point, so that careful consideration is needed so as to work out the best practical accommodation in this area.

Somewhat different from most 'development' work is help given to poor urban dwellers who are heroin addicts. One monk, Phra Chamroon, runs a curative regime of herbal medicine and moral discipline at his monastery. Its high cure rate has attracted the interest of doctors in the West. Some Thais criticize him for involving monks too closely with disturbed laypeople, but others would see his work as an extension of the meditative concern to purify the mind.

As in Burma, there are many fine meditation masters in Thailand, some of them lay, and meditation is increasingly popular among the educated urban classes. Some monks and laypeople downplay much of the conventional 'merit'-making religion, to concentrate on matters pertaining to overcoming attachment and attaining *Nibbāna*, the ultimate goal. They stress the centrality of meditation, and the peripheral importance of ceremonies, as Ch'an had done in China. L. S. Cousins has coined the term 'ultimatism' to refer to such forms of Buddhism in Thailand and elsewhere.[9]

Among the educated elite, one of the most well-known, if controversial, 'ultimatist' monks is Buddhadāsa. His interpretation of the doctrine of rebirth, which has become influential with many Thai scientists (over half of whom no longer believe in life after death), is that it only refers to a series of states within one life. Each time the thought of 'I' arises, one is 'reborn', but one's aim should be to be 'reborn' into a new kind of selfless, Nibbānic living, beyond the birth and death of ego-thoughts. Buddhadāsa's appreciation of some Mahāyāna ideas has led to him translating some of its *Sūtras* into Thai, and the art which he uses for spiritual education is drawn from various Buddhist traditions. It is also drawn from other religions, and he says that both *Dhamma* and God, properly understood, refer to a reality beyond concepts. While Buddhadāsa's interpretation of Buddhism is a this-worldly one, he is critical of other this-worldly developments such as the involvement of monks in development projects, which he sees as inappropriate.

The *Sangha* as a whole is wary of innovators such as Phra Chamroon and Buddhadāsa, and also of political monks, who vary from former Marxist student activists, to the fervently anti-Communist Phra Kittivuddho.

Sri Lanka

The British took over the island of Ceylon in 1815, and although they agreed to 'maintain and protect' Buddhism, the objections of Christian missionaries led to a gradual removal of the state's role in purifying the *Sangha*. The missionaries ran all the officially approved schools, though they made few converts. They were annoyed when their attacks on Buddhism were at first met by monks lending them Buddhist manuscripts and letting them stay in temples when on preaching tours. By 1865, however, monks began a counter-attack by printing pamphlets and accepting Christian challenges to public debates. A famous one at Pānadura in 1873 saw the victory of the monk Guṇānanda before a crowd of 10,000. This much-publicized event signalled a resurgence in Buddhism, which borrowed certain techniques from the Christianity it was opposing.

By the last decade of the century, a new style of Buddhism was developing, at least among the newly affluent, English-educated middle classes of the capital, Colombo. It tended to see the Buddha as 'simply a human being', and Buddhism as a 'scientific', 'rational' philosophy, 'not a religion', as it did not depend on blind faith. Such ideas were influenced by English concepts and Western interpretations of Buddhism. This style of Buddhism also advocated the adoption of new organizational forms, such as lay societies (e.g. the Young Men's Buddhist Association), Buddhist-influenced modern schools, and the use of printing and newspapers. H. Bechert thus refers to it as 'Buddhist modernism'. G. Obeyesekere and R. Gombrich prefer the more loaded term 'Protestant Buddhism'. This is because they emphasize that these developments were partly a protest against Christianity, and shared with Protestantism both a dislike of traditional 'ritualistic accretions' and a (re-)emphasis on the laity as individually responsible for their own salvation. The latter was aided by Western scholarship, which made the Pali Canon available in English translation: traditionally it was conveyed to the laity from its Pali form by the monks.

An important event occurred in 1880, when Colonel H. S. Olcott (1832–1907), and Madame H. P. Blavatsky (1831–91) arrived in Colombo. In 1875, this American journalist and Russian clairvoyant had founded the Theosophical Society in New York. In 1879, they established the headquarters of this syncretistic religious movement in

India. On arriving in Colombo, they appeared to embrace Buddhism by publicly taking the refuges and precepts, thus giving a great confidence-boost to some Buddhists, due to their being Westerners. Olcott set up a 'Buddhist Theosophical Society', which was in fact a vehicle of modernist Buddhism. He then organized a thriving Buddhist schools movement with a Western, English-language curriculum, in which the laity began to exercise leadership roles of a religious nature.

Out of this milieu arose Don David Hewavitarne (1864–1933), who reacted against an intolerant Christian schooling and was inspired by Guṇānanda and Olcott. In 1881, he adopted the title Anagārika ('Homeless One') Dharmapāla ('Defender of *Dhamma*'), and went on to become the hero of modern Sinhalese Buddhism, being regarded as a *Bodhisatta*. *Anagārika*-hood was a new status, mid-way between that of monk and layman, involving adherence to the eight precepts for life. While others did not follow his example in this respect, he was the model for lay activism in modernist Buddhism. In 1891, he visited Bodh-Gayā, the site of the Buddha's enlightenment, and was distressed by its dilapidated state and its ownership by a Hindu priest. He therefore founded the Mahā Bodhi Society, an international Buddhist organization whose aims were to win back the site for Buddhism by court action (achieved only in 1949), and establish an international Buddhist monastery at Bodh-Gayā. For the rest of his life, Dharmapāla worked for the resurgence of Buddhism, linking this to Sinhalese nationalism and calls for independence. In this work, the missionary zeal which he had been subjected to as a child was directed back at the Christian British. He was also critical of caste, and even of recourse to gods, as unbuddhist.

Christians and the influential modernist Buddhist minority criticized monks as not socially active enough. In time, this led to them becoming involved in social welfare activities, acting as prison and even army chaplains, and as paid school teachers. The more traditional activity of monastic scholarship also flourished. There were many contributions to this by the small group of Western monks led by the German Nyanatiloka (1878–1956), who had ordained in 1904 in Burma.

Independence and the advent of democracy in 1948 brought monks increasingly into the political arena. Liberal, socialist and Marxist ideas encouraged political activity among all sections of the population, and some monks saw it as part of their duty to guide their parishioners politically. *Sangha* political pressure groups developed which are now split along party lines. For many laypeople, though, the activity of the 'political monk' is a distasteful expression of *Sangha* factionalism and secular involvement.

Since 1948, a population-boom consequent on the eradication of malaria has broken up traditional village communities by driving many peasants off the land to the cities. Poor economic performance had led to different communities blaming each other for this, which is one of the roots of the Tamil–Sinhalese troubles which erupted in 1983. The Sinhalese majority have a long history of defending their culture against Tamil incursions from south India. In the post-war period, they sought to redress certain advantages which they saw the British as having given to the Tamils. In time these moves went too far, and led to Tamil demands for autonomy or independence for parts of the island where they predominate. In times of economic difficulty, this situation led to Tamil terrorist activity which has sparked off a period of inter-communal violence.

Mass education has led to rising material aspirations, and frustration at not being able to fulfil them. This has led some businessmen, peasants and the urban poor to be attracted away from the worship of ethical 'Buddhist' gods such as Viṣṇu, to those such as Kataragama, a war-like god once worshipped mainly by the Tamils. To gain his protection and aid, devotees go into ecstatic states in which they claim to be possessed, and accomplish feats such as pushing skewers through their cheeks. Traditionally, Buddhists usually saw possession as requiring exorcism. It is possible that, over time, Kataragama will be progressively 'Buddhicized', as has previously happened to gods who have risen in popularity.

In over 4,000 of Sri Lanka's 25,000 villages, the Sarvodaya Śramadāna ('Giving of Energy for the Awakening of All') movement has been active in promoting village renewal. Started in 1958 by A. T. Ariyaratne, this lay-led movement involves both laity and monks. Its aim is to foster 'development' in the widest sense, by arousing villagers from their passivity and getting them involved in choosing and working on projects, such as building a road to the village or organizing a marketing co-operative. It draws on Buddhist ideals such as generosity and lovingkindness, and seeks to get *all* sections of the community to participate and work together so as to experience their individual and communal potential for changing their economic, social, natural and spiritual environments. Women are particularly encouraged to speak up and be more active, and the movement has also sought to foster better Sinhalese–Tamil relationships.

The re-emphasis on lay involvement in religion continues, and the desire for Buddhism to permeate life has now led to middle-class weddings being held on monastery premises. The middle classes also increasingly practise meditation, most often a Burmese form of *Vipassanā*, whether for its day-to-day benefits or as a way to progress towards *Nibbāna*. There is also a trend for certain lay people to live celibate lives. As the urban laity have become more active, and more educated, there has been an erosion of their respect for monks, most of whom are still from rural backgrounds and many of whom are less educated. Thus they may look more to a lay meditation teacher than a non-meditating monk for guidance. Increasingly, however, monasteries have become 'meditation centres', this being a concept derived from the West and Burma. Other developments have included a revival of the forest meditation tradition, whose monks are highly revered. They represent a 'reformist' trend, whose aim is closer conformity to the ideals of the early *Sangha*. This trend is different from 'ultimatist' and 'modernist' ones, but can attract similar people. The respect accorded to the ten-precept nuns is also due to their simple meditative life. Many English-language Buddhist pamphlets and booklets have been produced since 1958 by the Buddhist Publication Society, run by pupils of Nyanatiloka. The best of their 'Wheel' pamphlets have done much to show the modern implications of ancient Buddhist texts.

Burma

The great Burmese ruler king Mindon (1853–78) gave much support to Buddhism and presided over the 'fifth' Great Council (1868–71). At this, recensions of the Pali Canon were cross-checked, and an orthodox version was inscribed on 729 stone slabs. The British conquered lower Burma in 1853, and in 1885 they took over the whole country, leading to some weakening in monastic discipline, due to the ending of the royal prerogative of purging the *Sangha*. The 1920s saw both the development of more accessible forms of *Vipassanā* meditation, to teach to the laity, and agitation by monks in favour of independence. While monastic leaders saw political activity as against the *Vinaya*, it was difficult to prevent some of the younger monks from developing a taste for it. Malcontented urban monks have therefore been active for or against certain parties or policies since this time. Leaders of the independence movement drew on a mix of socialism and nationalism, due to the dislike of Indian capitalists and landlords introduced by the British. Independence was gained in 1948, and U Nu, the first prime-minister, favoured a form of socialism as a means to the Buddhist goal of a just and peaceful society which did not encourage greed.

In 1956, Southern Buddhists celebrated '*Buddha Jayanti*', 2,500 years of the Buddhist era, when a Buddhist revival had come to be expected. U Nu presided over the 'sixth' Great Council (1954–6), held to commemorate this. Monks from a number of Theravādin countries attended, a new edition of the Pali Canon was produced, and efforts were made to stimulate Buddhist education, missionary endeavours and social welfare activities. Many 'meditation centres' for monks and laity were established, and this development later spread to Sri Lanka and Thailand. Of particular note was Sayagyi U Ba Khin, a layman who was a prominent and respected government official. Even in his seventies, he energetically combined his government work with the running of an International Meditation Centre, teaching *Vipassanā* meditation to laypeople from Burma and abroad.

In 1962, a *coup* brought a semi-Marxist military government to power, which has expended much energy on warfare with various ethnic minority groups fighting for independence from the Burmese. The government has not been anti-Buddhist, and its isolationist policies have in fact helped to preserve a devoutly Buddhist culture from the forces of secularization and tourism. Nevertheless, increasing discontent with the country's poor economic performance, and the government's dictatorial methods, led to mass anti-government demonstrations in 1988. Monks took part in these, and the public placed the administration of many towns and cities in the hands of committees of monks, due to the breakdown of government authority there.

Malaysia, Bangladesh, north-east and north India, Bhutan and Nepal

In Malaysia, Islam is the official religion, but Buddhism remains in the religious mix of the Chinese, who make up 45 per cent of the population. Buddhism of a Thai variety also exists near the border with Thailand. Missionaries from Sri Lanka have been active in the twentieth century, with converts being won, and Theravāda doctrine also being added to Chinese practice. Exiled Tibetans are also present and active as missionaries.

In Bangladesh, Buddhism is found among the 400,000 tribal people of the thinly populated Chittagong Hill Tract. In recent years, however, these people have been suffering repression, being pushed off their land by hydro-electric schemes and settlement by the majority Muslim Bengalis, backed by the power of the Bangladeshi army.

In the north-eastern Indian state Assam, 90,000 Buddhists were registered in the 1971 census, these being both Southern Buddhists and those of Nepali culture. Southern Buddhists also predominate in Tripura, Mizoram, and eastern parts of Arunachal Pradesh. In these three states, there were 181,700 Buddhists registered in the 1981 census.

In the independent state of Bhutan, which has only recently opened itself up to the outside world, Northern Buddhism continues to flourish and be supported by both the people and government. It also exists in neighbouring Sikkim, a small state incorporated into India in 1975, and the Darjeeling and Jalpaiguru districts of northern West Bengal. In both, it has been strengthened by the influx of Tibetan refugees. Northern Buddhism also exists in Ladakh, in the northern Indian state of Jammu and Kashmir, but it faces real problems from the rapidly increasing Muslim population of the state and the cutting off of communication with Tibet.

In Nepal, Buddhism has mostly remained as a junior partner in a syncretism of the Tantric forms of Hinduism and Buddhism. Renewal began in the 1930s, however, when Nepali Buddhists met monks from Burma and Sri Lanka working for the revival of Buddhism in India. In 1951, Nepal opened itself to the outside world, and the government pressure towards Hinduization abated. Southern Buddhist missions entered the country, so that the Theravāda is now a small but growing and very active religion, with an indigenous *Sangha* of monks and ten-precept nuns. Its presence has helped stimulate a general renaissance of Newar culture, and a renewal of traditional Newar Buddhism. Buddhism is also found among Tibetan-influenced minorities such as the Sherpas, and Tibetan refugees.

Tibetan refugees in India

When the Dalai Lama fled from Tibet in 1959, around 80,000 people accompanied or followed him. Most of them (50,000) settled in India, which granted land for this purpose. The Dalai Lama has an administrative centre at Dharamsāla in the northern state of Himal Pradesh, which also contains a third of the 120 monasteries established by the refugees. Flourishing lay communities exist in Orissa and Mysore. The unfamiliar Indian climate has led to much ill-health among the refugees, however, and though many communities have become self-supporting, unemployment remains a problem; the refugees therefore partly subsist on Indian and foreign aid. The monks must support themselves by growing food, tending small herds of cattle, and producing craft work for sale, so that less time is available for study. Learned *bLamas* are only found among the very old, and the refugees are faced with the dual tasks of recording and passing on their rich cultural heritage, and physical survival. Nevertheless, works of Tibetan Buddhism are being printed in India, and monks and learned laymen are studying at various universities in India, the West and Japan, thus stimulating an increase in studies of Tibetan Buddhist culture. The Tibetan diaspora has also led to refugees settling in the West, where they have been very active in spreading their tradition. A sign of the vitality of Northern Buddhism was a gathering, in 1985, of more than 200,000 pilgrims at Bodh-Gayā, with 10,000 even coming from Tibet.

RECOVERING OLD GROUND

Indonesia

The visit of Western Theosophists to Indonesia in 1883 re-awakened an interest in Buddhism both among the Chinese, who make up about 3 per cent of the population, and the predominantly Muslim Indonesians, who have always had a taste for mysticism. Buddhist missions followed from Sri Lanka (1929) and Burma (1934). In 1955 Ashin Jinarakkhita, a Chinese monk ordained in Burma, returned to Indonesia. Theravāda monasteries began to be built, helped by the interest aroused by the international celebration of *Buddha Jayanti*. Ordinations and many conversions followed from among the people of eastern Java who still adhered to the Śiva-Buddha syncretism, and also from the Chinese. In 1965, as a result of an attempted Communist *coup*, the government outlawed all organizations that doubted or denied the existence of God. This posed a problem for the 'non-theistic' Theravāda Buddhism. Jinarakkhita proposed that the Buddhist 'God' was the *Ādi*-Buddha, the primaeval Buddha of the region's previous Mantrayāna Buddhism, while more orthodox Theravādins said that *Nibbāna*, the 'unborn', was their 'God'. In general, the Buddhism favoured by Jinarakkhita has been somewhat syncretistic. While predominantly Theravādin in teaching, it uses some Sanskrit and Javanese texts, includes reference to some Mahāyāna Buddhas and *Bodhisattvas* in its devotion, and draws on elements of Chinese Buddhist ritual. The increase in Buddhist activity in Indonesia has led to greater activity among Chinese Buddhists and a revival in the old Śiva-Buddhism on the island of Bali. More traditional Theravāda was strengthened in 1970 by a Thai mission which started an indigenous *Sangha*. In 1977, there were two to three million Buddhist in Indonesia.

India

Since the nineteenth century, both Western and Indian scholars studied the Buddhist heritage of India through archaeology and textual research. From the 1890s, popular works on Buddhism appeared, and the poet Rabindranath Tagore included Buddhist themes in his plays. Dharmapāla's Mahā Bodhi Society developed centres in many cities and helped raise India's awareness of Buddhism. It gradually made some converts among educated Indians, and an ex-MBS member worked to convert some lower caste people in the south. In the 1920s and 1930s, the MBS was associated with the scholarly and popular writings of three notable Indian scholar-monks, R. Sankrityayan, A. Kausalyayan and J. Kashyap.

The re-awakening of Indian interest in Buddhism has led to the publication of many books on the religion. Some secularized intellectuals have become attracted to its 'rationalism' and its non-support of the caste system, but do not usually formally become Buddhists. Buddhism tends to be seen as part of Hinduism, whose strongly social nature retains its hold. The first prime minister of independent India, Jawaharlal Nehru, was such an 'intellectual' Buddhist. They are also found among the mainly middle-class people, of various religious affiliations, who attend ten-day 'meditation camps'. These teach a form of *Vipassanā* as a means to a harmonious way of life, and can be seen as a form of Buddhist modernism.

The most numerous 'new' Buddhists in India are ex-members of certain 'untouchable' castes, who are followers of Dr B. R. Ambedkar (1891–1956). Such 'Ambedkar' Buddhists, numbering around 4·5 million, are mainly concentrated in the western state of Maharashtra, where they comprise around 7 per cent of the population. The untouchable castes, known as 'scheduled castes' since 1935, comprise a traditionally economically depressed and socially shunned group, placed below even the *Śūdras* in the Hindu social system. They did dirty jobs such as street cleaning, and were looked down on, especially by Brahmins, as less than human. Ambedkar, though himself an untouchable, managed to get a good education, in India and abroad. He became a lawyer and, from the 1920s, worked for the emancipation of the untouchables from their degradation within Hinduism. He saw many social evils in India, and regarded the caste system as the root of them all. In 1936, he formed the Scheduled Castes Federation to help overcome Brahmin political power, which he saw as underpinning the caste system. As Minister of Law in the first post-independence government, he ensured that the constitution protected the rights of scheduled caste members.

In 1935, Ambedkar had declared he would convert from Hinduism to another religion, this being the way forward for scheduled caste members. He was courted by different religions, but rejected Christianity and Islam due to their non-Indian origin, and because their Indian members were affected by caste attitudes. He also found Christians rather individualistic and disliked Islam for its tendency to intolerance and its enforced seclusion of women in *purdah*. While he was also attracted to Sikhism, in 1950 he chose Buddhism, which he regarded as a rational and egalitarian religion, with emphases on love, equality and spiritual freedom. He wanted to avoid such things as expenditure on 'merit'-making activities, however, and saw himself as a 'neo-Buddhist'. For him, Buddhism was a social gospel whose monks the Buddha had intended to be the torch-bearers of a new ideal society. They should therefore be 'social workers and social preachers', like Christian missionaries, and teach Buddhism as a means to human dignity and a democratic society. In 1956, Ambedkar and around

500,000 scheduled caste members converted to Buddhism at a mass public 'consecration' ceremony. Other mass conversions followed, and still continue on a smaller scale. Ambedkar Buddhism focusses on the moral reform of the individual and society. It stresses devotion, but not meditation, and Ambedkar himself is taken as a fourth 'refuge', being regarded as a *Bodhisatta*. Its teachings are akin to those of modernist Southern Buddhism.

Conversion has meant that the Ambedkar Buddhists have overcome their sense of inferiority, and experienced a great enhancement of their dignity. They have been keen for educational advancement, and have experienced economic betterment, for example by greatly cutting down on the expense traditionally entailed by such things as weddings. These first generation Buddhists have had the task of developing a knowledge of their newly-adopted religion, a task which was not without its difficulties at first. The movement is mainly led by lay officials, who have undergone six months' training. By 1970, there were around forty monks, but training facilities for them were inadequate, so that few were learned. Ambedkar Buddhists are mostly ex-members of the Mahar and Jatav castes, and in fact now tend to be treated as a new (low) caste: they have not broken the mould. Nevertheless, their numbers continue to grow.

Buddhist pilgrims from many countries now visit sites associated with the Buddha's life in India, particularly Bodh-Gayā, the scene of the Buddha's enlightenment. Here there is a large Tibetan monastery, a Japanese temple and school for local children, a Thai temple, a rest-house run by Sinhalese monks of the MBS, a Burmese monastery, and a small Chinese temple. The local villagers are also starting to turn to Buddhism. In an important sense, Buddhism began at Bodh-Gayā, and it is fitting that this should now be a microcosm of the Buddhist world.

13

BUDDHISM BEYOND ASIA

As European powers expanded into Asia, particularly India, knowledge of Asian religions became more soundly based. Changes in European thought also led to some receptivity to ideas from non-Christian religions. In the eighteenth century, the Enlightenment's emphasis on 'reason' and 'science' weakened reliance on authoritative 'revelation' in religious matters, and a number of people thought that they saw a 'natural religion' held in common by people of all cultures, but best expressed in Christianity. In the nineteenth century, advances in geology and Biblical studies led to a weakening of Biblical literalism, and the concept of biological evolution seemed, to many, to cast doubts on the 'revealed' Christian account of creation. In this context, the idea of making a 'scientific', 'comparative' study of all religions came to be advanced.

These elements came together in the last two decades of the nineteenth century, when there was something of a vogue for (modernist) Buddhism among sections of the middle classes in America, Britain and Germany. Like Christianity, Buddhism had a noble ethical system, but it appeared to be a religion of self-help, not dependent on God or priests. Like science, it seemed to be based on experience, saw the universe as ruled by law, and did not regard humans and animals as radically distinct. Yet for those with a taste for mysticism, it offered more than science.

SCHOLARSHIP

The first Buddhist texts to be worked on were Sanskrit ones (mostly Mahāyāna) from Nepal, collected by the British resident B. H. Hodgson. The French scholar Eugène Burnouf used these to produce his *Introduction à l'histoire du bouddhisme indien* (1845), and a translation of the Lotus *Sūtra* (1852).

In Sri Lanka, missionaries began the study of Buddhism, though the best of their accounts still tended to give a distorted view of the Southern tradition as a pessimistic, inadequate religion. From around 1800, this was rectified by the work of English, German and Scandinavian scholars, such as V. Fausboll, who edited the *Dhammapada* and translated it into Latin in 1855. Two influential and popular accounts of the Buddha's life and teachings, based on Pali materials, were *The Buddha, His Life, His Doctrine, His Community* (1881, in German), of Hermann Oldenberg, and *Buddhism* (1878), of T. W. Rhys Davids, who had spent eight years in the colonial civil service in Sri Lanka. Also in England, the German-English F. Max Müller edited the fifty-one volume *Sacred Books of the East* series (1879–1910), which contained translations of a number of Buddhist texts. In America, Henry Clarke Warren co-founded the Harvard Oriental Series (1891), and produced an excellent anthology of translations from the Pali Canon, *Buddhism in Translations* (1896). Particularly important was the work of the Pāli Text Society, founded in England in 1881 by Rhys Davids (1843–1922). Its aim was to publish critical editions, in Roman characters, of the texts of the Pali Canon and its commentaries, along with translations. Interest in the Pali Canon arose because it was seen as preserving the 'original teachings' of the Buddha, who was regarded as a rational, ethical teacher, with ritual and supernatural elements of Buddhism being seen as later accretions. International co-operation enabled the PTS to publish most of the Pali texts of the Canon by 1910, and by 1989 it had produced 176 volumes of text, and 74 of translations, along with works of aid for textual study.

In the early twentieth century, Tibetan and Chinese texts were studied. In Russia, a team of scholars was led by T. Stcherbatsky, who studied Buddhist philosophy, and produced such works as *The Central Conception of Buddhism, and the Meaning of the Word Dharma* (1923), and *Buddhist Logic* (1930). Other scholars, mainly French and Belgian, studied the religious and historical aspects of the Mahāyāna, with L. de La Vallée Poussin producing translations of the *Abḥidharma-kośa* and key Yogācāra works. Knowledge of Zen Buddhism was greatly aided by the scholarly and popular writings of Dr D. T. Suzuki, for example his *Essays in Zen Buddhism, First Series* (1927).

Since the Second World War, the Franco-Belgian school has been continued by scholars such as E. Lamotte (1903–83). Advances in the study of Northern Buddhism were made by the travels and translations of the Italian G. Tucci, while Indian and Japanese scholars have made important contributions to international Buddhology. The discovery of texts from such places as the sands of Central Asia, and the cave-temples of Tun-huang in China, have also opened up new areas of research. Edward Conze (1904–79) advanced the study of the Perfection of Wisdom literature, and his *Buddhism* (1951), *Buddhist Texts Through the Ages* (1954), *Buddhist Scriptures* (1959) and *Buddhist Thought in India* (1962) have done much to disseminate knowledge of Buddhism. From the 1960s, the study of Buddhism has become established in many Western universities.

Western scholars have thus played a key role in bringing knowledge of Buddhism to the West. This has been expressed both in scholarly and popular works and in exhibitions of Buddhist art and artefacts. More indirectly, it has also led to treatments of Buddhism on television and radio. Works on Buddhism are now also being produced by a number of Buddhist publishers. In America there are Shambhala, Dharma and Snow Lion Publications, and in Britain there are Wisdom and Tharpa Publications.

THE INFLUENCE OF BUDDHISM THROUGH LITERATURE AND PHILOSOPHY

Another channel through which Buddhism has reached the West has been through the work of certain writers and philosophers. In Germany, Arthur Schopenhauer (1788–1860) was struck by what he saw as parallels between his philosophy and the ideas of Buddhism and Hinduism (which he conflated to some extent). His key work, *The World as Will and Representation* (1818 and 1844, in German), contains many references to Buddhism, particularly in its second volume. Schopenhauer regarded Buddhism as the best religion, and while Christian missionaries criticized it for its 'pessimism', he saw this as its strength, realistically assessing the presence of suffering in the world. Schopenhauer's interest in Buddhism influenced Wagner in the composition of his opera *Tristan and Isolde* (1855). In the 1830s and 1840s, the American Transcendentalist writers R. W. Emerson and H. D. Thoreau also drew on Indian themes. In developing their individualist, intuitive, and pantheistic philosophy, however, their Indian sources were mainly Hindu.

In England, Sir Edwin Arnold, who became editor of the *Daily Telegraph*, produced the *Light of Asia* (1879), a poem on the life of the Buddha. This led to quite a widespread interest in Buddhism among the middle classes in England and America, and aided the Buddhist renaissance in Sri Lanka. Arnold was a liberal Christian much attracted to Buddhism. His sympathetic account, in a somewhat rich, dramatic and sentimental style, portrayed the Buddha as a figure in some ways akin to Jesus. In 1885, he visited Bodh-Gayā and then travelled to Sri Lanka and Japan to rouse support for the restoration of it and other holy sites. This caused Anagārika Dharmapāla to visit the site, after which he founded the Mahā Bodhi Society.

The novels of the German writer Hermann Hesse used Buddhist themes, especially the influential *Siddhartha* (1922), and the Swiss psychoanalyst Carl Jung explored parallels between symbolic dreams and Tibetan *maṇḍalas*. In the 1950s, Jack Kerouac's *The Dharma Bums* and *On the Road* infused Zen themes into the anarchic Beat sub-culture. Aldous Huxley's *The Doors of Perception and Heaven and Hell* (1956) also stimulated an interest in Eastern meditation by (wrongly) comparing enlightenment to experiences had under the influence of mescaline. In the 1960s, this kind of association helped Buddhism catch the interest of people influenced by the Hippie movement.

THE THEOSOPHICAL SOCIETY: A BRIDGE BETWEEN EAST AND WEST

The first organized group in the West to advocate the adoption of Indian religious beliefs and practices was the Theosophical Society, founded in New York in 1875 (see p. 290). This grew out of the American vogue for spiritualism, and mingled Neo-Platonic mysticism, other elements of the Western esoteric tradition, Hindu and Buddhist ideas, and a religious version of 'evolution'. It saw individuals as spiritually evolving over many lives, through cycles of the universe, according to their 'karma' and knowledge. It did not accept that a human could be reborn at an animal level again, though. Ultimate reality was seen more in Hindu than in Buddhist terms: all beings were regarded as containing an inner *ātman*, or Self, which was a portion of the universal One or *Brahman*.

The co-founder Blavatsky was an eccentric, charismatic figure who had travelled widely. She had perhaps reached an area of Tibetan Buddhist culture under Russian control, and later introduced to America and Europe the image of Tibet as a mysterious and wonderful land. She claimed that her books, such as *The Secret Doctrine* (1888) were clairvoyantly dictated to her by members of a 'Brotherhood' of spiritual 'Masters' who lived in Tibet. They had 'chosen' her to teach an ancient religion – Theosophy, or 'Divine Wisdom' – which was the inner essence and basis of all known religions. Jesus and the Buddha had been past 'Masters' of this esoteric tradition. Olcott's strengths lay in organizational abilities, though it appears to have been he who wished to go to what he saw as the 'holy land' of India: one of the first of many Western pilgrims who followed in later years.

The Theosophical Society established branches in America, England, India and Sri Lanka. In the West, it attracted people who found the conventional structures of society inhibiting, for example intelligent, creative people with little formal education, or women chafing at their social position. From 1907, when Olcott died, its President was Annie Besant (1847–1933), an Englishwoman who had previously been an atheist and socialist. The society was at the height of its influence in the 1920s, when it had groomed the Indian Jiddu Krishnamurti (1895–1986) as the vehicle of a Messiah figure, seen as both the returning Christ and Maitreya Buddha. In 1929, Krishnamurti publicly rejected this role, and the Society subsequently declined in influence. The Society had, however, been successful in introducing a number of key Buddhist and Hindu concepts to people unfamiliar with scholarly writings.

IMMIGRATION, FOREIGN WARS AND TRAVEL

In the 1860s and 1870s, hundreds of thousands of Chinese immigrants came to the West Coast of America and Canada to work in the gold mines and on the railroads. After 1882, Japanese labourers followed. From 1868, significant numbers of Japanese and Chinese immigrants also came to work on the sugar plantations of Hawaii, which was annexed as an American territory in 1898. Asian immigration to California was halted in 1902, but continued in Hawaii, which thus became an important centre for the transmission of Buddhism to America. Japanese immigration to Brazil began in 1909.

Chinese religion kept a low profile in North America, though a Pure

Land mission was active to some extent among the Chinese. Today, most temples are hidden away in Chinatowns in big cities. They mostly follow traditional syncretistic folk religion, though some are mainly Buddhist and/or Taoist. Since 1950, the 'folk' temples have been declining, as their members age and die. There has been a steady growth of non-syncretistic ones, though, mainly of the broad T'ien-t'ai Buddhist tradition.

Japanese immigrants have been more obviously active in religious matters, many coming from an area where the Jōdo-shin sect was strong. This sect was also the most active in sending out missions. In 1889, the priest Sōryū Kagahi arrived in Hawaii and established the first Japanese temple there. He belonged to the Hompa Hongwanji sub-sect, which became for a long time the largest Buddhist denomination in Hawaii and North America. In 1899, Sokei Sonada came to San Francisco and established the sub-sect on the continent as the North American Buddhist Mission. During the Second World War, this was re-organized as the Buddhist Churches of America, and became independent of its Japanese parent body. To help pass on its traditions, the Mission and then Church organized a Young Men's Buddhist Association (1900), Sunday Schools, Buddhist women's societies, and educational programmes. These Western-influenced activities had already begun to develop in Japan itself at this time. The title 'Church' indicates further Westernization, as does the style of religious service, which are held on Sundays, use organs and include the singing of hymns such as 'Buddha, lover of my soul...'

After the war, two institutes for training priests were established. One of the Church's members was an astronaut killed in the 1986 Challenger space-shuttle disaster and, in 1987, the US Defence Department allowed the Church to put forward chaplains to work in the military. In 1987, the Church claimed 170,000 adherents, with sixty-six clergy and sixty-three temples in the USA. Most adherents are of Japanese descent. In Canada, in 1985, the related Buddhist Churches of Canada had eighteen member Churches and a membership of around 10,000. In Brazil, there are now around 500,000 people of Japanese ancestry. Various sects of Buddhism are found among them: Zen, Jōdo-shin, Jōdo, Shingon, Tendai and Nichiren, and Brazilian Buddhists, numbering between 100,000 and 200,000, are mainly of Japanese descent.

In Australia, Buddhism arrived in 1882 with a small group of immigrants from Sri Lanka. It also existed among Chinese settlers. However, it did not start to develop among other sections of the population until the 1930s.

In Africa, a Buddhist monastery was established in Tanzania in 1927 by immigrant labourers brought over from Sri Lanka. It still exists, though the number of Buddhists seems to be dwindling. Immigrants from Sri Lanka also seem to be behind the existence of Mahā Bodhi Societies in Ghana and Zaire, and a Buddhist society in Zambia, where some among the indigenous population are now starting to express an interest in Buddhism.

From 1860 to 1913, low-caste Indians came as indentured labourers to South Africa, mainly to Natal. In the 1920s and 1930s, increasing discrimination led some of them to Westernize and convert to Christianity, while others explored their Indian roots, strengthening their Hinduism. Some turned to Buddhism, attracted by what they saw as its freedom from caste and superstition, its social ethic, and its emphasis on the compassionate Buddha-nature within all. Links with Buddhists in south India led to the founding of a Buddhist Society in 1917. It was never a mass movement, however, its weakness being that it has had no temples or monks; the recent interest in Buddhism among Caucasians may remedy this, though.

After the Second World War, an interest in Buddhism was developed by some American servicemen taking part in the occupation of Japan, and in the Korean and Vietnam wars, and by some of the young people who travelled overland to 'mystic' India and Nepal in the sixties and seventies. Tibetan refugees also soon started to share their tradition with people in North America and Europe. From 1975, refugees from Vietnam, Laos and Cambodia have come to the West, their numbers reaching 884,000 by 1985: 561,000 in the USA, 94,000 in Canada, 97,000 in France, 91,000 in Australia, 22,000 in Germany, and 19,000 in Britain. The Vietnamese have established a number of temples in the West, and the Cambodians are now building Buddhist centres and ordaining as monks. In Britain, a community of Indian Ambedkar Buddhists has developed around Birmingham, numbering around 6,000 by 1988. Some have converted in Britain since 1973.

BUDDHIST MISSIONS AND ORGANIZATIONS

The USA

An important platform for Buddhist missions to Westerners was created by the convening of the World Parliament of Religions, organized by liberal Christians as an adjunct to the 1893 Chicago World Fair. The hope was to reveal the common elements in all religions, so as to foster brotherhood in worship, service to man, and opposition to materialism. The delegate who made the most impression was Swami Vivekānanda, a Vedāntic Hindu, but Anagārika Dharmapāla also made a very favourable impression. He and the Rinzai Zen abbot Sōen Shaku initiated a short surge of interest in Buddhism by their speeches at the Parliament. Dr Paul Carus resolved to publish works on Buddhism, especially Zen, through his Open Court Publishing Company, and himself produced *The Gospel of Buddha* (1894), a popular anthology of Buddhist texts.

In 1896, Dharmapāla returned to America for a year at the invitation of Carus, travelling widely and teaching Buddhist doctrine, psychology and meditation. He again returned in 1902–4. Carus also invited D. T. Suzuki (1870–1966), a lay student of Sōen Shaku, to work at his publishing company. After eleven years doing so, he returned to Japan in 1909, but he still kept up contacts with the West, publishing extensively in English on Zen from the late twenties, and lecturing at Columbia University in the fifties. Sōen Shaku returned to America in 1905–6, at the invitation of supporters in San Francisco. His close disciple Nyogen Senzaki founded Zen groups in California from the twenties to the fifties. Another disciple, Ven. Sōkei-an, founded the Buddhist Society of America, in New York City in 1930. This later became the First Zen Institute of America. Zen became the first form of Buddhism to really catch on among Caucasians, who found it very amenable to the pragmatic, energetic American disposition.

In post-war America, Zen continued to develop in the fifties 'Beat' period, and in the counterculture of the sixties and seventies, when Buddhism in general started to really take off, mainly in its Zen and Tibetan forms. While Rinzai was the first form of Zen established in America, Sōtō, which is popular in Hawaii, followed. In 1961, the Sōtō master Shunryu Suzuki (1904–71) opened the impressive San Francisco

Zen Center and, in 1967, established the Tassajara Mountain monastery. Sōtō Zen was also introduced by Reverend Master Jiyu Kennett, an Englishwoman born to Buddhist parents. After ordaining as a *bhikṣuṇī* of the Chinese *Sangha* in Malaysia, in 1962, she went to Japan and trained as the only woman in a Sōtō temple. In 1969, she went to America and, in 1970, she founded Shasta Abbey, in California, as the headquarters of the Zen Mission Society. A mixture of Rinzai and Sōtō is also taught, as at the cluster of buildings which forms the Zen Center of Los Angeles, established in 1956.

The four main schools of Tibetan Buddhism are all present in the USA, attracting a growing number of young people by their mixture of mysticism, symbolism, ritual and psychological insights. Chogyam Trungpa Rinpoche (1939–87), a bKa'brgyud *bLama*, established a thriving centre at Boulder, Colorado in 1971. This has since become the centre of the Vajradhātu organization, a network including many meditation centres, affiliated groups and a Buddhist Institute. Trungpa was a charismatic figure of somewhat controversial behaviour, whose teachings and popular writings, such as *Cutting Through Spiritual Materialism* (1973), presented the Tibetan tradition in such a way as would be attractive to those with a concern for 'psychological growth'. Another charismatic *bLama* is Tarthang Tulku Rinpoche, an ex-abbot of the rNying-ma school, who encourages study, publication of Buddhist works, and help for the Tibetan refugees in India.

In the Chinese tradition, Buddhist groups have become more active and have attracted Caucasians. Tripiṭaka Master Hsuan Hua has been particularly influential. Coming from Hong Kong in 1962 at the invitation of some Chinese-American disciples, he founded the Sino-American Buddhist Association in San Francisco in 1968. His reputation soon attracted Caucasian followers, who comprised two-thirds of the SABA membership by 1971. By 1977, the Association's headquarters was the 'The City of 10,000 Buddhas', a large former hospital in extensive grounds, in northern California. Here there is the Dharma Realm University, primary and secondary schools, and *Sangha* and lay training facilities. The Association emphasizes strict *Vinaya* for monks and nuns, meditation, and study of Chinese Buddhist texts. Through the Buddhist Texts Translation Society, it also translates such texts, along with explanations by Hsuan Hua. Study is of Ch'an, Lu, T'ien-t'ai, Pure Land, and Chen-yen, while meditation is Ch'an or Pure Land chanting.

Table 2

	Monastery/temples	Centres (meeting places other than private houses, hired premises or temples)
Tibetan	6	111
Zen	8	52
Theravāda	24	5
Chinese	8	5

In 1973, two American monks of this *Sangha* went on a 1,100 mile bowing pilgrimage across America. This journey for world peace took ten months, and is described in the book *Three Steps, One Bow*.

In 1960 the Sōka-gakkai, as 'Nichiren Shōshū of America', began to vigorously proselytize, starting in Los Angeles. Since 1967, it has worked beyond the Japanese-American community, so that 95 per cent of its members are now non-Asian. By 1970, it claimed 200,000 members in the USA, and by 1974, it had groups on over sixty university and college campuses. Its membership includes more Hispanics and Blacks than other Buddhist groups, and also media personalities such as the rock singer Tina Turner, and the actor Patrick Duffy, of the TV soap-opera 'Dallas'. Its simplicity, and the power of its practice has drawn in those who are seeking to overcome frustration or negativity and to enhance their creativity. Its numbers have continued to grow rapidly since 1970.

The Theravāda tradition is still young in the USA, its first *vihāra* being established by the Sinhalese in 1966 in Washington DC. Since then, others have been opened, and the tradition has started to flourish. Americans have ordained as monks and, from 1987, as ten-precept nuns, and meditation centres teaching Insight meditation are becoming popular.

Almost all extant forms of Buddhism, including some new eclectic and syncretistic ones, now exist in the USA. The American entries for the *International Buddhist Directory* indicate the situation in 1984. Apart from the Buddhist Churches of America, the biggest groups were as shown in Table 2.

Besides these, there were two hundred and fourteen Buddhist societies or groups, mostly of unknown affiliation. In 1987, forty-five different Buddhist organizations formed the American Buddhist Congress, a national body for co-operation, education and propagation.

Estimates for the number of American Buddhists vary widely. In 1979, Prebish put the figure at several hundred thousand, but in 1987, the American Buddhist Congress gave the figure of three to five million. Of these, perhaps 400,000 would be from Indochina, 170,000 would belong to the 'Buddhist Church', and perhaps 300,000 to Nichiren Shōshū.

As in other Western countries, most people find their way to Buddhism through meditation practice, with a little reading on Buddhism. They then become involved in wider aspects of the tradition. In Asia, devotional practices and contact with monks are usually the starting point. Followers are mostly from urban centres of the West and East Coasts and Hawaii. Non-Asian Buddhists tend to be 21–35, male, single, Caucasian, college-educated, and from Jewish or Catholic backgrounds. They feel uprooted to some extent, and see in Buddhism a non-traditional route to self-discovery and spiritual growth. Increasingly, Asian teachers are giving Caucasians authority to hand on the tradition, there being around fifty such teachers by the 1980s.

Canada

In Canada, the development of Buddhism has been similar to that in the USA. Numbers rose fourfold in the seventies, with approximately 50,000 Buddhists existing in the country by 1985. Apart from the Churches of the Jōdo-shin tradition, monasteries or temples had by then been established by several other traditions: Vietnamese (8), Chinese (4), Korean (3), Theravādin (1), Tibetan (1) and Zen (1). There were also many Centres of the Tibetan (22) and Zen (8) traditions, and six Theravādin societies. In 1981, the multi-denominational Buddhist Council of Canada was formed.

The United Kingdom

The first Buddhist missionary to Great Britain was Dharmapāla, who visited for five months in 1893, then in 1896 and 1904. On these occasions, he made contact with T. W. Rhys Davids, Edwin Arnold and

Theosophists. The second British monk (the first remained in South-east Asia) was Allan Bennett (1872–1923), who was inspired by the *Light of Asia* and appears to have been influenced by Theosophy. In 1902 he went to Burma, ordained as Ānanda Metteyya, and then formed a missionary society (1903). In 1907, the Buddhist Society of Great Britain and Ireland was formed, with T. W. Rhys Davids as its president, to receive a mission, and in 1908 Ānanda Metteyya and three Burmese monks arrived in Britain.

The Society was interested in a modernist version of Southern Buddhism, as both a world-view and an ethic. At first, progress was slow, but from 1909 to 1922, the *Buddhist Review* was published. The First World War held up development, and afterwards the Society struggled on until it collapsed in 1924. In this year, however, the lawyer Christmas Humphreys (1901–83) founded the Buddhist Lodge of the Theosophical Society, which absorbed the remnants of the previous Society in 1926. In 1943, the Lodge became the Buddhist Society, and its journal (*Buddhism in England*) became *The Middle Way*, which is still going strong. Under Humphreys, interest turned more to Zen and meditation practice. For many, his paperback *Buddhism* (1951 and still in print) has been their first book on Buddhism, though its interpretation is slanted by Theosophical ideas of the 'One' and the 'Self'.

Dharmapāla visited England from 1925 to 1927, to found a branch of the Mahā Bodhi Society (1926), and establish a monastery for Sinhalese monks (1928), which existed till 1939. 1928 also saw a visit from the Chinese reformer Ven. T'ai-hsu (1899–1947), while in 1936, D. T. Suzuki came to the World Congress of Faiths, in London, and lectured on Zen and Japanese culture in several English cities.

After the Second World War, a Sinhalese *vihāra* was established in London in 1954, and a Thai one in 1966. From the seventies, Buddhism started to put down firm roots, as seen by a more widespread commitment to Buddhist *practice*, as opposed to a still mostly intellectual interest, and by the development of a social dimension, with the establishment of an indigenous *Sangha* and many Buddhist centres. The strongest traditions are Theravāda, Tibetan, Zen, and a syncretistic group known as the Friends of the Western Buddhist Order. The 1987 *Buddhist Directory* for the United Kingdom indicated the presence of a number of forms of Buddhism. Of these, the largest were as shown in Table 3.

Table 3

	Monastery/ Temples	Centres	Society/Groups
Tibetan	3	19	17
Theravāda	12	3	28
FWBO	0	19	7
Zen	1	1	31
All	0	2	22
Total	16	44	105

Most of these are in England, though increasingly they are developing in Wales, Scotland, and, most recently, in Northern Ireland. The Buddhist Society, located in London, acts as a forum, especially through the pages of the *Middle Way*. It offers classes in Theravāda, Tibetan and Zen traditions, and has an annual summer school. Those interested in Buddhism are likely to be exposed to several traditions, and adherents of these interact to a fair extent: probably more so than in Asia, due to geographical separation. Besides the listings above, there is also a Buddhist prison chaplaincy organization, a Buddhist hospice project, a Buddhist animal rights group, a Buddhist Peace Fellowship (concerned with peace, ecology, and the human rights of Buddhists abroad), a 'Buddhism, Psychology and Psychiatry Group', and a Scientific Buddhism Association. All of these have been established in the 1980s. The growth of Buddhist monasteries and meditation centres has helped stimulate something of a revival in Christian meditation, and Christian monks and nuns sometimes learn techniques from Buddhist ones. Besides Asian Buddhists, there are probably between 10,000 and 100,000 Buddhists in Britain.

Some of the more important elements of Buddhism in Britain are as follows. In 1954, William Purfhurst travelled to Thailand to ordain, becoming Ven. Kapilavaddho. In 1956, he returned to England and founded the English Sangha Trust, whose aim was to establish an indigenous *Sangha* of the Southern tradition. In 1957, he disrobed due to bad health, but his disciple Ven. Paññavaddho continued the work of teaching *Vipassanā* meditation. There was, however, not much success in recruiting or retaining new monks. In 1962, a Thai-trained Canadian monk, Ānanda Bodhi, founded the Hampstead Buddhist Vihāra, under the auspices of the English Sangha Trust. Two years later, an invitation to his Thai teacher to visit England led to the establishment of a Thai *vihāra* in London, which opened in 1966. In 1967, Ānanda Bodhi moved on to found the Johnstone House Meditation Centre, in Dumfriesshire, Scotland, but Kapilavaddho re-ordained and returned as incumbent of the Hampstead Vihāra. By 1969, there were four monks at the *vihāra*, and there were regular meditation classes. In 1970, however, Kapilavaddho disrobed due to bad health, dying in 1971. The other monks also disrobed, largely due to a wish not to be confused with somewhat disreputable robe-clad Guru-figures who were then in evidence in England. They continued Buddhist activities, however, and this led to the establishment of two *Vipassanā* meditation centres.

In 1977, the well-known Thai meditation teacher Ajahn Chaa visited the Hampstead Vihāra, at the request of the English Sangha Trust. His Western pupil, the American monk Ajahn Sumedho, stayed on and organized the introduction of a *Sangha* of Western monks, trained in the forest tradition of Thailand. This soon moved to a rural site developed from a near-derelict country house in Sussex, with a nearby 108-acre forest as an integral part of a monastic settlement. Branch monasteries were then opened in Northumberland (1981) and Devon (1984). In 1985, the Amaravati Buddhist Centre was opened near Hemel Hempstead, in a group of wooden buildings which was formerly a camp school. This is the largest monastery of the group, and also acts as a centre for lay activities.

As of early 1988, this *Sangha* had sixty-three members, including monks, ten-precept nuns, and postulants (*anagārika*'s and *anagārikā*'s). A number of the older monks, who trained in Thailand, come from North America, but there are also ones from seven European countries, and an increasing number from Britain. Their leader is Ajahn Sumedho. They live a simple life, emphasizing *Vinaya*, meditation, and non-attachment in daily activities. For lay people, they offer weekend and ten-day introductions to meditation, emphasizing *Vipassanā* practice, and have regular teaching contacts with groups throughout the country. Senior monks travel to related monasteries recently established in Australia and New Zealand, and groups in South Africa and Switzerland.

A lay-led organization of the Southern tradition is the Samatha Trust. This was set up in 1973 by pupils of a Thai meditation teacher,

Nai Boonman, who had had links with the Hampstead Vihāra. It specializes in the teaching of breathing-based *Samatha* meditation, with classes in ten towns and cities, a meditation centre in Manchester, and a national meditation centre in rural Wales. Besides meditation, activities include Pali chanting and *Sutta* and *Abhidhamma* classes.

Another lay-led organization of the Southern tradition is the International Meditation Centre in Heddington, Wiltshire. This was founded in 1979 to provide a facility to teach *Vipassanā* meditation, and follows the teaching and example of Sayagyi U Ba Khin, founder of the International Meditation Centre in Rangoon, Burma. Regular ten-day courses are taught by Sayagyi U Ba Khin's closest disciples, Sayama and Saya U Chit Tin, or their assistants, in the practice of morality, meditation and wisdom, with the goal of achieving Nibbanic peace within. Each course begins with four formalities, recited in Pali by the participants: taking the three refuges and five or eight precepts, surrendering to the Buddha, and making a formal request to be taught the *Dhamma*. The first four days are devoted to the practice of mindfulness of breathing to develop Calm, and this is then used as a basis for the development of Insight-wisdom through *Vipassanā*. Other Southern-inspired groups offer *Vipassanā* shorn of devotional accompaniments.

All four schools of the Tibetan tradition are established, with the bKa'brgyud and dGe-lugs being strongest. In 1967, Ānanda Bodhi invited Chogyam Trungpa and another *bLama* to teach at Johnstone House. This led to its transformation into Samye-Ling monastery and Tibetan centre. This has acted as a place of quiet retreat for people of various religious backgrounds, and has worked to pass on not only Buddhist teachings and practices, but also Tibetan arts, crafts and skills. Its workshops and Tibetan art school have also been utilized in the building of an impressive new temple. There are also plans for a small college. Around a hundred people live in the community, which is led by Akong Rinpoche, a married *bLama*. Most of the residents are lay people, but a few are ordained. The centre has connections with many others in Britain and abroad. The main dGe-lugs centre is the Manjushri Institute, situated on the edge of the English Lake District. This was set up in 1976 by pupils of Thubten Yeshe Rinpoche, who had established a centre for Westerners in Nepal in 1969. The key function of the Institute is to act as a college for the study and preservation of the dGe-lugs tradition. Besides a few Tibetan *bLamas* and a number of Western monks and nuns, fifty or more lay people live in the community. The Institute also spawned Wisdom Publications, a rapidly growing Buddhist publishing house. There are many other smaller Tibetan Buddhist centres in Great Britain.

While Rinzai Zen is strong in the Buddhist Society, a key Sōtō centre is Throssel Hole Priory, in Northumberland. This was founded in 1972, as a branch monastery of Shasta Abbey, California. It acts as a training monastery for Western monks and nuns (also called 'monks', for egalitarian reasons), and a 'retreat' centre for intensive meditation: not, of course, as a 'retreat' from life, but as an opportunity to face and understand it. Throssel Hole's resident monks and lay visitors live a life emphasizing discipline, tidiness, meditation and hard work. The monks visit various groups, conduct weddings and funerals, and ordain people as lay Buddhists. They also conduct a lay ministry programme.

The Friends of the Western Buddhist Order is a lay movement of mostly Mahāyāna influence, and a very Western emphasis. It was founded in 1967 by Ven. Sangharakshita, an English monk with experience of the Southern, Northern and Eastern traditions. He had been a monk for seventeen years in India, ten of them working with the Ambedkar Buddhists. The movement consists of a network of four types of organizations: urban centres, offering meditation classes, 'retreats', and talks for the public; local groups; co-operatives, in which members work on a team basis with an emphasis on ethical livelihood which helps the personal development of the individual; and communities where many members live, often having a 'common purse'. The movement has spread from Britain to continental Europe, New Zealand, Australia, and the USA, and to India, where it does educational, medical and spiritual work among the Ambedkar Buddhists.

The Nichiren Shōshū (Sōka-gakkai) entered Britain in the 1980s; by the end of 1986 it claimed 3,000 followers and was growing rapidly. Besides its national headquarters, its only entry in the *Buddhist Directory*, it has five regional centres and over a hundred small groups, meeting in people's houses. Its adherents include a number of well-known people from the worlds of creative arts and public relations.

Monks and nuns of the Nipponzan Myōhōji Order, a small Nichiren sub-sect dedicated to working for world peace, have also been very active. A few monks of the Order first arrived in the late seventies and became involved in marches of the Campaign for Nuclear Disarmament. They then moved on to building 'Peace Pagodas'. Over sixty have been built in Japan, including ones at Hiroshima and Nagasaki, two in India, and one in Sri Lanka. In 1980, they opened the first consecrated Pagoda/*Stūpa* in the West, at Milton Keynes. Ones in Vienna (1983), Massachusetts (1985), and London (1985) followed. The London one is in Battersea Park, besides the Thames. It is 34 metres high and contains relics from Nepal, Burma, Sri Lanka and Japan. Unlike the Milton Keynes structure, which blends Japanese and ancient Indian designs, its form is primarily Japanese (see Frontispiece). The sect also hopes to build Pagodas in Moscow, and opposite the United Nations in New York. The yellow and white robes of their monks and nuns can sometimes be glimpsed in television news reports dealing with matters relating to nuclear weapons in various parts of the world.

The Pure Land tradition also has a small following in Great Britain. In 1976, the Shin Buddhist Association of Great Britain was formed by Rev. Jack Austin and Rev. Dr Hisau Inagaki, a lecturer in Japanese Buddhism at London University. Inagaki's father had been largely responsible for the establishment of Jōdo-shin Buddhism in Europe, and Rev. Austin had also been active in this field. In 1977, people meeting at Rev. Inagaki's house also formed the non-sectarian Pure Land Buddhist Fellowship. Both groups have a newsletter and attend services in private houses. Another Japanese tradition with a small following is the Shingon school.

The different forms of British Buddhism, while from diverse Asian roots, all share the need to work out an accommodation with Western culture. In this, the *Sangha* under Ajahn Sumedho and the FWBO perhaps lie at the two ends of a spectrum. The former have sought to introduce a mostly traditional monastic life-style, with no deliberate attempt to adapt to Western conditions. Ajahn Sumedho holds that 'If one trims the tradition down before planting the seed, one often severs or slightens the whole spirit.' To those who criticize the importation of 'Asian' customs, such as Pali chanting, he replies that only dogmatically clinging to traditions for their own sake should be avoided. Rather than dogmatically rejecting traditions and conventions, he prefers the middle way of *using* them skilfully. This could be characterized as a non-dogmatic, pragmatic traditionalism.

As to institutional forms, the monks and nuns led by Ajahn Sumedho continue the monastic traditions of the forest monasteries of Thailand. They have successfully introduced the close lay–monastic relationship of Thailand, and are supported by lay donations, both from Asian communities in Britain (and Thailand) and indigenous Britons. A periodic alms-round has even been instituted in Newcastle-upon-Tyne, in an area where a number of Buddhists live. Fairly traditional teachings are given, though rebirth is seen primarily as something to be observed in changing states of mind. As regards life after death, a somewhat agnostic attitude is conveyed.

The FWBO emphatically seeks to develop a Western form of Buddhism, and has criticized other Buddhist groups for importing what it sees as extraneous cultural accretions along with 'essential' Buddhism. It selects practices and teachings by the criterion of their contribution to the development of the 'individual', on which it puts much stress. While being syncretistic, paradoxically it has fewer dealings with other Buddhist groups than the more traditional ones. Another paradox is that it is the most antipathetic to certain features of Western culture, such as what it sees as 'pseudo-Liberalism'. Unlike other Buddhist groups, it is also very critical of Christianity, which it sees as both limited and harmful. On the other hand, it greatly admires the English mystic William Blake.

The FWBO is centred on the Western Buddhist Order, which had 300 members in 1987. They follow ten precepts (which are in fact like the usual five lay precepts), take a Sanskrit name, and are united by their commitment to the Buddha, *Dharma* and Order. Order members, known as *upāsakas* and *upāsikās*, live in communities (mostly single sex), alone, or with their families. The FWBO is very critical of the nuclear family, however, seeing it as a claustrophobic social institution which restricts the growth of the individual. The Western idea of an 'alternative society' has also been influential, so that the WBO is seen as the nucleus of a 'New Society' in which the values of human growth are paramount. The emphasis is on the movement being an economically self-sufficient society-unto-itself. The economic base is provided by 'Right Livelihood' co-operatives such as vegetarian restaurants, wholefood shops, building teams, an Arts Centre, and a printing press. Along with selected Buddhist practices, including chanting in English, Sanskrit and Pali, the FWBO members also practise such things as yoga, T'ai chi, and karate. In its teachings, it emphasizes the 'Higher

Evolution' of the 'individual', such that its ideal seems to be a kind of heroic, muscular, romantic superhumanism, which is influenced by some of the ideas of the philosopher Friedrich Nietzsche. It thus seems to neglect that aspect of the Buddhist path which ultimately aims at the transcending of I-ness and ego-attachment.

Continental Europe

In Germany, interest has long been focussed on the Southern tradition, which perhaps appeals to those from a Protestant culture. The first Buddhist society was started in 1903 by the Pali scholar Karl Seidenstüker, to promote Buddhist scholarship. Success was small, though. An influential figure in early German Buddhism was George Grimm (1868–1945), whose *The Doctrine of the Buddha, the Religion of Reason* (1915, in German) was one of the most widely read books on Buddhism, both in its original German, and in many translations. His interpretation of the *Suttas* saw the teaching that all phenomena are not-self as a way to intuit the true Self, which lies beyond concepts. As he felt that the Buddhist tradition had misunderstood the Buddha, he called his interpretation 'Old Buddhism', meaning the 'original' teaching. In 1921, Grimm and Seidenstüker formed the Buddhist Community for Germany, which became the Old Buddhist Community in 1935, under Grimm's leadership. As most German Buddhists did not accept Grimm's views, 'Old Buddhism' became a kind of sect. Another key Buddhist was Paul Dahlke (1865–1928), who developed an interest in Buddhism while in Sri Lanka in 1900. He followed a modernist version of Southern Buddhism, well-rooted in the Pali sources. He built the 'Buddhist House' in Berlin-Frohnau, a temple/meditation-centre opened in 1924, and also published translations of a number of *Suttas*.

A number of Germans became attracted to the monastic life in Asia. In Sri Lanka, Nyanatiloka ordained as a novice in 1903 (getting higher ordination in Burma), while his main pupil, Nyanaponika, became a novice in 1936. Both of these monks have produced much Buddhist literature, in English and German, which has been widely read by European Buddhists. The first European Buddhist nun, Sister Uppalavarna, was also a German, who was ordained in 1926. In the post-war period, mission societies from Sri Lanka (1952) and Burma (1957) were established, and a *Vipassanā* meditation centre was opened near Hamburg (1961).

Between the wars, some studies of Zen were made, but it was still little known or appreciated. This changed after the Second World War, especially due to the influence of a small book by Dr Eugen Herrigel. This was *Zen in the Art of Archery* (1948, in German), the fruit of five years of studying a Zen martial art. From the seventies, Zen centres have sprung up, and Jōdo-shin also established a presence. The post-war period also saw the introduction of the Arya Maitreya Mandala, which had centres in ten cities by 1970. This is a lay Order founded by *bLama* Anagārika Govinda (1898–1985), a German who had trained in both the Southern and Northern traditions, and was a follower of the Tibetan ecumenical *Ris-med* movement. From the seventies, other Tibetan groups have been established.

France has been strong in Buddhist scholarship. Its first Buddhist society was 'Les Amis du Bouddhisme', founded in Paris in 1929 by the Chinese reformer T'ai-hsu and Constant Lounsberry. There are now many refugees from Indochina living in France, who had set up three Vietnamese temples by 1984. The strongest tradition, with forty-six centres by 1984, was the Tibetan one, with Zen having five centres, and the Theravāda two, along with two monasteries. Nichiren Shōshū is also present.

In Italy, only a few Buddhist groups existed by 1970, but by 1986, there were over thirty centres and monasteries, and approximately twenty-five societies, mainly Tibetan and Zen.

The *International Buddhist Directory*, giving information for 1984 listed Buddhist organizations in Austria, Belgium, Denmark, Finland, Greece, Holland, Norway, Portugal, Spain, Sweden and Switzerland. In Western Europe as a whole, excluding the United Kingdom, it listed: 139 centres, one monastery, and one Institute of the Tibetan tradition; thirty-four centres and two monasteries of the Zen tradition, and twenty-five centres and two monasteries of the Theravāda tradition. The Jōdo-shin school has two temples in Switzerland and one in Belgium. In 1987, a two-year-old Spanish boy, son of a couple running a Tibetan Buddhist centre in Spain, was recognized as the reincarnation of Thubten Yeshe Rinpoche (1934–84), a dGe-lugs *bLama* who had been very active in establishing Tibetan centres and monasteries in the West. The boy now resides as spiritual focus of Kopan monastery, Nepal, which was established by *bLama* Yeshe.

A Buddhist Union of Europe was formed in 1975, as a common forum for discussion, co-operation, publications, and liaison with psychological and medical Institutes. By 1987, it included national Buddhist Unions of Austria, France, Germany, Italy, Holland, and Switzerland, and around fifty organizations (such as the London Buddhist Society), monasteries and groups. In 1987, it claimed that there were over a million Buddhists in Europe (including Asians). Besides 500,000 claimed for England (a figure which is far too high), other figures given were: 70,000 in Germany, 200,000 in France, 15,000 in Italy, and 6,000 in Austria.

In Eastern Europe, Buddhism has a small presence, with one centre or society each in East Germany, Czechoslovakia, Hungary and Yugoslavia. In Poland, however, as of 1984, there were six Tibetan Buddhist centres, three of Korean Son, and three of Zen. As early as the First World War, a Buddhist temple was established in Warsaw to serve the needs of Buryat and Kalmyk troops in the Russian army. In the USSR, Buddhists of the Baltic states claim to have a long Buddhist heritage, possibly going back to the thirteenth century (from the Mongols). They had a 'Buddhist Cathedral' built in St Petersburg (now Leningrad) in the period 1907–15, and were active between the two World Wars in translating texts into their languages. In 1988, there were reports of groups in the USSR who were building *Stūpas* and temples.

Australasia, South America and Africa

Since the 1930s, various short-lived Buddhist societies began to form in Australia. The longest established are the Buddhist Societies of Victoria and New South Wales, established in the 1950s. From the early seventies, Buddhism began to take root as teachers arrived from Asia. These included the British monk Phra Khantipalo, trained in Thailand, and *bLamas* Thubten Yeshe and Thubten Zopa (1974). The Tibetan, Theravāda, Zen, Chinese, Vietnamese, and Nichiren Shōshū traditions are now all present and active. In New Zealand, there were 6–7,000 Buddhists by 1981, the main traditions being Tibetan, Zen, Theravāda and FWBO.

Buddhism did not spread beyond the Japanese community in countries such as Brazil until after the Second World War. Since then, Tibetan Buddhism has established a small presence in Argentina, Brazil, Chile, Columbia and Venezuela, while the Nichiren Shōshū is active throughout the region. In Brazil, besides a number of Japanese sects, and the Tibetan tradition, the Theravāda tradition is also present.

In South Africa, Buddhism is now starting to develop among non-Indians. In 1984 there were eight Tibetan centres and one Theravāda one, specializing in Insight meditation. These centres also attract support from neighbouring Zimbabwe. The Nichiren Shōshū has also been active in West Africa from around 1975.

Today, Buddhism has become a world-wide phenomenon. In Asia, it has suffered losses under Communist rule, but shows signs of recovery. It is also having to adapt to a secularizing environment. Beyond Asia, it is increasingly being established and recognized as one facet of a diverse religious scene.

APPENDIX: CANONS OF SCRIPTURE

The Pali Canon is known as the *Tipiṭaka*, or 'Three Baskets', as its palm-leaf manuscripts were kept in three different baskets. It consists of the *Vinaya-piṭaka*, or 'Basket of (Monastic) Discipline', the *Sutta-piṭaka*, or 'Basket of Discourses', and the *Abhidhamma-piṭaka*, or 'Basket of Further Teachings'. The contents of the *Vinaya* (6 vols.) and *Abhidhamma* (7 texts in 13 volumes, in one edition) are discussed on pp. 224ff. and 83ff. respectively. The contents of the *Sutta-piṭaka* is as follows (the number of volumes are those of the PTS edition):

(i) *Dīgha Nikāya*, or 'Collection' of 34 'Long (Discourses)' (3 vols.).
(ii) *Majjhima Nikāya*, or 'Collection' of 150 'Middle Length (Discourses)' (3 vols.).
(iii) *Saṃyutta Nikāya*, or 'Collection' of 7,762 'Connected (Discourses)', grouped in fifty-six sections (*saṃyuttas*) according to subject matter (5 vols.).
(iv) *Aṅguttara Nikāya*, or 'Collection' of 9,550 'Single-item Upwards (Discourses)', grouped according to the number of items occurring in lists (from one to eleven) which the discourses deal with (5 vols.).
(v) *Khuddaka Nikāya*, which consist of 15 'Little Texts' in 20 volumes. This includes various miscellaneous texts, many in verse form, which contain both some of the earliest and some of the latest material in the Canon:
   (a) *Khuddaka-pāṭha*, a short collection of 'Little Readings' for recitation.
   (b) *Dhammapada*, or 'Verses on *Dhamma*', a popular collection of 423 pithy verses of a largely ethical nature. Its popularity is reflected in the many times it has been translated into Western languages.
   (c) *Udāna*, eighty short *Suttas* based on inspired 'Verses of Uplift'.
   (d) *Itivuttaka*, or 'As it Was Said': 112 short *Suttas*.
   (e) *Sutta-nipāta*, the 'Group of Discourses', a collection of 71 verse *Suttas*, including some very early material such as the *Aṭṭhakavagga*.
   (f) *Vimāna-vatthu*, 'Stories of the Mansions', on heavenly rebirths.

(g) *Peta-vatthu*, 'Stories of the Departed', on ghostly rebirths.
(h) *Thera-gāthā*, 'Elders' Verses', telling how a number of early monks attained enlightenment.
(i) *Therī-gāthā*, the same as (h), for nuns.
(j) *Jātaka*, a collection of 547 'Birth Stories' of previous lives of the Buddha, with the aim of illustrating points of morality. The full stories are told in the commentary, based on verses, which are canonical; together they comprise 6 volumes. While this is a relatively late portion of the Canon, probably incorporating many Indian folk tales, it is extremely popular and is often used in sermons.
(k) *Niddesa*, an 'Exposition' on part of (e).
(l) *Paṭisambhidā-magga*, an *Abhidhamma*-style analysis of certain points of doctrine (2 vols.).
(m) *Apadāna*, 'Stories' on past lives of monks and nuns in (h) and (i).
(n) *Buddhavaṃsa*, 'Chronicle of the Buddhas', on 24 previous Buddhas.
(o) *Cariyā-piṭaka*, 'Basket of Conduct', on the conduct of Gotama in previous lives, building up the 'perfections' of a *Bodhisatta*.

The Chinese Canon is known as the *Ta-ts'ang-ching*, or 'Great Scripture Store'. The standard modern edition, following a non-traditional order based on systematization by scholars, is the *Taishō Daizōkyō*, published in Japan from 1924 to 1929. It consists of 55 volumes containing 2,184 texts, with a supplement of 45 volumes. Its contents are:

(i) translations of the *Āgama*'s (equivalent to the first four Pali *Nikāyas*, and part of the fifth) and the *Jātakas* (219 texts in 4 vols.).
(ii) translations of Mahāyāna *Sūtras* (discourses), sometimes including several translations of the same text. These are grouped into sections on: the Perfection of Wisdom (see pp. 95ff.), the Lotus *Sūtra* (see pp. 92ff.), the *Avataṃsaka* (see pp. 118ff.), the *Ratnakūṭa* (a group of texts, some very early, such as the *Kāśyapa-parivarta*), the *Mahā-parinirvāṇa* (on the last days of the Buddha, and the 'Buddha-nature'), the 'Great Assembly', and general '*Sūtras*' (mostly Mahāyāna) (627 texts in 13 vols.).
(iii) translations of *Tantras* (see pp. 133ff.; 572 texts in 4 vols.).
(iv) translations of various early *Vinayas* (on monastic discipline) and some texts outlining 'discipline' for *Bodhisattvas* (86 texts in 3 vols.).
(v) translations of commentaries on the *Āgamas* and Mahāyāna *Sūtras* (31 texts in 3 vols.).
(vi) translations of various early *Abhidharmas* (see pp. 83ff.) (28 texts in 4 vols.).

(vii) translations of Madhyamaka, Yogācāra and other *Śāstras*, or 'Treatises' (129 texts in 3 vols.).

(viii) Chinese commentaries on the *Sūtras*, *Vinaya* and *Śāstras* (12 vols.).

(ix) Chinese sectarian writings (5 vols.).

(x) Histories and biographies (95 texts in 4 vols.).

(xi) Encyclopaedias, dictionaries, non-Buddhist doctrines (Hindu, Manichean, and Nestorian Christian), and catalogues of various Chinese Canons (64 texts in 3 vols.).

As can be seen, the Chinese Canon includes types of material (such as commentaries, treatises and histories) which are treated as extra-canonical in the Southern, Pali tradition.

The Tibetan Canon consists of the *bKa' 'gyur* (pron. *Kangyur*) and *bStan 'gyur* (pron. *Tengyur*). The former is the 'Translation of the Word of the Buddha', and consists in its sNar thang (pron. Narthang) edition of 98 volumes containing over 600 translated texts, grouped as follows:

(i) *Vinaya* (monastic discipline) (13 vols.).

(ii) Perfection of Wisdom (21 vols.).

(iii) *Avataṃsaka* (6 vols.).

(iv) *Ratnakūṭa* (49 *Sūtras* in 6 vols.).

(v) *Sūtra* (three-quarters of which are Mahāyāna; 270 texts in 30 vols.).

(vi) *Tantra* (more than 300 texts in 22 vols.).

The *bStan 'gyur* is the 'Translation of Treatises', consisting in its Peking edition of 3,626 texts in 224 volumes. These are grouped as follows:

(i) *Stotras*, or hymns or praise (64 texts in 1 vol.).

(ii) commentaries on the *Tantras* (3,055 texts in 86 vols.).

(iii) other commentaries and treatises: commentaries on the Perfection of Wisdom *Sūtras* and the *Vinaya*; Madhyamaka and Yogācāra treatises, *Abhidharma* works, tales and dramas, treatises on such topics as logic, medicine, grammar and chemistry, and other miscellaneous works (567 texts in 137 vols.).

The *bStan 'gyur* mainly consists of Indian works, but outside the above twofold Canon, there is an enormous literature written by Tibetans.

NOTES

1 *Compassion Yoga*, p. 36.
2 W. T. de Bary, *Sources of Chinese Tradition*, vol. I., p. 366.
3 R. Gombrich, 'A new Theravādin Liturgy', *JPTS* vol. IX, p. 67.
4 J. Blofeld, *The Tantric Mysticism of Tibet*, p. 151.
5 *The Soul of a People*, chapter 14.
6 Rōshi Jiyu Kennett, *Zen is Eternal Life*, pp. 299–300.
7 J. R. Hinnells (ed.), *A Handbook of Living Religions*, p. 379.
8 *Ibid.* p. 385.
9 *Ibid.* p. 315.

BIBLIOGRAPHY

BOOKS OF GENERAL USE

See Abbreviations under *Dial.*, *Medit.*, *Script.*, *Sources*, *Texts*, *Trad.*; all of these are anthologies of translations of Buddhist texts.

Bechert, H., and Gombrich, R. (eds.), *The World of Buddhism: Buddhist Monks and Nuns in Society and Culture*, London and New York, Thames and Hudson, 1984.

Conze, E. *Buddhist Thought in India*, London, Allen & Unwin, 1962; Ann Arbor, Mich., University of Michigan Press, 1967.

A Short History of Buddhism, London, Allen & Unwin, 1980.

Dumoulin, H. (ed.), *Buddhism in the Modern World*, New York, Collier, and London, Collier Macmillan, 1976.

Dutt, N. *Early Monastic Buddhism*, 2nd edn, Calcutta, Firma K. L. Mukhopadhyay, 1971.

Eliade, M. (ed.), *The Encyclopaedia of Religion*, (16 vols.) New York, Macmillan, and London, Collier Macmillan, 1987.

Gombrich, R. *Theravāda Buddhism. A Social History from Ancient Benares to Modern Colombo*, London and New York, Routledge & Kegan Paul, 1988.

Hinnells, J. R. (ed.), *A Handbook of Living Religions*, Harmondsworth, Middlesex, Penguin, 1985. Contains good article on 'Buddhism' by L. S. Cousins. Cf. articles on 'Hinduism', 'Jainism', 'Chinese Religions' and 'Japanese Religions'.

Lamotte, E. *History of Indian Buddhism* (tr. from French (1958) by S. Boin-Webb), Leuven, Belgium, Peters Press, 1988.

Malalasekera, G. P. *et al.* (eds.), *Encyclopaedia of Buddhism*, Colombo, Government of Sri Lanka, 1961 and following.

Morgan, K. W. (ed.), *The Path of the Buddha: Buddhism interpreted by Buddhists*, New York, Ronald Press, 1974; repr. Delhi, MB, 1986.

Nārada Thera, *The Buddha and His Teachings*, Colombo, Vajirarama, 1964; repr. Kandy, BPS, 1986.

Prebish, C. S. (ed.), *Buddhism: A Modern Perspective*, University Park and London, Pennsylvania University Press, 1975.

Robinson, R. H. and Johnson, W. L. *The Buddhist Religion: A Historical Introduction*, 3rd edn. Belmont, Calif., Wadsworth, 1982.

Saddhatissa, H. *The Buddha's Way* [deals with Theravāda teachings and practices], London, Allen & Unwin, 1971, repr. 1985; New York, Brazillier, 1972.

Warder, A. K. *Indian Buddhism*, 2nd edn, Delhi, MB, 1980.

The Wheel: a series of inexpensive booklets, by various authors, produced by the BPS, Kandy, Sri Lanka. These are Theravādin, often of a somewhat modernist type. Some of the better ones are referred to below by the numbers of the booklets, e.g. *Wheel* nos. 308/11 (this refers to one booklet). A catalogue of the booklets, and the booklets themselves, can be obtained from any of the following (as can other BPS publications):

London Buddhist Vihāra, 5 Heathfield Gardens, London, W4 4JU, England.

Vihāra Book Service, 5017 16th. Street NW, Washington DC 20011, USA.

Wat Buddha Dhamma, Ten Mile Hollow, Wiseman's Ferry, NSW 2255, Australia.

Zaehner, R. C. (ed.), *Concise Encyclopaedia of Living Faiths*, 3rd edn, London, Hutchinson, 1977. Contains good articles on the teachings of 'The Theravāda' (by I. B. Horner) and 'The Mahāyāna' (by E. Conze), and on the history of 'Buddhism in China and Japan' (by R. H. Robinson). Cf. articles on 'Hinduism', 'Jainism', 'Confucianism', 'Taoism' and 'Shintō'.

Zürcher, E. *Buddhism, Its Origin and Spread in Words, Maps and Pictures*, Leiden, Netherlands, Brill, 1959; New York, St Martin's Press, 1962.

(In the following lists, reprints are only mentioned when they are by publishers other than the original ones.)

DICTIONARIES, BIBLIOGRAPHIES, AND SURVEYS OF BUDDHIST LITERATURE

Wheel nos. 217/220, 313/315.

Ch'en, K. K. S. *Buddhism in China: A Historical Survey*, Princeton University Press, 1964, pp. 365–78 (on the Chinese Canon).

Conze, E. *Buddhist Scriptures: A Bibliography* (ed. & rev. L. Lancaster), New York, Garland, 1982.

Lancaster, L. 'Buddhist Literature: Its Canons, Scribes and Editors' in W. D.

O'Flaherty (ed.), *The Critical Study of Sacred Texts*, Berkeley, Calif., Berkeley Religious Studies Series, 1979, pp. 215–29.

Ling, T. *Dictionary of Buddhism*, New York, Scribner, 1972; repr. Calcutta, K. P. Bagchi & Co., 1985.

Norman, K. R. *Pāli Literature: Including the Canonical Literature in Prakrit and Sanskrit of all Hīnayāna Schools of Buddhism*, in J. Gonda, *A History of Indian Literature* (vol. VII, fasc. 2), Wiesbaden, Harrassowitz, 1983.

Nakamura, H. *Indian Buddhism, A Survey with Bibliographical Notes*, Buddhist Traditions Series, vol I, Delhi, MB, 1986.

Nyanatiloka, *Buddhist Dictionary: A Manual of Buddhist Terms and Doctrines*, 3rd rev. edn, Colombo, Sri Lanka, Frewin & Co., 1972; Kandy, Sri Lanka, BPS, 1986.

Renou, L. and Filliozat, J. *L'Inde Classique*, vol. II, Paris, Imprimerie Nationale, 1953.

Reynolds, F. *Guide to the Buddhist Religion*, Boston, G. K. Hall, 1981.

Sangharakshita, *The Eternal Legacy: An Introduction to the Canonical Literature of Buddhism*, London, Tharpa, 1985.

Winternitz, M. *A History of Indian Literature*, vol. II, University of Calcutta, 1933.

THE BUDDHA AND HIS INDIAN CONTEXT

Dial. 5–55, 143–220; *Script.* 19–66, 238–42; *Sources* 165–74, 185–97; *Trad.* 31–2, 48–51, 57–72; *Texts* 2, 5, 7–12, 20–2, 77, 101, 105, 113–18, 120; *Wheel* no. 216.

See Abbreviations under *Bvms.*

Basham, A. L. *The Wonder That Was India*, New York, Grove Press, 1959; repr. London, Sidgwick & Jackson, 1985.

Gombrich, R. 'The Significance of Former Buddhas in the Theravāda Tradition' in S. Balasooriya *et al.* (eds), *Buddhist Studies in Honour of Walpola Rahula*, London, Gordon Fraser, 1980, pp. 62–72.

Jayatilleke, K. N. *Early Buddhist Theory of Knowledge* [covers intellectual context of the Buddha's day], London, Allen & Unwin, 1963; repr. Delhi, MB, no date.

Johnston, E. H. *The Buddhacarita or, Acts of the Buddha* [of Aśvaghosa; text and translation], 2nd edn, New Delhi, Oriental Books Reprint Corp., 1972.

Ñāṇamoli, Bhikkhu. *The Life of the Buddha: As it Appears in the Pali Canon*, Kandy, Sri Lanka, BPS, 1972.

Pye, M. *The Buddha*, London, Duckworth, 1979.

Reynolds, F. E. 'The Many Lives of the Buddha: A Study of Sacred

Biography and Theravāda Tradition' in F. E. Reynolds and D. Capps (eds.), *The Biographical Process: Studies in the History and Psychology of Religion*, The Hague, Mouton, 1976, pp. 37–61.

Rhys Davids, T. W. *Buddhist Birth Stories* [trans. of *Nidānakathā*], London, Routledge, 1925; repr. Varanasi, India, Indological Book House, 1973.

EARLY BUDDHIST TEACHINGS: REBIRTH AND KARMA

Dial. 101–13; *Script.* 224–6; *Sources* 29–38; *Texts* 206; *Wheel* nos. 9, 47, 147/149, 221/224, 248/249.

Gombrich, R. '"Merit Transference" in Sinhalese Buddhism', *History of Religions*, 11, 2 (1971), 203–19.

Horner, I. B., and Geham, H. S. *Minor Anthologies*, vol. IV [trans. of *Vimānavatthu* and *Petavatthu*, on heavenly and ghostly rebirths], London, PTS, 1974.

Jayatilleke, K. N. *The Message of the Buddha*, London, Allen & Unwin, and New York, Free Press, 1975, pp. 90–116, 128–95.

La Vallée Poussin, L. de. 'Cosmogony and Cosmology: Buddhist' in J. Hastings (ed.), *Encyclopaedia of Religion and Ethics*, 13 vols., Edinburgh, T. & T. Clark, 1908–26; vol. IV, pp. 129–38.

McDermott, J. P. *Development in the Early Buddhist Concept of Kamma/Karma*, Delhi, MB, 1984.

Marasinghe, M. M. J. *Gods in Early Buddhism*, Vidyalankara, University of Sri Lanka, 1974.

Stevenson, I. *20 Cases Suggestive of Reincarnation*, 2nd edn, Charlottesville, University of Virginia Press, 1974.

Story, F. *Rebirth as Doctrine and Experience* [includes some Ian Stevenson case studies], Kandy, Sri Lanka, BPS, 1975.

EARLY BUDDHIST TEACHINGS: THE FOUR HOLY TRUTHS

Dial. 56–70; *Script.* 146–62, 186–9; *Sources* 199–206, 236–46; *Trad.* 15–25, 30; *Texts* 6, 14–19, 39–69, 80–1, 84–99, 102–3, 107–8, 110, 119; *Wheel* nos. 11, 140, 186/187, 191/193, 202/204, 308/311.

Bodhi, Bhikkhu (tr.), *The Great Discourse on Causation: The Mahā-nidāna Sutta and its Commentary*, Kandy, Sri Lanka, BPS, 1984.

Carter, J. R. *Dhamma: Western Academic and Sinhalese Buddhist Interpretations: A Study of a Religious Concept*, Tokyo, Hokuseido Press, 1978.

Collins, S. *Selfless Persons: Imagery and Thought in Theravāda Buddhism*, Cambridge University Press, 1982.

de Silva, P. *An Introduction to Buddhist Psychology*, London, Macmillan Press, 1979.

Harvey, P. *The Selfless Mind – Personality, Consciousness and Nirvāṇa in Early Buddhism*, London, Curzon Press, 1995.

Johansson, R. E. A. *The Psychology of Nirvana*, London, Allen & Unwin, 1969 and New York, Doubleday, 1970.

Kalupahana, D. J. *Causality: The Central Philosophy of Buddhism*, Honolulu, University Press of Hawaii, 1975.

Katz, N. *Buddhist Images of Human Perfection: The Arahant of the Sutta Piṭaka Compared With the Bodhisattva and the Mahāsiddha*, Delhi, MB, 1982.

La Vallée Poussin, L. de. *The Way to Nirvāṇa: Six Lectures on Ancient Buddhism*, Cambridge University Press, 1917; repr. New York, AMS Press.

Nyanatiloka Mahāthera (tr.), *The Word of the Buddha: An Outline of the Teaching of the Buddha in the Words of the Pali Canon*, 14th edn, Kandy, Sri Lanka, BPS, 1968.

Rahula, W. *What the Buddha Taught*, Bedford, Gordon Fraser, 1959, 2nd edn, 1967; New York, Grove Press, 1962; 2nd edn, New York, 1974.

ASOKA

Trad. 51–4; *Wheel* no. 265.

Basham, A. L. 'Asoka and Buddhism: A Re-examination', *JIABS*, 5, 1 (1982), 131–43.

Nikam, N. A. and McKeon, R. *The Edicts of Aśoka*, University of Chicago Press, 1959.

Przyluski, J. *The Legend of Emperor Aśoka in Indian and Chinese Texts*, Calcutta, Firma K. L. Mukhopadhyay, ,1967.

DEVOTION AND SYMBOLISM IN EARLY BUDDHISM

Harvey, P. 'Symbolism and Venerated Objects in Early Buddhism' in K. Werner (ed.), *Symbolism in Indian Religions*, London, Curzon Press, 1989.

Snellgrove, D. L. (ed.), *The Image of the Buddha*, London, Serindia; Paris, UNESCO, and Tokyo, Kodansha International, 1978.

THE *ABHIDHAMMA*

See Abbreviations under *Dhs.*, *Kvu.*, *Vibh.*, and *Vism.*

Aung, S. Z. (tr. with C. A. F. Rhys Davids), *Compendium of Philosophy* [trans. of Anuruddha's *Abhidhammattha-Saṅgaha*], London, PTS, 1910.

Guenther, H. V. *Philosophy and Psychology in the Abhidharma*, rev. edn, Delhi, MB, 1974; Berkeley, Calif., Shambhala, 1976.

Nyanaponika Thera. *Abhidhamma Studies*, Kandy, Sri Lanka, BPS, 1965.

Stcherbatsky, T. *The Central Conception of Buddhism and the Meaning of the Word 'Dharma'* [based on the *Abhidharmakośa*], London, Royal Asiatic Society, 1923; repr. Calcutta, Susil Gupta, 1956.

EARLY SCHISMS, FRATERNITIES AND SCHOOLS

Script. 192–7. See Abbreviations under *Kvu.* and *Mvs.*

Bareau, A. *Les Sectes Bouddhiques du Petit Véhicule*, Paris, L'École Française d'Extrême-Orient, 1955.

Cousins, L. S. 'The "Five Points" and the Origins of the Buddhist Schools' in T. Skorupski (ed.), *Buddhist Forum* vol. II, London School of Oriental and African Studies, 1990.

Frauwallner, E. *The Earliest Vinaya and the Beginnings of Buddhist Literature*, Rome, Istituto Italiano pe il Medio ed Estremo Oriente, 1956.

R. Gombrich. 'The History of Early Buddhism: Major Advances since 1950' in A. DasGupta (ed.), *Indological Studies and South Asian Bibliography–a Conference*, 1986, Calcutta, National Library, 1988, pp. 12–30.

Nattier, J. J. and Prebish, C. S. 'Mahāsaṅghika Origins', *History of Religions*, 16 (1976–7), 237–72.

MAHĀYĀNA THOUGHT – BOOKS OF GENERAL USE

Conze, E. *Thirty Years of Buddhist Studies* [collected essays], Oxford, Cassirer, 1967; Columbia, SC, University of South Carolina Press, 1968.

XIVth Dalai Lama, *Opening the Eye of New Awareness* (tr. D. S. Lopez and J. Hopkins), London and Boston, Wisdom, 1985.

Dutt, N. *Aspects of Mahāyāna Buddhism and Its Relations to Hīnayāna*, London, Luzac, 1930; rev. edn as *Mahāyāna Buddhism*, Delhi, MB, 1978.

Kiyota, M. (ed.), *Mahāyāna Buddhist Meditation: Theory and Practice*, Honolulu, University Press of Hawaii, 1978.

Snellgrove, D. L. *Indo-Tibetan Buddhism: Indian Buddhists and their Tibetan Successors*, London, Serindia, 1987.

Suzuki, D. T. *Outlines of Mahāyāna Buddhism*, London, Luzac & Co., 1907; repr. New York, Schocken Books, 1963.

Williams, P. *Mahāyāna Buddhism: The Doctrinal Foundations*, London, Routledge & Kegan Paul, 1989.

THE RISE OF THE MAHĀYĀNA

Script. 197–211; *Texts* 121–3; *Trad.* 85–9.

See Abbreviations under Lotus *Sūtra*.

Harrison, P. 'Who Gets to Ride in the Great Vehicle? Self-image and Identity Among the Followers of the Early Mahāyāna', *JIABS* 10, 1 (1987), 67–89.

Kent, S. A. 'A Sectarian Interpretation of the Rise of the Mahāyāna', *Religion*, 12 (1982), 311–32.

McQueen, G. 'Inspired Speech in Mahāyāna Buddhism', *Religion*, 11 (1981), 303–19 and 12 (1982), 49–65.

THE PERFECTION OF WISDOM LITERATURE AND THE MADHYAMAKA SCHOOL

Script. 162–4, 168–71; *Sources* 211–25; *Texts* 141–5, 161–7.

See Abbreviations under *Asta.*, *Mk. Panca.* and *Vc.*

Capra, F. *The Tao of Physics* [for comparisons to modern physics], London, Fontana, 1976.

Conze, E. (tr.), *Selected Sayings from the Perfection of Wisdom*, London, Buddhist Society, 1955; repr. Boulder, Colo., Prajna, 1978.

Huntingdon, C. W., and Wangchen, Geshe N. *The Emptiness of Emptiness* [trans. of Candrakīrti's *Madhyamakāvatāra*, with extensive intro.], Honolulu, University of Hawaii Press, 1988.

Lindtner, Chr. *Nagarjuniana: Studies in the Writings and Philosophy of Nagarjuna*, Buddhist Traditions Series, vol. II, Delhi, MB, 1987.

Robinson, R. H. *Early Mādhyamika in India and China*, Madison, University of Wisconsin Press, 1967; repr. Delhi, MB, 1976.

Ruegg, D. S. *The Literature of the Madhyamaka School of Philosophy in India*, in J. Gonda, *A History of Indian Literature* (vol. VII, fasc. 1), Wiesbaden, Harrassowitz, 1981.

Sprung, M. (ed.), *The Problem of Two Truths in Buddhism and Vedānta*, Dordrecht, Holland, and Boston, Reidel, 1973.

THE YOGĀCĀRA SCHOOL

Texts 156, 178–84.

See Abbreviations under *Lanka.*, *Ms.*, *Mv.*, and *Mvkb.*

Hall, B. C. 'The Meaning of *Vijñapti* in Vasubandhu's Concept of Mind', *JIABS*, 9, 1 (1986), 7–24.

Keenan, J. P. 'Original Purity and the Focus of Early Yogācāra', *JIABS*, 5, 1 (1982), 7–18.

Lamotte, E. (tr.), *Saṃdhinirmocana, l'explication des mystères, texte tibetain edité et traduit*, Louvain, Bureaux du Muséon, 1935.

The Treatise on Action by Vasubandhu (*Karmasiddhi-prakaraṇa*), (tr. L. Pruden), Berkeley, Asian Humanities Press, 1988.

Suzuki, D. T. *Studies in the Lankavatara Sutra*, London, Routledge & Kegan Paul, 1930.

TATHĀGATA-GARBHA THOUGHT

Texts 169, 185.

See Abbreviations under *Lanka.*, *Rv.* and *Srim.*

Brown, B. E. *The Buddha-nature: A Study of the Tathāgatagarbha and Ālayavijñāna*, Buddhist Traditions Series, vol. XI, Delhi, MB, 1991.

Keenan, J. P. See Yogācāra section.

Ruegg, D. S. *La Théorie du Tathāgatagarbha et du Gotra*, Paris, L'École Française D'Extrême-Orient, 1969.

THE *AVATAMSAKA SŪTRA* AND THE HUA-YEN SCHOOL

See Abbreviations under *Essays*, III.

Chang, G. C. C. *The Buddhist Teaching of Totality: The Philosophy of Hwa-yen Buddhism*, University Park, Pennsylvania State University Press, 1971; London, Allen & Unwin, 1972.

Cleary, T. (tr.), *The Flower Ornament Scripture*, vol. III, Berkeley, Calif., Shambhala, 1987.

Cook, F. H. *Hua-yen Buddhism: The Jewel Net of Indra*, University Park, Pennsylvania State University Press, 1977.

THE PATH OF THE *BODHISATTVA*

Script. 164–8, 183–4; *Sources* 38–45, 229–35; *Texts* 124–33; *Tradit.* 83–5, 90–1, 172–8, 271–6.

Cleary, T. (tr.), *The Flower Ornament Scripture*, vol. II (contains the *Daśabhūmika Sūtra*, on the ten stages of the *Bodhisattva*), Berkeley, Calif., Shambhala, 1986.

Dayal, H. *The Bodhisattva Doctrine in Buddhist Sanskrit Literature*, London, Routledge & Kegan Paul, 1932; repr. Delhi, MB, 1970.

Guenther, H. V. (tr.), *The Jewel Ornament of Liberation*, [of sGam-po-pa.], London, Rider, 1959; repr. Berkeley, Calif., Shambhala, 1971.

Kawamura, L. S. (ed.), *The Bodhisattva Doctrine in Buddhism*, Waterloo, Canada, Wilfred Laurier University Press, 1981.

Matics, M. L. (tr.), *Entering the Path of Enlightenment: The Bodhicaryāvatāra of the Buddhist Poet Śāntideva* [from Sanskrit], New York, Macmillan, 1970; London, Allen & Unwin, 1971.

Pye, M. *Skilful Means: A Concept in Mahāyāna Buddhism*, London, Duckworth, 1978.

THE MAHĀYĀNA BUDDHOLOGY AND PANTHEON

Script. 211–14, 232–3; *Texts* 134–9, 157, 159, 168, 207; *Tradit.* 94–5.

See Abbreviations under Lotus *Sūtra* and *Rv.* (vv.205–40).

Birnbaum, R. *The Healing Buddha*, Boulder, Colo., Shambhala, and London, Rider, 1979.

Blofeld, J. *Compassion Yoga: Mystical Cult of Kuan Yin*, London, Unwin, 1977; repr. as *Bodhisattva of Compassion: The Mystical Tradition of Kuan Yin*, Boston, Mass., Shambhala, 1988.

Cowell, E. B. (ed.), *Buddhist Mahāyāna Texts*, Sacred Books of the East, vol. XLIX [contains trans. of three main Pure Land texts focussed on Amitābha], Oxford, Clarendon Press, 1894; repr. New York, Dover, 1969.

Getty, A. *The Gods of Northern Buddhism: Their History and Iconography*, Oxford, Clarendon Press, 1928; 3rd edn, Rutland, Vt, and Tokyo, C. E. Tuttle, 1962; repr., New York, Dover, 1988.

Malalasekera, G. P. *et al.* (eds.), *Encyclopaedia of Buddhism*, Colombo, Government of Sri Lanka: vol. I, fasc. 3 (1964), 363–8 ('Akṣobhya'), 434–63 ('Amita'); vol. II, fasc. 3 (1967), 407–15 ('Avalokiteśvara'); vol. II, fasc. 4 (1968), 661–6 ('Bhaiṣajya-guru').

Schumann, H. W. *Buddhism: An Outline of Its Teachings and Schools*, London, Rider, 1973, pp. 98–117.

Tay, N. 'Kuan-yin: The Cult of Half Asia', *History of Religions*, 16 (1976–7), 147–77.

TANTRIC BUDDHISM

Script. 175–80; *Sources* 258–61; *Texts.* 186–8, 193; *Tradit.* 118–22.

Dasgupta, S. *An Introduction to Tantric Buddhism*, Calcutta University Press, 1958; repr. Berkeley, Calif., Shambhala, 1974.

Snellgrove, D. L. (tr.), *Hevajra Tantra, Part I, Introduction and Translation*, London, Oxford University Press, 1959.

Indo-Tibetan Buddhism: Indian Buddhists and their Tibetan Successors, London, Serindia, 1987.

LATER HISTORY AND SPREAD

Eastern tradition: *Script.* 171–5; *Texts* 208, 211; *Tradit.* 131–8, 158–60, 179–96, 202–7, 211–17, 225–31, 240–51, 329–44, 350–71.

See Abbreviations under *Plat.* (its introduction).

Northern tradition: *Sources* 174–84.

Anesaki, M. *Nichiren, the Buddhist Prophet*, Cambridge, Mass., Harvard University Press, 1916; repr. Gloucester, Peter Smith, 1966.

Batchelor, S. (ed., tr. and intro.), *The Jewel in the Lotus: A Guide to the Buddhist Traditions of Tibet*, London and Boston, Wisdom, 1987.

Bloom, A. *Shinran's Doctrine of Pure Grace*, Tucson, University of Arizona Press, 1965.

Ch'en, K. K. S. *Buddhism in China: A Historical Survey*, Princeton University Press, 1964.

Cleary, T. *Record of Things Heard* [Dōgen], Boulder, Colo., Prajna Press, 1980.

de Bary, W. T. *et al. Sources of Chinese Tradition*, vol. I, New York and London, Columbia University Press, 1960.

Dumoulin, H. *History of Zen Buddhism* (tr. P. Peachey), London, Faber; New York, Pantheon, 1963, McGraw-Hill, 1965; Boston, Beacon Press, 1969; new edn *Zen Buddhism–A History*: *India and China*, New York, Macmillan, and London, Collier Macmillan, 1988.

Foard, J. and Solomon, M. (eds), *The Pure Land Tradition*, Berkeley Buddhist-Studies Series, vol. III, Berkeley, Calif., forthcoming; available from MB.

Geiger, W. (tr.), *The Mahāvaṃsa, or the Great Chronicle of Ceylon*, London, PTS, 1920; repr. with addendum, 1980.

Hazra, K. L. *History of Theravāda Buddhism in South-East Asia, with special reference to India and Ceylon*, New Delhi, Munshiram Manoharlal, 1982.

Joshi, L. *Studies in the Buddhistic Culture of India*, 2nd edn, Delhi, MB, 1977.

Kitagawa, J. M. *Religion in Japanese History*, New York and London, Columbia University Press, 1966.

Ling, T. *The Buddhist Revival in India*, London, Macmillan Press, 1980.

Puri, B. N. *Buddhism in Central Asia*, Delhi, MB, 1987.

Rahula, W. *History of Buddhism in Ceylon: The Anurādhapura Period, 3rd Century B.C. to 10th Century A.D.*, 2nd edn, Colombo, Gunasena, 1966.

Snellgrove, D. and Richardson, H. *A Cultural History of Tibet*, London, Weidenfeld, and New York, Praeger, 1968.

Sunim, M. S. *Thousand Peaks: Korean Zen – Tradition and Teachers*, Berkeley, Calif., Parallax Press, 1987.

Takakusu, J. *The Essentials of Buddhist Philosophy* [on ideas of schools of Eastern Buddhism], Bombay, Asian Publishing House, 1956; 3rd edn, Honolulu, Office Appliance Co., 1956; repr. Westport, Conn., Greenwood, 1976.

Thich Thien-An. *Buddhism and Zen in Vietnam in Relation to the Development of Buddhism in Asia*, Rutland, Vt. and Tokyo, C. E. Tuttle, 1975.

Zürcher, E. *The Buddhist Conquest of China*, 2 vols., Leiden, Brill, 1959.

BUDDHIST PRACTICE: BOOKS OF GENERAL USE

Beyer, S. *The Cult of Tārā: Magic and Ritual in Tibet*, Berkeley, University of California Press, 1973.

Blofeld, J. *The Tantric Mysticism of Tibet: A Practical Guide*, New York, Dutton, 1970; repr. Boston, Mass., Shambhala, 1987.

Beyond the Gods: Buddhist and Taoist Mysticism, London, Allen & Unwin, 1974.

de Silva, L. *Buddhism: Beliefs and Practices in Sri Lanka*, 2nd edn, Colombo, n.p., 1980.

Earhart, H. B. *Religion in the Japanese Experience: Sources and Interpretations*, Encino and Belmont, Calif., Dickenson, 1974.

Ekvall, R. B. *Religious Observances in Tibet: Patterns and Functions*, University of Chicago Press, 1964.

Gombrich, R. *Precept and Practice: Traditional Buddhism in the Rural Highlands of Ceylon*, Oxford, Clarendon Press, 1971.

Kennett, Roshi J. *Selling Water by the River: A Manual of Zen Training*, New York, Random House, 1972; 2nd edn, *Zen is Eternal Life*, Berkeley, Calif., Dharma, 1976.

Ling, T. 'Sinhalese Buddhism in Recent Anthropological Writings: Some Implications', *Religion*, 1, 1 (Spring 1971), 49–59.

Spiro, M. E. *Buddhism and Society: A Great Tradition and its Burmese Vicissitudes*, New York, Harper & Row, 1970; London, Allen & Unwin, 1971.

Suzuki, D. T. *Shin Buddhism*, London, Allen & Unwin, and New York, Harper & Row, 1970.

Manual of Zen Buddhism, 2nd edn, London, Rider, 1974.

Swearer, D. K. *Buddhism and Society in Southeast Asia*, Chambersburg, Pa., Anima Books, 1981.

Tambiah, S. J. *Buddhism and the Spirit Cults in North-east Thailand*, Cambridge University Press, 1970.

Tucci, G. *The Religions of Tibet* (tr. G. Samuel), London, Routledge, and Berkeley, University of California Press, 1980.

van Kooij, K. R. *Religion in Nepal*, Leiden, Brill, 1978.

Welch, H. *The Practice of Chinese Buddhism*, Cambridge, Mass., Harvard University Press, 1967.

BUDDHIST PRACTICE: DEVOTION

Medit. 45–61; *Script.* 182–3; *Sources* 47–64; *Texts* 24–8, 170–7, 214; *Wheel* nos. 206/207, 262, 282/4.

Carter, J. R. (ed.), *The Threefold Refuge in the Theravāda Buddhist Tradition*, Chambersburg, Pa., Anima Books, 1982.

Corless, R. J. 'The Garland of Love: A History of the Religious Hermeneutics of Nembutsu Theory and Practice' in A. K. Narain (ed.), *Studies in Pali and Buddhism*, Delhi, B. R. Publishing Corp., 1979, pp. 53–73.

Gombrich, R. 'Buddhist Festivals' in S. Brown (ed.), *Festivals in World Religions*, London and New York, Longman, 1986, pp. 31–59.

'A New Theravādin Liturgy', *JPTS*, IX (1981), 47–73.

Robinson, R. H. *Chinese Buddhist Verse*, London, John Murray, 1955.

Wells, K. E. *Thai Buddhism, Its Rites and Activities*, Bangkok, Christian Bookstore, 1960; 3rd edn, Bangkok, Suriyabun Publishers, 1975.

See also Birnbaum, Blofeld, Cowell and Tay under 'The Mahāyāna Buddology and pantheon'.

BUDDHIST PRACTICE: ETHICS

Dial. 89–100, 114–39; *Script.* 24–30, 70–3, 83–93, 185–6; *Sources* 10–29, 130–4; *Texts* 2, 73 104; *Tradit.* 36–9, 39–44, 91–2; *Wheel* nos. 41, 104, 175/176, 280, 282/284, 346/348.

See Abbreviations under *Dhp.*, *Jat.* and *Khp.A.* (pp. 23–37).

Aitken, R. *The Mind of Clover: Essays in Zen Buddhist Ethics*, Berkeley, Calif., North Point Press, 1984.

Aronson, H. B. *Love and Sympathy in Theravāda Buddhism*, Delhi, MB, 1980.

Cousins, L. S. 'Ethical Standards in World Religions: Buddhism', *Expository Times*, 86 (1974), 100–5.

Hall, F. *The Soul of a People* [observations on Burmese life], London, Macmillan, 1902.

Horner, I. B. *Women Under Primitive Buddhism*, London, Routledge & Kegan Paul, 1930; repr. Delhi, MB, 1975.

King, W. *In the Hope of Nibbana: An Essay on Theravada Buddhist Ethics* [based on texts and observations in Burma], LaSalle, Ill., Open Court, 1964.

Lamotte, E. 'Religious Suicide in Early Buddhism', *Buddhist Studies Review*, 4, 2 (1987), 105–18.

McFarlaine, S. 'Buddhism' in E. Laszlo and J. Y. Yoo (eds), *World Encyclopaedia of Peace*, vol. 1, Oxford, Pergamon Press, 1986, pp. 97–103.

Miller, B. D. 'Views of Women's Roles in Buddhist Tibet' in A. K. Narain (ed.), *Studies in the History of Buddhism*, Delhi, B.R. Publishing Corp., 1980, pp. 155–66. This also contains an article by D. Paul, 'Portraits of the Feminine: Buddhist and Confucian Historical Perspectives', pp. 209–21.

Misra, G. S. P. *Development of Buddhist Ethics*, New Delhi, Munshiram Manoharlal, 1984.

Nagarjuna and Gyatso, Tenzin. *The Buddhism of Tibet and the Precious Garland*, London, Allen & Unwin, 1983.

Paul, D. *Women in Buddhism* [in Mahāyāna texts], Berkeley, Calif., Asian Humanities Press, 1980.

Ruegg, D. S. 'Ahiṃsā and Vegetarianism in the History of Buddhism' in S. Balasooriya *et al.* (eds), *Buddhist Studies in Honour of Walpola Rahula*, London, Gordon Fraser, 1980, pp. 234–41.

Saddhatissa, W. *Buddhist Ethics: Essence of Buddhism*, London, Allen & Unwin, 1970; New York, Brazillier, 1971; repr. London and Boston, Wisdom, 1987.

Stott, D. *A Circle of Protection for the Unborn*, Bristol, Ganesha Press, 1985.

Thich Nhat Hanh. *Vietnam – Lotus in a Sea of Fire*, London, SCM Press, and New York, Hill & Wang, 1967.

BUDDHIST PRACTICE: THE *SANGHA*

Script. 73–82, 93–6; *Sources* 67–73, 74–9; *Texts* 1, 3, 71, 210; *Tradit.* 33–6. See Abbreviations under *Essays*, 1, 314–62 and *Vin.*

Bechert, H. 'Theravāda Buddhist Sangha', *Journal of Asian Studies*, 29 (1970), 761–78.

Bloss, L. W. 'The Female Renunciants of Sri Lanka', *JIABS*, 10, 1 (1987), 7–32.

Bunnag, J. *Buddhist Monk, Buddhist Layman: A Study of Urban Monastic Organization in Central Thailand*, Cambridge University Press, 1973.

Carrithers, M. B. *The Forest Monks of Sri Lanka: An Anthropological and Historical Study*, Delhi, Oxford University Press (India), 1983.

Ch'en, K. K. S. 'The Role of Buddhist Monasteries in T'ang Society', *History of Religions*, 15, 3 (1976), 209–31.

de Groot, J. J. M. *Le Code du Mahāyāna en Chine: son influence sur la vie monacle et sur la monde laïque* [trans. of *Brahmajāla Sūtra*], Amsterdam, J. Müller, 1893; repr. New York, Garland, 1980.

Dutt, S. *Buddhist Monks and Monasteries of India*, London, Allen & Unwin, 1962.

Khantipalo, Bhikkhu. *Banner of the Arahants: Buddhist Monks and Nuns from the Buddha's Time till Now* [in ancient and Southern Buddhism], Kandy, Sri Lanka, BPS, 1979.

Prebish, C. S. *Buddhist Monastic Discipline: The Sanskrit Prātimokṣa Sūtras* [of the Mahāsāṃghikas and Mūlasarvāstivādins], University Park and London, Pennsylvania State University Press, 1975.

Satō, G. *Unsui: A Diary of Zen Monastic Life* (ed. B. L. Smith), Honolulu, University Press of Hawaii, 1973.

Suzuki, D. T. *The Training of a Zen Buddhist Monk*, New York, University Books, 1965.

Uchino, K. 'The Status Elevation Process of Sōtō Sect Nuns in Modern Japan' in D. L. Eck and D. Jain (eds), *Speaking of Faith: Cross-cultural Perspectives on Women, Religion and Social Change*, London, The Women's Press, 1986, pp. 149–63.

BUDDHIST PRACTICE: MEDITATION AND THE DEVELOPMENT OF WISDOM

Meditation in Southern Buddhism

Dial. 71–85; *Medit.*; *Script.* 103–33, 184–6; *Sources* 71–85; *Texts* 23–4, 29–35; *Wheel* no. 189/190.

See Abbreviations under *Vism.*

Cousins, L. S. 'Buddhist Jhāna', *Religion*, 3 (1973), 115–31.

Gunaratana, H. *The Path of Serenity and Insight: An Explanation of the Buddhist Jhānas*, Delhi, MB, 1985.

King, W. *Theravāda Meditation: The Buddhist Transformation of Yoga*, University Park, Pennsylvania State University Press, 1980.

Kornfield, L. *Living Buddhist Masters*, Santa Cruz, Calif., Unity Press, 1977; repr. Boulder, Colo., Shambhala, 1983.

Nyanaponika Thera. *The Heart of Buddhist Meditation: A Handbook of Mental Training Based on the Buddha's Way of Mindfulness*, Rider, 1962; New York, Samuel Weisner, 1971.

Swearer, D. K. (ed.), *Secrets of the Lotus* [on Insight and Zen meditation], New York, Macmillan, London, Collier-Macmillan, 1971.

Vajirañāña Mahāthera, P. *Buddhist Meditation in Theory and Practice: A General Exposition According to the Pāli Canon of the Theravāda School*, 2nd edn, Kuala Lumpur, Malaysia, Buddhist Missionary Society, 1975. Available from MB and from Wisdom Publications.

Meditation in Northern Buddhism

Medit. 133–9; *Script.* 227–32, *Sources* 99–115, 124–30, 140–61; Texts 189–92, 194.

Blofeld, J. *Mantras: Sacred Words of Power*, London, Unwin, 1978.

Chang, G. C. C. (tr.), *Teachings of Tibetan Yoga*, Secaucus, NJ, The Citadel Press, 1974; repr. as *Six Yogas of Naropa and Teachings of Mahamudra*, Ithica, NY, Snow Lion, 1977.

Fremantle, F. and Trungpa, C. *The Tibetan Book of the Dead: The Great Liberation Through Hearing in the Bardo*, Boulder, Colo., Shambhala, 1978.

Hopkins, J. *The Tantric Distinction: An Introduction to Tibetan Buddhism*, London and Boston, Wisdom, 1984.

Lessing, F. D. and Wayman, A. *An Introduction to the Buddhist Tantric Systems*, The Hague, Mouton, 1968; repr. Delhi, MB, 1978.

Norbu, N. *The Crystal and the Way of Light: Sutra, Tantra and Dzogchen* (ed. J. Shane), London, Routledge & Kegan Paul, 1986.

Tucci, G., *The Theory and Practice of the Mandala*, London, Rider, 1961; 2nd edn 1969.

Wayman, A. (tr.), *Calming the Mind and Discerning the Real*, New York, Columbia University Press, 1978.

Meditation in Eastern Buddhism

Script. 134–44; *Sources* 116–24, 161–4, 246–58, 261–9; *Trad.* 160–2, 199–201, 217–25, 231–40, 371–3, 376–93.

See Abbreviations under *Plat.* and *Essays*, I and II.

Chang, G. C. C. *The Practice of Zen*, New York, Harper & Row, 1959; London, Rider, 1960.

Chappell, D. W., and Ichishima, M. (tr.), *T'ien-t'ai Buddhism: An Outline of the Fourfold Teachings* [of Chegwan], Honolulu, University of Hawaii Press, 1984.

Gregory, P. (ed.), *Traditions of Meditation in Chinese Buddhism*, Kuroda Institute, Studies in East Asian Buddhism 4, Honolulu, University of Hawaii Press, 1986.

Hakeda, Y. S. (tr.), *The Awakening of Faith in the Mahāyāna*, New York and London, Columbia University Press, 1967.

Kiyota, M. *Shingon Buddhism: Theory and Practice*, Los Angeles and Tokyo, Buddhist Books International, 1978.

Ryukoku University Translation Centre, *The Sutra of Contemplation of the Buddha of Immeasurable Life*, Kyoto, Ryukoku University Translation Centre, 1984.

Sekida, K. *Zen Training: Methods and Philosophy*, New York and Tokyo, Weatherhill, 1975.

Suzuki, D. T. *An Introduction to Zen Buddhism*, London, Rider, 1949, 3rd edn 1983; New York, Philosophical Library, 1949, Grove Press 1964; prev. publ. Kyoto, Eastern Buddhist Society, 1934.

Suzuki, D. T. *Zen and Japanese Culture*, New York, Pantheon, 1959.

Suzuki, S. *Zen Mind, Beginner's Mind* [Sōtō teachings], New York, Walker/Weatherhill, 1972.

Swearer, D. K. (ed), *Secrets of the Lotus* [on Insight and Zen meditation], New York, Macmillan, and London, Collier-Macmillan, 1971.

THE MODERN HISTORY OF BUDDHISM IN ASIA

Bechert, H. 'The Buddhayāna of Indonesia: A Syncretistic Form of Theravāda', *JPTS*, 9 (1981), 10–21.

Buddhadāsa. *Towards the Truth* (ed. D. K. Swearer), Philadelphia, Pa., Westminster, 1971.

Chan, Wing-tsit. *Religious Trends in Modern China*, New York and London, Columbia University Press, 1953; repr. London, Octogon, 1970.

Gombrich, R. 'From Monastery to Meditation Centre: Lay Meditation in Modern Sri Lanka' in P. Denwood and A. Piatigorsky (eds), *Buddhist Studies, Ancient and Modern*, London, Curzon Press and Totowa, NJ, Barnes & Noble, 1983, pp. 20–34.

Ling, T. *Buddhist Revival in India*, London, Macmillan Press, 1980.

The Buddha, Marx and God: Some Aspects of Religion in the Modern World, New York, St Martin's Press, 1966.

Lopez, D. S. Jr, and Stearns, C. 'A Report on Religious Activity in Central Tibet', *JIABS*, 9, 2 (1986), 101–8.

Macy, J. *Dharma and Development: Religion as Resource in the Sarvodaya Self-help Movement*, West Hartford, Conn., Kumarian, 1983.

Malalagoda, K. *Buddhism in Sinhalese Society, 1750–1900: A Study of Religious Revival and Change*, Berkeley, Calif., University of California Press, 1976.

Murata, K. *Japan's New Buddhism: An Objective Account of Soka Gakkai*, New York and Tokyo, Walker/Weatherhill, 1969.

Niwano, N. *Buddhism for Today: A Modern Interpretation of 'The Threefold Lotus Sutra'*, Tokyo, Kosei, 1980.

Smith, B. L. *Contributions to Asian Studies Vol. 4: Tradition and Change in Theravāda Buddhism*, Leiden, Brill, 1973.

Sponberg, A. 'Report on Buddhism in the People's Republic of China', *JIABS*, 5, 1 (1982), 109–17.

Suksamran, S. *Political Buddhism in Southeast Asia: The Role of the Sangha in the Modernization of Thailand*, London, Hurst, 1977.

Swearer, D. K. *Buddhism in Transition* (on South-east Asia), Philadelphia, Westminster, 1970.

Welch, H. *The Buddhist Revival in China*, Cambridge, Mass., Harvard University Press, 1968.

Buddhism Under Mao, Cambridge, Mass., Harvard University Press, 1972.

BUDDHISM BEYOND ASIA

Wheel nos. 144/146, 159/161.

Almond, P. C. *The British Discovery of Buddhism*, Cambridge University Press, 1988.

Arnold, E. *The Light of Asia: Or the Great Renunciation, Being the Life and Teaching of Gautama*, London, Routledge & Kegan Paul, 1879 (repr. 1978).

The Buddhist Society. *The Buddhist Directory*, 5th edn, London, The Buddhist Society, 1991.

Campbell, B. F. *Ancient Wisdom Revived, a History of the Theosophical Movement*, Berkeley, University of California Press, 1980.

de Jong, J. W. *A Brief History of Buddhist Studies in Europe and America*, Varanasi, India, Bharat Bharati, 1976; 2nd rev. edn, Delhi, Sri Satguru, 1986.

Humphreys, C. *Sixty Years of Buddhism in England (1907–1967)*, London, The Buddhist Society, 1968.

Hung Ju, Bhikshu, and Hung Yo, Bhikshu. *Three Steps, One Bow*, San Francisco, Ten Thousand Buddha Press, the Buddhist Text Translation Society, 1977.

Jackson, C. T. *The Oriental Religions and American Thought – Nineteenth-Century Explorations*, Westport, Conn. and London, Greenwood Press, 1981.

Kashima, T. *Buddhism in America – the Social Organization of an Ethnic Religious Institution*, Westport, Conn., and London, Greenwood Press, 1977.

Katz, N. *Buddhist and Western Psychology*, Boulder, Colo., Prajna, 1983.

The Middle Way: Journal of the Buddhist Society, quarterly from the Buddhist Society, 58 Eccleston Square, London, SW1V 1PH, England. £8.50 per annum (in UK) [good news section for UK].

Oliver, I. P. *Buddhism in Britain*, London, Rider, 1979. For a review showing its shortcomings, see *Buddhist Quarterly*, 12 (1980), 99–102.

O'Neil, K. *The American Buddhist Directory*, New York, Crises Research, 1985.

Peiris, W. *The Western Contribution to Buddhism*, Delhi, MB, 1973.

Prebish, C. S. *American Buddhism*, Belmont, Calif., Wadsworth, 1979.

Schumann, H. W. 'Buddhism and Buddhist Studies in Germany', serialized in *The Mahā Bodhi* (journal of the Mahā Bodhi Society) in 1971.

Subhuti, Dharmachari. *Buddhism for Today: A Portait of a New Buddhist Movement*, Salisbury, Wiltshire, Element Books (with the FWBO), 1983.

Trungpa, C. *Cutting Through Spiritual Materialism*, Berkeley, Calif., Shambhala, 1973.

Welbon, G. R. *The Buddhist Nirvāṇa and its Western Interpreters*, University of Chicago Press, 1968.

Wisdom Publications. *The International Buddhist Directory*, London and Boston, Wisdom, 1984. For a comprehensive mail order book catalogue on Buddhism, write to Wisdom Publics., 402 Hoe Street, London E17 9AA, United Kingdom; also 361 Newbury Street, Boston MA 02115, USA and P.O. Box 1326, Chatswood, NSW 2067, Australia.

World Fellowship of Buddhists Review. Quarterly from World Fellowship of Buddhists, 33 Sukhumvit Road, Bangkok, 10110, Thailand. $8 per annum [good international news section].

INDEX OF CONCEPTS

Primary entries are shown in bold type

Abhidhamma (Skt *Abhidharma*), 3, **83–4**, 86, 87, 88; canonical, 322, 323–4; in China, 148; later Pali works of, 142; Madhyamaka view of, 96–7; momentariness in, 84, 105, 107; Sarvāstivādin, 85, 97; study of in West, 301, 314; two levels of truth in, 83, 98–9; Vibhajjavāda/Theravādin, 83–4, 143; Mahāyāna version of, 104, 106

abortion, 202–3, 338

access concentration, 247, **249**, 250, 251, 253, 257; and Zen meditation, 271, 274

action, right, 68, 69, 70, 206, 207

Ādi (Primordial) Buddha, 127, 261, 297

ahiṃsā (*see* non-violence)

ālaya-vijñāna (storehouse consciousness), **107–9**, 333; and Ch'an school, 156; 'ālaya which is beyond', 108, (as basis of all) 117; and *Dharma*-body, 127; and *Nirvāṇa*, 112; as the *Tathāgata-garbha*, 117; worlds depend on, 118

alms, 11, 149, 229–30, 198; -bowl, 220; -round, 229, 238, 317

anatta (Skt *anātman*; *see* not-self)

animal(s); *Bodhisatta* as an, 15; and karma, 41; killing of, 10, 76, 201, 202, 203, 204, 205; rebirth as, 33, 71, (in Theosophy) 303; responding to kindness, 25, 211; treatment of, 201, 205, 211

'annihilationism', 14, 58

Arahat's (Skt *Arhat*'s), 24, **64–5**, 330; and cessation of cognition and feeling, 252; compared to the Buddha, 29; and compassion, 65, 93; as '*Dhamma*-become', 28; female, 216, 222; fetters destroyed by, 72; and 'I am' delusion, 65, 72, 93; can be gods, 72; and other Holy persons, 35, 71; images of, 170; laypeople as, 218; Mahāyāna on, 91, 92, 93, 124, 127, 131; and *Nibbāna*, 61; power of, 182; regression of, 88; relics of, 27, 78; and sixth stage *Bodhisattva*, 123; as 'true Brahmins', 2; Zen liking for, 166

Arahatness, 64, 72

Arahatship, 27, 71, 222, 232, 257, 276

Arhat's (*see Arahat*'s)

art, 161, 240; Mahāyāna, 189; Zen, 167, 277–9
asceticism; in Buddhism, 191, 203, 220, 229, 235; unacceptable when harsh, 19, 23; non-Buddhist, 10, 11, 13
astrology, 172, 243; and karma, 41
ātman (Skt, Pali *atta*; *see* self)
attachment; with hatred and delusion, 61, 64 69; to morality, 71, 154, 186; and *Nibbāna*, 61, 64; and views on self, 52, 54; to worlds, 72
auspicious actions, 42–4, 198

'becoming' an object or holy being, 189, 267, 277
beings; all have Buddhaness, 104, 122; all been good to one in past, 38; all been one's mothers, 245; all have the *Tathāgata-garbha*, 122; as conventional entities, 51–2; as empty *dharmas*, 121; holy beings of the Mahāyāna, 121–38; kinds of, **33–6**; 'sameness' of, 121
bhavaṅga consciousness, 84, 106
bhikkhu's (Skt *bhikṣu's*; *see* monks)
bhikkhunī's (Skt *bhikṣuṇī's*; *see under* nuns)
bLama's (pron. *Lama's*), **134**, **218**, 241, 260, 296; bowing to, 173; female, 215; as a refuge, 179; as *sprul-skus*, 238; visualization of, 268; Western, 319
blessings, 181, 241
bodhi (*see* enlightenment)
bodhi-citta (thought of enlightenment), 91, 117, 122, 127, 246
Bodhi-tree(s), 21; at Anurādhapura, 141, 191; at Bodh-Gayā, 21, 22, 68; and devotion, **77–8**, 79, 171, 173, 191, 193; and power-for-good, 180, 190; symbolism of, 79, 155, 172
Bodhisatta (*see also Bodhisattva*'s), 15, 28, 35, 323; Ambedkar as a, 299; Dharmapāla as a, 291; king as a, 142
Bodhisattva's (*see also Bodhisatta*; *Bodhisattva*-path; Great Beings), 323, 330; advanced, 113; as heavenly saviour beings, 124; Holy *Bodhisattvas*, 122–3, 126, 128, 178, 258; and killing, 202; king as an incarnation of, 144; lay *Bodhisattvas*, 93, 285; their 'merit', 126; motivation of, 246; precepts of, 228; relation to other beings, 122; as self-sacrificing heroes, 94; can stay within *saṃsāra*, 103–4; their task, 104; their vows, **122**, 126, 127, 129, 178, (taking of them) 210, 221; as wiser than *Arhats*, 91
Bodhisattva-path, 118, **121–4**, 125, 333–4; acceleration on, 134, 212, 258; as central to the Mahāyāna, 89, 91, 93; and Communism, 281; as hugely long, 122, 134; in *Mahāvastu*, 89; and the perfections, 96, 122–4, 286; in Theravāda tradition, 93
Bodhisattva-yāna, 92, 93
body; body, speech and mind in religious practice, 258, 266; meditation on parts of, 247; mindfulness of, 254; *Nibbāna*/*Nirvāṇa* as within, 59, 138; touching *Nibbāna* with, 252; in Tantric meditation, 138, 267;

world as within, 59; in Zen meditation, 270, 271
bowing, 149, 154, **172–3**, 197, 258
Brahmajāla code, 228, 230
Brahman, 10, 99; in Theosophy, 303
Brahmins, 10, 73, 141; and Asoka, 76; in the Buddha's time, 9, 11, 15, 16, 24, 29, 36
breath, meditation on, **248–9**, 254, 270, 277
'brightly shining mind', **56**, 197; in Mahāyāna, 113, 114–15, 117, 129, 197; and meditation, 251; in Theravāda, 84
Buddha, meaning and application of term, 1
Buddha, the (*see also* Gotama Buddha in Index of proper names); as an *Arahat*, 29, 177; authority of, 30; as a compassionate protector, 181; cosmic importance of, 16; devotion to, 2, 170–82, 190–5; as 'Lord' or 'Blessed One', 23, 177; nature and style of his teaching, 25, 29, 29–31; and politics (*see also Cakkavatti*), 16, 75; as a 'refuge', 172, **177**, **178**; sensitivity of, 27; as a spiritual physician, 47; spiritual power of, 67, 77, 78, 79, 181; spiritual sovereignty of, 16, 78; symbolic representations of, 79–80; as teacher of gods, 22, 37
Buddhas, 1; earthly, 125, 126; cannot be female, 216; five Vajrayāna Buddhas, 135; heavenly, 123, 125, 126, 128, **129–30**, 178; 'Laughing Buddhas', 131; the nature and role of (Theravāda) **28–9**, (and *Dhamma*) 28, 71, 177, (in *Mahāvastu*) 89, (in Mahāyāna) 28, **125–8**, 178, 334; as omniscient, 127; of past and future (*see also Bodhisattvas*; and Maitreya and Metteyya in Index of proper names), 1, 15, 94, 323, 324, (devotion to) 78, 171, 177 (in the Mahāyāna) 125, 190; perfect Buddhas, 1, 15; power of, 182; as rare, 1; solitary Buddhas, 92, 93
Buddha-force, 180
Buddha-images (*see* images of holy beings)
Buddha Jayanti, 294, 296
Buddha Lands (*see also* Pure Lands), 126–7
Buddha-nature (*see also Tathāgata-garbha*), **114**, 333; and Ch'an school, 154, 155, 156, 157; and compassion, 186, 306; and *Dharma*-body, 259; and equality, 149; and ethics, 196; and human potential, **197**; and *Mahāmudra* meditation, 268; in *Mahā-parinirvāṇa Sūtra*, 323; and Nichiren school, 167; and Pure Land schools, 157, 164, 259; and the Sōka-gakkai, 285; and Son school, 160; and *Tathāgata-garbha*, 114; and T'ien-t'ai school, 151; and Zen meditation, 271, 273, 276, 277; and Zen school, 165, 166, 178, 196
Buddha-potential, 114
Buddha-recollection, 152–3, 179
Buddha-recitation hall, 239
Buddha-vehicle, 93
Buddhahood (*see also* enlightenment), 22; as attained in

Akaniṣṭha heaven (in Mahāyāna), 124; as Mahāyāna goal, 38, 92; and *Nibbāna*, 22, 29; and *Nirvāṇa*, 93, 104; and Zen, 271, 276
Buddhaness, 127; and *dharma*-ness, 127; as within all beings, 104, 122
Buddhism, 1; beyond Asia, **300–21**, 342–3; early developments in, **73–94**, 330–1; later history and spread of, **139–69**, 335–6; in modern Asia, **280–99**, 326, 341–2; Southern, Eastern and Northern Buddhism defined, 4; Western influence on, 290
'Buddhist Hybrid Sanskrit', 4, 90
Buddhists, populations of, 5, 8
Buddhology of the Mahāyāna, **125–8**, 334

Cakkavatti ('Wheel-turning') emperor, 16, 27, 75, 81, 119
cakra's (psychic centres), 267
Calm (*Samatha*) meditation, **246–53**, 257–8, 339, 340; in Britain, 313–14; and Insight meditation, 251, 253–4, 255, 256; and *Mahāmudra* meditation, 268–9; and *Nibbāna*, 63, 254; and Pure Land meditation, 258; and Tantric visualization, 266; and Zen meditation, 270, 271, 273
Calm, vehicle of (*see Samatha-yāna*)
cankers, four, 57, 61, 118
Canons of scripture, 3, **323–4**; Chinese, 4, 158, 159, **234**, **323–4**; non-Theravādin early ones, 3; Pali, 3, 32, 141, **322–3**, (access to) 290, 301, (printed versions of) 233, 294, 301, (on stone slabs) 293; Sanskrit, 3, 300; Tibetan, 4, 146, 282, **324**
caste and class, 10, 11, 24, 140, 204; and Ambedkar Buddhism, 298, 299; Buddhist antipathy to, 25, 297, 306; monks and, 145, 219, 228; in Nepal, 219; in Sri Lanka, 227–8, 291
cave temples, 172, 302
celibacy (*see also* chastity), 10, 146, 149, **225**; abandoning of, 145, 164, 219; among laity, 293
cessation; of cognition and feeling, 27, 251, 252, 253; of *dukkha*, 47, 55, 60, 68
chanting, **175–6**, 210, 238, 241, 242; and meditation, 232, 247; in Nichiren school, 190, 285–6; of the precepts, 176, 199; protective, 180–2; of Pure Land *Sūtras*, 187
chaplains, prison and army, 291, 305, 312
chastity (*see also* celibacy), 208
Chinese Buddhism, **148–58**; in South-east Asia, 294, 296–7; in the West, 304–5, 308, 309, 310, 320
Chinese Canon (*see* Canons of scripture)
circumambulation, **78**, 167, 173, 186, 193
citta ('mind/heart/thought'; (*see also bhavaṅga* consciousness; 'brightly shining mind'), **50**; in *Abhidhamma*, **84**; cultivation of, 68; as empirical self, **52**; mindfulness of, 255; as a momentary 'mind-set', 52, 107; in Yogācāra thought, 107–9, 111
cognition (*saññā*), 49, 50, 56, 257

commentaries, 141, 142, 323, 324
commitment: fear of, 21, 249; levels of, 196
compassion, 38, 69, 94, 207, 209, **210–11**; and the *Arahat*, 65, 93; and Avalokiteśvara, 131, 182, 186; and the *Bodhisattva*, 121, 123, 131; and the Buddha, 22, 181; and the Buddha-nature, 186, 306; and *dukkha*, 197; for evil doers, 197; great, 245–6; and Great Brahmā, 37; as an 'immeasurable', 29, **209**, 245; and *Mahāmudrā* meditation, 269; and monasteries, 211; as part of right directed thought, 69; and Pure Land practice, 187; and Sōka-gakkai practice, 286
conceit of 'I am', 54, 65, 72, 164
concentration (*samādhi*), 65, 68, 70, 246–7, 253; and mindfulness, 247, 253; momentary, 253–4; one-pointed, 246, 251, 266, 274, 277; in Zen, 271
conception, 58, 60, 202; Gotama's, 16
conceptual proliferation, 99, 103; *Nibbāna* as without, 62
Conditioned Arising (*paṭicca-samuppāda*), **54–60**, 63, 329, 330; in *Abhidhamma*, 83; and emptiness, 97–8, 99; insight into, 71, 123, 256; in Mādhyamika thought, 97–8, 99, 100; as a Middle Way, 69
conditioned phenomena (*saṅkhāra*'s); going beyond, 253; 'three marks' of, 52
conscience, 200–1, 212
consciousness, (discriminative), **49–50**, 54, 55, **57–8**, 106; and *Nibbāna*, 63, 64, 67, 330; in Yogācāra thought, 107–9
constructing activities (*saṅkhāra*'s), 49, 55, 57, 63
construction of the unreal, 111, 117
constructions, mental, 105, 108, 110–11, 117
constructs of language, 99, 103
continuity of character/personality, 52, 107
contraception, 202
conventional truth, 98–9, 100, 123, 128
cosmology, 32–7, 329; of Mahāyāna (*see also* Pure Lands), 90
councils, 3; first, 73; second, 74; 'third', 87; 'fifth', 293; 'sixth', 233, 294
craving, 23, 47, **53**, 55, **59**; cessation of, 61; for *Nibbāna*, 61
cultural adaptation, 149–50, 316

Dalai Lamas (*see also* Index of proper names), **131**, **147**, 191
dāna (*see* giving)
dating; of the Buddha, 9; of scriptures, 3
dead, rites for the, 43, 150, 195, 203, **211–12**, 281
death; caused by birth, 60; a good, 211; the great, 271, 275; *Nibbāna* beyond, 65–8
death penalty, abolition of, 76, 159
Deathless, the, 22, 23, 27, **60**, 62, 103, 255
debate in Tibetan Buddhism, 147, 234
decline of Buddhism, 67, 140–1, 153
defilements; alien, 56, 113, 115; and *Nirvāṇa*, 116; and purity, 113;

and the *Tathāgata-garbha*, 114–16
delusion, 2, 61, 64, 65, 109
Dependent Origination (*see* Conditioned Arising)
deva's (*see* god(s))
development work, 211, 288, 292–3, 294, 341, 342
devotion (*see also* faith, *and under* Amitābha, Avalokiteśvara, Bhaiṣajya-guru, *Bodhi*-tree, Buddha (the), images, Lotus *Sūtra*, and *Stūpa*), **77–82**, **170–95**, 330, 342; in Ch'an, 154, 157; and joy, 48, 55, 173, 189, 247; and meditation, 232, 244, 247, 310, 314; and 'merit', 173; *mudrās* in, 266
dge-bshes (pron. *geshe*; doctor of Buddhology), 234, 238
Dhamma (Skt *Dharma*), **2**, 28, **84**, **177**, 329; and the Buddha, 28; the Buddha's decision to teach it, 22; as Conditioned Arising, 54, 177; experiential understanding of, 23, 70, 177; and the first council, 73; gift of, 198; and God, 289; as an 'island', 26; as like a raft, 31; made available by Gotama, 164; as *Nibbāna*, 28, 54, 68; as from perfect wisdom, 90; power of, 67; as profound and subtle, 22; as a 'refuge', 26, 172, **177**, 178; *Saṅgha* as depending on, 26; 'seeing' it (*see Dhamma*-eye); slander of the, 130; as social justice, 75; timeless truths of, 15
dhamma's (Skt *dharma*'s), **50**, **83–4**, 331; and *Dhamma*, 84; and emptiness, 99; as empty, 97–8, 105, 121, 257; and Insight meditation, 254, 255, 256; Madhyamaka on, 97–8, 99; mindfulness of, 255; as not-self, 52, 97; and 'own-nature', 85, 87, 97; 'sameness' of, 99; Sarvāstivāda on, 85, 86; the unconditioned *dhamma*, 52, 87; Vibhajjavāda/Theravāda on, 87; Yogācāra on, 110–11
Dhamma-become, 28, 71
Dhamma-eye, 23, 28, 68
Dhamma-wheel, 23, 80, 186
dhāraṇī's ('preserving' chants), 135, 182, 257
Dharma (*see Dhamma*),
dharma's (see *dhamma*'s),
Dharma-body (*see also* Three-body doctrine), 86, **126**, **127–8**; as Amida/Amitābha Buddha, 168, 259; as the *Dharma*-refuge, 178; as innately pure, 155; and meditation, 259, 261, 267, 269, 270, 276; as *Nirvāṇa*, 116; and 'Self', 118; symbolized by the *Vajra*, 135; and the *Tathāgata-garbha*, 116, 118; as ultimate reality, 128, 138; as Vairocana Buddha, 161; as Vajrasattva, 135; and Vajrayāna Buddhas, 261; and the Won School, 284
dharma-ness as Buddha-ness, 127
Dharma-realm, 108, 112, 113, 116, **119-20**, 128
dhyāna (*see jhāna*)
directed thought, right, 68, 69, 70, 209
Disciple, vehicle of the (*see also* Śrāvakayāna), 92, 93
discipline (*see also Vinaya*); in Ch'an/Zen, 156, 166, 272–3; moral, 59

discrimination, 108, 110
divine abidings (*see* immeasurables)
dream; *dharmas* as like a, 97; experience as like a, 110; of Gotama's mother, 16; meditation in, 267; and visions, 90, 133
drugs, 207, 289, 303
duality, subject/object, 108, 111; overcoming of, 257, 269, 277
dukkha (suffering, unsatisfactoriness; *see also* suffering; Four Holy Truths), **47–53**, 59; its causes, 53–60; cessation of, 55, 60, 68; and ethics, 196–7; meditation on, 255
Dzokchhen (*see rDzogs-chen*)

early Buddhist teachings, **32–72**, 329–30
early schools of Buddhism, **85–9**, 331
Eastern Buddhism, **4**, **5**, 6–7, 8; alms-round in, 230; and *Bodhisattva* vows, 210, 221; divination slips in, 243; ethics in, 200, 203, 204, 210, 212, 215; festivals in, 194–5, 200, 208; images in, 179; meditation in, 232, 235, 257–60, 270–9, 340–1; monasticism in, 220, 225, 226, 228, 236, 237, 239, 242, (nuns) 222, (study) 232, 234; protective chanting in, 242; *upāsakas* and *upāsikās* in, 208
'easy path,' 153, 163, 164
economic development, 205, 299
education, 181, 280, 284, 291, 299; and monks, 142, 221, 233–4, 242, 291
effort, right, 68, 69–70, 79, 246, 253
Eightfold Path; and the *Bodhisattva*-path, 122; Holy, 23, 27, 47, **68–72**, 122; ordinary, 68, 69, 122; and the Risshō-kōseikai, 286;
elements, four physical, 49, 62, 63, 84; meditation on, 252
emptiness, xvi, 95, **99–100**, **101–2**, 332; Clear Light of, 212; as *Dharma*-body, 127; as *Dharma*-realm, 120; and interpenetration, 119; meditative insight into, 90, 123, 256, 258, 267, 269, 273, 275; *Nibbāna/Nirvāṇa* as, 62, 103, 256; Hua-yen on, 120; and sexual equality, 216; in Tathāgata-garbha thought, 114, 116–17, 118; and the Won school, 284; Yogācāra on, 108, 111; and Zen art, 279
empty; *dharmas* as, 97–8, 105, 121, 257; of self, 50, 97, 255
Enjoyment-body Buddhas, **126–8**, 178
enlightened person; as 'hard-to-fathom', 28, 66; state of beyond death, 65–7
enlightenment (*see also* Buddhahood); of the Buddha, 22, 28, 32; in the Mahāyāna, 112, 116; original, 276; in the Vajrayāna, 135
environment, effect of greed on, 37
eons, 15, 33, 35
equality, 149, 215–16, 298
equanimity, 65, 209, 210, 245; and meditation, 251, 256
'established church', 147, 168
'eternalism', 14, 58
ethics (*see also* moral virtue; precepts; social ethics), 76, 161, **196–216**, 337–8; in Jōdo-shin, 168, 196

evil; 'necessary', 201; the problem of, 37, 115–16; victory over, 19–21, 194
evolution; biological, 300; in Theosophy, 303; of a world-system, 33, 36, 37
evolving consciousness and rebirth, 58
existence and non-existence; beyond, 117; Middle Way between, 69, 97–8
exorcism, 181, 238, 292
experience and knowledge, 14, 30, 70

factors of enlightenment, 65, 255
factors of personality, (*see khandha*'s)
faith (*see also* devotion), 28, 30, **31**, 70, 81, **170**; in one's Buddha-nature, 271; and Conditioned Arising, 55; in Japanese Buddhism, 163; and meditation, 55, 170, 247, 256; in Nichiren school, 167, 190; in Pure Land schools, 152, 163–4, 189, 258; as route to Pure Lands, 127, 130; in Zen, 166, 271
family relationships, ethics of, 76, 213, 214, 215
fatalism, 13; and karma, 40, 41
feeling, 49, 55, 59; cessation of, 27, 251, 252, 253; mindfulness of, 255
female Tantric 'deities' (*see also* Tārā), 134, 137, 216, **262–4**
festivals, 172, **191–5**, 200, 208, 337
fetters, spiritual, 71–2, 196, 257
fighting between Buddhist schools, 146, 168
first sermon of the Buddha, 23, 30, 53, 193
five points of Mahādeva, 74, 88, 331
forest meditation tradition, 232, 235, 238, 293, 338; in the West, 313, 317
form, realm of (pure), 34, 72
formless mystical states, 18, 27, 62, 251, **252**
formless realm, 34–5, 67, 251, 252
Four Holy Truths, 23, 32, 46, **47–72**, 329–30; chant on, 176; and Conditioned Arising, 55; as known simultaneously or not, 87; in the Mahāyāna, 92, 100, 123, 286; mindfulness of, 255; as within the body, 59
fraternities, monastic, **2**, **74**, 85, 88, 90, 331; in Sri Lanka, 142, 227–8, 232; in Thailand, 227, 287
free will, 13, 57
funerals, 212, 241

gestures (*mudrā*'s); of images, 19–20, 183, 266; and devotion, 175; and meditation, 266
ghosts, 33, 181, 195, 209, 239
giving, 76, 123, **198–9**, 207, 209, 210, 292; of one's life, 203; and 'merit', 42–3
God concept; no creator accepted, **36–7**, 300; and *Dhamma*, 289; and karma, 39; and Mahāyāna thought, 125, 127, 297; and *Nibbāna*, 297; and sin, 56
god(s) (*deva*(s)), 4, **34–7**, 329; the *Bodhisatta* may be a, 15; aiding the Buddha, 16, 22; the Buddha as not a, 28; at the Buddha's death, 27; 'Buddhist', 292; attitude of Dharmapāla to, 291;

Holy persons may be, 35, 71, 191; lovingkindness to, 209; named gods (*see also* Hindu gods; Māra), (Brahmā) 11, 22, 29, 35–7, 209, (four great kings) 190, 264–5, (Indra) 35, 119, 135, (Radiant) 36, 37, (Sakka) 35, (Saman) 191, (Tusita) 35; nature gods, 4; protection by, 181, 190; sharing 'merit' with, 43; shrines for, 172; as taught by the Buddha and his disciples, 22, 37, 177; Vedic, 10, 35, 135
grace, 124, 130, 164, 187
gradualism in Ch'an/Zen, 154, 160, 276
grasping, 49, 55, 59; 'groups of grasping', 49–50
Great Beings, 124, 126, 127, 128, **130–3**, 191
Great Man, 81, 126
Greek; art, 81; language, 9; philosophers, 11
guilt, 40, 200, 206
Gurus, 134, 138, 179

Haiku poems, 168, 279
happiness, 196, 250, 251
hatred and ill-will, 61, 64, 69, 209, 248, 249
healing, 26, 130, 181, 189
heaven(s) (*see also* gods; Pure Lands), **34–7**, 38, 76, 214; Akaniṭṭha/Akaniṣṭha, 124, 126; Tāvatiṃsa, 35, 193; Tusita/Tuṣita, 15, 16, 35, 89, 124, 194
hell, **34**, 163, 167; care for beings in, 131, 133, 209
'hereditary temples', 237, 239, 280
hermits, 218, 232, 235
higher knowledges, 251, 252–3
hindrances, five, 21, 57, **249–50**, 251, 255, 257; and spiritual ignorance, 56; and guilt, 200
'Hīnayāna' ('Inferior vehicle'), 92, 94
Hindu gods (*see also* Śiva and Viṣṇu in Index of proper names), 81; and the Mahāyāna, 128, 131, 134
Holy (*see also Saṅgha* (Holy), Four Holy Truths, *and under Bodhisattvas* and Eightfold Path), 23, 29; persons, 71, 178; Tenfold Path, 69, 72
human rebirth, **38–9**, 202, 203, 245
humility, 173, 198, 217
Huns, 139, 150

I; attachment to, 209; feeling of, 51, 52, 53
'I am' attitude/conceit/delusion, **54**, 65, 72, 197, 262; *Arahat's* lack of, 65, 72, 93
iconoclasm, 138, 154
iconography (*see also* images of holy beings); of Amitābha, 188, 189; of Avalokiteśvara, 131, 133, 182–5; of the Buddha, 21, **80–2**; of Great Beings, 131; of Kṣitigarbha, 168; of Maitreya, 130–1; of Mañjuśrī, 132–3
ignorance (*see* spiritual ignorance)
images of holy beings (*see also* iconography), **80–2**, 161, 170, 172, 173, 262–3, 264; attitudes to, 154, 172, 173, **179–80**; of the Buddha, 20, 21, 80–2, 170, 174, 179; gestures of, 20, 21, 82, 266
images, meditative, 110, **249**, 251, 267, 270

immeasurables, the four, 209, 245, 247
immigrant Buddhists, 304–6
impermanence, **50**, 52, 173, 197, 210, 255
incarnation (*see* Transformation-body)
initiation, 219, 260
Innate vehicle (Sahajayāna), 138, 268
'inner' and 'external', fiction of, 109
insight, 46; and the *Arahat*, 65; and cessation, 252; into Conditioned Arising, 69, 123, 256; defilements of, 256; into emptiness, 90, 123, 256, 258, 267, 269, 273, 275; and first sermon, 23; and the higher knowledges, 252; and ignorance, 56; and karma, 39, 42; and mind-to-mind transmission, 154; spontaneous, 257; sudden, 160, 276; and Tantric visualization, 266
Insight (*Vipassanā*) meditation; and Calm meditation, 251, 253–4; in Eastern and Northern Buddhism, 257–8, 340; and Pure Land meditation, 258, 259; and *Mahāmudra* meditation, 268, 269; in Southern Buddhism, **253–7**, 293, 294, 298, 339; in the West, 309, 312, 313, 314, 318, 321; and Zen, 270, 273
Insight, vehicle of (*see Vipassanā-yāna*)
interpenetration, 119, 161
interviews, Ch'an/Zen, 156, 157, 274
intuition, 138, 154, 156, 272, 274

Jātaka stories, xv, 15, 78, 89, 233, 323; and ethics, 198, 203, 206, 211, 241
jewel; -net of Indra, 119; -trees, 119, 129, 259; wish-granting, 133, 136
jewels, the three, 177, 181
jhāna's (Skt *dhyāna*'s; meditative trances), 70, 210, 249, **250–1**, 253, 339; in the life of the Buddha, 19, 21, 27; and Ch'an/Zen, 153, 271, 275; and 'five points of Mahādeva', 88; and heavenly rebirths, 35, 36, 39, 123; in the Mahāyāna, 123, 129, 153, 257, 258, 271, 275; transcendent and ordinary, 254; and the Yogācāra school, 105
joy, 48, 55, 65; and chanting, 176; and defilements of insight, 256; and devotion, 48, 55, 173, 179, 189, 247; and ethics, 196, 199, 211; as a factor of enlightenment, 65; and meditation, 48, 248, 250, 251; and 'merit', 172
joy, sympathetic, 209, 245
Just Sitting, 270–1, 275, 276

kami's, 128, 161, 162, 169, 190
karma, **39–44**, 57, 329; and the *Arahat*, 64; belief/disbelief in, 13–14, **44–6**; in Brahmanism, 11; and children, 213; and Confucianism, 149; and intention/will, 40, 49, 57, 201; in Jainism, 13, 40; as known by meditative experience, 14, 21, 44; and right understanding, 69; and the Sōka-gakkai, 285; and suffering, 44, 53; and Theosophy, 303; in Yogācāra thought, 105, 107–9, 110

kasiṇa-maṇḍala's ('universal circles'), 248, 251, 258, 259, 264
kenshō ('seeing of one's nature'), 275–6
khandha's ('groups', factors of personality), the five, **49–50**, 56, 83; birth and re-arising of, 60; as consciousness and mind-and-body, 58; as empty, **50–3**, 99, 255; and *Nibbāna*, 61; and the 'person', 85; and views, 54, 66
kings; as *Bodhisattas*, 142, 144; and social welfare, 142
Knowledge-body, 127
kōan's, **157**, 160, 166, 168, 270, **273–5**
Kṣatriya's, 10, 15, 24, 141
kung-an (*see kōan*)

Lama (*see bLama*)
language; -constructs, 99, 103; nature of, 98, 108–9; limitations of, 62, 103
latent tendencies, 56, 57
latter-day *Dharma* (Jap. *mappō*), 153, 162, 163, 228
lay; disciples (*see also upāsaka*'s); ordination, 200; patrons, 73; ritual specialists, 182, 241; stewards, 226, 230
lay–monastic relationship, 198, 213, 214, 217, 221, **240–3**, 338
lay people (*see also upāsaka*'s), 93, 208, 213; activism and leadership by, 291, 292, 293, 299, 313, 314; as *Bodhisattvas*, 93, 285; celibacy among, 293; and Ch'an school, 156; Holy persons among, 178, 218; meditation by, 241, 244, 293, 294, 310; and Tantric Buddhism, 134
letting go, 61, 97, 164, 253
liberation of living beings, 192, 195, 211
literacy, 233, 242
livelihood; right, 68, 89, 90, 200, 203–4, 315, 317; wrong, 202, 207
logic, 102, 147, 234
lotus symbolism, 131, 136, 259, 285
lovingkindness, 42, **209–10**, 214, 337; and the *Arahat*, 65; and the *Bodhisattva*, 123; and Brahmā, 29; meditation on, 245, **247–8**; and *parittas*, 181; and past rebirths, 38; power of the Buddha's, 25; and the Sarvodaya Śramadāna movement, 292

magic, 134, 145, 146, 150, 161, 261
Mahāmudrā meditation, 268–9, 272, 340
Mahā-siddha's 134, 138, 145, 330
Mahāyāna ('Great Vehicle'), 2, 32, 81, **89–94**, 331; Buddhahood as goal of, 38, 92; Buddhology of, **125–8**, 334; in Central Asia, 140; pantheon of, **129–38**, 334; and the 'intermediary existence', 60; meditation in, **257–79**, 331, 340; and 'merit' sharing, 44; motivation, 245; philosophy of, **95–120**, 331–3; refuges in, 178–9; in South-east Asia, 143, 144, 159, 289; in Sri Lanka, 142, 143; *Sūtras* of, 4, 90–2, 95, 323–4; women in, 216, 338
manas (*see* mind-organ)
maṇḍala's, 260, 264–5, 267, 340
mantra's 3, 10, 134, **135–6**, 138, 176, 179, 186–7; and meditation, **260–1**, 266, 268
Mantrayāna ('*Mantra*' Vehicle; *see*

also Northern Buddhism Tantric Buddhism), 4, **135–6**, 260, 261; in China (*see* Chen-yen in Index of proper names); in Japan (*see* Shingon); in Korea (*see* Milgyo); refuges in, 179; in South-east Asia, 143, 297; in Sri Lanka, 142, 143

mappō (*see* latter day *Dharma*)

marriage, 193, 206, 207, 213, 214–15, 216

married clergy, 217; in Japan, 164, 170, 228; in Korea, 220, 283, 284; in Nepal, 219; in Tibet, 218

married tantric practitioners, 138

'marvel of the pairs', 26, 194

māyā (magical illusion), 97

meditation, 50, 59, 70–1, **244–79**, 339–41; on Amitābha's Pure Land, 258–60, 340; attitude to in Sri Lanka, 232; on the breath, 248–9, 254, 270, 277; in Ch'an/Zen, 153, 157, 165, 166, 270–9, 340, 341; and chatter, 207; as cultivation/purification of the mind, 56–7, 68, 245; and devotion, 232, 244, 247, 310, 314; in Eastern Buddhism, 148, 257–60, 270–9, 331, 340; on the elements, 248, 252; and faith, 55, 170, 247, 256; on foundations of mindfulness, 254–5, 257, 339; on a *kōan*, 273–5, 340, 341; and the laity, 241, 244, 293, 294, 310; life of, 235; on lovingkindness, 210, 245, 247–8, 339; and 'merit', 198; in Northern Buddhism, 257–8, 260–70, 331, 340; and rebirth, 35, 36; and study, 231–5; in Southern Buddhism, 246–57, 339; and Tantric visualization, 266–7, 340; teachers of, 153, 156, 244, 260, 273, 294, 339; and wisdom, 244, 246, 250, 255, 261; and the Yogācāra path, 112

'meditation camps', 297

'meditation centres', 293, 294, 331, 341; in the West, 314, 315, 309, 318, 321

meditation hall, 171, 235, 239

memories, 105, 107

memory of previous lives, 21, 29, 251

merchants, Buddhist, 24–5, 140, 148

'merit', **42–4**, 57, 172, 198, 199; and alms, 229; and Amitābha, 230; and ascetic monks, 229; and *Bodhisattvas*, 122, 123 124, 126; and the Buddha, 21; and chanting, 173, 181, 199; of copying out *Sūtras*, 91; and criminals, 76; criticism of concern over, 153–4, 289; 'demerit', 201; and devotion, 173; and festivals, 191; field of, 178, 198, 240; and giving one's life, 203; and the Holy *Sangha*, 178; -making ceremonies, 199, 288, 289, 298; and the *Maṇi-mantra*, 186; and meditation, 198; and pilgrimage, 190; and sacralized water, 193; shared act of, 214; store of, 124, 126; and ordinations, 44, 220, 221; transference/sharing of, (in the Mahayāna) 94, 123, 124, 126, 150, 195, 212, 260, (in the Theravāda) **43–4**, 172, 198, 212, 329

Middle Way; in ideas, 58, 69, (in Mahāyāna thought), 96, 98, 106, 111; of practice, 23, 47, 68, 73, 200

mind (*see also citta*; brightly shining mind); of no-mind, 272; original, 273, 275; straightforward, 273
Mind; absolute, 152; Buddha, 273; one, 120, 160; pure, 212, 259, 277; shining, 269; ultimate, 277
mind-and-body, 55, 58; *Nibbāna* as beyond, 62; stopping of, 63, 160
mind-organ (*mano*, Skt *manas*); in early Buddhism, 58–9, 107; in Yogācāra thought, 107, 108, 109, 112, 272–3
mind-reading, 22, 251, 252
mind-to-mind transmission, 154, 155, 160, 166
mindfulness, 68, **70**, **254**, 339; of breathing, 248–9, 268, 271; and conscience, 200; four foundations of (*sati-paṭṭhāna*'s), 254–5, 257, 268, 270; and Insight meditation, 253, 254–5, 256; and intoxication, 207; and *jhāna*, 250; and *Mahāmudra* meditation, 268–9; and Pure Land meditation, 258, 260; spontaneous, 269; as a tool of meditation, 246, 247, 253; transcendence of, 269, 272; of walking, 254; and Zen, 270, 272, 273
missions; Buddhist, 77, 144, 294, 295, 296, 297 (to the West), 305, 307–21; Christian, 159, 168, 280, 290, 298, 301, 302
modernism, Buddhist, 290, 291, 293, 298, 299; in the West, 300, 312, 318
momentariness, 55, 84, 105, 107
monasteries; as 'meditation centres', 293; as temples, 170; and wealth, 157; welfare roles of, 211, 241
monastic; day, 238–9; discipline (*see Vinaya*); fraternities (*see* fraternities); life, 73, 217–18, (economic base of) 229–31, 280, (as unnecessary) 164; names, 220; robes, 220; *Saṅgha*, **217–43**
monastic–lay relationship, 198, 213, 214, 217, 221, **240–3**, 338
monasticism, role of, 217–20
monks (*bhikkhu*'s; *see also* monastic; *Saṅgha*, monastic), **217–43**, 326, 329; as chaplains, 291; and education, 142, 221, 233–4, 242, 291; medical activities of, 211, 242, 288, 289; and money, 74, 208, 226, 230, 291; numbers of, 217, 223, 280, 281, 284; respect for, 173, 218; role of in modern society, 288–9; as soldiers, 168, 202; and politics, 243, 291–2, 294; and welfare/development work, 211, 241, 243, 288, 291, 292, 342; wandering, 140, 241; Western, 291, 308, 309, 311, 312–13, 314–15, 316–17, 318, 320
moral virtue (*see also* ethics, and precepts), 68, 70–1, 123, 196, 200, 210; and faith, 170; and meditation, 246; and stages of purification, 256
mudrā's (*see* gestures)

nature, 37, 203, 277, 288
nature spirits, 172, 336
neither-cognition-nor-non-cognition, sphere of, 18, 67, 211, 252
nembutsu (Ch. *nien-fo*), 130, **152–3**,

187, **189**, 258, 337; in Ch'an liturgy, 157, 273; Japanese attitudes to, 163, 164, 167
New Religions (of Japan), 219, 285–6
Nibbāna (Skt *Nirvāṇa*), 19, 22, 23, 27, **60–8**, 330; beyond death, 65–8; and the body, 138, 252; and consciousness, 63, 64, 67, 97; as the Deathless, 27, **60**, 62, 103, 255; as *Dhamma*, 28, 54, 68; during life, 61–4; as emptiness, 62, 103, 256; and ethics, 196; as 'further shore', 31, 63; as 'God', 297; and Holy *Saṅgha*, 178; as a long-term goal, 38; in Mahāyāna thought, **93**, 96–7, 98, **103–4**, 108, **112–13**, **123**, **124**, 127, 134, 152; and meditation in Southern Buddhism, 251, 252, 253, 254, 255, 256; as not-self, 52; potential for, 56; pseudo-, 256, 275; Stream-enterers' glimpse of, 23, 68; and transcendental action, 39; as the unconditioned, 52, 54, 61, 62, 87, 98, 103; Vibhajjavāda/Theravāda on, 64, 87; Western attempts to understand, 343; 'without standstill', 113, 124
nidāna's (links), the twelve, **54–60**
nien-fo (*see nembutsu*)
nikāya's (*see* fraternities)
Nirvāṇa (*see Nibbāna*)
no-mind, 117, 272
no-thought, 272, 273, 275, 277
non-attachment, 199, 235
Non-returners, 35, **71–2**, 124, 178, 252
non-sensuality, 69, 210, 225
non-violence, 13, 38, 76, **202–5**, 316, 338
Northern Buddhism (*see also* Mantrayāna, Tantric Buddhism; Tibet), **4**, **5**, 6–7, 133; asceticism and 'merit' in, 229; astrology in, 243; and the *Bodhisattva* vows, 210, 221; the *bLama* in, 134, 218; blessings in, 241; ethics in, 204–5, 208, 212, 215; festivals in, 194; history of, 144–7, 158, 334, 335, (modern) 281–2, 295, 296, 297; images in, 179; lay ritual specialists in, 241; *Maṇi-mantra* in, 186; meditation in, 232, 235, 245, 257–8, 260–70, 340; monasticism in, 220, 225, 226, 231–2, 234–8, 242, (nuns), 208; mystery plays in, 241; offerings in, 175; *upāsakas* and *upāsikās* in, 208
not-self (*see also* empty, and self), **50–3**, 54, 55–6, 83–4, 85, 97, 123, 329; and ethics, 197–8; and Insight meditation, 255, 256; and suffering, 50–1, 54, 197–8
nothingness, sphere of, 18, 251, 252
novices, 220, 227
nuns, **221–4**, 217, 229, 326, 339; and Arahantship, 216, 222, 276; *bhikkhunī/bhikṣuṇīs* type, (start of their Order) 24, 221–2, 229, (present lack of in Southern and Northern Buddhism) 142, 208, 222, 223–4, (Western) 224, 308; eight precept type, 222–3; Japanese type, 219, 222, 339 (Western) 315; numbers of, 221, 223, 281, 284; ten precept type,

208, 222–3, 232, 293, 295, 338, (Western) 309, 313, 315, 318

objectless thought, 64, 97, 112
observance days (*uposatha*'s), 172, **192**, 193, 203, 204, 208, 225
offerings, 173–5
Once-returners, 71, 78
one-pointedness of mind, 246, 250, 251, 274, 277
one-vehicle, 93
oral traditions, 3, 15, 233
ordinary (*lokiya*); Path, 68, 122; right view/understanding, 46
'ordinary person' (*puthujjana*), 71
ordination, 23, 143, 193, **220–1**; lay, 200; temporary, 193, 221, 223; and *Vinaya*, 236; of women, 24, 221–4
ordination line, 2, 142, 143, 222, 223–4
original; Buddhahood/enlightenment, 271, 276; face, 157, 273, 276; mind, 273, 275; nature, 271; purity, 275, 333; sinlessness, 56; vow of Amitābha, 163
other-power, 153, 157, 164, 179
other religions, attitude to and relationship with (*see also* Bon, Brahmanism, Christianity, Confucianism, Hinduism, Islam, Jainism, Shintō, Taoism), 4–5, 27, 298
outcastes/untouchables, 24, 204, 228, 298–9
own-nature, **85**, 87, **97**, 100, 103

Pagodas (*see also* *Stūpa*'s), ii, 79, 170, 316
Pali, xx, 3, 9, 233, 284
Pali Canon (*see* Canons of scripture)
Pali literature, non-canonical, 3–4, 141, 142, 328
pantheon, Mahāyāna, 129–33
parinibbāna (final *Nibbāna*), 27, 67; of the relics, 67–8; and *Stūpas*, 78
paritta's, 135, **180–2**, 183, 209, 241
Path (*see also* Eightfold Path, and *Bodhisattva*-path); of Seeing, 123, 258, 276; Tenfold, 69, 72
patience, 41, 123, 210
pāṭimokkha (monastic code), 224–8, 236
peace (*see* non-violence)
perception (*see also* cognition); in Theravāda, 84; in Yogācāra, 108
perfections; and the *Bodhisattva*-path, 94, 96, **122–4**, 136, 199, 210; of Gotama, 15, 21, 28, 81; and the Nichiren school, 190; in Southern Buddhism, 199, 210; vehicle of the, 134
Perfection of Wisdom (Skt *Prajñā-pāramitā*) literature, xiv, xvi, xviii, **95–104**, 122, 302, 323, 324; in China, 148, 150, 156; and Mañjuśrī, 133
persecution; of Buddhists, (China) 5, 150, 157–8; (by Communists) 280–3; (India) 139, 140, 141, (Korea) 160–1, (in Tibet) 146; of Christians, 168
person, concept of a, **49–53**, 84, 85, 97, 98–9, 255–6
pessimism (*see also* happiness, and joy), 48, 301, 302
physics, 100, 332
pilgrimage, 76, 77, **190–1**, 193, 235
politics and Buddhism, 16, 75; in

Eastern Buddhism, 162, 167, 168, 243, 286; in Northern Buddhism, 146, 243, 281–2; in Southern Buddhism, 243, 291–2, 294
population of Buddhists, 5, 8
powers (*see also* psychic powers); of Avalokiteśvara, 183, 186; of the Buddha, 26, 67
power-for-good, 180, 182, 190
Prajñā's (female consorts), 262
Pratyeka-buddha's (*see* Buddhas, solitary)
prayer, 94, 127, 179, 183; -flags, 187, 191; -offerings, 133; -wheels, 186
precepts, ethical, 192, 198, **199–208**, 210; attachment to, 71, 196; the eight, 208, 222–3, 291; the five, 176, 192, **202–7**, (the first) 202–5, (the last four) 205–7, (positive sides of) 207; the ten, 208, 220, 222–3; the ten great (of Zen), 200, 207, 229; the three pure, 200
priest-like roles of monks, 217, 241–2
priests (*see* married clergy)
printing, 158, 159, 233, 234
projections into worlds, 124, 126
protection; by chants (*see paritta*'s); by gods, 43–4, 163, 181, 190, 194; by magic spells in Brahmanism, 11; by power of 'merit', 161; by rites, 162, 182, 241–2
'Protestant' Buddhism, 290
psychic forces, 261, 266
psychic powers (*see also* powers), **26**, 110, 150, 251, **252**; of the Buddha, 26, 81, 191; of the Buddha's disciples, 24, 65
psychology, Buddhist, 84, 329, 330, 342
'public monasteries', 237, 239, 280
pūjā ('reverencing'), 172
puñña (*see also* 'merit'), 42
pure abodes, 35, 36, 72, 124
(pure) form realm, 34, 36, 72, 124; and meditation, 250, 251
Pure Lands, **126–7**, 128, 129, 130; of Amitābha (*see also* Sukhāvatī), **129–30**, 167–8, 259; in Northern Buddhism, 212, 262, 264, 267
purgatory, 130
purification and meditation, 250, 256–7, 260
purity of mind, depth, 207
purity and defilement, 56, 113, 114–16
purposelessness in Zen, 271, 277

'rains' period (*see Vassa*)
'rationalism' of Buddhism, 290, 297, 298, 301
rDzogs-chen (pron. *Dzogchhen*) meditation, 268, 269–70, 340
realms, the three, 34, 36, 250, 251, 252
rebirth, 11, 13, **32–9**, 329; as an animal, 33, 71, 303; belief/disbelief in, 14, **44–6**, 69; during life, 45, 60, 289, 317; and ethics, 197; and gender, 215–16; and a good death, 211; good rebirth as a goal, 76, 196; and karma, 39, 41; meditation affects, 35, 36, 39, 44, 123; meditative memory of, 14, 21, 29, 251; period between two, 58, **59–60**, 212, 267; in a Pure Land, 126–7, 130, 152, 163, 189, 212, 258, 259, 267; and suffering, 48
recollection of the Buddha, 153, 179

reformism, 293
reformists, early, 75
refuge(s); extra, 179, 299; oneself and *Dhamma* as a, 26; the three, 71, 173, **176–9**, 256, 337
refugees, Buddhist, 139, 295, 296, 306, 319
regret, 40, 41, 196, 200, 211
relics, 27, 67, 77, **78**, 180, 190, 191; at Anurādhapura, 141; hairs as, 170; in images, 180; in London Peace Pagoda, 316; *parinibbāna* of the, 67–8
renunciation, 17–18, 207, 217, 220
repentance, 173, 257
representation, 108, 110, 332
representation-only, 106, 111, 112
ritual; appeal of in early Japan, 161; dances, 194; healing, 189; of *paritta*-chanting, 182; tantric, 134, 138, 163; and T'ien-t'ai meditation, 257; water-pouring, 21, 78, 192, 193, 195, 212
rosaries, 176, 186, 187

sacrifice, 10, 11, 29, 76
salvation; by grace, 164; of sinners, 164
samādhi (*see* concentration)
Samaṇa's 11–14, 17, 27, 73
Samatha (*see* Calm meditation)
Samatha-yāna ('vehicle of Calm'), 253, 270, 273
sameness; of beings, 121; of *dharmas*, 99, 199
saṃsāra ('wandering on', conditioned world of rebirth), **32**, 103, 104, 112, 113, 258
samurai, 162, 163, 165, 168; ethic of, 205
Saṅgha ('Community'), three meanings of, 217
Saṅgha, Holy, **71**, 172, **177–8**, 217
Saṅgha, monastic (*see also bLama*'s; monks; nuns), 2, 26, 141, **217–43**, 326, 338–9; early, 23, 24–5, 73–5; as a field of 'merit', 198; and Holy *Saṅgha*, 178, 217; indigenous, 141, (in Britain) 311, 312; a local, 225; as politically autonomous, 149; purification of by rulers, 77, 290, 293; and voting, 73
Sanskrit, xx, 9, 25, 29, 233, 234, 284
Sanskrit Canon (*see* Canons of scripture)
Śāstra's ('Treatises'), 95, 324
sati-paṭṭhāna's (*see under* mindfulness)
satori, 195, 275
scholarship on Buddhism, Western, 300–2, 342
science and Buddhism, 284, 300
schisms, **74**, **75**, 77, 142, 226, 236, 331
schools of thought (*vāda*'s), **2**, **74**, 83, **85–9**, 331; Mahāyāna on the early, 92–4
scriptures, **3–4**, 233, **322–4**, 327, 328; in Ch'an/Sŏn/Zen schools, 154, 160; -readers, 218
secularization, 240, 287, 294
self (Pali *atta*, Skt *ātman*; *see also* not-self; person), 14, **51**, 52–3, 54, 65, 66; and the *ālaya*, 109; and the Puggalavāda, 85; and the *Tathāgata-garbha*, 118; in the *Upaniṣads*, 10, 13; in the West, 303, 311, 318
Self-existent body, 127, 128
self-immolation, 203, 338
self-power, 153, 157, 164, 167, 179
self-reliance, 26, 30, 217
selfishness, undermining of, 122, 197

sense-bases, the six, 55, 58–9
sense-desire, realm of, 34, 36, 71, 250, 251
sensual desire, 19, 21, 249
serene observation meditation, 271, 274
sexes, development of, 37
sexual; behaviour, 205–6; symbolism, 266; yoga, 138, 147, 218, 267
shame, 200–1
sick, care for the, 210–11, 214, 228
signs (*nimitta*'s), meditative, 249, 251
similes; arrow, 66; blaze of light, 128; cataracts, 111; chariot, 52; clear lake, 250, 271; extinguished fire, 61, 66–7; further shore, 31, 62; holographic image, 120; mirage, 111; purification of gold ore, 57, 249, 251; raft, 31; television screen, 84; watching television, 109
sin, 164, 189
sinlessness, original, 56
skilful (or wholesome); actions, 41–2, 49, (the ten) 207; *cittas*, 84; criteria of what is, 41–2; states, 69–70
skilful means (Skt *upāya-kauśalya*), 92, **121–2**, 125, 134, 260, 334; and adaptability, 150, 165, 201–2; of Avalokiteśvara, 183; and levels of teachings, 93, 125, 151; and projection into worlds, 124; and transcending of views, 100, 101–2; and wisdom as complementary, 135, 263, 266; Yogācāra theories as, 106
social ethics, 75, 76, 149, 205, 213–16
society, development of, 37
Southern Buddhism, **4**, **5**, 6–7, 143; alms-giving in, 229–30; astrology in, 243; in China, 144, 281; blessings and protections in, 241; ethics in, 43, 198, 199–200, 204, 208, 211–12, 215; festivals in, 192–4; in Indonesia, 296–7; meditation in, 210, 246–57, 339–40; 'merit' and asceticism in, 229; in modern India, 295, 298, 299; monasteries and village life in, 240–1; monasticism in, 220, 225, 227, 230–3, 236–7, 238, 242, 339, (nuns) 222–3, 339; in Nepal, 295; sermons in, 241; temple boys in, 230, 239–40, 241; temporary ordination in, 220, 221, 223; *upāsakas* and *upāsikās* in, 208; welfare roles of monasteries in, 211, 241; in the West, 311, 312, 313–14, 318
speech; false, 206; right, 68, 69, 206–7
spiritual ignorance, 55, 56, 57, 59, 70, 72; in Mahāyāna thought, 103, 115
spontaneity, 138, 156, 258, 268–70, 272–3, 277
sprul-sku's (pron. *trulku*'s), 147, 238
Śrāvakayāna ('vehicle of the Disciples'), **92**, 93, 105, 148, 151, 159, 166; as a level of practice, 94, 245
stages; of the *Bodhisattva*-path, 122–4; on the Holy Eightfold Path, 71–2; of purification, 256–7
state religion, Buddhism as a, 145, 161, 287
storehouse consciousness (*see ālaya-vijñāna*)
Stream-enterers, 23, 35, 68, **71**, 178, 222, 256; some gods as, 35, 191

'stream-entry', **23**, 28, **68**, 71, 87, 123
study, monastic, 135, 151, 231–4, 238, 239
Stūpa's (relic mounds), 27, **77–9**, 141, 170, 171, 191; at Borobuḍur, 144; devotion at, 27, 172, 173, 191; and *maṇḍalas*, 264; and 'merit', 172; of sand, 172, 192; in the West, ii, 316, 320
subject/object duality, 108, 110, 111; transcending of, 111, 112, 127, (in meditation) 257, 269, 272, 277
sudden awakenings/insights, 154, 160, 276
suffering (*see also dukkha*), 2, 11, 13, 23, 36, 47–9; and not-self, 197–8
suicide, 53, 203, 337
Sūtra's (*see also under* Mahāyāna); recitation of, 238, 239, 242; spurious, 234
Sutta's, 3, **73–4**, 83, 91, **322–3**
symbolism; of *Bodhi*-tree, 79, 155, 172; in early Buddhism, 77–81, 330; of lapis lazuli, 189, 259; of light (*see also* brightly shining mind), 129; of lotus, 131, 136, 259, 285; of seeds, 39, 86, 107; sexual, 266; of sword, 133; tantric, 134; of *Vajra*, 135; of wish-granting jewel, 133
syncretism; Ch'an/Pure Land, 157; in Chinese religion, 158; in the Friends of the Western Buddhist Order, 317; with Hinduism in Nepal, 295; in Indonesian Buddhism, 297; Mahāyāna/Śaivism, 143, 144, 159, 297; with Shintō, 162
T'ang monasteries, 157, 211, 231, 242, 338
Tantra's, 133–4, 323, 324
Tantrayāna, 134
Tantric Buddhism (*see also* Mantrayāna and Northern Buddhism), **133–8**, 334, 336; and Ch'an, 153; female holy beings in, 134, 137, 138, 216; meditation in, **260–70**, 340; in South-east Asia, 143, 144; in Sri Lanka, 142
tantric; college, 234; priests, 219; rituals, 238
Tathāgata ('Truth-attained One'), 23, 65; 'has *Dhamma* as body', 28; and the *Dharma*-body, 127; as 'hard-to-fathom,' 66
Tathāgata-garbha (*see also* Buddha-nature), **114–18**, 120, 122, 127, 197, 333
temples, 170, 173; devotion at, 172, 173
temple boys, 230, 239–40, 241
thang-ka (hanging scroll), 132, 185, 265, 266
thought of enlightenment (*see bodhi-citta*)
thought-only, 106, **109–10**, 112, 126, 134, 179; in Tantric meditation, 257, 261, 266
Three-body doctrine, **125–8**, 178
'three marks' of conditioned phenomena, 50, 71, 105; and ethics, 196–8; meditation on, 255, 256, 257
three natures, **110–11**, 112, 113, 120
'threefold knowledge', 21, 252
thunderbolt (Skt *Vajra*), 83, 135
thusness, **102–3**, 108, **111**; in *Avataṃsaka Sūtra*, 119, 120, 128; and Ch'an/Zen school, 155, 156,

275, 276, 277, 279; and Clear Light, 271; and *Dharma*-body, 127, 128; and *Mahāmudra* meditation, 269; and T'ien-t'ai school, 151
Tibetan Canon (*see* Canons of scripture)
time, 35, 63, 68, 85, 101, 125
timeless, *Nibbāna* as, 63, 68
Ti-ratana (*see* jewels, the three)
transcendent; action, 39; all the Buddha's teachings as, 89; Calm, 258; *citta*, 113; *jhāna*, 254; knowledge, 112; level of the Path, 68; moment of faith, 189; right understanding/view, 46
Transformation-body, **126**, **128**, 130, 131, 147, 178; as an incarnation, 144, 166
translations, 145, 146, 150, 151, 234, 300–2
trulku (*see sprul-sku*'s)
truth; asseveration of, 181–2; experience as criterion of, 30; love of, 207; two levels of (*see also* conventional truth, and ultimate truth), **98–9**, 110, 128, (in Hinduism) 140
Truths, Four Holy, 47–72
truthfulness as a perfection, 210

ultimate truth, 83, 98–9, 100, 123, 155, 156
ultimatism, 289, 293
unborn, 60, 62, 68, 103
unconditioned, 52, 54, **61**, **62**, **87**, 98, 103
unconscious, the, 84, 107, 108, 134
understanding, right (*see* view/understanding, right)
'undetermined questions', 65–6
universities, Buddhist, 135, 139, 145, 147, 233, 284
unskilful/unwholesome actions, results of, 196, 200
unsui (a Zen trainee), 229, 339
'unthinkable'; details of karma as, 41; nature of reality as, 119, 259
untouchables (*see* outcastes)
upāsaka's and *upāsikā*'s ((devout) lay disciples), 200, 208, 217, 317
uposatha (*see* observance days)

Vajra, 135, 136, 266
vajrācāra's, 219
Vajrayāna (*see also* Mantrayāna), 135
Vassa (the 'rains'), 73, **193**, 221, 223, 236
Veda's, 10, 134, 136, 140
vegetarianism, 138, 140, **203–4**, 338; and Asoka, 76; in Eastern Buddhism, 187, 204, 219, 228, 229, 280; in Jainism, 13
veterinary care, 76, 211
view/understanding, right; 46, 68, 69, 70, 198; transcendent and ordinary, 46
views, 14, **53–4**; on existence and non-existence, 69, 98; on the existing group, 54, 71; transcending of, 96, 100–2; on self, 51, 54, 66, 71
vigour, 123, 210, 235, 240
vihāra (monastic 'dwelling'), 170
Vinaya (monastic discipline), 2, 73, 217, 222, **224–9**, 235, 236; for the laity, 213; its rules on deportment, 75, 227; its rules on eating, 208, 226; *Saṅgha* as dependent on, 26; school (Lu), 152; as a text (*see* Index of

proper names); in the West, 305, 313
Vipassanā (*see* Insight meditation)
Vipassanā-yānā ('vehicle of Insight'), 253, 270
visionary experiences, 90, 119, 125, 126, 133; after death, 212; and Mahāyāna art, 189
visualization, 258; of the Buddha, 80, 90; in Pure Land meditation, 187, 258–60; in Tantric meditation, 179, 238, 266–7, 268, 277; in T'ien-t'ai meditation, 257
visualized beings, the nature of, 261, 267
volition, 57; and karma, 49
vows; attachment to, 71, 196; of a *Bodhisattva*, **122**, 124, 126, 127, 129, 178, 210; in Eastern Buddhist practice, 189, 257; and pilgrimage, 190; precepts as, 199

war, 53, 202
water, sacralized, 193
wealth, 205; and contentment, 207
welfare activities (*see also under* monks), 142, 157, 211, 280, 284; in the West, 312
will; and karma, 62; as relatively free, 57
wisdom, 46, 53, **59**, 68, **244**; the Buddha's, 22; and compassion, 121; and the Eightfold Path, 69, 70; and faith, 127, 170; flashes of, 255; and Madhyamaka school, 105; and Mañjuśrī, 133; and meditation, 244, 246, 250, 255, 261; perfect, 90; perfection of (*see also* Perfection of Wisdom literature), 96, 123–4, 210; and skilful means as complementary, 135, 263, 266; and the Sōka-gakkai, 286; and transmuted faults, 261
women (*see also* female Tantric 'deities', and Kuan yin); ordination of, 24, 221–2; role and status of, **215–16**, 222, 293, 298, 337, 338; and Theosophy, 303
world; as in body, 59; as body of Vairocana Buddha, 120; in Buddhist cosmology, **33–7**; as a harmonious organic whole, 120; and the *maṇḍala*, 267; as thought-only, 109–10, 128; and *Vajra*-sceptre symbolism, 135
world mountain, 264
world-systems, 33, 36, 37
wrathful *yi-dam*'s, 262
writing, introduction of, 233; in Japan, 161, 162; in Tibet, 145

yi-dam ('chosen deity'), 260, 261–4, 267; as a refuge, 179
yoga, 10, 18, 339; and the Buddha, 18, 19, 22; Hindu, 246; sexual, 138, 147, 218, 267; six yogas of Naropa, 267, 240

zazen ('sitting meditation'), 165, 166

INDEX OF PROPER NAMES

Including named historical individuals, holy beings, texts, Buddhist schools and fraternities, Pure Lands, geographical locations, historical periods, peoples, religions and political movements (but see Index of concepts for the three main cultural areas of Buddhism, types of meditation, and spiritual vehicles (*yānas*), such as the Mahāyāna). Primary entries in bold type.

Abhidhammattha-saṅgaha, 142
Abhidharma-kośa, 86, 104, 151, 301
Abhidharma-samuccaya, 104
Afghanistan, 81, 139, 169
Africa, Buddhism in, 306, 321
Āgama's, the five, 323
Aggañña Sutta, 37
Ājīvaka's, 13, 76
Akṣobhya Buddha, 261, 262, 265, 266, 334
Ambedkar, B. R., 298–9
Ambedkar Buddhists, 298–9, 306, 315
America, Buddhism in United States of, 169, 300, 343; among immigrants in, **304–5**, 342; missions and organizations, **307–10**, 315; Theosophy and, 303, 304
Amida Buddha (*see* Amitābha)
Amitābha (Jap. Amida) Buddha, **129–30**, 131, 148, 334; absolute faith in, 258; and Avalokiteśvara, 183, 189, 259; as the Buddha-refuge, 178; in Ch'an/Zen, 157, 273; devotion to, 152–3, 162, 163–4, **187–9**, 219, 239, 242, 273; and the *Dharma*-body, 168, 259; and the dying, 130, 212; and ethics, 168, 196; hymns to, 187, 305; images of, 188, 189; and meditation, 187, 257, **258–60**, 262, 267; Nichiren on, 167; and Pure Land schools, **152–3**, **163–4**, 168
Amitāyur-dhyāna Sūtra, 258
Amitāyus Buddha, 129, 258
Ānanda, 24, 26, 73, 222
Ānāpāna-sati Sutta, 254
Anatta-lakkhaṇa Sutta, 51
Aṅguttara Nikāya, xiv, 322
Anurādhapura, 141, 191
Arnold, Sir E., 303, 310, 342
Aryans, 9, 10, 11, 29
Asaṅga, 104, 105, 107, 110, 114, 122, 202; works of, xvi, xvii, 104–5

Asoka, emperor, 9, **75–7**, 202, 203, 213, 330

Aṣṭasāhasrikā 'Perfection of Wisdom' *Sūtra*, xiv, 95

Atīśa, 146, 147

Avalokiteśvara *Bodhisattva* (*see also* Kuan-yin), **131**, **133**, 334; and Amitābha, 183, 188, 189, 259; appearing to Shinran, 164; and Dalai Lamas, 131, 147; devotion to, 162, **182–7**; iconography of, 131, 136, 182–5; *mantra* of, 136; and pilgrimage sites, 191; power of, 183, 186; skilful means of, 183; and Tārā, 137; vow of, 183; Zen understanding of, 186

Avalokiteśvara Sūtra, 182, 183

Avataṃsaka Sūtra, **118–20**, 127, 128, 152, 323, 324, 333

'Awakening of Faith in the Mahāyāna', Treatise on, 114

Bali, 5, 144, 297

Bangladesh, 5, 169, 295

Bashō, Matsuo, 168, 279

Bhaiṣajya-guru Buddha, 130, 148, 189, 334

Bhāvana-krama, 257

Bhutan, 5, 147, 169, 205, 287, 295

bKa'brgyud (pron. Kagyu) school, 146, 147; and meditation, 232, 235, 267, 268; in the West, 308, 314

bKa'-gdams (pron. Kadam) school, 146, 147

Blavatsky, H. P., 290–1, 303–4

'Blue Cliff Records', 273

Bodh-Gayā, 22, 191; in modern Buddhism, 224, 296, 299; restoration of, 291, 303

Bodhi-caryāvatāra, 123, 334

Bodhidharma, 153, 154

Bodhisattva-bhūmi, 122, 202

Bon, 5, 145, 146, 194

Brahmajāla Sūtra, 228, 230, 338

Brahmanism, 9–11, 51, 80; in Cambodia, 143; comparison to Confucianism, 158

Britain, Buddhism in, 300, 306, **310–18**, 342, 343

British in Asia, 143, 290, 293, 294

Buddha, the (*see* Gotama Buddha in this index, and *see also* Buddha in Index of concepts)

Buddhacarita, 15, 328

Buddhadāsa, 289, 341

Buddhaghosa, xviii, 4, 87, 142, 247

Buddhavaṃsa, xiv, 15

Burma (*see also* South-east Asia), 5, 77, 140, **143**, 169; Buddhism in modern, 289, 293, **293–4**, 336, 337; missionaries from, 295, 296, (in West) 311, 318; monastic hierarchy in, 237; nuns in, 223; *rite de passage* in, 220; and Sri Lanka, 142, 143, 294; temporary ordination in, 220, 223; and *Vipassanā* meditation, 253, 293

Cambodia (*see also* South-east Asia), 5, 143, 169, 282

Canada, Buddhism in, 304, 305, 310

Candrakīrti, 96

Central Asia, 85, 139, 140, 169, 302, 335; and China, 148; and Tibet, 145

Ceylon (*see* Sri Lanka)

Ch'an school (*see also* Lin-chi Ch'an, Sŏn, Thien, and Zen), 130–1, 152, **153–7**, 158, 165, 335; devotion in, 154, 157; and equality, 215; iconoclasm in, 154;

and meditation, 232, 235, **270–9**, 283; monastic code of, 228, 230; syncretism with Pure Land, 157; in the USA, 308; and 'ultimatism', 289; and manual work, 230, 240
Chen-yen school (*see also* Milgyo and Shingon), 151, 308
Chih-i, 151, 257
China, 5, 8, **148–58**, 169, 335, 337; history of Buddhism in, (early) 148–51, (later) 157–8, (modern), **280–2**, 341, 342, 336; and Indian civilization, 148; monasticism in, 220, 228, 231, 232–3, 237, 239, 242, (nuns) 222; rites for the dead in, 150, 212, 281; schools of Buddhism in, 151–7, 332, 335; Southern Buddhism in, 144, 281; status of women in, 222, 338; and Tibet, 145; translations in, 150, 151, 234; wandering preachers in, 241
Chinul, 160, 165
Chittagong, 5, 295
Ch'ont'ae school (*see also* T'ien-t'ai), 160
Christianity; aid to Buddhism by Christians, 303, 307; Buddhist influence on, 312; criticism of by the FWBO, 317; in Ceylon, 143, 290, 291; in China, 280; in Korea, 282; in Japan, 168, 284, 285; in Vietnam, 159; comparisons to, 76, 164, 197, 217, 298, 300; its influence on Buddhism, 280, 284, 290, 291, 299, 305, 312; texts of in Chinese Buddhist Canon, 324
Chu-she school, 151
Communism and Buddhism, 5, 217, 230, 240, 280–3, 291, 341; in China, 237, 280–1, 342; in South-east Asia, 237, 282–3, 288, 289, 297, (Marxism) 289, 294; in Tibet, 234, 242, 281–2
Confucianism, 5, **148–9**, 158, 192, 194, 280; and Brahmanism, 158; and Ch'an monastic code, 230; in Japan, 161, 162, 169, 204; in Korea, 159, 160, 283; Neo-Confucianism, 158, 160, 169; social ethic of, 215, 240, 338; in Vietnam, 159
Confucius, 148
Conze, E., 302; works of, xiv, xvi, xvii, xviii, 326, 327, 331, 332

Dalai Lama (present one; *see also* in Index of concepts), 243, 281, 282, 296, 331
Daśa-bhūmika Sūtra, 118, 122, 333
dGe-lugs (pron. Geluk) school, 147, 228, 232, 234, 238, 257; in the West, 314, 315, 319
Dhamma-cakka-pavattana Sutta (*see also* first sermon, in Index of concepts), 23
Dhammapada, xiv, 301, 322
Dhamma-saṅgaṇī, xv, 83
Dharmaguptaka school, 152, 225
Dharmapāla, Anagārika, 291, 297, 303, 307
'Diamond-cutter Perfection of Wisdom *Sūtra*', xviii, 95, 155, 234
Dīgha Nikāya, xiv, 15, 322
Dīpaṅkara Buddha, 15, 125
Dōgen, 165–6, 228–9, 236, 271, 335
Dohā-kośa, 138

Eisei, 165

Europe, Buddhism in, 169, 313, 318–20

Fa-hsiang school, 151
Fa-tsang, 119, 152
'fire sermon', 61
France; Buddhism in, 319; and Indochina, 282
Friends of the Western Buddhist Order, 311, 312, **315**, 316, **317–18**, 320, 342

Gaṇḍavyūha Sūtra, 118–20, 259
'Gateless Gate', 273
Gautama Buddha (*see* Gotama Buddha)
Geluk (*see* dGe-lugs)
Germany, Buddhism in, 300, 318–19, 343; monks from, 291, 318
Gotama Buddha (*see also* Śākyamuni Buddha; Buddha in Index of concepts); 1, **14–27**, 328–9; assassination attempts on, 25; background to, 9–14; 'biographies', 15, 81, 89; birth and early life, 17; charisma and psychic powers, 25–6; his dates, 9; enlightenment and after, 21–2; first sermon, 23; and nature, 16, 25; passing away, 26–7; prior to his birth, 15–16; renunciation and quest for enlightenment, 17–21, 47; temptations by Māra, 19–21, 26
Gupta dynasty (320–540), 81, 139

Hakuin, 168, 273
Hawaii, Buddhism in, 304, 305, 307, 310
'Heart Perfection of Wisdom *Sūtra*', 95, 99
Hevajra Tantra, 138
Hinduism, 9, 76, 139, 191, 298, 306; and Buddhism's decline in India, 140–1; and Buddhism in modern India, 297, 298; Buddhist influence on, 140; and Confucianism, 158; its influence on Buddhism, 134, 136, 145; its influence in the West, 302, 303, 307; its opposition to Buddhism, 140, 143; Sāṃkhya school of, 101; in syncretism with Buddhism, 143, 144, 159, 295, 297
Hōnen, 163, 164
Hong Kong, 8, 282
Hsüan-tsang, 90, 151
Hua-yen school, (*see also* Hwaom, and Kegon), 118–20, 152, 232, 333
Hui-nêng, 154–5
Hwaom school (*see also* Hua-yen), 160

India, 5, 169; Buddhism in modern, 295, 296, 297–9, 341
Indian Buddhism, late, 4, 139–41, 334, 335
Indonesia, 5, 8, 144, 169, 296–7, 341
Islam (*see also* Muslims), 139, 140, 294–5, 298

Japan, 5, 8, **161–9**, 336; abortion in, 202–3; Buddhism from in the Americas, 304–5; history of Buddhism in, (early) 161–2, (later) 167–9, (modern) **284–7**; married clerics in, 219, 228; and meat-eating by monks, 219; modernization in, 205; monasticism in, 220, 228, 231, (nuns) 219, 222, 339; New Religions in, 219, 285–6; schools of Buddhism in, 163–7, 237; and this-worldliness, 219; Zen arts in, 277

Jainism, 13, 30, 51, 73, 76, 81, 139

Jātaka's (*see also* Index of concepts), xv, 323

Java, 144, 296

Jesus, 38, 304

Jinarakkhita, A., 296–7

Jizō *Bodhisattva* (*see* Kṣitigarbha)

Jñāna-prasthāna, 86

Jōdo-shin school (-shū) (*see also* Pure Land schools), 165, 168, 187, 189, 336; beyond Asia, 305, 310, 316, 319; and ethics, 168, 196; an married clerics, 219

Jōdo school (-shū) (*see also* Pure Land schools), 163, 167, 305

Kadam school (*see* bKa'-gdams)

Kagyu school (*see* bKa'brgyud)

Kālāma Sutta, 30

Kamalaśīla, 96, 257

Kaniṣka I, emperor, 81, 85, 86

Karaṇīya-metta Sutta, 181, 209–10

Kashmir, 139, 295

Kathāvatthu, xv, 87, 88

Kegon school (*see also* Hwa-yen), 161, 232, 237

Khmer Rouge, 54, 282

Khuddaka Nikāya, 322

Korea, 8, **159–61**, 169, **283–4**, 306; Buddhism from, beyond Asia, 310, 335; and married 'monks', 220; monasticism in, 220, 233, 237, (nuns) 222; and monks' militia, 202

Kṣitigarbha (Jap. *Jizō*), *Bodhisattva*, 133, 203

Kuan-yin (*see also* Avalokiteśvara), 131, 183, 184, 186, 334; festivals of, 195

Kūkai, 162

Kumārajīva, 150, 151

Kusha school, 86

Kyeyul school (*see also* Lu), 160

Kyoto, 162, 163; pilgrimage sites at, 191

Ladakh, 295

Lalitavistara, 15, 16

Lamotte, E., xvi, 301, 326, 333, 337

Lam-rim chen-mo, 257

Laṅkāvatāra Sūtra, xv, 104, 108, 114, 116, 117, 153; and vegetarianism, 204

Laos (*see also* South-east Asia), 4, 144, 169, 282, 283

Lao-tzu, 148, 150

The Light of Asia, 303, 342

Lin-chi, 157

Lin-chi Ch'an school (*see also* Rinzai Zen), 157, 160, 165, 270

Lokottaravāda school, 89

'Lotus' *Sūtra*, xv, **92**, **125**, 153, 323; and Avalokiteśvara, 131, 182; devotion to, 166, 190, 285; and Nichiren school, 166, 167, 190; and Risshō-kōseikai, 286; and Sōka-gakkai, 285; and T'ien-t'ai/Tendai school, 151, 166–7, 257; first translation of in the West, 300

Lu school (*see also* Kyeyul, and Ritsu), 152, 228, 308

Madhyamaka school, **95–104**, 332; in China, 151, 152, 156, 332; and conceptual constructions, 105; and Tathāgata-garbha thought, 113, 116–17; in Tibet, 146, 147;

and the Yogācāra, 96, 105, 106, 110, 111, 116–17
Madhyamaka-kārikā, xvi, 96
Madhyānta-vibhāga, xvi, 105
Madhyānta-vibhāga-kārikā-bhāṣya, xvi, 105
Mahā Bodhi Society, 291, 297, 299, 306, 311, 343
Mahā-nidāna Sutta, 54
Mahā-parinibbāna Sutta, 26
Mahā-samaya Sutta, 91
Mahā-sati-paṭṭhāna Sutta, 254
Mahā-sudassana Sutta, 119
Mahā-vibhāṣā, 86
Mahādeva, 88; five points of, 74, **88**, 331
Mahāpajāpati, 24
Mahāsaṅghika fraternity, 75, 85, 88–9, 331
Mahāsthāmaprāpta *Bodhisattva*, 131, 188–9
Mahāvaṃsa chronicle, 141, 335
Mahāvastu, xvi, 89
Mahāyāna-abhidharma Sūtra, 104, 107, 116, 117
Mahāyāna-saṃgraha, xvi, 104, 113
Mahāyāna-sūtrālaṃkāra, 117
Mahinda, 77, 141, 193
Maitreya *Bodhisattva* (*see also* Metteyya), 118, 119, 124, 130, 148, 304
Maitreya/Maitreyanātha the teacher, xvi, xvii, 104, 114
Majjhima Nikāya, 322
Malay peninsula, 144, 169
Malaysia, 5, 8, 294–5
Maṅgala Sutta, 181
Mañjuśrī *Bodhisattva*, 119, 132, 133, 262
Māra (the tempter), 35, 162, 163; conquest of, 19–21, 26; cannot be female, 216
Metteyya *Bodhisatta* (*see also* Maitreya), 15, 35
Mi-la-ras-pa (pron. Milarepa), 146, 207
Milgyo school (*see also* Chen-yen), 160, 260
Milinda, king, 4
Milindapañha, xvi, 4, 84
Mogallāna, 14, 24, 195
Moggaliputta, Tissa, 77, 87
Mo-ho Chih-Kuan, 257
Mon country, 77; people from 143, 144
Mongkut, king, 287
Mongolia, 5, 146, 147, 169, 281
Mongolians, 144, 146, 147, 158, 165, 167, 202, 281
Muslim countries, 207
Muslims (*see also* Islam), 139, 141, 191, 204, 294, 295, 296

Nāgārjuna, xvi, xviii, 95, 96, 97, 99, 211
Nara sects, 161, 237, 187
Nepal, 5, 14, 144–5, 169, 219, 295, 336; texts from, 300; and Western Buddhism, 314, 319
New Zealand, Buddhism in, 313, 315, 320
Newars, 145, 219, 295
Nichiren, 166, 167, 190, 285, 335
Nichiren school, **166–7**, 168, **190**, 219, 285–6; beyond Asia, 305, 309, 315–16, 319, 320, 321; sub-sects of, 237, 287, (Nichiren Shōshū), 190, 285, 286, 309, 315, 319, 320, 321
Nidānakathā, 15, 16, 17–18
Nidāna-saṃyutta, 54
Nikāya's the five, 3, 322–3
Nyingma school (*see* rNying-ma)

Olcott, H. S., 290–1, 304

Padmasambhava, 145
Pai-chang, 230
Pakistan, 10, 81, 139, 169
Pāli Text Society, xviii, 301, 322
Parakkama Bahu I, king, 142
Paramārtha, 151
Parinirvāṇa Sūtra, 151, 323
Paṭṭhāna, 83
Perfection of Wisdom *Bodhisattva*, 216
Petavatthu, 43, 323, 329
'Platform *Sūtra* of the Sixth Patriarch', xvi, 155, 234
Prabhūtaratna Buddha, 190
Prasannapadā, 96
'Precious Garland of Advice for the King', 211, 338
Puggala-paññatti, 83
Puggalavāda school, 85
Pure Land schools, 129, 335; in the Americas and Europe, 305, 316; in China, **152–3**, 158; devotion in, **187–9**, 232; in Japan (*see* Jōdo and Jōdo-shin); in Korea, 159; meditation in, **258–60**; *Sūtras* of, 129, 152, 334, 340; syncretism with Ch'an, 157; in Vietnam, 159
Pu-tai, 130–1

Rājagaha, 24, 73
Ratana Sutta, 181, 182
Ratnagotra-vibhāga, xvii, 114, 115, 116
Ratnasambhava Buddha, 261, 262
Rhys Davids, T. W., xiv, xv, 301, 310, 311, 329
Rinzai Zen school (*see also* Lin-chi Ch'an), 165, 166, 167, 231, 270, 273–6; in the West, 307, 308, 315
Risshō-kōseikai, 286
Ritsu school (*see also* Lu), 165, 228
rNying-ma (pron. Nyingma) school, 145–6, 218, 235, 267, 268; in the West, 308, 314
Russia, interest in Buddhism in (*see also* Soviet Union), 301, 304

Saichō, 162, 219, 228
Śaivism, 140, 143, 144, 159
Sakya school (*see* Sa-skya)
Śākyamuni Buddha (*see also* Gotama Buddha), 14, 125, 126, 127; his helpers, 133; images of, 189, 195; lifespan of, 125, 190; and Nichiren school, 167, 190; and the Risshō-koseikai, 286; and Zen, 166, 167
Sāmañña-phala Sutta, 13, 253
Samantabhadra *Bodhisattva*, 133
Samantabhadra Buddha, 262, 270
Samatha Trust, 313–14
Saṃdhinirmocana Sūtra, 104, 333
Saṃmitīya-nikāya-śāstra, 85
Saṃyutta Nikāya, xvii, 322
San-lun school, 151
Śāntarakṣita, 96, 145
Śāntideva, 121, 123
Saraha, 138, 268
Sāriputta, 14, 24, 54
Sarvāstivāda school, 77, **85–6**, 87, 88, 106, 127; its biography of the Buddha, 15; in Central Asia, 140; in China, 151; its list of *dhammas*, 84; Mādhyamika critique of, 97; monastic code of, 225, 231, 339; in South-east Asia, 143, 144
Sa-skya (pron. Sakya) school, 146

Sautrāntika school, 86, 105, 106
Sāvatthī, 16, 26, 194
Shaku, Sōen, 307
Shan-tao, 153, 187
She-lun school, 108, 151
Shingon school (*see also* Chen-yen; and Mantrayāna in Index of concepts), 162, 163, 165, 167, 168, 237, 260, 287, 340; outside Asia, 305, 316
Shinran, 163, 164, 167, 219, 228, 335
Shintō, 161; integrated with Buddhism, 5, 128, 162, 190, 194, 214; in modern Japan, 285, 287; separated from Buddhism, 169, 284
Shōtoku, prince, 161
Sigālovāda Sutta, 213–14
Sikhism, 298
Sikkim, 147, 169, 295
Śikṣā-samuccaya, 121
Singapore, 8, 297
Sinhalese, 141, 292, 293; monastery of, 311
Śiva (the Hindu God), 140, 144, 191, 297
Sōka-gakkai (*see also* Nichiren (Shō-shū)), **285–6**, 341; in the West, 309, 315
Sŏn school (*see also* Ch'an), 159, 160, 284, 335; in Poland, 320
Sōtō Zen school (*see also* Ts'ao-tung Ch'an), **165–6**, 196, 200, 270–1, 276; monastic discipline in, 229, 236; nuns in, 339; in the West, 307, 308, 315
South Africa, Buddhism in, 306, 313, 321
South America, Buddhism in, 304, 305, 320
South-east Asia (*see also* Burma, and Thailand), 4, **143–4**, 159, 335; alms-round in, 229; Buddhism in modern, **282–3**, **287–9**, **293–4**, **296–7**, 342; nuns in, 223, 232; refugees from in the West, 306; temporary ordination in, 220, 221, 223; welfare services of monasteries in, 241
Soviet Union (*see also* Russia), 5, 147, 320
Sri Lanka, 4, 5, 77, 140, **141–3**, 168; alms-round in, 229; attitude to meditation and Arahatship in, 232, 293; Buddhism in modern, **290–3**, 301, 336, 338, 341; caste in, 227–8; communal strife in, 202, 292; missions from, 294, 295, 296, (to West) 311, 318; monasticism in, 142, 228, 230, 231, 232, 236, (nuns) 223, 338; and South-east Asia, 143, 144
Śrīmālā-devī siṃhanāda Sūtra, xvii, 114, 115
Sthaviravāda (*see also* Theravāda), 75
Sthiramati/Sāramati, xvii, 114
Sukhāvatī ('Happy Land'), 129, 130, 152, 189; conditions for rebirth in, 130, 152, 164
Sukhāvatī-vyūha Sūtra's, 129–30, 152
Sukhāvatī-vyūhopadeśa, 152, 258, 259
Śūnyatāvāda, 95, 96, 128
Śūraṅgama Sūtra, 156, 186
Sutta-nipāta, xvii, 322
Suvarṇa-bhāsottama Sūtra, 126
Suzuki, D. T., 118, 126, 301, 307, 311; works of, xv, 331, 333, 336, 339

T'ai-hsu, 311, 319

Taishō Daizōkyō, 234, 323
Taiwan, 8, 158, 169, 194, 283
Tamils, 142, 202, 292, 293
T'an-luan, 152
Taoism, 5, 148, 149, 150, 152, 336; and Ch'an, 153, 272; hostile to Buddhism, 157; in Japan, 161, 162; in Korea, 283; in syncretism with Buddhism, 158; in the West, 305
Tārā, 137, 183, 261, 264, 336
Tathāgata-garbha Sūtra, 114
Tathāgata-garbha thought, **113–18**, 128, 333
Tendai school (*see also* T'ien-t'ai), **162**, 163, 165, 166, 168, 219, 228; sects of in modern Japan, 237, 287; in Brazil, 305
Thailand (*see also* South-east Asia), 5, 8, **143**, **144**, 169, 336, 337; Buddhism in modern, 202, **287–9**, 336, 337, 338, 341, 342; missions from, 294, 297, (to West) 311, 313; and Mon country, 77; monasticism in, 221, 227, 233–4, 236–7, 238, (nuns) 223, 224; pilgrimage in, 235; and Sri Lanka, 228
Theosophists, 290–1, 296, 303–4, 311, 342
Thera-gāthā, xvii, 24, 323
Theravāda school (*see also* Southern Buddhism), **2**, **32**, **77**, **86**, 142, **143**, 326, 327, 335, 337, 339, 341; *Abhidhamma* of, 83–4, 87; on the *Arahat*, 93; beyond Asia, 309, 310, 312, 319, 320, 321; biography of the Buddha in, 15; *Bodhisatta*-path in, 93; on the Buddha as beyond contact, 67; on Conditioned Arising, 60; faith in, 31; on first schism, 74; and 'Hīnayāna', 94; and images, 179, 180; in Indonesia, 296–7, 341; on 'intermediary existence', 59; on 'merit' sharing, 43, 44; monastic code in, 225; in Nepal, 295; on *Nibbāna*, 64, 87; refuges in, 176–8; respect for monks in, 218; in south India, 86, 139; and 'Śrāvakayāna', 94; sudden awakenings in, 276; temples in, 170, 172; in Vietnam, 159
Therī-gāthā, xvii, 24, 216, 323
Thien school (*see also* Ch'an), 159, 336
Tibet (*see also* Northern Buddhism in Index of concepts), 5, **145–7**, 169, 220, 331, 334, 335, 336; Buddhism from, beyond Asia, 306, 307, 308, 310, 311, 312, 314–15, 319, 320, 321; Buddhism in modern, 234, 242, **281–2**, 341; nuns in, 234, 242; refugees from 295, 296, 306; women in, 215, 338
'Tibetan Book of the Dead', 212, 340
T'ien-t'ai school (*see also* Ch'ont'ae; Tendai), 151, 158, 257–8, 340; in the West, 305, 308
Tipiṭaka ('Three Baskets'), 322
Triṃśatikā-kārikā, xviii, 105
Tri-svabhāva-nirdeśa, xviii, 105
Trungpa, Chogyam, 308, 314, 343
Ts'ao-shan, 157, 274
Ts'ao-tung Ch'an school (*see also* Sōtō Zen), 157
Tsong-kha-pa, 147, 194, 257

Udāna, xviii, 62, 322
Upaniṣad's, 10, 11, 99

Vaibhāṣika's, 86, 106
Vairocana Buddha; as the *Dharma*-body, 127, 161, 261; in the Hua-yen/Kegon school, 118, 120, 161; in Tantric Buddhism, 261, 265, (Shingon) 162, 167
Vajradhāra, 262
Vajrasattva, 135, 262
Vasubandhu; author of *Abhidharma-kośa*, 86; the Yogācārin, xvi, xviii, 104, 113, 152, 332, 333
Vesālī, 24, 74
Vibhajjavāda, 85, 86–8, 106, 143
Vibhaṅga, 83
Vietnam, 8, **159**, 169, 203, **282**, 306, 336, 338; Buddhism from in the West, 310, 319, 320
Vigraha-vyāvartanī, 96
Vijñānavāda, 106
Vimalakīrti-nirdeśa Sūtra, 93
Viṃśatikā-kārikā, xviii, 105
Viṃśatikā-kārika-Vṛtti, xviii, 105
Vinaya, xviii, 3, 73, 224, 236, 322, 323, 324
Viṣṇu; Hindu God, 140; Buddhist god, 292
Visuddhimagga, xviii, 4, 142, 247, 256

Won school, 284

Yamāntaka, 262
Yeshe, Thubten, 314, 319, 320
Yogācāra school, 95, **104–13**, 332–3; in China, 151, 152; on consciousness, 107–9, 276; and Mādhamikas, 96, 105, 106, 110, 111, 116–17; on path and goal, 112–13, 258; and Tathāgata-garbha thought, 113, 114, 116–17; and thought-only, 109–10, 261; and the 'Three Body' doctrine, 125

Zen schools (*see also* Ch'an, Sōtō Zen, and Rinzai Zen), 2, 96, 153, **165–6**, 167, 219, 335, 336, 341; in the Americas 303, 305, 307, 308, 309, 310; arts of, 277–9, 341; Buddha-refuge in, 178; and D. T. Suzuki, 301; ethics in, 166, 196, 337; in Europe and Australasia, 311, 312, 315, 319, 320; and faith, 166; flower offering verse in, 173; *Jūkai* festival in, 200, 208; meditation in, 268, **270–9**, 340, 341; in modern Japan, 237, 287; monasteries and temples in, 171, 239, 339; rites for dead beings in, 203; sexual equality in, 215; trainees in, 230; vegetarianism in, 204; on Avalokiteśvara's help, 186